Manteo and the Algonquians
of the Roanoke Voyages

Also by Brandon Fullam

*The Lost Colony of Roanoke:
New Perspectives* (McFarland, 2017)

Manteo and the Algonquians of the Roanoke Voyages

BRANDON FULLAM

McFarland & Company, Inc., Publishers
Jefferson, North Carolina

ISBN (print) 978-1-4766-7801-6
ISBN (ebook) 978-1-4766-3824-9

LIBRARY OF CONGRESS AND BRITISH LIBRARY
CATALOGUING DATA ARE AVAILABLE

© 2020 Brandon Fullam. All rights reserved

No part of this book may be reproduced or transmitted in any form or by any means, electronic or mechanical, including photocopying or recording, or by any information storage and retrieval system, without permission in writing from the publisher.

Front cover: Theodor de Bry's engraving of
"The Marckes of sundrye of the Chief mene of Virginia"
(including the marks, letters and lines), 1590

Printed in the United States of America

McFarland & Company, Inc., Publishers
Box 611, Jefferson, North Carolina 28640
www.mcfarlandpub.com

To the unnamed
and unsung Algonquians
of the Roanoke voyages,
whom history has failed to record

Acknowledgments

I'd like to extend a few words of heartfelt thanks to my wife, Ann, and my daughter, Alexis, who were my first string supporters, reviewers, and constructive critics on this project; to my granddaughter, Evelyn, who helped search my working manuscript in the endless effort to avoid the spelling inconsistencies of Algonquian names and places that plagued the late 16th century accounts; to Mike Gayle, my technical support specialist and graphic designer, for his essential help and expertise in the preparation and production of the illustrations; to Lea Abbott, formerly of the State Office of Archaeology in Raleigh, for his valuable input regarding the various archaeological sites covered in this book; to W. Stephen Lee, who provided unique insights on the early transcription and origins of "The Legend of the Coharie"; to Joel Rose of the Sampson County Historical Society for personally acquainting me with the local county historical sites; to Stuart Parks of the Outer Banks History Center for graciously furnishing many maps and documents from the Center's archives for my perusal; and finally to the many fine folks at McFarland & Company who made the publication of this and my previous book possible, particularly Charlie Perdue, whose editorial commentary and advice are always right on target.

Table of Contents

Acknowledgments vi

Preface 1

Introduction 5

Manteo	9	Pemisapan	131
Andacon	89	Piemacum	132
Cossine	90	Pooneno	139
Ensenore	92	"Raleigh"	141
Eracano	100	Skiko	142
Granganimeo	102	Tarraquine	145
Menatoan	112	Tetepano	146
Menatonon	113	Towaye	148
Okisko	122	Wanchese	149
Osacan	129	Wingina	157

Appendix A: "Manteo and Jack Straw" 193

Appendix B: "The Legend of the Coharie" 199

Chapter Notes 203

Bibliography 211

Index 217

Preface

"There is properly no history," Ralph Waldo Emerson wrote in 1841, "only biography." While the precise relationship between the disciplines of history and biography may be debatable within the halls of academia, it is clear that a "proper" understanding of past events must include at least to some extent the lives and stories of the individuals who shaped those events. In that regard, then, Emerson's words serve to illustrate a nagging deficiency in our perception of the historical time frame covered in this book: the Anglo-Algonquian contact period between 1584 and 1590, when the first serious efforts by the English were made to colonize the New World. That "contact" period obviously implies interaction with the native people, who in this case dwelt in the northeastern part of present-day North Carolina. Yet most of the individual Algonquian Indians whom the English met are barely remembered, if at all, in spite of the pivotal roles they played in the very early years of American colonial history. The fundamental rationale for this book is that the "history" of the Anglo-Algonquian contact period cannot be fully understood without a better sense of the identities, perspectives, and endeavors of those specific native Indians who interacted, for better or worse, with their English counterparts. It is the intent of this book to highlight those individual Indian participants and to tell their stories.

The essential defect in what we know of these individual native people is due, of course, to the fact that the accounts of that historical contact period are subjective, seen entirely through the eyes of the English participants. That problem is further complicated because a number of the accounts exhibited an intentionally distorted view about the land that was soon to be called "Virginia" and the portrayal of the native inhabitants who dwelt there. Many of those late 16th century chronicles, in fact, had portions altered, extracted, or suppressed prior to publication in order to present a favorable view to prospective colonists and investors. Consequently, the native Indians were often marginalized and sometimes portrayed as compliant subordinates, who would learn to "honour, obey, feare and loue vs," as Thomas Harriot wrote. The native Indians represented in the following pages were never passive bystanders in these colonization ventures. On the contrary, almost all of them were continually and actively engaged with the English during the contact period, and a few of them directly affected the course of colonial history in America.

In total there were nineteen native Indians identified by name in the early accounts of the Anglo-Algonquian contact period, commonly referred to as the Roanoke voyages. Those nineteen are the subjects of this book, each one treated as a separate entry in what may be considered a volume of biographical narratives and sketches. Of these, the first and most comprehensive biographical narrative is that of Manteo, the Croatoan Indian who sailed to England twice and was directly and continually involved with the English from 1584 through 1587 and beyond. Ironically, Manteo was arguably more actively and personally engaged in the various stages of the Roanoke voyages than any single Englishman. There is even some fragmentary evidence suggesting Manteo's activities and potential whereabouts after he and the English colonists had disappeared from the historical record. One of these sources is a fascinating entry in the 1631 journal of John Winthrop, Governor of the Massachusetts Bay Colony.

After Manteo, the remaining eighteen Algonquians are presented alphabetically in the book. Among them are especially important names like Ensenore, Granganimeo, Menatonon, Wanchese, and Wingina, to name a few, whose close interactions with the English had significant consequences and determined the course of events. Interspersed among these are the concise sketches of a number of Indians such as Andacon, Cossine, and Eracano, who played strategic roles, but what is known about them was confined to a single event or two, and they were only briefly mentioned in the accounts. On the occasions when more than one of the nineteen native Indians participated in the same historical event, the emphasis is maintained on the role played by the individual Algonquian highlighted in that particular entry. It is my hope that by concentrating on their individual narratives in this manner, the result will bring each of the nineteen Algonquians into sharper focus and thereby provide a better and more complete understanding of the Anglo-Algonquian story.

A secondary purpose in writing this book was to draw attention to the surprising amount of misinformation contained in published material, both past and present, dealing with this topic. I first became aware of the extent of the problem a number of years ago when I was researching the late 16th century accounts for my previous book, *The Lost Colony of Roanoke: New Perspectives*. Some of the misinformation appears in the form of assumptions and conclusions which are not supported by the original texts, and many times they are simply factual errors that are directly contradicted by those texts. As expected, the most notorious purveyor of misinformation related to the Roanoke voyagers and the Algonquians they encountered is the Internet, where errors are endlessly repeated, often verbatim, on site after site. Such errors distort the historical record as well as our understanding of the Anglo-Algonquian contact period. Consequently, when these mistakes are associated with a particular Algonquian represented in this book, an attempt will be made to set the record straight.

The greatest challenge in writing this book had to do with source material, since the Algonquians obviously left no written records of their own. Nevertheless, despite their aforementioned deficiencies, the existing eyewitness accounts from the Anglo-Algonquian contact period were mandatory starting points, and there is a wealth of information to be gleaned there in a close reading of the details, cross-references, and even in the contradictions and omissions to reevaluate significant events and reconstruct the actions and motivations of the particular Algonquians who participated in them. Those primary source accounts were collected by Richard Hakluyt in his exhaustive *The principall Navigations, Voiages and Discoveries of the English Nation…*, and published in two editions between 1589 and 1600. John White's 1585–6 drawings of individual Indians and villages were also useful, as were his *La Virginea Pars* map and the later White/de Bry engraved map published in 1590. Textual excerpts and images from all of these sources are used frequently throughout the book to support various points and deductions and to provide a more authentic representation of late 16th century language and sensibilities.

Another valuable source of material was the seminal two volume *The Roanoke Voyages 1594–1590*, edited by historian David Beers Quinn and first published by the Hakluyt Society in 1955. Many useful late 16th century documents are contained therein, including a few with firsthand references to Manteo and Wanchese. Also helpful was Humphrey Dyson's 1618 comprehensive book of *Proclamations pvblished during the Raigne of the late Queene Elizabeth*, which provided original reports on several noteworthy occurrences in London during Manteo's and Wanchese's stay there. Particularly informative were the Elizabethan sumptuary laws in effect at that time which shed new light on the two Algonquians' social status in English society. *The Colonial Records of North Carolina* supplied information about the conditions and eventual fate of the nineteen Algonquians' tribes. Secondary sources included the published works of archaeologists, geographers, historians, philologists, and others, all of which provided grist for the narrative mill. Particularly beneficial was the work that has been done in the field of ethno-history, which has revealed a great deal about the complex cultural environment within which dwelt the nineteen Algonquians highlighted in this book.

A note should be mentioned here about the orthography of the Algonquian words used in the book. English spelling had not yet been standardized in the late 16th century, when the Roanoke voyages took place, and the problem of spelling inconsistencies was exacerbated as the English voyagers struggled to transpose the Algonquian names they heard from the native Indians into their phonetically equivalent English forms. To make matters even worse, the spellings were further distorted as these Algonquian words were cited and miscopied over and over again in subsequent documents. As a result, for example, the word we know today as "Roanoke" can be found in the early accounts as "Roanoac," "Roanoak," "Roanocke," "Roanaac," "Raonoak," "Roonok," "Roonock," and "Croonoake." To maintain a semblance of consistency throughout the book, therefore, whenever possible I have chosen to use the spellings of tribal and place names as they appeared on White's *La Virginea Pars* map and/or the White/de Bry engraving. In the abovementioned example, "Roanoac" was used on both maps, and that form is used throughout the book when referring to the village, tribe, or individual members of that tribe. Exceptions to this practice would be when referring to the island of Roanoke or when quoting lines from the early texts, in which case the original spellings are retained.

Introduction

In mid–July 1584, two English vessels anchored at an inlet along the Outer Banks of present-day North Carolina. Three days later initial contact was made with the native people who dwelt there, marking their entry into the historical record. Those native Indians were descendants of the large Algonquian linguistic group that over the centuries had migrated southward along the coastal plain. By 1584 the Algonquian-speaking people occupied areas that reached from Canada all the way to North Carolina. The native people with whom the English interacted in 1584 were the southernmost branch of that Algonquian migration, whose long-established territory at that time extended along the Tidewater Region from the Neuse River nearly to the Chesapeake Bay.

Often referred to as "Carolina Algonquians," they were made up of a number of separate tribal divisions, each ruled by a "king" or principal weroance, whose realm was comprised of the main village where he dwelt as well as a number of secondary villages spread throughout his territory. These tribal divisions included the Roanoac, Secotan, Weapemeoc, Chawanoac, Croatoan, Moratuc, and Pomouik. The Neusiok have occasionally been included in this group, but their language affiliation is not certain. The Chesepians have been categorized as one of the "Virginia" Algonquian tribes to the north, but their territory may have extended from the Chesapeake Bay area into present-day North Carolina. In 1586, at least, the Chesepians were part of a coalition of tribes organized by the Roanoac weroance, Pemisapan.

The Carolina Algonquians were bordered in the west by a powerful tribe they called Mangoaks, who were part of another language group, the Iroquoian, and they dwelt on the inner coastal plain beyond the Tidewater Region. To the south of the Carolina Algonquians, and also farther west in the Piedmont past the Mangoaks, were Siouan speaking tribes. To the north were two autonomous Algonquian tribes, one of which was the abovementioned Chesepians. The other was the Powhatans, led by a weroance named Wahunsunacock, who in 1584 would have been in his mid-thirties. By the time the Jamestown colonists arrived at the Chesapeake Bay in 1607, Wahunsunacock had destroyed the Chesepians and had expanded his Powhatan chiefdom to include at least thirty tribes.

Amadas and Barlowe, the co-captains of the 1584 English expedition, were well received by the native Indians, and good relations were quickly established. The English remained at the Outer Banks for a few weeks trading with the Indians and venturing out occasionally on short exploratory excursions. In mid–September they arrived back in England where the voyage was hailed as a great success. Word quickly spread throughout London, no doubt by Walter Raleigh and his supporters, that a promising settlement location had been found in the New World, that the climate was healthy, that the land was fertile, and that wild game was abundant. Regarding the native inhabitants, they were found to be exceedingly friendly and polite, and would willingly embrace the English and their ways when they returned the following summer. As proof of this latter point, Amadas and Barlowe had brought back to England two of the native Indians, who would soon be seen clothed in English attire and speaking a bit of the Queen's English.

Barlowe's account of the voyage, however, written months later and not published until 1589, contained a few details that contradicted the promotional portrayal of the Algonquians as a naturally peaceful and compliant people, who would be ready and willing to accept the English as overseers. The Algonquians, in truth, could be fiercely aggressive, particularly when provoked, and warfare among the tribes was a fairly common occurrence. Their wars, Barlowe wrote, were "very cruell and bloody" and as a result, he continued, "the people are maruelously wasted, and in some places the countrey left desolate." At the time of the Amadas-Barlowe voyage, in fact, a "deadly and terrible warre" was still being waged by the Secotans against the Pomouiks in revenge for an incident that had occurred two years earlier. William Strachey wrote later of the Algonquians that "they seldome make wars for lands or goodes … [but] principally for revenge, so vindicative and jealous they be, to be made derision of, and to be insulted upon by an enemy." Success in war was publicly acclaimed and richly rewarded. Captured warriors would expect to be tortured and killed, and women and children were adopted into the conquering tribe. These were the Algonquian people whom the English encountered during the Roanoke voyages: hospitable to strangers but fierce adversaries when wronged.

With the return of the English to the Outer Banks on June 26, 1585, Anglo-Algonquian relations started on a downward spiral from which the native Indians in particular would never fully recover. One reason for the decline can be attributed to the prior experiences and predispositions that this new group of Englishmen brought with them in their attempt to establish the first colony at Roanoke. These men arrived with a determination that allowed little time for appeasing the Indians and none at all for tolerating defiance against English authority. They were mostly trained and experienced soldiers who had fought in Ireland during the bloody repression of the rebellious Gaelic lords. Walter Raleigh himself, who sponsored and organized the Roanoke expeditions, would always be associated with his previous involvement in the infamous 1580 massacre at Smerwick in County Kerry, where unspeakable atrocities were committed. Raleigh's half-brother, Humphrey Gilbert, was fond of lining the entranceways to his camp with the severed heads of rebel fighters and civilians alike. Ralph Lane had soldiered in Ireland as well as in Northumberland and Westmorland during the earlier Northern Rebellion of Catholic nobles. Following the execution of the rebellion's leaders, Queen Elizabeth ordered the public hanging of more than 400 commoners in the surrounding villages as a warning to potential troublemakers. It was probably due to Lane's reputation as a disciplinarian that Elizabeth instructed Raleigh to appoint him governor of this first colony at Roanoke. Such was the mindset in Elizabethan England toward dissidents, and that was the mentality that the English brought with them to Roanoke in 1585.

The immediate objectives of the newly arrived Englishmen were to locate commercially viable commodities, precious metals, pearls, and whatever else might return a profit for themselves and investors in London who had a stake in the Roanoke voyages. They also hoped to find the fabled all-water passage to the South Sea, which was believed to lie not very far to the west of the mainland opposite the Outer Banks. Their broader goal was to establish a permanent, fortified base in the New World from which they could launch the most profitable of all enterprises: privateering ventures against the Spanish treasure ships headed back to Spain laden with gold and silver extracted from their colonial holdings to the south. As to the native Indians, the stated intention was "that they may in short time bee brought to ciuilitie, and the imbracing of true Religion." In reality, though, the Indians were seen by nearly all the Englishmen involved in the 1585 venture as little more than a potential source of information about the location of the abovementioned precious metals and the passage to the South Sea. Ralph Lane admitted as much when he wrote in 1586 that, except "for that the discouery of a good Mine ... or a passage to the South-sea, or some way to it, nothing els can bring this Countrey ... to be inhabited by our nation."

Far more destructive and terrifying to the native Indians than the cultural predispositions of the English were the pathogens the English unwittingly carried with them to Roanoke. Although this facet of the Roanoke voyages has not been sufficiently probed, there is enough evidence in the contemporary accounts to conclude that epidemic diseases spread by contact with the English were responsible for the rapid depopulation of a number of Carolina Algonquian villages in 1585–6. Having had no previous exposure to European diseases such as smallpox, measles, influenza, and others, none of the Indians had developed immunities, leaving them extremely vulnerable to viral infection. Furthermore, since they knew nothing of contagions, their close proximity to one another within their village environments insured that the disease would spread rapidly. These afflictions were both dreadful and inexplicable to the native Indians, who eventually realized that the outbreaks of the terrible sickness were almost always preceded by the appearance of the English. As relations deteriorated further, conflicts inevitably occurred, and the English responded with deadly force to incidents that Thomas Harriot conceded could easily have been ignored.

In the end the Roanoke voyages failed to establish a permanent English settlement in the New World and the once-promising relations with the Carolina Algonquians were irreparably shattered. Also altered forever were the lives of the nineteen Algonquians who are included in the following pages.

Manteo

Manteo, the Croatoan

Manteo was a principal member of the Croatoan tribe that inhabited the island of the same name on the Outer Banks. Because of his involvement with all of Sir Walter Raleigh's colonization ventures in the New World and his two trips to England, Manteo has emerged as the most fascinating and complex of the late 16th century Algonquians who interacted with the English between 1584 and 1587. Manteo's mother, unnamed in the historical accounts, was a leading figure among the Croatoans, very possibly holding the status of a queen or ruling weroansqua (spelled variously "weroanza," "weroanequa," etc.). Since the ruling hierarchy of most Carolina Algonquian tribes was passed down through matrilineal descent, it is likely that Manteo's mother had no—or no surviving—male siblings, in which case her governing position among the Croatoans would rightly have descended through her own mother to herself. Manteo's standing as a young weroance and important member of the Croatoan tribe was thus inherited from his mother. Manteo was born at Croatoan perhaps about 1564, assuming that he was approximately twenty years old when the Amadas-Barlowe reconnaissance expedition arrived from England on July 13, 1584.

The English knew him as "Manteo," but this was almost certainly not what he had been called at Croatoan in his youth or early adulthood. It is even very possible that "Manteo" was a new name that he took in the summer of 1584 prior to his departure to England with the Amadas-Barlowe expedition. Algonquians acquired multiple names over time, the earliest ones being terms of affection, and later "nicknames" of a sort, describing individual personality traits. Algonquian boys learned at an early age that they were expected to become proficient hunters, at which time they would be given new and suitable names to mark their achievements. Young men looked forward to earning additional and more prestigious names by accomplishing feats of valor as warriors. The earliest firsthand explanation of this Algonquian naming practice was provided by William Strachey, secretary of the Jamestown colony in 1610:

> Both men, women, and children have their severall names; at first according to the severall humour of their parents; and for the men children, at first, when they are young, their mothers give them a name, calling them by some affectionate title, or, perhaps observing their promising inclination give yt accordingly.... When they become able to travel into the woods, and to goe forth a hunting, fowling, and fishing with their fathers, the fathers give him another name as he finds him apt and of spirit to prove toward and valiant, or otherwise changing the mother's, which yet in the family is not so soone forgotten; and if soe be yt be by agility, strength, or any extraordinary straine of witt he performes any remarkable or valorous exploite in open act of armes, or by stratagem, especyally in the tyme of extreamity in the wars for the publique and common state, upon the enemie, the king, taking notice of the same, doth then not only in open view and solemnely reward him with some present of copper,

or chaine of perle, and bedes, but doth then likewise (and which they take for the most eminent and supreme favour) give him a name answearable to the attempt.[1]

Weroances often had several names. Strachey wrote that the Jamestown colonists knew the paramount chief as Powhatan, but "his owne people sometimes call him Ottaniack, sometyme Mamanatowick, which last signifies 'great king'; but his proper right name, which they salute him with (himself in presence), is Wahunsenacawh."[2] A weroance might change his current name to reflect an advancement in prestige or political position, or to mark a personal transformation. The choice of a new name was important and meaningful, and was taken to reflect the nature of his transition or to symbolize his new identity. The English looked upon such name changes as curiosities but did not understand their significance, occasionally at their own peril. In 1586, for example, the Roanoac weroance Wingina changed his name to Pemisapan, meaning "a wolf who watches from a distance"[3] to signify his final transition from one who had tolerated the English, to a dedicated enemy who quietly assembled an alliance of distant tribes to fall upon the unsuspecting English and slaughter them as they slept. Likewise, the Jamestown colonists did not recognize the ramifications of Opechancanough's name change to Mangopeesoman in 1621, which foreshadowed the coordinated massacre of the English colonists on March 22, 1622.[4]

The arrival of the English was a transitional event of great significance for the Algonquian tribes. There are several examples from the historical record of other leading Indians who adopted names of a spiritual nature upon interacting with the English newcomers and later functioned as intermediaries between the two cultures. Colonial historian Karen Kupperman cited as examples the Patuxet Algonquian known to the Mayflower Pilgrims as Squanto, which was actually the name of a fearful deity, as was Hobbomock, the name of another influential Indian who acted as translator and liaison between the English and the local Pokanoket tribes. "Squanto and Hobbomock and many other Indian leaders," Kupperman wrote, "adopted the names of gods as they took up English association to indicate that they were entering a liminal state with all the power and danger that that entailed."[5]

Among the 16th and 17th century Algonquian tribes, "manitou" or "mantóac" was the universal expression for the collective supernatural forces that pervaded the world. Thomas Harriot, who learned the Algonquian language from Manteo and Wanchese, described mantóac as the general name for their "many [lesser] gods ... of different sorts and degrees," but did not include the "one onely chiefe and great God, which hath beene from all eternitie."[6] Kupperman identified several leading Algonquians, including Manteo, who assumed a manitou identity when they began their association with the English. One of these Indians was Munetute, who acted as intermediary between the Jamestown colonists and the Powhatan tribes, and was thought by them to have supernatural powers which made him immune to English weapons. Another was Manedo, an Algonquian Abenaki Indian in Maine whose name was similar to Manteo's and who—like Manteo—had also been to England. Kupperman called Manteo and these Algonquians "boundary crossers," leading Indians who continually transitioned between two cultures and understood their roles in spiritual terms.[7]

For these select "boundary crossers," then, there were spiritual overtones attached to their new roles, which were formalized by the traditional Algonquian practice of adopting new and appropriately spiritual names. This, in turn, would help explain Manteo's willingness to embrace the English and travel to England on two separate occasions, and could shed some light on his motivation and gradual transition to becoming the most anglicized and acculturated of all the native Indians encountered by the English during the Roanoke voyages.

Croatoan, Manteo's home and birthplace, was the name of the island on the Outer

Banks extending at that time from just north of what is now known as Cape Hatteras to about half way along present-day Ocracoke Island. It was also the name of the tribe residing there as well as the principal village on the island. "Croatoan" is believed to translate literally from the Algonquian as "talk-town" or rather "council-town," signifying that it was the leading weroance's—weroanza's probably in this case—main residence, the place where council meetings were held and the center of tribal activities.[8] According to the depiction on the White/de Bry map, there were three villages on the island of Croatoan. Based on archaeological findings, the northernmost village (north is to the right on the White/de Bry map below) near present-day Buxton was the location of the principal village of Croatoan. That archaeological location, called the Cape Creek site, was once situated in the maritime forest which centuries ago extended over much more of the Outer Banks than today. Coastal Indian villages were generally positioned on the sound-side of the barrier islands within the maritime forest, which provided better protection from the elements and a canopy for shelter. The extensive midden at the Cape Creek site was referred to by archaeologist William G. Haag as "the best midden found on the Outer Banks" and indicates that a large population once resided there.[9] As illustrated below, the principal village of Croatoan was located very close to the unmarked inlet called Chacandepeco on later maps, just north of the island. Chacandepeco is said to mean "dips and disappears into shallows,"[10] and is where John White took depth soundings on his way to Roanoke Island in 1590, three years after his colonists and Manteo were left there. The Chacandepeco inlet closed during a storm 1672.

Archaeological evidence of two other villages to the southwest of Buxton have also been found, which generally correspond with the locations on the White/de Bry map. The Croatoans were known to be frequent visitors at Roanoac and Dasamonquepeuc and, prior to 1585–86 at least, were certainly allied with the chief Roanoac weroance, Wingina. Archaeological findings on Roanoke Island and Croatoan confirm that the Roanoacs and Croatoans were closely linked and that there was continual contact between the two.[11] The fact that Manteo was born at Croatoan and that his home was located there, however, is an indication that the Croatoans were probably a separate tribe from the Roanoacs, rather than an extension of it, as some have suggested, although the organizational relationship between the Roanoacs and the Croatoans is not very clear. From his base at Roanoac and Dasamonquepeuc, Wingina may have exercised a degree of influence over a larger area than has previously been thought.

Because of Croatoan's proximity to Wokokon—present-day Ocracoke—it is possible that Manteo could have been involved very early in the initial Anglo-Algonquian contact. In a marginal notation of his *Principal Navigations*, Richard Hakluyt identified Wokokon as the location where the Amadas-Barlowe reconnaissance voyagers landed in 1584. If Hakluyt's note was correct, then the Croatoans may have been the first native Indians to witness the Englishmen's arrival. Manteo, as a young Croatoan weroance, would have been immediately informed about it and could possibly have been among the first to interact with Amadas and Barlowe soon after their arrival on July 13, 1584. In that event one might wonder if he could have been the bold but unidentified native Indian who initiated the actual first Anglo-Algonquian contact when he was rowed to the shoreline adjacent to the English ships and "came along the shoreside towards vs, and … walked vp and downe vpon the point of the land next vnto vs … neuer making any shewe of feare or doubt."[12] It was this first friendly encounter on July 16, 1584, that led to Granganimeo's formal arrival the following day, which in turn offered the promise of a mutually beneficial Anglo-Algonquian relationship.

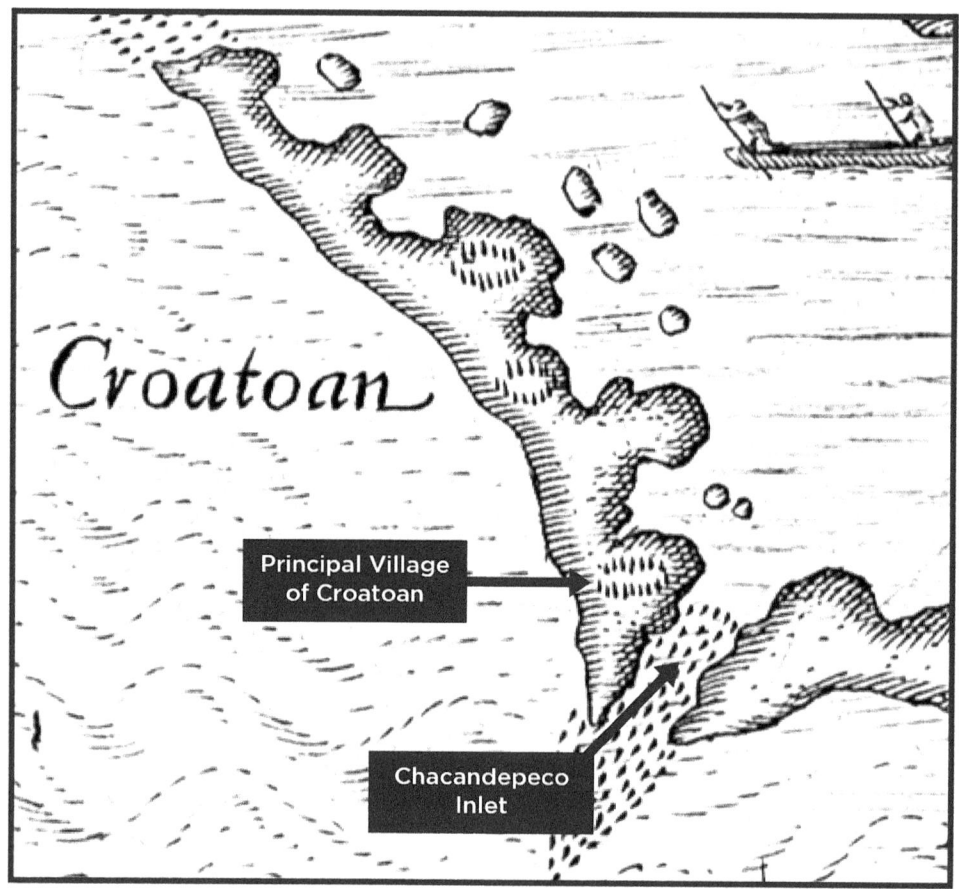

Part of the 1590 White/de Bry map showing the three villages on Croatoan and the Chacandepeco inlet.

Manteo's appearance, attire, and comportment would change dramatically over the course of the next three years, as will be seen, and so it would be instructive to understand what he looked like to the English at the time of the first Anglo-Algonquian contact. Unfortunately, other than a single reference in Barlowe's account—which was probably not added until years later—to both Manteo and Wanchese as "lustie men," meaning "vigorous, lively, spirited," there is no evidence in the historical sources pertaining specifically to Manteo's physical characteristics or appearance when the English arrived in July of 1584. There were two passing comments recorded about Manteo's and Wanchese's appearance by non–English observers, but these occurred months later, after their voyage to England, and by which time their attire had changed. One of these comments was made by Leopold von Wedel, a nobleman from Pomerania (the northern part of present-day Poland and Germany), who visited London in October 1584. After Raleigh allowed him to see Manteo and Wanchese, von Wedel wrote in part, "In face and figure they were very much like white Moors."[13] His comment, though, is not particularly helpful, since at that time the term "Moor" was not ethnically or geographically precise.[14] The best that can be gathered from von Wedel's comment is that Manteo and Wanchese were not very dark-skinned.

The other very brief reference to Manteo's physical appearance is from a Spanish account by Hernando Altamirano, one of the Spaniards who met with Grenville and the

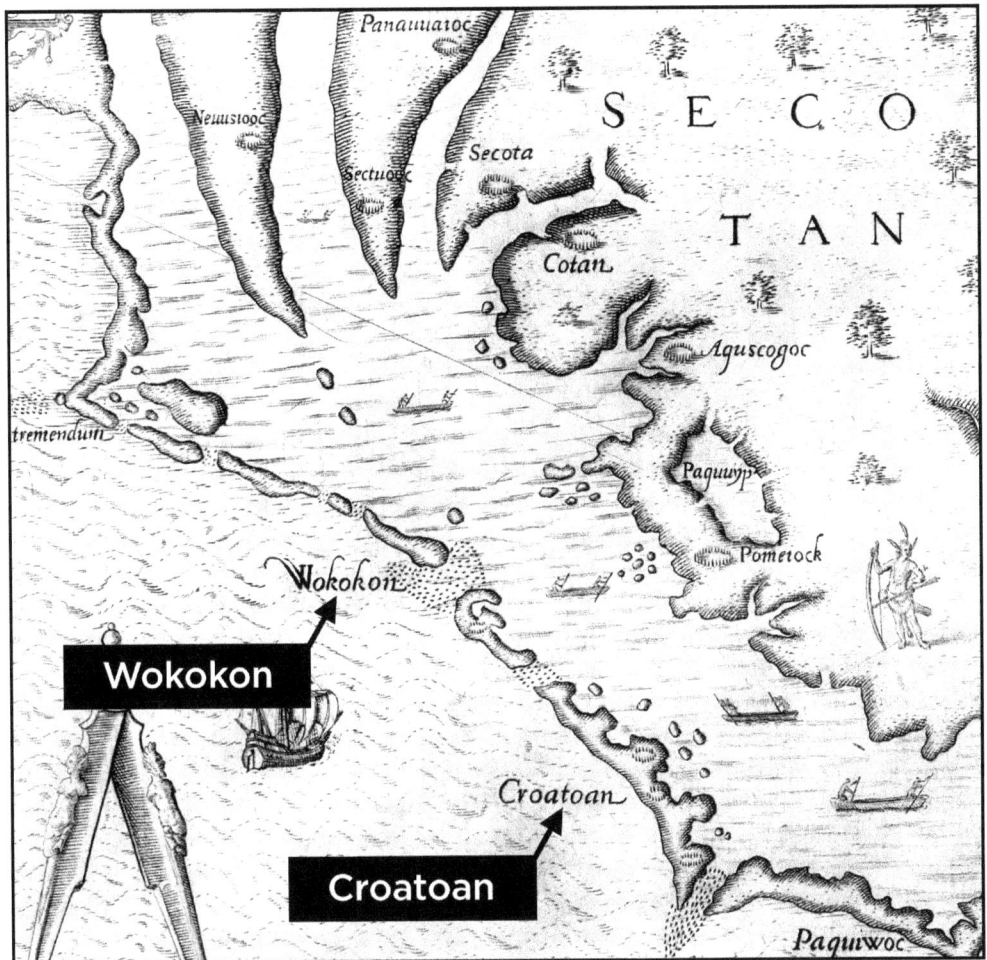

Location of Manteo's Croatoan and its proximity to Wokokon on the White/de Bry map.

English in May 1585, at the island of St. John in the Caribbean. Grenville's fleet had stopped there en route to Roanoke Island with Manteo and Wanchese on May 11 to build a new pinnace to replace the one lost in a storm. Altamirano noted that "They [the English] were accompanied by two tall Indians whom they treated well…."[15] This notation, however, was made a number of months after von Wedel's and offers little information about Manteo's appearance when the English arrived at the Outer Banks nearly a year earlier. All that can be said about Manteo (and Wanchese) from these accounts, then, is that they were tall and not particularly dark skinned.

There were more detailed reports about the physical traits of the eastern Algonquians *in general* from their late 16th and early 17th century English contemporaries. As the Spaniard Altamirano noted above, Manteo was considered to be "tall" by comparison and that was indeed true of the eastern Algonquians. Skeletal analysis has indicated that the average height of European men in the 16th century was about 5 feet 6 inches, so it can probably be safely approximated that Algonquian men of the time may have averaged about 5 feet 10 inches or perhaps even taller. John Smith of the Jamestown colony wrote of Wahunsonacock (Chief Powhatan) that "he is of personage a tall well proportioned man…." Regarding the Virginia Algonquians in general, Smith wrote, they were "generally tall and straight, of a comely proportion."[16]

One of the most telling visual examples of Anglo-Algonquian height difference can be found in the following illustration from Smith's *Generall Historie of Virginia*. The illustration was intended to depict Smith's capture of Opechancanough, the Pamaunkey chief, in 1608. Although the details of events in his *Generall Historie* may not always be completely reliable, the illustration at least demonstrates that there must have been a fairly considerable height discrepancy between the Pamaunkey weroance and Smith, who is believed to have been slightly shorter than average, perhaps about 5 feet 4 or 5 inches tall.

Smith also added that they "are of a colour browne when they are of any age, but they are borne white. Their hayre is generally blacke, but few haue any beards.... They are very strong, of an able body and full of agilitie, able to endure to lie in the woods vnder a tree by the fire, in the worst of winter, or in the weedes and grasse, in Ambuscado in the Sommer."[17] In his *Historie of Travaile Into Virginia Britannia* Strachey explained how and why they achieved their brown appearance:

> They are generally of a cullour browne or rather tawny which they cast themselves into with a kind of arsenick stone ... or rather red tempered oyntments of earth, and the juyce of certain scrused [crushed] rootes, when they come unto certaine yeares, and this they doe (keeping themselves still so smudged and besmeared) eyther for the custome of the countrye, or the better to defend them ... from the stinging of muskitoes.

"C Smith taketh the King of Pamaunkee prisoner 1608."

However, he went on to say, "they are from the womb indifferent white, but as the men, so doe the women, dye and disquise themselves into this tawny cowler, esteeming yt the best beauty."[18]

The most accurate assessment of what Manteo must have looked like to the English in the summer of 1584 can be inferred from the depictions of other Carolina Algonquians produced by artist and cartographer John White during the 1585–6 colonization attempt at Roanoke. White's detailed water colors included the native Algonquians' manner of dress, hair arrangements, and adornments. Engravings of 23 of White's drawings were published by Theodor de Bry in

1590 to illustrate Harriot's *Briefe and true report*. Although de Bry's engravings captivated the public and provided Europeans with their first views of the New World and its native inhabitants, they were not identical in style and detail to the original watercolors produced by White in 1585–86, copies of which would not be published until the 19th century. De Bry was in London after the return of the first colonization attempt in 1586, and he met with Hakluyt, who had seen White's watercolors. Hakluyt persuaded de Bry to publish Harriot's *Briefe and true report* and to illustrate the book with White's drawings. It is possible that White redrew some of his originals to accommodate de Bry's requirements, which could account for the differences.

Compare, for example, the 1590 de Bry engraving below of "A weroan or great Lorde of Virginia" with White's earlier watercolor from 1585–86. Although the de Bry engraving adds background figures, the subject lacks much of the detail of the original and his posture has been "idealized" somewhat to appeal more to European sensibilities. The reversed figure in the engraving is the result of the standard practice of cutting the copper plate from a reflected image of the original.

Neither de Bry's engraving nor White's original watercolor, both produced well after Manteo had assumed English attire, could of course be he, even though the watercolor has

Left: De Bry's engraving of "A weroan or great Lorde of Virginia." **Right:** White's original 1585–86 depiction of an Algonquian leader.

been portrayed as such, especially online. Nevertheless the watercolor in particular offers a number of useful details about the appearance and attire of a neighboring Indian of Manteo's comparable status, and as such suggests how Manteo probably appeared to the English when they first arrived in the summer of 1584.

The following descriptive text, provided by Thomas Harriot for de Bry, accompanied the engraving in de Bry's 1590 publication:

> The Princes of Virginia ... weare the haire of their heades long and bynde opp the ende of the same in a knot vnder thier eares. Yet they cutt the topp of their heades from the forehead to the nape of the necke in manner of a cokscombe [a crest of hair at the top of the head sometimes called a roach or 'Mohawk style'], [sticking a fair long feather] of some berd att the Begininge of the creste vppun their foreheads, and another short one on both seides about their eares. They hange at their eares ether thicke pearles, or ... the clawe of some great birde.... Moreouer They ether pownes [tattoo], or paynt their forehead, cheeks, chynne, bodye, armes, and legs.... They weare a chaine about their necks of pearles or beades of copper ... and wear they also braselets ohn their armes. They hange before them the skinne of some beaste verye feinelye [finely] dresset in suche sorte, that the tayle hangeth downe behynde. They carye a quiuer made of small rushes holding their bowe readie bent in on hand, radie to defend themselues.[19]

White's original picture depicts a weroance posing with what would be considered "ceremonial" adornments worn only for important occasions. Normally a warrior or weroance would be dressed for more utilitarian purposes. It was important, for example, that there were no obstructions of any kind on the sides of the head such as feathers, long hair, or jewelry that could interfere with a bowstring, a primary consideration in hunting or war. It was for that reason that the Powhatan Algonquian warriors to the north had the right side of their heads below the roach shaved clean using oyster shells.[20] From the description above it does not appear that "the Princes of Virginia," i.e., the important young weroances, followed that practice, but it is possible that the rest of their tribesmen may have done so or at least kept the right side cut short. In any case the adornments depicted above would not usually be worn, especially when they were "radie to defend themselues," and any long hair would have been tied up securely in a knot. For Manteo, though, the upcoming voyage to the place called England would undoubtedly have been a highly anticipated event, possibly requiring traditional ceremonial attire. On the day of his departure, then, he may have been dressed for the occasion in much the same manner as the weroance in White's portrait.

"We brought home ... two of the Sauages"

With Manteo and Wanchese aboard, Amadas and Barlowe left the Outer Banks sometime in August and arrived in England in mid–September of 1584. There are no existing reports about the voyage itself, but the fact that it took only about a month to reach England would indicate that the trip was relatively fast and uneventful. For Manteo, however, the voyage was anything but uneventful. It is impossible to know his thoughts about the passage, of course, but one can at least begin to conceive of Manteo's reactions by comparing elements of that experience with what he had known previously. Prior to this ocean voyage the largest water crafts Manteo or any of his people had known were dugout canoes, painstakingly made, without the use of metal tools, from large felled tree trunks hollowed out by burning and scraping with shells in the manner illustrated below:

The following is Harriot's text accompanying this 1590 de Bry engraving and describing in detail the meticulous "manner of makinge their boates."

De Bry's engraving of "the manner of makinge their boates."

The manner of makinge their boates in Virginia is verye wonderfull. For weras they want Instruments of yron, or other like vnto ours, yet they knowe howe to make them as handsomelye, to saile with whear they liste in their Riuers, and to fishe with all, as ours. First they choose some longe, and thicke tree, according to the bignes of the boate which they would frame, and make a fyre on the grownd abowt the Roote therof, kindlinge the same by little, and little with drie mosse of trees, and chipps of woode that the flame should not mounte opp to highe, and burne to muche of the lengte of the tree When yt is almost burnt thorough, and readye to fall they make a new fyre, which they suffer to burne vntill the tree fall of yt owne accord. Then burninge of the topp, and bowghs of the tree in suche wyse that the bodie of thesame may Retayne his iust lengthe, they raise yt vppon potes laid ouer cross wise vppon forked posts, at suche a reasonable heighte as rhey may handsomlye worke vppó yt. Then take they of the barke with certayne shells: thy reserue the, innermost parte of the lennke, for the nethermost parte of the boate. On the other side they make a fyre according to the lengthe of the bodye of the tree, sauinge at both the endes. That which they thinke is sufficientlye burned they quenche and scrape away with shells, and makinge a new syre they burne yt agayne, and soe they continne somtymes burninge and sometymes scrapinge, vntill the boate haue sufficient bothowmes. This god indueth thise sauage people with sufficient reason to make thinges necessarie to serue their turnes.[21]

    The ships of the 1584 Amadas-Barlowe expedition were not named in the account, but it is believed that they may well have been the large 200 tun[22] *Bark Raleigh* and the smaller, perhaps 30–40 tun *Dorothy*. Both of these vessels were far greater in size and capability that anything Manteo had known before, a further demonstration of the strange abilities the English seemed to possess. The ships were wonders in themselves, massive and tall and yet capable of catching the wind as they plowed through the sea, while his familiar Croatoan coastline quickly faded away in their wakes. Manteo had never been out of sight of land, whether it was his home on the barrier islands or the mainland or the islands that dotted the sounds. Now he was a participant in an extraordinary journey to a strange and unknown destination so distant that for weeks nothing but the ocean could be seen in every direction.

The lack of any further details about this historic voyage from the Outer Banks to England has led to several improbable speculations concerning Manteo and Wanchese. It has been suggested, for example, that the two Indians may have been coerced or even seized and taken to England against their will. Paul Hulton, former curator at the British Museum, referred to them as "the Indians captured by Amadas and Barlowe,"[23] and historian David Beers Quinn called them "captives."[24] However, there is no evidence whatsoever in the contemporary sources to support that conclusion. On the contrary, given the fact that very friendly and cooperative relations had just been established with the coastal Algonquians, a prerequisite for Raleigh's colonization attempt the following year, it does not seem remotely possible that Amadas and Barlowe would have jeopardized everything by abducting two of the native Indians and forcibly carrying them away.

Furthermore, it ignores the far more likely conclusion that both Manteo and Wanchese had specific objectives, albeit different, for undertaking the voyage. The Roanoac Indian Wanchese may very well have been sent by his principal weroance, the cautious Wingina, to estimate the numbers, strength, and intentions of the English. Manteo, on the other hand, particularly given the previously mentioned spiritual nature of his association with the English, would have seen this voyage as a personal journey of discovery to further understand their remarkable powers and capabilities, which could perhaps be harnessed for his own and his tribe's future benefit. Both Manteo's and Wanchese's actions and behavior upon their return to the Outer Banks the following year strongly support those two very different motivations. Far from having to be coerced, or even persuaded, it is much more likely that Manteo would have looked forward to the extraordinary voyage with eager anticipation.

It has also been speculated that scientist and mathematician Thomas Harriot may have accompanied Amadas and Barlowe on the reconnaissance voyage to the Outer Banks and had begun interacting with Manteo as early as August of 1584, during the return trip to England. That notion was based on the fact that Harriot and Manteo seemed to have acquired a working knowledge of each other's language relatively quickly, about two and a half months after they arrived in London in September. Consequently, it has been theorized, the language instruction may have started a month earlier during the voyage. Again there is no evidence to support this. Harriot is not mentioned or referred to at all in Barlowe's account, and his name was certainly not included among the list of "particular Gentlemen, and men of accompt [account], who then were present." Given Harriot's standing and his close association with Raleigh at that time, it is highly unlikely that a person of his importance would have been omitted from such a list of gentlemen if he had actually been among them. In addition, to assume that either Harriot or Manteo was incapable of quickly acquiring at least a minimal facility with the other's language in two and a half months does them both an injustice. Harriot's reputation as a brilliant scientist was well known, and Manteo, as mentioned, would have been highly motivated to assimilate as much as he could of the English manitou. The first step in that process would be to comprehend their strange language, an aptitude Manteo very likely possessed, since in all of the subsequent accounts, he appears to have been intelligent, perceptive, and alert.

Quinn and others have also suggested that John White, artist and future governor of the 1587 colony, may have been on that reconnaissance voyage as well and consequently would have made Manteo's acquaintance as early as 1584. That assumption is based entirely on a single sentence White penned in a 1593 letter to Richard Hakluyt in which he mentioned "my fift and last voiage to Virginia,"[25] a term then applied to the entire east coast of North America. Those who propose that White must have been on the 1584 reconnaissance voyage argue that White took only four known voyages to "Virginia," and therefore the fifth must have been made in 1584. White, however, almost certainly *did* actually sail five separate times for what was called Virginia, but the 1584 voyage was not one of them: He was obviously part of the Grenville-Lane colonization attempt at Roanoke in 1585–86, and in 1587 he sailed to "Virginia" as governor in the second colonization effort. In 1588 he made an unsuccessful voyage to resupply the 1587 colony, and in 1590 he made his "fift" and last voyage to Roanoke Island in a failed attempt to find his "lost" colony. What Quinn and others seem to have overlooked, however, was White's *first* voyage as artist aboard the ship *Aid* with Martin Frobisher's expedition in 1577 to discover the Northwest Passage. The persuasive evidence for White's presence on that expedition are the sketches and watercolors of scenes and native Inuits produced during the voyage, attributed to him, and purchased a century later from his family descendant.

White's 1588 attempt aboard the *Brave* to resupply his colony, although he was forced to abandon the effort near the Azores and return to England, must be counted as one of the voyages he undertook to Virginia, and was so documented by at least one of his contemporaries. There is a line accompanying the illustrations in Harriot's *A Briefe and true report*, published by Theodor de Bry in 1590, stating that the images were "Drawne by Ihon White who was sent thither [to Virginia] speciallye and for the same purpose by the said Sir Walter Raleigh the year abovesaid 1585 … and also the year 1588."[26] Again, neither Harriot nor White was mentioned in Barlowe's account and no drawings or documents exist to demonstrate that White was there in 1584. The 1584 voyage was purely a reconnaissance effort, intended primarily to claim the new land for England and to locate a potential site for Raleigh's subsequent colonization attempt in 1585. Amadas and Barlowe accomplished those goals in the few weeks that their ships remained anchored at the Outer Banks. There would have been little practical reason for Raleigh to send either White or Harriot at that point. It is much more likely that White, who was not part of Raleigh's inner circle at Durham House in London, did not meet Manteo until late April or May of 1585, when final preparations were made for Raleigh's first colonization expedition. The assumption that either White or Harriot was part of the 1584 reconnaissance voyage appears to be without merit.

The ships arrived "in the West of England about the middest of September," 1584, and then from there Manteo and Wanchese were transported to London. One can only imagine Manteo's reaction when he first laid eyes on London, a densely populated city that would soon approach 200,000. It should be remembered that until this time the largest "town" Manteo had seen consisted of about twenty native dwellings. The village of Roanoac, which Manteo's Croatoans visited frequently, reportedly had just nine houses, and its sister village of Dasamonquepeuc probably had no more than that. "Their townes are but small," Harriot wrote, "& neere the sea coast but few, some containing but 10 or 12 houses: some 20 the greatest that we haue seene haue bene but of 30 houses."[27] Manteo and his fellow Algonquians had only heard about, but not actually seen, "the greatest citie, called Skicoak, which this people affirme to be very greate."[28] Harriot and an exploratory party spent part of the winter of 1585–86 near Skicoac, the town he referred to as "the greatest that we haue seene." This was the chief village of the Chesepian tribe on the present-day Elizabeth River well to the north of Roanoac, and it contained thirty dwellings. By comparison, the enormity of London was inconceivable. The route Manteo took to London after disembarking "in the West of England" was not recorded, but if they approached the city by way of London Bridge, he may have seen the severed heads of traitors often impaled on pikes at the bridge's gatehouse.

When Manteo arrived in England, London was on the verge of becoming one of the great commercial centers in Europe as people flocked there from other parts of England, Wales, and continental Europe. In 1580 Queen Elizabeth had attempted to restrict London's swelling population by issuing a proclamation which prohibited new building within three miles of the city "where no former house had been known to have been within living memory."[29] The proclamation apparently had little effect and was probably not strictly enforced, however, since London's population growth continued unabated.

With London's rapid growth, increasing prices, and poor land usage policies, also came rising poverty, unemployment, and crime. Much has been written about the crowded narrow streets, the filthy conditions, disease, and the poverty that existed in London during this time, but if Manteo caught even a glimpse of the city's seedy side it would have been purely by accident. Raleigh's purpose in bringing the two Algonquians to London was basically twofold: One reason was to learn from Manteo and Wanchese about their homeland, particularly its valuable commodities, and their language, all of which were assigned to Harriot. Raleigh's other reason was to use the two native Algonquians for marketing purposes, to help drum up financial support for his planned colonization venture the following year. That goal involved the careful orchestration of their activities, including interactions with London's prosperous citizenry. Most of those interactions occurred at Raleigh's London residence or at court, precluding any association with the lower classes and their environs which were looked upon with disfavor and linked to the periodic plagues that struck London, the last of which had occurred just two years earlier. Manteo and Wanchese were also seen occasionally in public to be sure, touring London's imposing cathedrals and palaces and probably also at fairs and other public venues. They would have been accompanied by a small retinue which likely included Raleigh or Harriot, or perhaps both, and the two Algonquians' fascination with London's attractions would have been matched by that of London's curious onlookers.

An early reference to Manteo, although not by name, appeared in a line from Arthur Barlowe's journal, completed some weeks after he returned to England. Barlowe mentioned "these men which we haue brought with vs to England," but his account would not be published until 1589. The first printed reference to Manteo, again not by name, was published shortly after his arrival in London in September of 1584. The reference appeared in a notice in one of the early English "news-letters" printed by Arthur Collins announcing the return of the 1584 expedition sent out by Raleigh to America. The notice reported that "two gentlemen the one called Philip Amadis; the other Arthur Barlow ... returned ... and brought with them two savage men of that countrie."[30] Another reference was printed about three months later, in mid–December, in the official bill confirming Raleigh's patent for the "discoverie and Inhabitinge of certeyn Foreyne Landes." The document acknowledged the discovery of "a Land called Wyngandacoia ... and some of the people borne in those parties [were] brought home into this our Realme of England by whose meanes & direction ... great commodities of that Lande are revealed & made knowen vnto vs."[31] It is clear that Harriot and Manteo had acquired a working proficiency with each other's language by December 1584.

Manteo's name was recorded in a line which was apparently added to the very end of the Barlowe account a number of years later by Richard Hakluyt. The line, which was appended after the list of gentlemen who were on the voyage, read "We brought home also two of the Sauages being lustie men, whose names were Wanchese and Manteo." As mentioned, however, Barlowe's account did not appear in print until it was published by Hakluyt in his

1589 *The Principal Navigations, Voyages, Traffiques and Discoveries of the English Nation*, but that first edition did not contain the abovementioned line. The line containing Manteo's (and Wanchese's) name, was not included until the publication of the 1600 edition. Since Barlowe's original journal has not survived, it is not known if it actually contained the two Algonquians' names and were initially omitted by Hakluyt, or whether Hakluyt simply inserted the names later for the sake of clarity and continuity between the account of the Amadas-Barlowe voyage in 1584 and that of the subsequent voyages, when Manteo played a significant role. In any case, if Manteo's name was not widely known to the London public, it was certainly well known among Raleigh's inner circle by the fall of 1584, and it would be familiar to all the Roanoke voyagers thereafter.

Manteo's arrival in England coincided with the rapid ascension of Sir Walter Raleigh's standing in Queen Elizabeth's court as well as in her personal favor. Raleigh had already gained fame and notoriety as a result of his military actions against the Irish in Munster in 1580 and the suppression of the Desmond Rebellion there, which included his participation in the infamous massacre at Smerwick. Upon the death at sea of his half-brother, Sir Humphry Gilbert, on September 9, 1583, Raleigh petitioned the queen to transfer Gilbert's rights for discovery in America to him. Queen Elizabeth responded by granting "to our trusty and welbeloued seruant Walter Ralegh" his own Letters Patent "for the discovering and planting of new lands."[32] Raleigh's first act under his new charter was to commission the 1584 Amadas-Barlowe reconnaissance expedition which returned to England with Manteo and Wanchese.

Manteo was in England for seven months, from mid–September 1584, to April 9, 1585, time enough to comprehend the strange and powerful manitou of the English in general and Raleigh in particular. An account of the voyage was apparently submitted to Queen Elizabeth in October, about the same time that Manteo and Wanchese were presented at Hampton Court, where all the trappings of Elizabethan grandeur were on display. Shortly thereafter Raleigh was elected to Parliament and in December 1584, he introduced the abovementioned bill confirming his patent for discovery in "Virginia." On January 6, 1585, Sir Walter Raleigh was knighted by Queen Elizabeth and was granted the title of Lord and Governor of Virginia. Although it is not known whether Manteo witnessed the ceremony, he would almost certainly have understood from his own observations and his conversations with Harriot that Raleigh's prestige and influence had been heightened even further. The rise of Raleigh's status and authority—his enhanced manitou—would not have escaped Manteo's notice and may have contributed to his continued identification with the English.

During Manteo's entire stay in England he lived at Raleigh's sumptuous Durham House on the bank of the Thames River in west London. Durham House, situated near the bend in the Thames, had its own chapel, great room, stables, and private rooms where Manteo resided. From Durham House he could see the imposing architectural wonders of Southwark Cathedral on one side and Whitehall Palace and Westminster Abbey on the other. He would have visited these grand structures in person as Raleigh exhibited the two Algonquians around London, including the formal occasion when Raleigh presented them to the Queen's court. Durham house had been built by Bishop Thomas Hatfield more than two centuries earlier and was granted by Queen Elizabeth to Raleigh in 1583. It is believed that Raleigh's study was situated in a turret at Durham House overlooking the Thames. Also lodged at Durham House was the scientist, astronomer, and mathematician Thomas Harriot, who set up a twelve foot telescope on the roof of Durham house, the first astronomical telescope in England.[33] It was at Durham House that Harriot worked tirelessly learning the

Algonquian language, and he devised a phonetic Algonquian alphabet in the process. Both Manteo and Wanchese seem to have taken to the work at hand at Durham House quickly and constructively, and they soon acquired at least a basic proficiency with the English language. Manteo would become the primary English/Algonquian interpreter and guide during the years that followed. It was possibly during one of these language sessions at Durham House that Harriot discovered to his surprise that "Wingandacoa," the expression originally thought to be the native Algonquian name for the territory ruled by their primary weroance, Wingina, actually was an Algonquian compliment extended to Amadas and Barlowe meaning "You have good clothes."

In mid–October, about a month after Manteo arrived in London, Raleigh was called on at Durham House by the abovementioned nobleman Leopold von Wedel and his retinue from Pomerania. During the visit Raleigh exhibited Manteo and Wanchese to von Wedel, who wrote about the experience. Although von Wedel would have been unaware of the nuances of English social structure, his comments provide us with some insight into

Part of John Norden's 1593 map of Westminster, showing Durham House.

the way Raleigh intended Manteo and Wanchese to be perceived in Elizabethan England. Von Wedel wrote in the October 18th entry of his journal that Raleigh "allowed us to see them [Manteo and Wanchese]. In face and figure they were very much like white Moors. Normally they wear no shirt, just a wild animal skin across the shoulders and a piece of fur over the privies, but now they were dressed in brown taffeta. No one could understand what they said…." If, according to von Wedel, "no one could understand what they said," it could either mean that Manteo and Wanchese had spoken in Algonquian, or that their rough English was not yet refined enough for von Wedel's retinue—whose native language was Slavic—to recognize.

It is most notable that Manteo and Wanchese had already discarded their native dress and were now clothed in English attire. What Von Wedel could not have known—nor could Manteo and Wanchese for that matter—was that English attire was strictly regulated by the Sumptuary Laws or Statutes of Apparel which had been reformed by Queen Elizabeth in 1562 and again in 1574. These statutes were supposedly put in place to prevent the "superfluity" of spending on the "excess of apparel" which could "ruin … many good families" and lead to the "decay of the wealth of the realm."[34] In actuality, however, the statutes prescribed in great detail both the color and type of material one was permitted to wear based entirely on his or her social status. Consequently, in the strict class structure of Elizabethan society, one's social standing could easily be observed by one's attire. For example, "silke of the colour purpura [purple]" could only be worn by the royal family, but other noblemen were permitted to have purple linings inside their cloaks. On the other end of the social spectrum were the lower classes, who wore wool, linen, or sheepskin clothing, but were permitted to have taffeta or velvet buttons or trimming.

The fact that both Manteo and Wanchese were "dressed in brown taffeta" says something about their perceived standing, at least initially, in the class structure of London society in 1584. "Taffeta," unfortunately, was a term that could be applied to a range of material, including fabrics reserved only for the higher classes, but by "taffeta" in this instance von Wedel probably meant that their clothing was made of a plain-woven fabric that is the same on both sides.[35] The color of their taffeta, however, is more instructive. Just as purple garments were reserved exclusively for the royal family, brown attire was assigned decidedly to the lower classes. The color brown represented poverty and humility, and brown dye was made from a root commonly found in England, as opposed to the "richer" color dyes which were scarcer and often had to be imported. Brown dye was cheap and readily available, and brown clothing was seen throughout the poorer sections of English society. By exchanging their original native dress for brown English attire, almost certainly a plan designed by Raleigh, Manteo and Wanchese would now be seen as having submitted—symbolically at least—to the dictates of Elizabethan societal authority.

All of this was part of Raleigh's effort to assure those potential investors and participants in the upcoming colonization expedition that there was nothing at all to fear from the "sauages" in America. Manteo and Wanchese were presented as living proof that the native Indians not only could be readily enlightened and civilized, but also that they would soon speak the Queen's English, demonstrations of which would have delighted both investors and the nobility. The *brown* attire would have been a not-so-subtle hint to all, except the two Algonquians themselves, that the native Indians would have a place in the new colonial society in "Virginia," but that their role would be more or less subservient. After all, Harriot would later write, "it [is] probable that they shoulde desire our friendships & loue, and haue the greater respect for pleasing and obeying vs."[36]

A briefe content of certayne clauses

of the Statute of King Henry the eight, and Queene Mary,
with some moderations thereof, to be observed accor-
dyng to her Maiesties Proclamation
above mentioned.

¶ Mens apparrel.

None shall weare in apparell any	Sylke of the colour of purpure, Cloth of golde tissued, nor furre of Sables.	but only the	Kyng. Queene. Kynges	Mother. Chyldren. Brethren and sisters. Uncles & Auntes.	and except	Dukes, Marquesses, & Earles, who may weare ý same in Dublets, Jerkins, linings of Clokes, Gownes, and Hose. And those of the Garter, Purple in Mantels only.
	Cloth of Golde. Syluer. Tinseld Satten. Sylke, or cloth myxt or embrodered with any golde or syluer.				excepte	All degrees above Viscountes, and Viscountes, Barons, and other persons of lyke degrees, in Dublets, Jerkins, lynynges of Clokes, Gownes, and Hose.
	Wollen cloth made out of the Realme, but in Cappes only. Veluet Crymson or Scarlet. Furres Blacke Jenets. Lusernes. Embroderie, or Taylers worke, hauyng golde, or syluer, or pearle therein.				excepte	Dukes, Marquesses, Earles and Viscountes, Barons, and Knyghtes, beyng companions of the Garter, or any person beyng of the pryuie Counsel. / theyr chyldren.
	Veluet in Gownes, Coates, or other uttermost garmentes. Furre of Libardes. Embroderie with any sylke.				excepte	Men of the degrees above mentioned, Barons sonnes, Knyghtes, and Gentlemen in ordinarie office attendant upon her Maiesties person, and suche as haue ben employed in Imbassages to foraigne pryncees.
	Cappes, Hattes, Hatbandes, Capbandes, Garters, Bootehose, Sylke Netherstockes. Enamelled Chaynes, Buttons, Aglets.	trimmed with	Golde, or Syluer, or Pearle.		excepte	Men of the degrees above mentioned, the Gentlemen attendyng upon the Queenes person in her hyghnesse priuie chaumber, or in the office of Cupbearer, Caruer, Shewer, Esquier for the body, Gentlemen ushers, or Esquires of the Stable.
	Satten, Damaske, Silke Chamlet, or Taffata, in furre whereof the hynde groweth not within the Queenes dominions, excepte Foynes, graye Jenets and Budge.	Gowne, Coate, Hose, or uppermost garmentes.			excepte	The degrees and persons above mentioned, and men that may dispende, C. li. by the yeere, and so valued in the subsidie booke.
	Hatte, Bonnet, Gyrdle, Scaberdes of swordes, daggers, &c. Shoes and Pantophles.	of Veluet.			excepte	The degrees and persons above named, and the sonne and heyre apparant of a Knyght.
	Sylke, other then Satten, Damaske, Taffata, Chamlet, in Dublets: and Sarcenet, Chamlet, or Taffata, in facyng of Gownes and Clokes, and in Coates, Jackets, Jerkins, Coyfes, Purses, beyng not of colour Scarlet, Crymson, or Blewe. Furre of Foynes, graye Jenets, or other, as the lyke groweth not in the Queenes dominions.				excepte	Men of the degrees and persons above mentioned, sonne of a Knyght, or sonne and heyre apparante of a man of CCC. Marke lande by yeere, so valued in the subsidie bookes, and men that may dispende, xl. li. by the yeere, so valued, ut supra.
None shall weare	Spurres. Swordes. Rapiers. Daggers. Skaynes. Woodknyues, or Hangers. Buckles of Gyrdles.	Gylt, Syluered, or Damasked.			excepte	Knyghtes and Barons sonnes, and other of hygher degree or place, and Gentlemen in ordinarie office attendaunt upon the Queenes Maiesties person, which Gentlemen so attendaunt, may weare al the premisses, sauyng gylte, syluered, or Damasked Spurres.

Page from the Sumptuary Laws regarding "Mens apparel."

There is no doubt that Raleigh intended to use Manteo and Wanchese principally for commercial purposes, to attract investors for his colonization enterprise and to convince Queen Elizabeth that America was ripe for English expansion. Raleigh's friend, the chronicler Richard Hakluyt, was also an Anglican priest and he attached a religious purpose to the enterprise as well. His *Discourse of Western Planting* had already been written "at the requeste and direction of the righte worshipfull Mr. Walter Raghly, nowe Knight," and "before the comynge home of his twoo barkes [the Amadas-Barlowe ships]." The *Discourse* was a twenty-chapter promotional piece advocating the many benefits that would result from the initial 1584 reconnaissance voyage and future colonization enterprises. The leading argument in Hakluyt's *Discourse* was that "This westerne discoverie will be greately for thinlargement of the gospell of Christe, whereunto the princes of the refourmed relligion are chiefely bounde, amomgest whome her Majestie ys principall."[37] Hakluyt's passage was a reminder to Queen Elizabeth that since the establishment of the reformed church—when England broke from the authority of the Pope—the Roman Catholic King Phillip II of Spain had gotten a big lead in the race to acquire new souls in America. It was not too late, though, Hakluyt advised, because "God hath his tyme for all men who calleth some at the nynth, and some at the eleventh houer. And if it please him to move the hart of her Majestie to put her helping hande to this godly action, she shall finde as willinge subjects of all sortes as any other prince in all Christendome."[38] Manteo and Wanchese, dressed in English clothing and learning to speak English, were living examples of such "willinge subjects" who, as Harriot predicted, would "in short time be brought to ciuilitie, and the imbracing of true religion."[39]

At Durham House Manteo and Wanchese participated in hours of sessions with Harriot, and they would have appreciated and taken a keen interest in the occasional tours of London's attractions with Raleigh. One of those attractions was the Palace of Westminster, not far from Durham House, which they certainly saw many times from a distance and probably visited several times as well. In February 1585, while preparations were in progress for Raleigh's first colonization attempt, the talk circulating throughout London was the upcoming execution of William Parry for allegedly attempting to assassinate Queen Elizabeth. Parry had confessed after being "examined" three times, but he vehemently denied the charges afterwards, to no avail. Manteo could easily have noticed the excited crowds gathering at Westminster's Old Palace Yard for Parry's public execution on March 2, 1585, and one might wonder how Raleigh or Harriot may have explained the event to him or what effect it may have had. Ironically, the Old Palace Yard at Westminster was where Raleigh himself would be publicly executed thirty-three years later, on October 29, 1618.

At some point, almost certainly before the fleet set sail from England to Roanoke in April 1585, the mindset of the two Algonquians split dramatically. While Wanchese grew increasingly skeptical and wary, Manteo's opinion of the English flourished. It has been suggested that the English may have treated Manteo more favorably than Wanchese, but there is no evidence to support that supposition. All that can be surmised is that perhaps Manteo was more motivated than Wanchese and may have begun to work longer and more closely with Harriot, but even that is guesswork. Both Wanchese and Manteo had been exposed to the wonders—the manitou—of the English and their world, but while one apparently grew to fear it, the other seems to have embraced its potential. Such power could defeat the enemies of the Secotans, particularly Piemacum, whom both Wanchese and Manteo had "oftentimes … perswaded vs to surprise." Manteo came to believe that a closer association—if not integration—with the English would not only enhance his own standing, but would also benefit the coastal Algonquians in general and his mother's tribe at Croatoan in particular. The two Algonquians were probably assured by Harriot, who normally had a more benign attitude toward the native Indians than most of the other Englishmen, that the purpose of the English was to live side by side with their Indian friends in an atmosphere of friendship and cooperation. Hakluyt had already stated in his *Discourse* that the intention of the English was to "use the natural people there with all humanitie, curtesie, and freedome."[40] Wanchese seems to have been unconvinced.

Raleigh's efforts to garner support for his 1585 colonization voyage to America were successful. Notable merchants and financiers as William Sanderson and George Carey backed the venture. Francis Walsingham, Queen Elizabeth's principal secretary, was a prominent supporter and members of his household joined the venture, as did Thomas Cavendish and Anthony Rowse, both members of Parliament. The Queen herself donated £400 worth of gunpowder and offered her ship, the *Tyger*, to be used as the flagship of the fleet. Raleigh hoped to lead the venture personally, but the Queen, unwilling to allow her favorite to venture too far on a potentially dangerous expedition, forbade him to sail with the fleet. Instead Raleigh's cousin, Richard Grenville, would lead the voyage, and Ralph Lane, soldier and expert on fortifications was recalled from Ireland and would be governor of the colony. Philip Amadas, co-leader of the 1584 reconnaissance expedition, would be Admiral, and Thomas Cavendish was the High Marshal responsible for military order and discipline. The colony, in fact, would be made up mostly of seasoned military men, whose attitudes and experience—particularly against the Irish—would unfortunately leave little room for tolerance and patience in their dealings with the tribes in Virginia. Manteo and Wanchese most likely stayed close to Harriot as final preparations were made, as well as during the voyage, since they had spent much time with him at Durham House and he was the only Englishman who possessed a familiarity with the Algonquian language. Both Wanchese and Manteo would have been anxious to return to their homeland, although for different reasons and with completely different intentions.

"We passed by water to Aquascogok"

The seven-vessel fleet sailed from Plymouth, England, on April 9, 1585. During the voyage Manteo and Wanchese experienced more of the Englishmen's remarkable capabilities: On May 12 Grenville was anchored off the island of St. John in the Caribbean where they built a fort, constructed a new pinnace to replace the one lost during the ocean crossing, and awaited the rest of the fleet to rendezvous at that location. It was there that the Spaniard Hernando Altamirano saw Manteo and Wanchese, the "two tall Indians" whom the English "treated well." The erecting of the fort and then the construction of the pinnace, which was amazingly completed in less than twelve days, would have further reinforced in both Wanchese and Manteo the impressive prowess of the English. So too would have the ease with which Grenville captured two Spanish frigates on May 29 and 30. On June 5 they also witnessed an extraordinary event at Hispaniola, present-day Haiti/Dominican Republic. Grenville had two banquet houses built on the beach, where he provided the Spanish Governor and all his men with a lavish feast, accompanied by "the sound of trumpets, and consorte of musicke." The Spanish were so delighted that they afterwards drove a number of white bulls onto the beach and singled out three of them for a sporting exhibition whereby they were "to bee hunted by horsemen after their maner." One of the bulls "tooke [to] the

Sea" and had to be "slaine with a musket." On June 8 Manteo and Wanchese watched as the English stopped at a small island "to take Seales," strange dog-like beasts of the sea they had never seen before.[41] These "seales" would have been Caribbean monk seals, a species of seal native to those waters and "which in that place wee vnderstood to haue bene in great quantitie," but are now extinct.

The fleet anchored at Wokokon on June 26, and shortly thereafter Manteo made his first appearance at Croatoan since his departure the previous year. It must have been with great amazement and possible confusion that the Croatoans first laid eyes on him. The Manteo who was well known at Croatoan and Roanoac and the surrounding areas prior to August 1584, was quite different from the Manteo who returned from England ten months later. Whereas Wanchese quickly reverted to his native dress and ways, here now was a transformed Manteo, clothed like an Englishman and able to speak in their strange tongue. If Manteo's long journey to England was undertaken primarily to discover and perhaps adopt the powerful manitou of the English, then the trip must have been seen as a success. He undoubtedly told his mother and fellow tribesmen of the wonders he had witnessed on his remarkable journey to England and of the bright future he envisioned for the Croatoan people.

Manteo returned to Wokokon with the news that there were some Englishmen already at Croatoan. These turned out to be men dropped off by George Raymond, captain of the *Red Lyon*, who had separated from Grenville's fleet earlier and set off on a privateering venture. On July 6 Grenville sent Captain Aubry and Captain Boniten to retrieve the men at Croatoan, and on the same day he sent Manteo and one of the principal Englishmen, John Arundel, to the mainland presumably to announce Grenville's upcoming tour of Pamlico Sound. In the meantime Grenville "sent word of our arriuing at Wocokon, to Wingina at Roanoak," most likely dispatching Wanchese to convey the news.

Although Manteo's whereabouts during the next few days were not recorded in the English account, he had to have returned to Wokokon with John Arundel on July 8 in time to guide Grenville's exploratory expedition through Pamlico Sound. Manteo's ability as translator combined with his familiarity with the mainland villages accessible via the sound would have made him an indispensable part of this excursion. The weeklong expedition was led by Grenville with at least forty other leading Englishmen in four vessels. Guided by Manteo, they toured a number of locations in the sound and visited the villages of Pomeiock, Aquascogoc, and Secotan. They also visited "the great lake called by the Sauages Paquique [Lake Mattamuskeet]" and "diuers other places." The tour was intended, in part at least, to initiate a relationship between the local weroances and the newly arrived English who would soon be their neighbors. John White accompanied this expedition and his drawings at Pomeiock and Secotan were among the first images he produced of the New World.

Harriot wrote the following text which was published along with de Bry's engraving of the village of Pomeiock:

> ... They are compassed abowt with poles starcke faste in the grownd, but they are not verye stronge. The entrance is verye narrowe as may be seene by this picture, which is made according to the forme of the towne of Pomeiooc. There are but few howses therin, saue those which belonge to the kinge and his nobles. On the one side is their tempel separated from the other howses, and marked with the letter A. yt is builded rownde, and couered with skynne matts, and as *yt* wear compassed abowt. With cortynes without windowes, and hath noe ligthe but by the doore. On the other side is the kings lodginge marked with the letter B. Their dwellinges are built with certaine potes fastened together,

Village of Pomeiock, drawn by John White during the visit in July, 1585.

and couered with matts which they turne op as high as they thinke good, and soe receue in the lighte and other. Some are also couered with boughes of trees, as euery man lusteth or liketh best. They keepe their feasts and make good cheer together in the midds of the towne as yt is described in they 17. Figure. When the towne standeth fare from the water they digg a great poude noted with the letter C. wherhence they fetche as muche water as they neede.[42]

All went well during Grenville's excursion of Pamlico Sound until an unfortunate incident occurred on July 16 which would damage future Anglo-Algonquian relations, and tested Manteo's allegiances, probably for the first time. The English discovered that a silver cup evidently belonging to Grenville was missing and was believed to have been "stollen from vs" by "one of the Sauages" during the stop at the village of Aquascogoc on July 13. Grenville apparently demanded that the cup be given back, and it seems that the weroance there promised to locate and return it. In the meantime Manteo guided Grenville's party to the village of Secotan, where they stayed for four days, from July 15 to 18. By July 16 no word had been heard from Aquascogoc about the missing cup, and so Grenville dispatched Philip Amadas and about ten men back to Aquascogoc to retrieve it. When the cup was not promptly handed over to Amadas, he responded with an extraordinarily excessive act of reprisal. He ordered his men to immediately burn the village to the ground, and as the panicked Indians fled he also burned their corn harvest.

It is not known whether Grenville ordered Amadas to take such harsh action in the event the cup was not returned, but in any case Amadas's reprisal at Aquascogoc is difficult to reconcile. This was the same Philip Amadas who, along with his co-captain Arthur Barlowe, had established such friendly and promising relations with the native tribes there the previous summer. And now, barely two weeks after the return of the English to establish Raleigh's first colony, Amadas took such severe actions that could only have put those good relations in serious jeopardy. Of course the only surviving account of the 1584 reconnaissance expedition was written by Barlowe, not Amadas, and it is possible that the former's glowing account of their interactions with the Indians may have been edited somewhat for propaganda purposes to exclude any negative occurrences. Since Amadas apparently did not put his account of the voyage into writing—or if he did, it may have been suppressed—it is possible that Amadas's view of his experiences with the natives in July and August of 1584 were less promising than Barlowe's, and that it carried over to the confrontation over the missing cup.

It is rather likely, though, that the account of the cordial interaction with the Indians written by the more level-headed Barlow was accurate, and that Amadas's reprisal at Aquascogoc was the result of his intemperate nature. Philip Amadas, who was sometimes called "little Amadas" due to his short stature, apparently had an equally short temper.[43] The previous January or February, two or three months before Grenville's fleet sailed from England, Amadas was involved in an incident on the Thames River which was serious enough that a complaint was lodged with the High Court of Admiralty. Amadas and three or four others had been testing the viability of one of Raleigh's boats, a four-oared vessel called a double-wherry, a good sized "boate with four oares which could not carry aboue fifteene men with their furniture, baggage, and victuall for seuen dayes at the most."[44] This was almost certainly one of the "two double wherries" Grenville transported to Roanoke Island and which Ralph Lane would later use in his exploratory venture up the Moratuc (Roanoke) River. Amadas, who was steering the double wherry on the Thames, overtook another boat and, instead of maneuvering around the smaller craft, he steered directly at it and attempted to ram into it several times. "Vile and vnreverente speeches" ensued during which Amadas, in what must have been a fit of temper, hurled the "helme staffe"—part of his own steering system—at the two rowers in the other boat. One of those rowers threw an object back at Amadas but instead struck one of his men who "blede abundantlye, and was soe wounded that he was not able to rowe."[45] The record of the outcome of the High Court of Admiralty's hearing on the matter has not been found, but the episode speaks to the tempestuous nature of Amadas's personality.

Since the accounts are otherwise silent about the time spent at Aquascogoc, perhaps there was more to the story than the incident involving the silver cup. If Grenville's party encountered hostility at Aquascogoc upon their arrival on July 13, it might partially explain their willingness to exact such an excessive reprisal on July 16. There is some indirect evidence, however slight, to suggest that Manteo and the Englishmen may not have been received with the same level of hospitality at Aquascogoc as they were at Pomeiock and certainly at Secotan. Their visit to Pomeiock on July 12 was cordial and comfortable enough for John White to complete three drawings or watercolors depicting "A Chieff Ladye of Pomeiock," "An Ageed Man of Pomeiock," and a the above depiction of the entire palisaded "Tovvne of Pomeiock." Similarly, Grenville's party stayed at Secotan for three full days, where they "were well entertained." White produced at least four drawings during that time, "On[e] of the chief Ladyes of Secota," "On[e] of the Religeous men in the towne of Secota," "A younge gentill woeman daughter of Secota," and a detailed drawing of the large, unenclosed "Tovvne of Secota." The stay at Aquascogoc, on the other hand, was apparently short and likely not very pleasant, and John White produced no drawings there. The brief visit and lack of drawings by White, however, can possibly be attributed to the controversy over the lost cup rather than any pre-existing hostility on the part of the Indians.

It has also been supposed that intertribal conflicts or local village politics at that time may have resulted in different attitudes toward the English at Secotan, where things went very well, than at Aquascogoc, where they did not. That supposition, though, is highly unlikely. Both Secotan and Aquascogoc were allied villages in the current war being waged between the weroance Piemacum south of the Pamlico River and the Algonquian tribes to the north. The weroances of Secotan and Aquascogoc would probably have been receptive to potential allies as powerful as the English in the war against Piemacum. It is possible, in fact, that Manteo may have guided Grenville there with that particular purpose in mind. Soon after Manteo had acquired a basic fluency in English, Barlowe wrote, he and Wanchese "oftentimes since perswaded vs to surprize Piemacum his towne, hauing promised and assured vs, that there will be found in it great store of commodities. But whether their perswasion be to the ende they may be reuenged of their enemies, or for the loue they beare to vs, we leaue that to the tryall hereafter."[46]

It seems clear that, early on at least, Manteo's intention was to enlist the might of the English against Piemacum, the common enemy of all the tribes between the Pamlico River and Albemarle Sound including Manteo's Croatoans and Wanchese's Roanoacs. It would have made sense, therefore, to introduce Grenville and the English party to the weroances of several villages allied against Piemacum, particularly Aquascogoc and Secotan, which were closer to the hostile territory of Piemacum than either the Roanoacs or the Croatoans. The unfortunate incident involving the missing cup and Amadas's excessive response not only completely upended Manteo's purpose, but was a turning point in Anglo-Algonquian relations which would affect the tribal balance of power in the months to come.

For Manteo, the incident had to have been both troubling and problematic. He would not have accompanied Amadas back to Aquascogoc, since Amadas's purpose there required

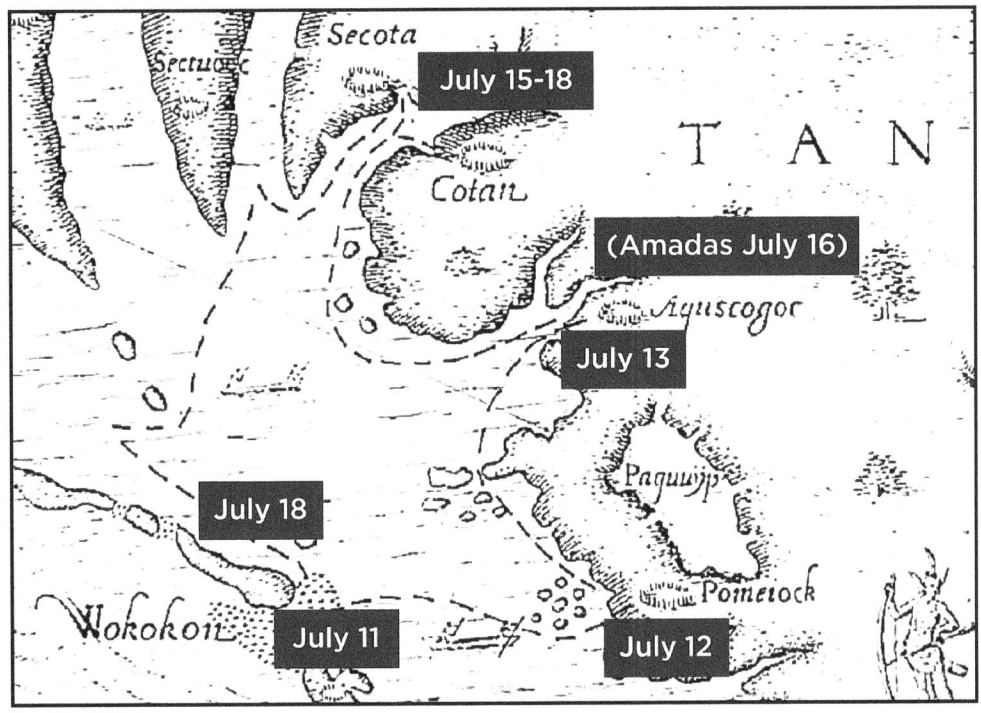

Route taken by Grenville during tour of Pamlico Sound, July 11–18.

no translation and Manteo's linguistic skills and role as liaison between the two cultures were needed during the three day stay at Secotan. He certainly learned about the incident, much to his dismay, as soon as Amadas returned to Secotan with the news. Manteo understood far better than the English what Amadas's excessive actions had inflicted on the Aquascogocs: not only was the tribe's village destroyed, but their entire corn supply—vital to their survival—was also ruined. The Carolina Algonquians planted their corn in April, May, and June, in order to have a sufficient harvest from early summer through October.[47] When Amadas "spoyled their corne" on July 16, the full planting cycle had already been completed. The existing corn supply from the first harvest was certainly destroyed when the village was burned, and it seems that the unharvested crop in the fields was also ruined, leaving the Aquascogoc Indians short of food for the remainder of the summer and into the fall. The severity of the damage done was irreparable, both to the Aquascogocs in particular and to Manteo's overall plan to create an alliance between the English and the tribes north of the Pamlico River.

Nothing more was recorded about the disastrous event at Aquascogoc, and it was only mentioned at all in a single line of one account, that of Grenville's voyage written by an unidentified narrator as a simple matter of fact, barely worthy of attention. The English considered the reprisal to be nothing but a logical and deserving reaction to an offense—however slight in the scheme of things—committed against them. The incident lends some insight into the mindset of the first English colonizers, mostly hardened military men as mentioned, who did not apparently hold appeasement of the local tribes very high on their list of priorities. Amadas's excessive reprisal at Aquascogoc, too often overlooked or underestimated, was a pivotal event in the 1585 colonization effort. It sent the first unmistakable signals to the surrounding tribes that perhaps an association with the dangerously unpredictable Englishmen was not in their best interests after all.

Manteo and the First Colony

By July 27 the fleet was anchored at Hatorask, the inlet near Roanoke Island, and two days later Manteo and Granganimeo, brother of the chief weroance of the Roanoac tribe, boarded the flagship *Tyger* for a meeting with Grenville and other prominent Englishmen. It is important to note that neither Wanchese, who had traveled to England with Manteo, nor Wingina, the leading weroance of Roanoac and Dasamonquepeuc, attended this important meeting. Granganimeo had been instrumental in establishing friendly relations with the Amadas-Barlowe expedition in 1584 and would continue to work to that end with Grenville and the new group of Englishmen. Manteo had immediately established himself as an important translator and facilitator, but Wanchese had abandoned the English soon after his return to his Roanoac village. Wanchese had promptly reported his negative assessment of the English to Wingina, who would have already been offended by Grenville's failure to respect Algonquian tradition requiring a formal greeting ceremony to be hosted at the village of the local weroance. Instead Grenville had remained aboard the *Tyger* attending to other tasks and announced that this meeting would be held there. It was decided at the meeting that the site for the new colony would be located towards the north end of the island, perhaps a mile or two from Wingina's village. By July 29, the day of the meeting, the good ties that had been established the previous summer by Granganimeo with the English were beginning to unravel.

For the next few weeks the English were occupied with several activities. First there was the task of unloading the supplies and equipment from the ships and then ferrying everything through the shallows to the north end of Roanoke Island where the colony was to be located. At the same time others were charged with clearing the site and building houses and other structures at the settlement site. Ralph Lane, governor of the colony and an expert in fortifications, supervised the construction of a fort complete with cannon and surrounded by a ditch. Manteo would have been kept busy during this time guiding and acting as intermediary for the excursions sent out to make further contact with other mainland villages, particularly those accessible via Albemarle Sound, to gather information about the geography to the west and the possible location of precious metals. The English also bartered for "furres" and "deere skinnes" during these expeditions and especially for freshwater mussel "pearles," which the local Indians were known to possess in good quantity. "One of our company," Harriot wrote, "had gathered together from among the Sauage people about fiue thousand: of which number he chose as many as made a faire chaine, which for their likenesse and vniformity in roundnesse, orientnesse, and pidenesse of many excellent colours, with equality in greatnesse, were very faire and rare."[48]

On August 2 Amadas was sent in the pinnace across Albemarle Sound on an exploratory expedition to Weapemeoc, where he visited several villages. A translator would again have been required at these contacts and Manteo most likely joined in the expedition perhaps accompanied by Harriot and possibly White, although there are no existing drawings of Weapemeoc villages or their inhabitants to confirm his presence there. On August 25 Grenville and most of the fleet set sail for England, leaving Governor Ralph Lane and his colony of 107 men, primarily soldiers, at Roanoke Island. For Lane the outlook seemed bright, particularly after the departure of Grenville, with whom he was not on the best of terms. Lane's optimism was reflected in his letter to Richard Hakluyt dated September 3, a little over a week after Grenville sailed for England. Of the land that by this time was called "the Countrey of Virginia," Lane wrote, "it is the goodliest and most pleasing Territorie of the world: for the continent is of an huge and vnknowen greatnesse, and very well peopled and towned, though sauagely, and the climate so wholsome, that wee had not one sicke since we touched the land here." Regarding the native Indians Lane added, "The people naturally are most curteous, and very desirous to haue clothes, bvt especially of course [coarse] cloth rather then silke, course canuas they also like well of, but copper caryeth the price of all...."[49]

In late October or early November Lane sent a group northward beyond Weapemeoc territory on an extended expedition into the land of the Chesepians, possibly to search out a better harbor than Hatorask, the inlet at Roanoke Island which proved to be inadequate. The party included John White and Harriot who together charted and mapped a portion of present-day Virginia Beach and Currituck Sound. They spent several months there and were visited by a number of neighboring Indians from different tribes who had heard about Harriot, the strange Englishman who could speak to them in their own native tongue. Manteo would not have joined this expedition for several reasons. In Harriot's absence there was a more pressing need for Manteo's services at Roanoke Island as well as the abovementioned short excursions to nearby villages. The duration of the Chesepian exploratory expedition was open-ended, and since Lane "had for a time appointed [them] to be resident there," they were expected to be away for most if not all of the winter. Furthermore, Manteo was not at all familiar with the Chesapeake Bay region, other than by hearsay—he had heard rumors of the previously mentioned "greatest" Chesepian town "called Skicoak"—and so his presence there would have been of limited value.

Ralph Lane's account of the 1585–86 colonization venture at Roanoke, which was published in Hakluyt's 1589 *Principal Navigations*, is unfortunately woefully lacking regarding Lane's and Manteo's activities at Roanoke Island and elsewhere for about the four month period leading up to early March of 1586. It is possible that portions of the account were suppressed prior to publication because they contained details about the settlement and its defenses that the English wanted to conceal from the Spanish. It is also very likely, however, that it contained information that was damaging to the rosy picture that had been painted about the friendly native Indians and the wonderful opportunities to be had in America. The short excursions to the mainland villages, guided by Manteo, would certainly have continued at this time, perhaps to barter for corn as well, but the weroances would have been increasing reluctant to provide food for the English colonists as the winter approached and native food stores dwindled.

A far more serious cause for alarm among the villages visited by the English was the strange sickness and death that seemed to follow a day or two later. No one, not even the oldest Indians among them, had ever witnessed anything like this terrible illness that swept through certain villages and left so many dead in its wake. The native healers could neither explain it nor cure it. Time-honored remedies including "winauk [sassafras]," normally used for "the cure of many diseases" were powerless against this mysterious and deadly disease. Although the Indians—as well as the English—did not understand the nature of infectious diseases, they understood very well that there seemed to be a cause and effect relationship between visitations by the English colonists and the occurrences of the strange and deadly sickness. This inevitably led to strained relations and probably many of the conflicts which were later excluded from Lane's account.

What can be said with confidence about Manteo is that, whatever problems occurred during that time period, he must have acquitted himself honorably, at least in Lane's opinion. By the time the account resumed in early March, Manteo had emerged as an indispensable asset of such importance to the English that he now carried an English firearm, an extraordinary development. The native Indians had first seen such a weapon, a matchlock arquebus, demonstrated the previous summer. As Barlowe had written, "When we discharged any piece, were it but an harqubuz [arquebus], they would tremble thereat for very feare." English swords were the most sought-after trade items by the Indians, and they "would haue giuen any thing for [them], but wee would not depart with any."[50] It would have been unthinkable to allow such a powerful weapon as a firearm to fall into the hands of an Indian, and Manteo's possession of one speaks volumes about the trust the English now placed in him. It also indicates the degree of assimilation and acculturation that had taken place in Manteo by early 1586.

The arquebus was an advancement in firearms development using a mechanism called a "matchlock." When the trigger bar was raised, a metal lock or clamp called a "serpentine," which held a slow burning matchcord, was lowered into a flashpan where a small amount of powder would ignite the main charge in the breach and propel a lead projectile from the barrel. In the decades leading up to the mid–16th century the arquebus was a rather clumsy and heavy weapon requiring the use of a resting stick, shown in the illustration below, to support the weight and lend some stability during the aiming process.

Whereas Barlowe referred to the weapon as a "harqubuz" or arquebus, Lane called them "calieuers [calivers],"[51] terms which were often used interchangeably. By the time of the Roanoke voyages, however, English gunsmiths were producing a lighter version of the arquebus. The light arquebus or caliver did not require a support stick, and was of far more practical use in the New World. It was these lighter weapons that were used by Lane's soldiers, and the one now carried by Manteo. Even though these firearms were lighter and more adaptable to the conditions at Roanoke Island and its environs, they still required a great amount of skill and care, since the loading and firing processes were fairly complicated and the proximity of the burning matchcord to the powder presented a constant danger.

From an English perspective there had been a remarkable change in Manteo's appearance and status even from mid–October 1584, when he was viewed with Wanchese at Durham House wearing common brown taffeta. Although his attire is not described in the account of the 1585 colonization venture, since he now carried a light English arquebus

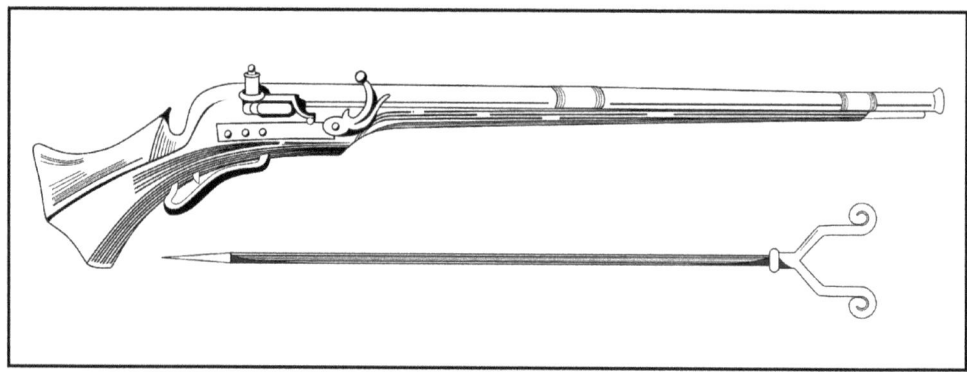

Heavy arquebus and required support rod (courtesy Michael Gayle).

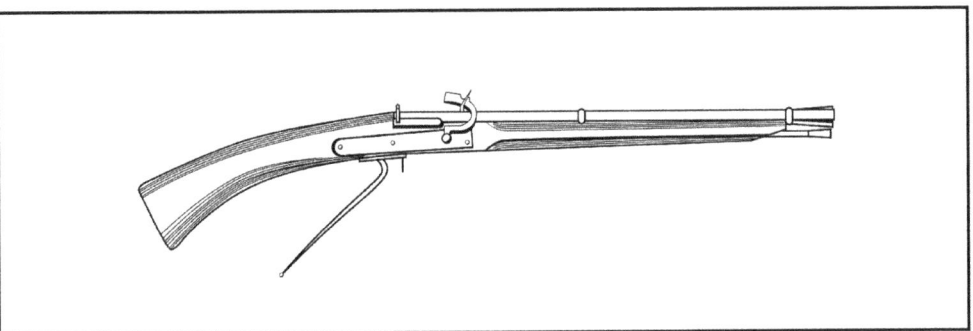

Late 16th century caliver similar to what Manteo possessed (courtesy Michael Gayle).

or caliver, a weapon which was not available to lower class Englishmen, he probably also wore English clothing somewhat more suitable to his new status. Like clothing, the type of personal weaponry allowed was directly connected to social status. The lower classes might possess knives or daggers, but not rapiers or swords, and certainly not any type of firearm, which was only within the means of the relatively wealthy, or consigned to soldiers serving under the authority of a lord or someone of high status. Manteo, now fluent in his native Algonquian as well as at least satisfactory English, was the principal guide and translator for Governor Lane and had been given a weapon that was beyond the reach of most Englishmen. Whether or not he was now attired in traditional English breeches, and a shirt and doublet, or perhaps a soldier's light corselet, is not known, but he probably had long since discarded the simple brown taffeta.

"The Conspiracie of Pemisapan"

As indicated above, very little is known about Lane's activities during the fall and winter of 1585–86 or the specific events that influenced Manteo's emergence as a trusted ally of the English. One consequential event that did occur during that time period was the unexpected death of Granganimeo, Wingina's brother. It was he who had been primarily responsible for the good relations established throughout the first contact period with the English the previous summer, and despite the growing opposition to the colonists at Roanoke, he continued to promote cooperation and cordial interactions with Lane and his men. Granganimeo's death had serious implications. In addition to Manteo, of course, there had been two key Indians, each with his own following among the Roanoac tribe, who actively supported cooperation with the English. The first was old Ensenore, the former chief weroance and father of Wingina and Granganimeo. The second was Granganimeo himself, whose death now severely weakened the pro–English faction. As noted, native opposition to the English presence at Roanoke Island had already been on the rise due to the colonists' constant demand for food even as the Indians' own stores grew short with the approach of winter. Even worse was the strange sickness that continued to claim so many lives, very likely including Granganimeo's, and was attributed to a dreadful power exercised by the English.

No one recognized the ramifications of Granganimeo's death more than Manteo, who had now lost an important ally in his efforts to maintain an increasingly difficult and delicate existential balance between the two cultures. He also understood the ominous impact that Granganimeo's death had on Wingina, who likely blamed his brother's death directly on the English. As mentioned earlier, Wingina now changed his name to Pemisapan—"a wolf who watches from a distance"—and turned irrevocably against the English. Manteo, of course, immediately realized the significance of Wingina's name change and the personal transformation it represented. Lane, however, noted that Wingina had changed his name, but neither he nor any of the Englishmen ever understood its importance or its consequences. It is generally thought that Pemisapan's conspiracy to destroy the English was not undertaken until March of 1586, but it really was initiated months earlier, immediately following his brother's death, which may have occurred as early as the beginning of November 1585. At that time Wingina became Pemisapan and quietly started to encourage factions in other villages to resist the English. The tide now turned decidedly against Lane and his men.

Some villages that had already experienced clashes with the English, certainly Aquascogoc among them, had already been primed for Wingina's message of resistance. A number of villages had suffered severe losses due to the infectious diseases carried by the English, which had already been taking a deadly toll among an Indian population with no natural immunities. Many Indians had concluded that the English had the inexplicable ability to strike down whom they chose "without weapons." For a short time it was believed that the deadly sickness—or any other misfortune that befell the villages for that matter—was intentionally caused by the English for "offending or not pleasing vs,"[52] but that conclusion was soon dispelled. Although Lane's account is silent about any conflicts with the Indians during that winter, Harriot made a vague reference to such clashes that occurred "towards the ende of the yeare [1585]." His *A Briefe and true report* was composed after his return to England and was written in part to counter the negative stories that were being circulated by many of Lane's returning men, a good indication that relations with the Indians were not as friendly as they were being portrayed to the public. Harriot tried to put a positive spin on those relations with the "naturall inhabitants" by writing that they "are not to be feared, but that they shall haue cause both to feare and loue vs, that shall inhabite with them." He closed his comments, however, by admitting that "some of our companie towards the ende of the yeare, shewed themselves too fierce, in slaying some of the people, in some townes, vpon causes that on our part, might easily enough haue been borne withal."[53] Another reference to unspecified atrocities by Lane's men was also recorded by the unknown chronicler of Grenville's 1586 relief voyage. In describing Lane's hasty departure from Roanoke, he wrote that "they left all things confusedly, as if they had bene chased from thence by a mighty army: and no doubt so they were; for the hand of God came vpon them for the cruelty and outrages committed by some of them against the natiue inhabitants of that countrey."[54]

It is evident, then, that the gap in Lane's narrative omitted a number of deadly conflicts between the English and Indians that had occurred in several villages during the winter of 1585–6. Harriot probably did not witness many of these clashes since he was at that time encamped to the north among the Chesepians. Whether or not these bloody conflicts were inspired by Wingina/Pemisapan, initiated by Lane's men, or brought about in reaction to the deadly disease, Manteo would have been an essential asset at this time by either attempting to restore peaceful relation with the Indians or by alerting Lane to their hostile intentions. By March, when Lane's account resumes, Pemisapan's efforts to unite the tribes against the English were solidifying, and Manteo had emerged as Lane's trusted and essential ally.

It was then that Lane, accompanied by Manteo and a party of about fifty men, led an expedition westward across Albemarle Sound and up the Chowan River into Chawanoac territory, ruled by the physically disabled weroance, Menatonon. When they arrived at the principal village of Chawanoac, Lane found that an assembly of Indians from various neighboring tribes had already gathered there, apparently at Pemisapan's behest, as part of his ongoing strategy of consolidating their forces against the English at Roanoke. Although it is doubtful that the gathering could have numbered the "three thousand bowes" mentioned by Lane, he did at least have the element of surprise in his favor. He immediately dispersed the assembly, seizing the crippled Menatonon, whom he held as prisoner for two days. The interrogation of Menatonon, no doubt with Manteo translating, revealed that there was a "greate quantitie of Pearle" to be found several days to the north in the land of the Chesepians. In addition Lane learned that there was a place called "Chaunis Temoatan" far up the Moratuc River in the land of the Mangoaks where a strange metal called "wassador" could be found in abundance. Wassador was said to be the color of the English copper, "very soft, and pale." The Indians who lived at Chaunis Temoatan used a flat bowl and "they say that they take the saide mettall out of a riuer that falleth very swift from the rockes and hils."[55] Lane suspected that Chaunis Temoatan was a likely source of high-grade copper, but since "they call by the name of Wassador euery mettall whatsoeuer," he may have wondered if it could be the elusive gold that the English eagerly sought. Lane released Menatonon, but not before taking his son Skiko hostage and shipping him back to Roanoke Island in the pinnace.

Lane now focused on preparations for an expedition up the Moratuc River in search of Chaunis Temoatan and its reputed source of "the marueilous and most strange Minerall." To reach Chaunis Temoatan, said to be many days journey upriver, Lane had to pass through the territory of the Moratucs, an Algonquian tribe dwelling along the river of the same name, present-day Roanoke River. He set out about mid–March with Manteo and thirty or forty men plus his two large mastiffs in two double wherries, one of which was most likely the vessel that Amadas had tested out on the Thames River in January or February of 1585. In the meantime, however, Pemisapan had learned about Lane's intentions and saw an opportunity to destroy the expedition as it ventured farther from Roanoke Island. He dispatched messengers to the Moratuc villages along the river with a two part plan. First they were to remove their corn supplies and abandon their villages as the English ascended the river, thus preventing them from replenishing their provisions. Then, when the English were weakened and nearly starved, they would be vulnerable to a surprise attack.

Lane and his party headed up the river intending to trade "our copper to haue had corne of them [the Moratucs] … with whom before wee were entred into a league, and they had euer dealt kindly with vs." Through Manteo's earlier role as intermediary and translator, the Moratucs had apparently been on friendly terms with the English in the fall of 1585, but by March of 1586 Pemisapan's efforts to turn the tribes against the English were bearing fruit. For three days Lane's group traveled up the river through Moratuc territory, but "wee could not meete a man, nor finde a graine of Corne in any of their Townes." With just enough supplies remaining for two days, they continued upriver in the hope of finding a food source, "but it fell out very contrary to all expectation." Eventually "our whole victuall spent, lying on shoare all night, wee could neuer see man, onely fires we might perceiue made alongst the shoare where we were to passe,"[56] intentionally set to lure the weakening Englishmen further on.

By this time Lane and his men were nearing the territory of the Mangoaks, and contact with the Indians finally seemed imminent. With their provisions gone and their situation becoming desperate, the English were elated to hear Indians calling from an elevated bank on shore to whom they thought was Manteo, who was in Lane's boat. When Manteo called back, they began to sing, whereupon the English concluded that this was a sign of friendship and started towards the shore. Manteo, however, quickly snatched up his light arquebus and warned Lane that this was all a ruse and that the English must prepare for an attack. The Indians immediately let loose "a vollie of their arrowes amongst them in the [foremost] boat," but thanks to Manteo's forewarning they managed to escape unharmed. Manteo's quick action had saved the English from the ambush, but the men were now exhausted and nearly starved. They decided to turn back downriver and managed to reach Albemarle Sound, but only after eating the two mastiff dogs Lane had brought along and then chewing on sassafras leaves. The Weapemeoc villages on the sound had also been deserted, but the nearly starved Englishmen were fortunate enough to find some fish in the weirs near one of the villages. The fish sustained them until they reached Roanoke, where they arrived on the morning of April 4, the day after Easter.

Manteo's actions on the Moratuc River had immediate and far-reaching consequences. First, of course, he prevented an ambush and very likely saved the expedition from disaster. He had obviously already earned Lane's trust prior to this Moratuc experience, and now his vital importance to the English was clearly recognized by the English and Indians alike. He had not only thwarted Pemisapan's orchestrated plot to destroy Lane and his companions on the Moratuc River, but he also caused a further setback for Pemisapan. After the death of Granganimeo, it was only old Ensenore who continued to counsel for cooperation with the English, but his advice carried significant weight with a number of Roanoac Indians. Pemisapan, thinking his plot had been successful, had spread the word that Lane and his companions were destroyed on the Moratuc River, that their god was not able to protect them, and that the English did not possess supernatural powers, as Ensenore claimed. As part of his final plan Pemisapan had also prohibited the Roanoac Indians from planting any corn or building weirs for the remaining English at Roanoke who would therefore eventually starve.

Thanks to Manteo, however, the expedition returned safely, and Pemisapan was now forced to retract his previous statements and prohibitions against the English and "change [his] disposition toward vs." He now reluctantly ordered weirs to be built for the English and fields prepared for their corn crop. By mid–April "he had sowed a good quantitie of ground, so much as had bene sufficient, to haue fed our whole company" and "besides that he gaue vs a certaine plot of ground for our selues to sowe."[57] These were all encouraging developments for Lane and his men. The April planting would provide an early July harvest, and Grenville was expected to return any day now from England with additional supplies and colonists. Furthermore, in a remarkable turn of events, Menatonon now sent word to Lane that he had commanded Okisko, the weroance of Weapemeoc, to submit to the authority of "the great Weroanza of England, and after her to Sir Walter Raleigh." Consequently twenty-four "of his [Okisko's] principallest men" were sent to the settlement at Roanoke to affirm that they were prepared to acknowledge the English queen as their true sovereign. All appeared to be going Lane's way. His only concern was that if Grenville's return was delayed, as turned out to be the case (he did not arrive until July), the English might have to rely in the meantime on Pemisapan's fragile cooperation.

Everything changed on April 20, when old Ensenore died, "being the onely friend to our nation that we had amongest them."[58] Ensenore's death was also a severe blow to Manteo, who lost the last powerful pro–English voice among the Roanoacs. Manteo now stood as the single remaining weroance fully and openly supporting the English, identifying with them in fact, but his influence among the Indians was limited to the Croatoans and to a lesser degree perhaps a handful of Granganimeo's and Ensenore's former followers who may have befriended Lane and his men. A few days after Ensenore's death Pemisapan abandoned Roanoke Island for his mainland village of Dasamonquepeuc, and refused to provide corn for the English or to continue building the promised weirs. Lane was consequently compelled to divide his men, sending some to Hatorask where shellfish was more readily available and others to Croatoan where they would have sustenance as well as a vantage point from which to sight Grenville's supply ships, which were now overdue.

Meanwhile at Dasamonquepeuc Pemisapan revived his plot to assemble a confederation of neighboring tribes with the single purpose of destroying the English once and for all. The plan involved assembling a large force of allied Indians at Dasamonquepeuc under the pretense of honoring Ensenore, a traditional practice following the death of a great weroance. The assault was to take place on June 10, once the tribes were assembled and the strategy laid out. In its initial stage a select group of about twenty-five Indians, approaching silently in the dead of night, was to set fire to the reeds covering the roofs of the dwellings where Lane, Harriot, and "all the rest of our better sort" slept. As the unarmed and disoriented men evacuated the burning buildings, they would be immediately slain. In the meantime the combined force of allied Indians, who would have crossed over to Roanoke Island in the night, would fall upon the remaining leaderless and disorganized Englishmen and destroy them.

Lane, however, learned about Pemisapan's plot from Skiko, Menatonon's son, whom he still held in chains as his prisoner and had threatened to behead, and also from an unnamed Roanoac Indian informant. Taking matters into his own hands, Lane prepared a ruse of his own whereby he sent a message to Pemisapan saying that he had received word that the English supply ships were in sight off Croatoan and that he wanted to stop at Dasamonquepeuc to borrow a few of Pemisapan's men to assist him. Pemisapan sent word back that he would personally come over to Roanoke Island, but when he delayed his departure, hoping to give his confederated Indians more time to assemble, Lane decided to act. On the morning of June 1, Lane and his men arrived at the shore near Dasamonquepeuc and informed one of Pemisapan's sentries that he wished to confer with him. They were then escorted to the village where Pemisapan sat with seven or eight of his weorances and followers. Lane and his men immediately attacked, and in the ensuing battle a number of Pemisapan's warriors were wounded or killed while the rest fled into the woods. Pemisapan himself, one of those wounded in the initial volley and presumed dead, managed to flee from the scene but was pursued into the woods where he was beheaded by one of Lane's men.

Although Manteo is not mentioned in Lane's account of the assault at Dasamonquepeuc, his presence there—at least in the initial phase—can be taken for granted. Lane had learned from his experience on the Moratuc that Manteo should be kept close by in all dealings with the Indians, particularly hostile ones. Furthermore, Manteo would have been needed to translate Lane's message to Pemisapan's sentry at the shore, a message Lane had designed to mislead the weroance and put him off guard. Lane's attack force consisted of 28 armed men including himself. During the attack, Lane noted, he tried to avoid injuring "Manteos friends," Croatoans who were known to visit both Roanoac and Dasamonquepeuc often. Nevertheless, a few Croatoans were apparently hurt during the attack, a fact that would be revealed the following year when the Croatoans brought up this very incident with Manteo and Edward Stafford during their first visit to Croatoan in 1587. At that time they were even shown an unfortunate Croatoan who had been permanently disabled in Lane's assault.

Manteo had demonstrated his loyalty and importance to the English and had even been issued the aforementioned light arquebus, but there is no indication that he actively participated in the assault. He was certainly ready to use his weapon against other Indians on the Moratuc River, but that was under different circumstances. There Lane's party was about to be attacked and Manteo's reaction was purely defensive. Here at Dasamonquepeuc Lane's surprise attack was an offensive operation preplanned and carried out by English soldiers using a "watch-word agreed vpon (which was, Christ our victory)." Manteo's part in the operation was narrowly defined: to convince Pemisapan that Lane and his men had arrived there with innocent intentions. He must also have warned Lane, however unsuccessfully, to be on the lookout for his Croatoan people once the attack started.

Pemisapan's plot to destroy the English had been effectively thwarted, and many of his followers had also been either killed or scattered. Nevertheless Lane's initial hope of establishing a viable colony had faded considerably by early June. Not only had the English alienated almost all of the surrounding tribes, but none of their initial objectives had been met. No precious metals had been found and the fabled all-water route to the South Sea, thought to lie within reach to the west, had not been located. Lacking these two discoveries, Lane wrote, "nothing els can bring this Countrey … to be inhabited by our nation." Furthermore, the inlet at Roanoke had proved to be inadequate for any vessel larger than a pinnace, making that location unsuitable for either a growing colony or a military base. Most importantly, Grenville's supply ships—expected to arrive by Easter—were long overdue.

On June 8 word arrived at Roanoke from an outpost at Croatoan that a large fleet was approaching, but it was not Grenville's. Sir Francis Drake, with an impressive fleet of "fiue and twentie ships," had raided several Spanish settlements to the south and, as had likely been prearranged with Raleigh, was headed to Roanoke Island with doors, locks, equipment, and possibly eleven slaves taken in the raids for use by Lane's colony.[59] The large fleet anchored off Hatorask, where Drake conferred with Lane, who by this time had lost faith in both Grenville's resupply and the future potential at Roanoke. And so it was that after much consideration and persistent stormy weather, Lane chose to evacuate the Roanoke settlement and return to England with Drake. In the Englishmen's haste to board Drake's ships a number of Harriots's papers and charts, as well as some of John White's drawings, were lost overboard. Three hapless Englishmen who were absent from the settlement during the rushed evacuation were apparently also left behind.

"…and so departed for England"

On June 19 Drake's fleet weighed anchors, and—with Manteo and another Indian named Towaye aboard—sailed for England, arriving at Plymouth on July 27. Given the circumstances surrounding the hasty abandonment of Roanoke Island in 1586, it is noteworthy that Manteo chose to sail with the fleet back to England, taking with him another Indian, Towaye. Manteo's reliability and his value to the English had been well-established, and it is more than likely that he had received assurances that the English planned to resume their colonization efforts in the general area, and that he would play an important role in those plans. The assurances probably came from either Lane or Harriot or both. Lane had already outlined his intentions—if only Grenville had arrived in time with fresh supplies—to relocate the colony northward where there was a better harbor. Harriot, who had worked long and hard with Manteo in England, was Raleigh's close friend and would be instrumental in promoting his next colonization attempt. Both he and Lane knew Manteo very well by this time and almost certainly helped Raleigh define the important strategic position to which Manteo would be appointed the following year.

Raleigh was deeply disappointed when he learned that Lane and all the colonists (with the exception of the three left stranded) had arrived back in England in late July, having put an abrupt end to his first colonization effort. There is some evidence, in fact, indicating that both Lane and Drake fell temporarily out of favor in certain circles for abandoning the colony.[60] To make matters worse, Raleigh had already dispatched a separate relief ship to Roanoke Island but, arriving at Hatorask only a week after Drake had evacuated the colony, the ship returned to England with all the provisions intended for the colony. Furthermore, Grenville's long-awaited resupply fleet, loaded with the promised fresh provisions and additional colonists for the Roanoke settlement, had gotten a late start and arrived at the inlet at Roanoke about two weeks after Drake had departed with Lane and his colonists. Finding the settlement abandoned and unable to determine the colonists' whereabouts, Grenville sailed back to England, but not before leaving a contingent of fifteen men well-provisioned at Roanoke in order to maintain possession of the country for England. He also captured three natives, two of whom managed to escape overboard. The third captive Indian was brought to Grenville's home town of Bideford where he was eventually baptized and died there three years later.

Manteo's second stay in London lasted almost ten months, during which he once again dwelt at Raleigh's Durham House on the Thames River. This time he was accompanied by the Indian Towaye, who may have been Manteo's servant or assistant, or perhaps was intended to play another role in the next colonization venture. When Manteo was in England the previous year, London had been focused for a time on the execution of William Parry at the Old Palace yard at Westminster, not far from Durham House. Now, Manteo returned to London just as the city became embroiled in another conspiracy, this one of such magnitude that it would remain the talk of the land for seven of the nearly ten months he was in London. The conspiracy was called the Babington Plot, one of the most sensational and controversial episodes in 16th century English history, and one which must surely have captured Manteo's attention.

The Catholic Mary, Queen of Scots, had once ruled Scotland for 25 years and was considered by English Catholics to be the rightful queen of England. After abdicating her throne in 1567, Mary fled to England expecting to find protection from her cousin Queen Elizabeth, but instead was placed under house arrest and had been held prisoner by Elizabeth ever since. During the many years of her imprisonment a number of unsuccessful attempts, including the previously mentioned alleged Parry Plot in 1585, had been hatched to assassinate Elizabeth and replace her with Mary. Queen Elizabeth's advisors, particularly her principal secretary and spymaster Francis Walsingham, had continually encouraged her to execute Mary and thus remove the Catholic threat, but, since there was no hard evidence to implicate Mary in the plots, the queen had always refused those requests. On July 17, ten days before Manteo's arrival in England with Drake's fleet, Walsingham announced that he had uncovered evidence of another plot not only to assassinate Elizabeth by planting gunpowder under her bed, but also to incite a rebellion at which time forces from France and Spain would invade England. Over the ensuing weeks, evidence of the plot emerged in the form of letters and secret ciphers which Walsingham's spies had been intercepting for some time. Seven conspirators, including a Catholic priest named John Ballard and a young gentleman named Anthony Babington, were apprehended and tortured, after which they confessed on August 22.

According to one contemporary chronicle, the city was so excited over foiling the "most wicked and detestable conspiracie against her Maiestie … [that] for ioy the citizens of London caused the bels in the churches to be rung, and bonfires in their streets to be made, and also banqueted every man according to his abilitie, some in their houses, some in the streetes with singing of Psalmes & praising God, for preseruing her Maiestie and people of this land."[61] The queen was so taken with the outpouring of affection for her and the public rejoicing over the apprehension of her "most devilish and wicked minded subjects" that she expressed her appreciation to the people in a letter to the Lord Mayor of London that "should be communicated in some general assembly to the most louing subjects the commoners of that city."[62] On September 7 the conspirators, including Ballard and Babington, were indicted "first, for intending treason against the Queenes owne person: secondly, for stirring ciuill wars within the realme: and thirdly, for practicing to bring in forraine power to invade the realme." On September 20 they were dragged through the streets of London on sleds to St. Giles Field, less than a half mile from Durham House, where they were hanged, drawn, "bowelled" while still alive, and quartered. The following day seven others who had been added to the indictment were hanged, drawn, and quartered, but were spared being disemboweled.

What added notoriety on the European continent concerning the Babington Plot was the fact that for the first time Mary, Queen of Scots had been implicated. Anthony Babington had written to Mary in cipher informing her about the plot, and in her secretary's ciphered reply she asked for more information. Both communications were intercepted by one of Walsingham's spies, and one of them, probably Thomas Phelippes, forged a postscript to Mary's reply requesting additional information and names. The Babington letter and Mary's reply with the forged postscript were used against her at the trial conducted at Fotheringay Castle in October, and, although she protested her innocence, she was found guilty of treason. On December 5 proclamations of Mary's death sentence were announced with great fanfare and the blare of trumpets all throughout the city. The news was once again greeted with "great and wonderful reioycing of the people of all sorts, as manifestly appeared by ringing of bels, making of bonfires, and singing of Psalmes in every of the streetes and lanes of the city."[63] Elizabeth signed the death warrant on February 1, 1587, and Mary was beheaded at Fotheringay Castle on February 10 before an assembly of more than 300 onlookers.

Manteo was certainly aware, at least in general terms, of the public events surrounding the Babington Plot and must have witnessed many of the loud and excited demonstrations conducted in the streets near Durham House. His English fluency and comprehension, which would have improved considerably over the past year, would now have significantly enhanced his understanding of the current incidents and also allowed him to converse about these topics, which surely came up frequently in conversation at Durham House. Raleigh, in fact, had a long association with Walsingham and was probably privy to the spy operations conducted in uncovering the Babington Plot.[64] He and Raleigh had worked closely together on a number of occasions and Raleigh had once devised a plot, undoubtedly with Walsingham's knowledge and most likely with his approval, to work at Queen Elizabeth's court under the pretense of assisting the Spanish ambassador. On another occasion Elizabeth sent Walsingham to the Netherlands to personally deliver a letter he had written defending Raleigh against remarks made against him by the Earl of Leicester.[65] And, of course, Walsingham was a prominent supporter of Raleigh's colonization ventures in the New World. Raleigh's association with Walsingham as well as his inside information about the affairs of state must have made for interesting conversation during Manteo's stay at Durham House.

Raleigh, though, was often called away from Durham House on official business for extended periods or to see to his duties as newly appointed Captain of the Queen's Guard. During his absence Manteo had the occasion to interact with a select group of noted visitors or temporary lodgers at Durham House. Among these was an admirer of Harriot, Henry Percy, the 9th Earl of Northumberland, who was a devotee of math, philosophy, science, and was called the "Wizard Earl." Others included William Warner who was working on blood circulation, and the mathematician Robert Hues who had sailed around the world with Thomas Cavendish. Hues and Cavendish, along with Harriot, were known as "the three magi." Also at Durham House were scientist Nathaniel Torporley, geographer Emery Molyneux, and astrologer Thomas Allen.[66] The common thread among all of these interesting visitors at Durham House in 1586–7 was Harriot, with whom Manteo had the closest connection and who very likely would have engaged the transformed Croatoan in many of their discussions.

Raleigh was also preoccupied at the time relocating Englishmen on land in Ireland allotted to him by Queen Elizabeth following the Desmond Rebellion. After many years of bloody fighting the Earl of Desmond had been finally caught and executed, and his head was sent to London to be displayed on a spike at London Bridge. Desmond's lands in Munster had been seized and the Irish population there virtually disappeared ... killed, starved, or fled. A plan for re-colonizing the lands was organized by a group which included Walsingham, who would have consulted with Raleigh since Queen Elizabeth had awarded her favorite with 42,000 acres.[67] As Raleigh's busy schedule periodically required his presence elsewhere, Manteo would have found himself with more time to absorb the peculiarities of English culture, an opportunity he would not have squandered.

Raleigh nevertheless remained undeterred by the failure of the first colony and made preparations for a second colonization venture, one in which Manteo was to play an important role. Harriot was putting the finishing touches on his *A Briefe and true report of the new found land of Virginia* during this time, very possibly fine-tuning the Algonquian nomenclature with Manteo's help. One main purpose of the report, though, was to encourage and promote Raleigh's next colonization effort and also, as mentioned, to dispel the damaging rumors about the conditions and Indian problems at Roanoke now being spread by some of Lane's men. To that end, Manteo would have provided tangible verification of the potential cooperation and friendship that could be cultivated among the native people.

On January 7, 1587, a new commission and a Grant of Arms were issued for the establishment of a colony to be called "The Cittie of Rawley in Virginia." The artist John White was named to be governor, a somewhat odd choice for a leadership position, but he would have twelve named assistants who would act in a supervisory capacity to oversee the management of the colony. As arranged by Raleigh, the document granted individual coats of arms to White and each of the twelve assistants, which in effect bestowed upon them the status of gentlemen, suitable to their new positions. Many of the prospective colonists seem to have been recruited by White in London, where the promise of "ayre ... so temperate and holsome" and "soyle so fertile" in the new colony would have been a promising alternative to the current and often unhealthy conditions in London. Most enticing was Raleigh's pledge to grant tracts of land to the colonists, "the least that hee hath graunted hath beene fiue hundred acres to a man onely for the aduenture of his person."[68] Grenville, too, seems to have had a hand in recruiting prospective colonists from London and Bideford. Hakluyt wrote that there would be "one hundred and fiftie men to be sent thither" to the "newe Colonie," but the list published later in his *Principal Navigations* of those who "safely arriued in Virginia, and remained to inhabit there" totaled 117, consisting of ninety-one men, seventeen women, and nine children. It is possible that the rest of the 150 either changed their minds or would have been among the additional colonists who were scheduled to join the original settlers once the colony had been established. It is worth noting that neither Lane, Amadas, Harriot, or any of the principal men from the 1585–6 voyage joined this venture, and of all the new recruits there were only two among them who had been to Roanoke previously.

Unlike the previous colony, which was made up primarily of military men whose dependence upon the native Indians for a continual food supply contributed to the growing hostilities, the new colony would have a completely different arrangement and purpose. The 1587 colony was designed and planned for agricultural self-sufficiency, and for the first time would include women and children, essential elements for a permanent, thriving colony. However, it had become very clear from the reports that Lane, Harriot, and probably White brought back after the 1585–86 venture that both Roanoke Island and its Hatorask inlet at the Outer Banks were inadequate for either a growing colony or a commercial operation. The new colony, therefore, was to be located about fifty miles farther north on the mainland which was easily accessible via the wide and deep entrance to the Chesapeake Bay. It is possible that Raleigh had also foreseen that a privateering station would be established nearby. There were indications, in fact, that he may have arranged with George Carey for the captain of one of his privateering ventures, William Irish, to make a stop at the Chesapeake colony later that summer.[69]

As ill-suited as Roanoke Island was, however, it was not to be eliminated from Raleigh's plans, and here Manteo would play an important role. Raleigh would maintain control of Roanoke, where Manteo was to be installed as lord and chief of the Roanoac and Croatoan tribes, probably supported by a small force stationed at Lane's old fort. En route to the Chesapeake Bay, a stopover was to be made at Roanoke Island where contact would be reestablished with the contingent of men left there by Grenville the previous year. A ceremony would be conducted there whereby the loyal Manteo, "by the commandement of Sir Walter Ralegh, was [to be] christened in Roanoak, and called Lord thereof, and of Dasamonguepeuk, in reward of his faithfull seruices."[70] This would not merely be a symbolic gesture, but rather a significant, consequential event. By his christening and title conferral, Manteo would become the first native Indian to have an official English title, and would oversee both the village of Roanoac and Dasamonquepeuc, the previous domain of Wingina/Pemisapan. Manteo, therefore, would hold the position of Raleigh's assignee, a status sanctioned by the original 1584 royal charter granting Raleigh rights to the New World. It is clear that the primary colony was to be located at the Chesapeake, but it also seems that Roanoke Island was intended to be a separate satellite entity of sorts, perhaps a protectorate of the Chesapeake colony, which, if all went according to plan, would eventually have the military presence of privateers. The Roanoac-Dasamonquepeuc villages and environs were to be ruled by Manteo, now a thoroughly anglicized native Indian, who, it was hoped, could consolidate the neighboring tribes in Raleigh's name and thereby tighten his grip on the New World.

"The mistaking of these Sauages somewhat grieued Manteo"

The three-vessel fleet carrying Governor John White, Manteo, and approximately 117 men, women, and children set sail from England on May 8, 1587, and on June 19 arrived at

Dominica in the Caribbean, the first stop after the trans-Atlantic voyage. It was most likely here that the flagship *Lyon*'s master pilot, Simon Fernandez, learned through his Caribbean contacts that the Spanish not only knew about Raleigh's plan to establish a colony at the Chesapeake Bay, but were about to sail from Havana to locate it. Discovery by the Spanish, perhaps the colonists' greatest fear, had to be avoided at all costs. Consequently this disturbing news would have eliminated the possibility of landing the colony at the original Chesapeake destination. It required a reassessment of potential locations.[71] The logical decision was made to proceed to Roanoke Island and land the colonists there, at least temporarily. Roanoke, after all, was familiar territory to both White, Fernandez, and of course Manteo. The old settlement site and Lane's fort were located there, and they expected to find Grenville's small contingent of men waiting there as well. Most importantly, Roanoke Island was situated inside the barrier island chain and was shielded from Spanish ships patrolling the coast.

The decision to divert the colonists to Roanoke would have had a direct impact on Manteo's designs and expectations. Raleigh's original plan for Manteo and the 1587 voyage was to make a temporary stop at Roanoke Island, just long enough to make contact with the men left by Grenville the previous year in order to assess the local conditions and current Indian relations, and then to perform the ceremony whereby Manteo was to be baptized and installed as the Lord of Roanoac and Dasamonquepeuc. Once that was accomplished and a company of men assigned to the fort at Roanoke, probably including the fifteen left by Grenville, the colonists were to sail on to the Chesapeake Bay and establish the The "Cittie of Rawley" at a suitable location there. In the meantime it is presumed that Manteo's Croatoans, who were frequent visitors to Roanoac and Dasamonquepeuc, would become more permanent residents in Manteo's new domain. With the entire colony now diverted to Roanoke Island, Manteo's role would have become far more complicated. He would have immediately foreseen the problems created by the unexpected presence of a governor and well over 100 additional English men, women, and children temporarily settled on Roanoke Island. For one thing it would likely create additional problems with his impending role as Lord of Roanoac and Dasamonquepeuc. It would also allow less time for him to organize and oversee his new realm as planned, and require a greater commitment to assisting a large group of essentially inexperienced colonists.

They arrived at the inlet off Roanoke Island on July 22 and towards evening White along with "fortie of his best men," and almost certainly Manteo, went ashore expecting to be met by the fifteen men Grenville had left there the previous year to maintain possession of the territory. There was no sign of them, however, as White would later write, "sauing onely wee found the bones of one of those fifteene, which the Sauages had slaine long before." The following day White and some of the colonists walked towards the north end of the island where the fort and settlement houses were located, still hoping to find signs of the fifteen men. When they reached the place, they "found the fort rased downe" but the settlement dwellings remained, although they "were ouergrowen with Melons of diuers sortes, and Deere within them, feeding on those Melons: so wee returned to our company, without hope of euer seeing any of the fifteene men liuing."[72] Manteo is not mentioned, but he most likely accompanied White and the others to the settlement looking for the men who were intended to remain with him at Roanoke Island as part of the original plan.

While the provisions and equipment were being unloaded, some of the men went to work repairing the existing dwellings and building new ones. On July 25 the flyboat arrived with the remaining colonists and the rest of the supplies obtained during the stop in the

West Indies. Three days later one of White's assistants, George Howe, wandered two miles from the settlement to catch crabs, and was killed by some of Pemisapan's former followers. The small band of Indians "shot at him in the water, where they gaue him sixteen wounds with their arrowes: and after they had slaine him with their woodden swords, they beat his head in pieces."[73] They had come to Roanoke Island either "to espie our company, and what we were, or else to hunt Deere," and they fled back to the mainland after killing Howe. The fact that George Howe thought it was safe enough to venture so far from the settlement—unarmed and alone—is an indication that he was either remarkably naïve, or that he was just one of many who had been convinced by the propaganda disseminated to prospective settlers back in London that there was nothing to fear from the local Indians. In any case the brutal killing must have been a shock to the rest of the colonists, some of whom may now have had second thoughts about the wisdom of the venture.

As noted, Manteo was now heavily relied upon by the colonists for his opinions and advice as well as his language skills. Not only was he alone qualified to speak both Algonquian and English, but he was also one of the very few who had direct experience with Raleigh's previous colonization effort. And, of course, his knowledge of the area surrounding Roanoke Island far exceeded everyone else's. Aside from White and Edward Stafford, both of whom had been to Roanoke once before with Lane's colony, this was the first venture to the New World for all but two of the rest of the 1587 colonists, many of whom had probably never been outside of London. Their expectations were based entirely upon what they had been told in London about the opportunities in Virginia, and they were quickly learning the difference between expectation and reality.

On July 30, probably as a result of Manteo's suggestion, White sent Manteo, Edward Stafford, and a party of twenty men to Croatoan where they would hopefully get "some newes of our fifteene men, but especially to learne the disposition of the people of the countrey toward vs, and to renew our old friendship with them." As Manteo and the Englishmen approached the village, the Croatoans at first were frightened by what appeared to be hostile strangers. Manteo, of course, had for almost two years now been attired in English clothing and carried a caliver or light arquebus, and he was now unrecognizable to his own tribesmen. As soon as Manteo saw their distress, he called out to them in their Algonquian tongue, whereupon the Croatoans dropped their bows and arrows and welcomed their leader and the Englishmen, who assured them that "our comming was onely to renew the old loue, that was betweene vs and them at the first, and to liue with them as brethren and friends." Manteo would have had numerous questions and answers to translate, but he would have made time first to reunite with his mother, the queen of the Croatoans, whom he hadn't seen in more than a year. His mother had witnessed his gradual transformation the previous year during Lane's tenure, and one can only wonder what she must have thought about and discussed with her son, who after two trips to England had become virtually acculturated. It seems very likely that Manteo would have told her and the other leading tribesmen about his imminent installation as Lord of Roanoac and Dasamonquepeuc and what that meant for their tribe's future.

One of the concerns brought to Manteo's attention by the Croatoans was the need for a "token or badge" that they could wear so that the English would recognize them as friends and allies whenever "we met them any where out of the Towne or Island." This plea was made precisely because "diuers of them were hurt the yeere before" during Lane's assault at Dasamonquepeuc on June 1, 1586. It will be recalled that Manteo had warned Lane about the possible presence of Croatoans, and Lane had tried to avoid injuring any of "Manteo's friends" during the attack, but he was evidently unsuccessful, a fact he failed to mention in his account. To stress this point with Manteo and Stafford, the Croatoans exhibited one of their tribesmen who still lay crippled from wounds accidentally inflicted by Lane's men. Unfortunately, it seems that such tokens or badges were not supplied to the Croatoans, because a very similar and even more regrettable mistake would occur in the not too distant future.

The following day the Croatoans verified what Manteo had already concluded, that George Howe had been slain by a remnant of Pemisapan's followers, who now were associated with Wanchese, the Roanoac Indian who had accompanied Manteo to England in 1584, but had turned against the English soon after his return. The English also learned what happened to the fifteen men Grenville had left at Roanoke Island in 1586: They had been attacked and routed by a combined force of tribesmen from Aquascogoc, Secotan, and Dasamonquepeuc. Two of the Englishmen were taken by surprise and killed in the initial stages of the battle. The few who were wounded, along with the rest of the men, made it to a boat and managed to escape to parts unknown. Stafford also conferred, via Manteo, with the Croatoans about the possibility of reestablishing friendly relations with the people of Secotan, Aquascogoc, Pomeiock, and Dasamonquepeuc, and "if they would accept our friendship, we would willingly receiue them againe, and that all vnfriendly dealings past on both parts, should be vtterly forgiuen and forgotten." The Croatoans agreed "that they would gladly doe the best they could, and within seuen dayes, bring the Wiroances and chiefe Gouernours of those townes with them, to our Gouernour at Roanoak, or their answere."[74]

It is not surprising that, for practical reasons alone, White would wish to restore some semblance of peace with adversaries such as Wanchese and the former followers of Pemisapan at Dasamonquepeuc, even in spite of the fact that a few of the Indians there were responsible for the recent killing of George Howe. So too it is understandable that he would want to mitigate the animosity that probably had been simmering at Aquascogoc ever since Amadas's excessive reprisal over the missing cup two summers earlier. Both of those villages had a history of conflict with the English and both had participated in the assault on the contingent of men Grenville had left at Roanoke. What is noteworthy, however, is the fact that White also sent peace offerings to Secotan and Pomeiock, two villages where the English had been treated very well during Grenville's excursion through Pamlico Sound in July of 1585. White had spent a day at Pomeiock and three days at Secotan with Lane and Manteo, and some of White's best known watercolors reflect the cordial and cooperative atmosphere the English experienced during those visits. White's assessment, that the once friendly villages of Secotan and Pomeiock should now be included among the hostile villages that required offerings of peace, is further evidence that the void in Lane's account from late fall of 1585 to early March of 1586 had originally included quite a number of serious conflicts that were afterwards deleted by Raleigh or Hakluyt. It is also an indication that by the time Lane vacated Roanoke Island with Drake on June 19, 1586, the English had alienated virtually all the tribes from Albemarle Sound to the Pamlico River, and this would have an impact on the 1587 colonists' relocation options in the months to come.

On August 1 Manteo and the Englishmen returned to Roanoke to await the arrival of the Croatoan emissaries who had been sent with White's offerings of peace. By August 8, when none of those weroances had shown up and White had not yet heard any word from them, he made an impulsive and unfortunate decision. Since it was a remnant of Pemisapan's followers from Dasamonquepeuc who had killed George Howe, and since Indians from Dasamonquepeuc had participated in the assault on Grenville's contingent of men left at Roanoke, White determined to retaliate with force. Instead of waiting to confer with the Croatoans about the status of his offer, or at least to inform them of the possible consequences in the event his offers were rejected, White prepared to attack Dasamonquepeuc immediately. Shortly after midnight on August 9, White, Stafford, Manteo, and 23 others crossed from Roanoke Island over the sound to the shoreline not far from Dasamonquepeuc. Manteo guided the group through the woods in the dark of night, and then waited as the Englishmen circled around and took up positions so that their adversaries would be caught between the attackers and the shoreline.

It is a virtual certainty that Manteo strongly cautioned White about the possibility that some of his Croatoans might be present, since they were frequent visitors at Roanoac and Dasamonquepeuc. As mentioned, he had warned Lane of that same possibility prior to his morning assault on Pemisapan's camp there the previous summer. That attack had killed the Roanoac weroance and a number of his followers, but also injured several Croatoans, in spite of Lane's stated efforts to avoid them. Just eight days ago the Croatoans had reminded the English of that unfortunate event and displayed one of their tribe who still lay crippled from Lane's assault. The sight of his disabled tribesman was certainly fresh in Manteo's mind. Lane's attack had had been carried out during daylight, and White's imminent midnight attack could only make distinguishing friend from foe much more difficult.

Manteo's fears were well founded. What neither he nor any of the English were aware of was that Wanchese and all of Pemisapan's former followers, fearing retaliation after the killing of George Howe on July 28, had fled from Dasamonquepeuc in such haste that they left their crops unharvested. When the Crotoans learned of this a few days later, a number of them went to Dasamonquepeuc to gather the precious ripening crops, never imagining that White would decide to launch a sudden attack on the village. Now, the only Indians at Dasamonquepeuc were Croatoans and among them were women and children. When the attack started, the terrified Croatoans fled into the tall reeds near the water where one of them was instantly "shot ... through the bodie with a bullet." As the attackers approached the reeds to finish them off, one of the Croatoans recognized Stafford and, calling out his name, ran towards him as the astonished Englishman lowered his weapon. Another Croatoan, the wife of a weroance, was about to be killed until the startled attacker saw that she carried a child on her back. White and the other Englishmen finally realized their terrible mistake and halted the assault. As with Lane's attack at Dasamonquepeuc the previous year, Manteo played a role as a guide, but not in the actual assault. White wrote that Manteo "behaued himselfe toward vs as a most faithfull Englishman," whose only role was "to be our guide to the place where those Sauages dwelt." If he had been involved in the actual attack, the identity of the Croatoans would likely have been recognized almost immediately. It is also probably safe to conclude that the English had not supplied the Croatoans with the badges or tokens they so earnestly requested, although—even if they had—the badges may have been ineffective in the dark.

We do not know how many casualties there were among the Croatoans, but it can be presumed that there were more than just the one shot "through the bodie" during the initial assault. The attack itself, hastily executed in the middle of the night and without the benefit of hearing back from the Croatoan emissaries who had been sent out on White's behalf, was impulsive and ill-advised. It was also uncharacteristically aggressive, a quality often found among the English, but not in White, who rarely displayed determination or assertiveness. This was demonstrated in the account of the 1587 voyage, during which he was the ostensible commander of the fleet but repeatedly failed to exercise any semblance of authority.[75] He was usually, in fact, somewhat submissive and occasionally helpless to grasp or control important events that directly affected him. His talents as an artist and cartographer were without doubt, but his leadership abilities were questionable. Given his reticent tendencies, it seems possible that White was prodded into launching the unfortunate attack by one or two of his more belligerent colonists, perhaps close friends of George Howe who wanted revenge.

Be that as it may, White's reaction to his mistake typified the standard English response to injuries, intended or not, inflicted on the Indians. To him the incident was unfortunate, but if responsibility for the error were to be assigned, it should be placed elsewhere, on the darkness for instance—which one could only expect in a midnight attack of his choosing—if not the Croatoans themselves. White's weak excuse for attacking women was that "it was so darke, that they being naked, and their men and women apparelled all so like others, wee knew not but that they were al men." His primary disappointment seemed to be that he and the English "were deceiued" and that the failure of their goal—to punish Pemisapan's former followers—was the greatest regret. "Finding our selues thus disappointed of our purpose," White wrote, they gathered all the ripened crops and took them "and the other Sauages with vs ouer the water to Roanoak."[76]

According to White's very questionable assessment, Manteo did not merely mirror his own reaction to the attack, but went so far as to attribute the injuries suffered by his fellow Croatoans to their own foolishness. Although Manteo "somewhat grieued" about "the mistaking of these Sauages," White wrote, "he imputed their harme to their owne folly." That Manteo "grieued" over this mistaken assault is undoubtedly true, but it seems inconceivable that he could then have openly reproached his own people for the death and injury that they had endured. This is particularly implausible considering the fact that this same debacle had happened the previous year, under similar circumstances and at the same location. Manteo had cautioned Lane prior to the attack at that time, when Lane was unsuccessful in "looking as watchfully for the sauing of Manteos friends." With the recently exhibited Croatoan who had been permanently disabled in Lane's attack still fresh in his mind, Manteo almost certainly would have warned White to be alert to the possibility that Croatoans could be among the Indians at Dasamonquepeuc, where his people often visited. That possibility would have been further enhanced by the knowledge among the Croatoans that Manteo was soon to be appointed lord of both Roanoac *and* Dasamonquepeuc.

In typical fashion White went to some length in this passage to deflect any responsibility away from himself, even using an improbable indirect quote he ascribed to Manteo. White has Manteo "saying to them [the Croatoans] that if their Wiroances had kept their promise in comming to the Gouernour at the day appointed, they had not knowen that mischance." It should be noted that this was not the first time White attempted to indemnify himself from what could conceivably be looked upon later as wrongdoing, nor would it be his last. As alluded to above, he as governor was the commander of the 1587 fleet, but when the colony was diverted to Roanoke Island instead of the Chesapeake, White uttered not a word of objection yet placed the responsibility for altering Raleigh's plan entirely on the pilot Simon Fernandez and thus deflected any potential blame away from himself.[77]

It is worth taking a closer look at White's use of the above-referenced indirect quote, supposedly relating Manteo's conversation with the Croatoans immediately following the attack. Although White could have visually observed that Manteo "grieued" following the assault, one must seriously question the credibility of his description of what Manteo said to his fellow Croatoans. In the first place White's use of an indirect quote of something Manteo actually said in his native tongue presupposes a fluency in Algonquian, an ability which White did not possess. The only Englishman who was at all fluent in Algonquian was Harriot, and Harriot was not part of this 1587 colonization venture.

White may have tried to convince Manteo that the fault lay with the Croatoans, but he could not have known what Manteo and the Croatoans actually said about the attack afterwards. Furthermore, the Croatoans must have been understandably agitated and upset, particularly since just over a week earlier they had begged the English for the badges to prevent exactly this sort of incident from happening. It is virtually impossible to believe that Manteo could have blamed his Croatoan people for the injuries caused by White's rash and ill-advised assault, and it is equally absurd to think that the Croatoans themselves would have been at all amenable to an assertion that placed the blame for their injuries squarely on "their owne folly." Again, it seems more than likely that White's version of this unfortunate incident was fabricated to absolve him from any blame in the matter.

Manteo, Lord of Roanoac and Dasamonquepeuc

On August 13, four days after the unfortunate attack at Dasamonquepeuc, the promised ceremony was held at the English settlement whereby Manteo was baptized into the Church of England and installed as Lord of Roanoac and Dasamonquepeuc. As mentioned previously, this ceremony had been ordered by Raleigh during the colony's planning stage in London, and it represented an important step in what was expected to be both Raleigh's and Manteo's future. As already noted, Raleigh's original plan seems to have intended the territory surrounding the villages of Roanoac and Dasamonquepeuc to be governed by Manteo as a satellite possession, associated with the main colony at the Chesapeake and enlarging Raleigh's territorial possessions. Because the Chesapeake had since been eliminated as a settlement location, the 1587 colonists would send out exploratory expeditions, guided by Manteo, to search for another mainland site suitable for a permanent agricultural colony. In the meantime the colony would spend the winter at Lane's old Roanoke settlement. It can be reasonably concluded that once the colonists had relocated to their new settlement site the following spring, the original plan to station a company of men with Manteo at Roanoke Island would be even more essential. The site for the new settlement would not be decided for several more months, necessitating next year's resupply ships from England to stop first at Roanoke where they would be informed about the colony's new location.

It is interesting to note that, as far as we can tell, no arrangement was made for Manteo to take a Christian name upon his being baptized, and certainly none was mentioned in White's reference to that event. In an unforeseen turn of events White would shortly depart for England, and Manteo was not mentioned again in his 1587 account after the baptism and installment ceremony on August 13. In a separate document later published by Hakluyt listing "all the men, women and children, which safely arriued in Virginia, and remained to inhabite there [in] 1587," he was still recorded as "Manteo," one of the two "Sauages [the other was Towaye] that were in England and returned home into Virginia with them." And White would continue to refer to him as "Manteo" in a 1590 comment about Croatoan, "which is the place where Manteo was borne, and the Sauages of the Iland our friends." The decision about a Christian name was probably left to Manteo himself who may have wished to maintain his Algonquian name, particularly if he saw his baptism and the new title bestowed upon him as confirmation of his ultimate acquisition of the powerful manitou that his name implied.

On August 18 White's daughter Elyoner Dare, wife of Ananias Dare, gave birth to a daughter, the first English child born in America. The following Sunday she was baptized and "because this child was the first Christian borne in Virginia, shee was named Virginia." This single reference, by the way, in addition to her inclusion on a list published by Hakluyt of "The names of all the men, women and children, which safely arriued in Virginia, and remained to inhabite there," was the only mention of Virginia Dare in all the Roanoke accounts. Overshadowed by Virginia's arrival was another child born shortly thereafter to colonist Margery Haruie [Harvie], wife of another of White's assistants named Dyonis Haruie. Neither the given name nor the gender of this child was recorded on the abovementioned list, which included the two "Children borne in Virginia." The Haruie child appeared directly below Virginia Dare only as "Haruie."

By this time all the supplies for the colony had been unloaded and transported to the settlement, and the colonists prepared letters to send back to England. On about August 21, however, a controversy arose over which one of the colonists should return to England to organize and coordinate the resupply effort for the colony. One of White's assistants, Christopher Cooper, initially agreed to go, but he was discouraged from doing so by his friends and soon changed his mind. Finally White's other assistants and some of the other colonists, "the whole company" according to White, came to him with the plea that White himself be the one to return to England. This was a very unusual and revealing development. The fact that the colonists implored their duly appointed governor to virtually abandon his colony, relinquishing both the administration of it and the upcoming important relocation decisions, is a good indication that there was a general consensus that the colony would fare better under someone else's leadership. It would further suggest that White's previously mentioned submissive nature and his lack of authority were evident to the colonists during the voyage from England. That, and perhaps the poor judgement he displayed in his hasty decision to attack Dasamonquepeuc, may have provided sufficient reason for the majority of colonists to want someone else directing the colony. They had risked everything on this venture to the New World, but their early optimism was quickly fading. The promise of "fiue hundred acres to a man" in the new The Cittie of Rawley was now in doubt, and one of their own, George Howe, had been brutally killed by Indians who were supposed to be peaceful and cooperative. Although White could not be blamed entirely for every misfortune that had occurred, he was apparently deemed sufficiently responsible to warrant a change of leadership.

White initially refused, citing the legitimate criticism he would likely receive back in England for abandoning his colony, particularly after being primarily responsible for persuading the majority of the colonists to take part in the venture. He also worried that in his absence the belongings he left behind would be "pilfered away" by the colonists, again a sign that he may not have had the level of respect normally attributed to a governor. White finally agreed to go, but—in an extraordinary attempt to absolve himself from blame once again—only after he was provided with a written "bond vnder all their hands and seales for the safe preseruing of all his [White's] goods," and attesting that "through their extreame intreating" the entire colony finally convinced him to leave against his will. To ensure that he would be legally indemnified, White "thought good to set downe" the entire text of the document verbatim in his account, a portion of which follows:

May it please you, her Maiesties subjects of England, we your friends and countrey-men, the planters in Virginia, doe by these presents let you and euery of you to vnderstand ... wee all of one minde and consent, haue most earnestly intreated, and vncessantly requested Iohn White, Gouernour of the planters in Virginia, to passe into England ... and he not once, but often refusing it, for our sakes, and for the honour and maintenance of the action, hath at last, though much against his will, through our importunacie, yeelded to leaue his gouernement, and all his goods among vs and himselfe in all our behalfes to passe into England ... we doe assure ourselues by these presents, and will you to giue all credite thereunto, the 25 of August 1587.[78]

Despite White's protestations and explanations, his agreement to leave his colony is difficult to justify. As governor his primary obligation was to preside over the administration of the colony, and as mentioned, he and Stafford were two of only four Englishmen with any prior experience in colonization at Roanoke. Stafford was never expected to remain at Roanoke, and in fact he sailed back to England with White. Once those two departed, the only semblance of authority remaining were the handful of assistants who had been appointed in London, none of whom had any experience in governance or colonization. The latter part of White's account covering his last days at Roanoke Island is taken up with explanations for his departure, but nothing is mentioned about who would lead the colony in his absence. It is probable that the leadership role would have fallen to one of the assistants, possibly Roger Bailey, the first of the twelve assistants listed in the 1587 Grant of Arms, or White's son-in law, Ananias Dare, but that is only speculation. What can be said with confidence is that the colonists' dependency on Manteo's guidance, already fairly substantial, could only have been heightened once White departed.

The plan was for White to return the following spring or early summer with fresh supplies, equipment, additional colonists, and whatever other necessities might be required. In his absence the colonists would select a new settlement site which would be located somewhere on the mainland approximately fifty miles—a probable prescribed jurisdictional designation—from Manteo's existing base at Roanoac/Dasamonquepeuc. At some time prior to White's departure it was agreed that the colonists would leave carved messages at the Roanoke fort as a contingency plan so that upon his return with the supply ships there would be a "written" record of sorts indicating where the colony had relocated. On August 27, 1587, just five weeks after John White arrived with the colonists, he boarded the *Lyon* and departed from Roanoke Island, leaving behind 119[79] men, women, and children, including his daughter Elyoner Dare and his nine-day-old granddaughter, Virginia. He fully expected to return in the early summer of the following year.

"They were prepared to remoue from Roanoak 50 miles into the maine"

Manteo and the entire 1587 colony disappeared from the historical record on August 27, but the colonists' plans and expectations were known. Therefore, it is possible to reconstruct their activities with a fair degree of confidence for at least ten months thereafter, during which time Manteo would have played a vital part. The colonists had agreed to remain at Roanoke only temporarily and eventually relocate to the mainland. The crucial question on everyone's mind in the late summer of 1587 was precisely *where* on the mainland their settlement should be. With White's unanticipated departure, the leadership of the colony was undoubtedly delegated to the assistants, but none of them, as mentioned, had been to the New World before. White, at least, had first-hand knowledge of the geography, as demonstrated by his maps, one of which was later published by de Bry, and it covered nearly all of the Outer Coastal Plain from the Chesapeake Bay to Cape Fear. Although it is reasonable to assume that White must have left a hand-drawn copy of the map with his assistants, its practical usefulness would have been rather limited. For one thing his map of the mainland was not entirely accurate, which would only further hinder such inexperienced observers who had no first-hand familiarity with the geography. Consequently it would have been of little help in selecting a location for the new settlement. More importantly, a map told nothing about intertribal alliances and allegiances nor could it identify potential areas where the colonists might be welcomed. Finally, none of the colonists could speak Algonquian and so they were powerless to communicate or negotiate effectively with any of the Indian groups they would inevitably encounter.

Given the colonists' shortcomings, it was obvious that no one but Manteo possessed all the requisite qualifications for proposing and exploring potential sites to relocate the colony. Finding a suitable settlement location could not be accomplished without Manteo's knowledge of the surrounding areas and his ability to act as interpreter and intermediary with the various tribes. That fact was clear even before White left and it would have been agreed, either formally or otherwise, that Manteo would be the guiding force in the search for an alternative settlement site. The selection of that new settlement location on the mainland was of vital importance, and it was probably pursued in earnest during the month or two following White's departure. The elimination of the Chesapeake Bay area as a settlement location did not alter the original purpose and nature of the colony, which was basically agricultural. Since the planting season started in April, the colonists had to be at the new settlement location in time to build the necessary structures and dwellings and to prepare their fields for the first planting. Consequently the move from Roanoke to the new location, although it probably was done in stages, had to have been accomplished by March of 1588, certainly prior to the first planting in April. Manteo would have spent much of the late summer and fall with the principal colonists who were designated to seek out potential mainland settlement locations.

It is very likely that Manteo guided that exploration party *southward*. The important lesson that was learned from the first failed attempt at colonization at Roanoke Island in 1585–6 was that the inlet there was inadequate and could only be navigated by small vessels. The 1587 colony's survival as a viable settlement depended upon their anticipated regular contact with—and periodic supplies from—England. Obviously this could only be accomplished if their mainland settlement location was *accessible* for re-supply. That accessibility would have been available via the wide entrance to the Chesapeake Bay, but that had now been eliminated due to the clear and present danger from the Spanish. The only other viable inlet that provided accessibility to the mainland happened to be at Wokokon, present-day Ocracoke Inlet, located just south of Manteo's Croatoan Island. The English had been well aware of the Wokokon inlet since the first reconnaissance voyage in 1584. Grenville had stopped there en route to Roanoke the following year and, with Manteo as guide and translator, spent over a week exploring present-day Pamlico Sound and visiting a number of native villages. It is believed, in fact, that the main purpose of Grenville's tour of the sound with Manteo was to search out alternative settlement locations for possible future colonization.[80] The information obtained during that excursion, which Manteo directed, could now have played an important role in the choice of resettlement locations for the colonists at Roanoke. The proximity of Wokokon to Manteo's Croatoan and his personal familiarity with the neighboring tribes in that particular area would have made Manteo an even more indispensable asset in the site-selection process.

It should be noted, however, that Manteo's own sphere of influence and the traditional inter-tribal alliances had changed dramatically since the first arrival of the English. Prior to 1584–85 the Croatoans were allied with, and—as some have suggested—perhaps even a sub-tribe of the Roanoacs and their chief Wingina. At that time Wingina was at "mortall warre" with the chiefs of Pomouik and "the countrey Newsiok [Neusiok]," two adjoining territories south of the land called Secotan on White's map. At the time of the initial Anglo-Algonquin contact in 1584, both Manteo and Wanchese were allies and both had tried to persuade the English to attack Pomouik. In 1584 Wingina and all the tribes north of the Pamlico River on the map below, including the Roanoacs, the Croatoans, and all the villages located in the large area labeled "Secotan," were allied against Piemacum, the weroance of the Pomouiks, and his allies the Neusiok, as well as "the next king adioyning towards the setting of the Sunne [the Mangoaks or possibly the small Woccon tribe]," and conceivably the Cwareuuock ("Coree" on the map).

By the time the 1587 colony arrived, however, Wingina/Pemisapan was already dead, having been killed the previous June by the English, with whom Manteo was now firmly allied against the remnants of Pemisapan's followers. Furthermore, Manteo was now the lord and chief of Roanoac and Dasamonquepeuc as well as the heir apparent weroance at Croatoan. This new realignment may have opened the door to previously unavailable alliances.

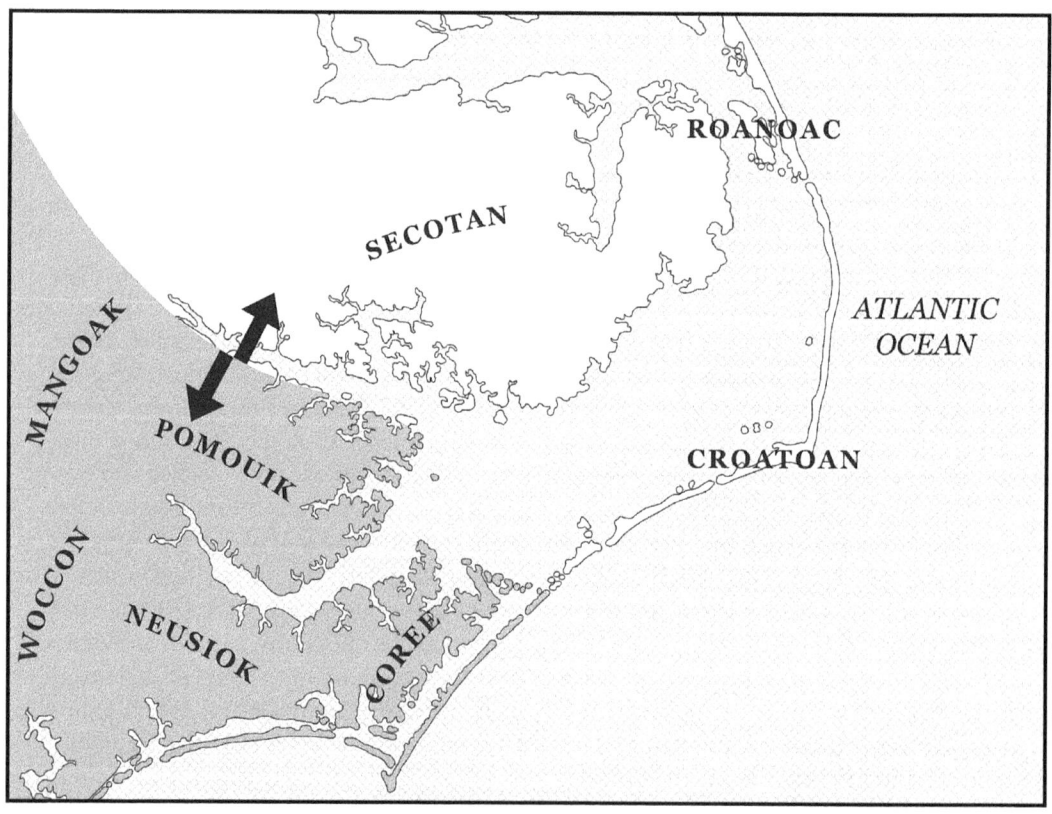

Map of Tribal Territories and Alliances in 1584 (courtesy Michael Gayle).

It is known, for example, that the Coree Indians, who lived south of the Neuse River, traditionally established temporary hunting and fishing camps on the Outer Banks and probably had some association or at least a familiarity with the nearby Croatoans. It is also widely thought that the Corees were related to the Neusioks, who dwelt on the south side of the lower Neuse River. Therefore, if the Corees were related to the Neusioks, and the Neusioks had been allied with the Pomouiks against Wingina, as is evident from the 1584 testimony of both Manteo and Wanchese, then there may have been a unique opportunity in 1587–88 for a favorable Anglo-Indian alliance among these different native groups. Those tribes—the Coree, Neusiok, and Pomouik, along with the English colonists, would now have shared a common enemy, the hostile Secotan tribes north of the Pamlico River. Such an alliance would also benefit Manteo—whose new realm now included Roanoac, Dasamonquepeuc, and Croatoan—by weakening the strength and influence of the Secotan tribes that would now find themselves encircled by enemies. An alliance like this could only have been arranged by Manteo, and it would also have the important benefit of providing the colonists with an opportunity for a suitable relocation site on the mainland near the all-important Wokokon inlet.

The Pamlico River was the approximate dividing line that separated the Pomouik tribe from their Secotan enemies to the north, who were by 1586 also hostile to the English. If Manteo were to broker an alliance between the 1587 colonists and one or more of the tribes located south of the Pamlico River, his best chance may have been with Piemacum, the principal weroance of the Pomouiks. For one thing the Pomouiks are known to have been part of the Algonquian language group, as were the Croatoans, whereas the language affiliation of the Neusiok and Coree tribes is uncertain. Archaeologist William Haag wrote that the form of the word "Neusiok" is an indication that they "were of Algonquian stock,"[81] but it is possible that the word was the Algonquian name for that tribe and was thus recorded as such by the English. The same could be said of the Coree tribe, which was recorded as the Algonquian-sounding "Cwareuuock" by White. According to linguist Blair Rudes, words with endings spelled by the English "-euuock," "-uuok," -ock," and "-iok," and the like, all had Algonquian suffixes meaning "people of."[82] Since no 16th century Englishman is known to have visited the Neusiok or the Cwareuuock, it would seem that these words must have been Manteo's Algonquian terms for those tribes and were phonetically recorded that way by White. What these now-extinct Neusiok and Cwareuuock tribes called *themselves* is not known. The Neusiok lived on the lower Neuse River in present-day Craven and Carteret Counties and may have been part of the Iroquoian language group like their Mangoak (later to be called Tuscarora) neighbors to the west. The Cwareuuock (Coree) may also have been Iroquoian, but during their seasonal presence on the Outer Banks they most likely interacted occasionally with Manteo's Croatoans.

On the map below, the shaded area comprising present-day Carteret and Pamlico Counties as well as the southern portions of Beaufort and Craven Counties was uniquely positioned to satisfy *all* of the colonists' concerns in 1587–88. It was shielded from Spanish ships in the Atlantic, and, of great importance, it was removed from the territory of all the now hostile Secotan Indians. It was also located more than fifty miles to the south of Manteo's Roanoac and Dasamonquepeuc, fulfilling the fifty-mile restriction mentioned above. Most notably, that area was accessible for future re-supply via the Wokokon inlet, the only proven navigable channel in Pamlico Sound. The Pomouiks, who dwelt across the Pamlico River from the Secotans, may very well have been receptive to discussions with Manteo that could bring the English into an alliance with them against their perennial enemies. As far as the physical suitability of the Pamlico River is concerned, it is worth mentioning that

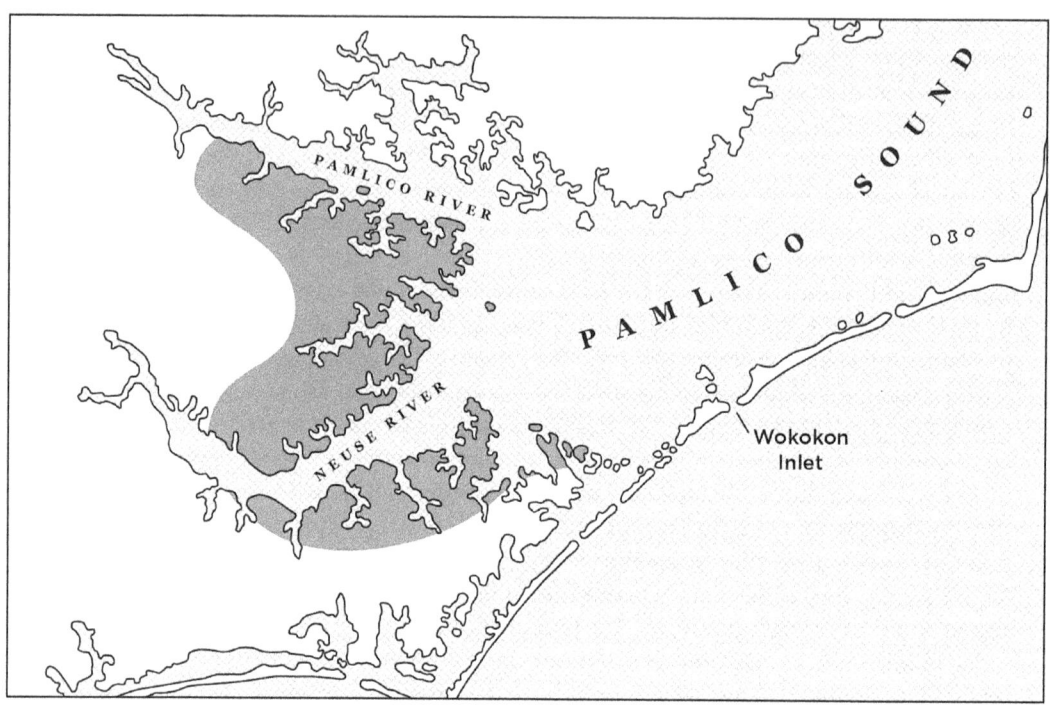

Potential settlement locations in 1588 (courtesy Michael Gayle).

archaeologist William Haag, who surveyed all of Pamlico sound in the late 1950s, noted in his report that the "Pamlico River ... might be the one they [the 1587 colonists] would look upon with favor as a new homesite."[83]

Since the colony was to be self-sufficient and agricultural, it can be concluded with a fair degree of conviction that the colonists were settled in at their new mainland location by March of 1588. As mentioned previously, planting was done from April through June so that a corn harvest was available from early summer through October. It is possible that an outpost was also established at Croatoan to watch for White's returning ships sailing up the coast, after which the supplies and additional colonists could be guided through the nearby Wokokon inlet to the mainland settlement. It is also probable that some Croatoans had already occupied Roanoac and Dasamonquepeuc, Manteo's new domain. Everything would have been in place for White's return, which was expected as early as the beginning of June. No one could have known that England was at that time preparing for a major attack by Spain's armada, and that John White's return would be delayed for two years.

What became of Manteo or the colonists after the summer of 1588 would be largely conjectural, but there are plausible assessments that can be made about their condition and the options available to them. By the late summer of 1588, when it had become abundantly clear that White would not return that year—if ever—the colonists, along with Manteo, were left in a critical situation. For the colonists, their survival depended upon the arrival of regular supply fleets, and the first and most essential of these was more than two months overdue. With critical supplies and materials running low, the colonists would now have to sustain themselves for at least another year while becoming increasingly dependent on the neighboring Indians, a factor which contributed to the failure of Lane's colony in 1586. Their position had quickly become desperate and their prospects grim.

It has been proposed by this author elsewhere[84] that the colonists, faced with the reality of their permanent abandonment in the fall of 1588, would have given up hope about colonization and made an attempt to intercept English ships to the north at the cod fisheries off Newfoundland. These fishing routes were well-known to the English, and a few English ships had, in fact, previously sailed to Newfoundland from the Hatorask and Wokokon inlets in 1585 and 1586. It is known from the Roanoke accounts that the 1587 colonists had in their possession, in addition to a few small boats, a seaworthy 30–35 tun pinnace capable of ocean travel. This was the same pinnace that Edward Stafford had commanded as part of the three-vessel fleet that had sailed from England to Roanoke the previous year. It is also known that when White did finally manage to return to Roanoke Island in 1590, he searched for both the colonists and the pinnace, as well as Manteo, but they were nowhere to be found.

A voyage up the coast to Newfoundland would have been far more preferable a choice than a perilous 3,500 mile solo trans–Atlantic voyage essentially due east to England, or the even farther and more dangerous circuitous route through the Spanish waters of the Caribbean. In the 16th century "New-found-land" was used to describe the shoreline from Labrador as far south as the present-day Gulf of Maine. English fishing fleets would naturally follow the codfish migrations, which would range from the polar current at Labrador during the summer southward to the Gulf of Maine in the fall, putting the potential contact with English ships less than 1,200 miles north of Croatoan. The pinnace was capable of reaching those fishing routes in perhaps six weeks or less. That route would also keep the vessel close enough to the coastline to search out a safe harbor in case of bad weather and also provide access to fresh water and provisions. English ships had been engaged in North Atlantic cod fishing near Newfoundland since shortly after Cabot's discovery of the "new founde land" in 1497, and that territory had become an English possession in 1583 when Raleigh's half-brother, Sir Humphrey Gilbert, claimed the land in the name of Queen Elizabeth. The shorter voyage along the accessible coast would also require less cargo space for provisions and correspondingly more room for colonists. Finally, as mentioned above, the Outer Banks-to-Newfoundland route was a familiar one. Ships from the first Grenville colonization venture at Roanoke had sailed from Croatoan to Newfoundland in the summer of 1585. Several of Drake's ships sailed on to Newfoundland in June of 1586 after evacuating Lane's colony from Roanoke Island. And then a few weeks later in 1586 some of Grenville's belated ships, intended for the resupply of Lane's colony at Roanoke, headed to Newfoundland after learning that Lane's colony had already departed with Drake.

There would have been some debate about the timing of the voyage to Newfoundland. The cod fishing season generally ran from May through October, and so by the time they had given up all hope of White's return—perhaps by late August or early September—it would probably have been too late to attempt a voyage that year. Since the voyage to Newfoundland could possibly take about a month and a half, they could not risk arriving at Newfoundland after the English fishing fleet had already headed back to England. In addition it would have taken a considerable amount of time to properly outfit the pinnace and gather all the necessary stores and supplies for the voyage, and so in all likelihood they could not sail until the following spring. If all went well, though, the colonists could have hoped to make contact with English ships at Newfoundland in the early summer of 1589.

The Newfoundland option, of course, would have directly affected Manteo. Whether or not Manteo would have sailed with the colonists to Newfoundland is debatable, although without the continued occupation of the English, his position would quickly have become untenable. He was known by all the neighboring tribes to be firmly allied with the English, whose intentions were clearly made known by the attack on what was thought to be remnants of Pemisapan's followers at Dasamonquepeuc. To the surrounding Secotan tribes Manteo was now considered an enemy who most likely could not survive without the presence of an English colony nearby. Furthermore even if he vacated Roanoac and Dasamonquepeuc and remained a weroance at Croatoan, his presence there may have endangered his own people as well as his mother, or at the very least complicated the Croatoans' relations with other tribes. Manteo may well have had little choice but to depart with the English aboard the pinnace. In addition, by his baptism and official installment the previous year as Lord of Roanoac and Dasamonquepeuc—by Raleigh's explicit command—Manteo had completed his transformation as a virtual Englishman. He very likely would have felt a sense of loyalty and responsibility to the English, conceivably requiring him to join the Newfoundland voyage in an attempt to make contact with Raleigh, who, for all Manteo knew, may have been planning another venture to the New World. Finally, there is a fascinating clue, to be seen in the next section, which seems to support the Newfoundland hypothesis concerning Manteo in particular.

Ironically, if Manteo and the colonists sailed for Newfoundland in the spring of 1589, as proposed, they would have escaped a destructive event that has only recently been identified.[85] New evidence from Spanish colonial records has indicated that a major hurricane struck present-day North Carolina in August of 1589. National Oceanic and Atmospheric Administration models show that both Croatoan and the potential resettlement areas in present-day Carteret, Pamlico, Beaufort, or Craven counties would most likely have been inundated by the storm surge, in which case the soil would have been contaminated for perhaps a year by increased saline levels. If Manteo and the colonists remained at any of these locations after White had failed to return in the summer of 1588, they would have been victimized by this powerful hurricane and surge and, if some survived, would have been forced to abandon the Outer Banks and the mainland settlement and flee farther inland.

Manteo and Jack Straw

Although nothing else can be said with certainty about Manteo or his whereabouts after 1588, there are two separate and mutually exclusive sources, each of which supports one of the two abovementioned theories regarding Manteo's activities and whereabouts post–1588. The first of these is particularly interesting because it provides supporting evidence directly from an early 17th century primary source that Manteo may possibly have reached the coast of present-day New England and had been active in the formative years of the new colonies there. The case is based on the following fascinating lines which appeared in the April 4, 1631, entry of the official journal of John Winthrop, Governor of the Massachusetts Bay Colony:

> Wahginnacut, a sagamore upon the River Quonehtacit [Connecticut River] which lies west of Naragancet, came to the governor at Boston, with John Sagamore, and Jack Straw (*an Indian which had lived in England and had served Sir Walter Raleigh*[?], *and was now turned Indian again*) and divers of their sannops [male Indians], and brought a letter to the governor from Mr. Endecott to this effect: That the said Wahginnacut was very desirous to have some Englishmen to come plant in his country, and offered to find them corn, and give them yearly eighty skins of beaver, and that the country was very fruitful, &c. and wished that there might be two men sent with them to see the country.[86] (italics added)

A few words should be included here about the Governor Winthrop manuscript. The original manuscript was contained in three notebooks, two of which were later printed by Noah Webster in 1790. In 1825–26 the complete three-journal manuscript was published by the Massachusetts Historical Society after it was carefully transcribed by Society member James Savage, who corrected a few minor errors in the Webster publication. The work appeared in two volumes titled *The History of New England from 1630 to 1649, by John Winthrop, Esq., First Governor of the Colony of the Massachusetts Bay*. In 1850 Savage began revising his work, added additional notes, and his second edition was published in 1853. In the early 20th century James Kendall Hosmer, a member of the Massachusetts Historical Society, edited the notes to the 1853 Savage edition, and it was then published by Charles Scribner's Sons in 1908. Hosmer's 1908 edition contained a bracketed question mark after Winthrop's "Sir Walter Raleigh" reference, as shown in the above excerpt.

The question mark had no further comment or explanation in the notes and did not appear in the earlier editions, and so it seems to have been inserted simply to express editor Hosmer's recognition of the implications concerning the Raleigh reference. Other New England historians have taken note of the entry as well. In 1836 Samuel Gardner Drake, founder of the New England Historic Genealogical Society, wrote of Winthrop's passage, "There accompanied Wahgumacut to Boston an Indian named Jackstraw, who was his interpreter.... Captains Amidas and Barlow sailed to America in his [Raleigh's] employ, and on their return carried over two natives from Virginia, whose names were Wanchese and Manteo. It is barely possible that one of these was afterwards Jack-Straw."[87] Heman Packard De Forest wrote in his 1891 *History of Westborough, Massachusetts*, that the possible connection to Manteo "is highly interesting."[88] And D. Hamilton Hurd, writing about the place called Jack Straw's Hill and the "famous Indian whose name it bears," included the following in his 1889 *History of Worcester County, Massachusetts*:

> Nearly a half-century before white people lived there, it named the country around ... [and] bears the name of the first Christian Indian in the English Colonies, a man for several years in the service of Sir Walter Raleigh, and baptized by his order.... After the abandonment of the Roanoke Colony by the English, he appears to have left his home and served as interpreter for traders and explorers along the coast as far as Maine.[89]

It is also very likely that James Hosmer, a historical society member himself, was aware of a paper titled "Manteo and Jack Straw" that had been presented by Judge William T. Forbes of Worcester, Massachusetts, at the American Antiquarian Society's meeting on April 24, 1901. "It is the purpose of this paper," Forbes stated, "to show that Manteo, the faithful friend of Sir Walter Raleigh and his colonists, from 1584 to 1587, the first Christian Indian in the English Colonies, and Jack Straw, who in his old age enjoyed the hospitality of Gov. Winthrop, in Boston, and of Gov. Bradford, in Plymouth, were probably the same person."[90]

The chronology of events contained in Forbes's paper and the identities of several historical references are somewhat disjointed and difficult to sort through, and so what follows is an explicated version of Forbes's investigation into the early colonial records in the Massachusetts archives: (The full text of Forbes's original paper is included in Appendix A).

According to Forbes the Indian referred to as "Jack Straw" in Winthrop's journal was well known to the early explorers and settlers of New England after 1623. His name was first mentioned in the colonial documents in *A Declaration of the Affairs of the English People That First Inhabited New England*, an account written by Phinehas Pratt. Pratt was one of about sixty settlers who sailed to New England in 1622, two years after William Bradford and the Pilgrims established the Plymouth Colony. After landing at Plymouth, Pratt and a group of settlers sailed northward to form a new colony at Wessagusset, about twenty-five miles north of Plymouth in present-day Weymouth. The Wessagusset colony failed, however, and Pratt returned to Plymouth. He later purchased property just north of Boston, where in 1662 he wrote his *Declaration*, which contained the following passage, in Pratt's original difficult spelling, about the early settlements and the naming of Jack Straw:

> … These Caled [the] name of [their] place Mountwooliston. They Continued neare a yeare as others had don before them; but famin was [their] final aforthrow. Near vnto [the] place is a Town of Lator Time Caled Brantry.
> Not long after the oferthrow of the first plantation in this bay Capt. Louit cam to [the] Cuntry.
> At the Time of his being at Piscataway a Sacham or Sagamor Gave two of his men, on[e] to Capt Louit & an other to Mr. Tomson, but on[e] that was ther said "How can you trust these Salvagis & call[ed] the nam[e] of on[e] Watt Tylor & the other Jack Straw after the names of the two greatest Rebills that ever weare in Eingland."
> Wott Tylor said when he was a boy Capt. Doomer found him upon an Island in great distress."[91]

Pratt's passage requires further clarification. In Forbes's paper Pratt's excerpt begins with "Near vnto…," but in order to give a better sense of the chronology and locations involved, part of Pratt's preceding sentence has been added in the above passage. "Mountwooliston" (Mt. Wollaston) is located in present-day Quincy, and "Brantry" (Braintree) is immediately south of Quincy. Weymouth, where Pratt lived and wrote his *Declaration*, is just east of both Quincy and Braintree. "The oferthrow of the first plantation in this bay" probably refers to Pratt's failed Wessagusset settlement in 1622–3, believed to have been located at Weymouth's Fore River.

Pratt's narrative then shifts about sixty miles north near the present-day Maine–New Hampshire line to "Piscataway" where "Capt. Louit cam[e]." Piscataway was a later spelling of "Piscataqua" the location of David Thompson's (Pratt's "Mr. Tomson") 1623 settlement at present-day Odiorne Point, believed to be the first settlement in New Hampshire. Christopher Levett (Pratt's "Capt. Louit") spent a month there in the autumn of 1623 before heading up the coast of Maine to start his own (unsuccessful) settlement at Casco Bay at present-day Portland. It should be mentioned here that, unlike many of the early settlers, Levett apparently established very cordial relationships with the Abenaki Algonquians he met. This in turn may help to explain the following incident that occurred at Piscataqua.

At some time during Levett's month-long visit with Thompson at Piscataqua, a native chief "gave two of his men" to Levett and Thompson, probably to act as intermediaries and interpreters, which would mean that at least one of the Indians had some fluency in English. It was not unheard of for settlers to occasionally encounter a coastal Abenaki Indian who, from his contact with English cod fishing vessels, knew a few English words and expressions. An Algonguian interpreter, though, would require a broader familiarity with English, one that—as Forbes pointed out—Manteo would have possessed. In any case, there was a less tolerant Englishmen present who—unlike Levett—seems to have had less than cordial contacts with the Indians and did not "trust these Salvagis." The annoyed Englishman named one of the Indians "Watt Tylor & the other Jack Straw, after the names of the two greatest Rebills that ever weare in Eingland." The Algonquian names of these two Indians were unfortunately not mentioned.

Jack Straw and Watt Tylor were indeed two of the most famous rebels who "ever weare in Eingland." In 1381 Tylor and Straw were major figures in the Peasants' Revolt, the first popular uprising in England, set in motion by social and economic discontent. To many

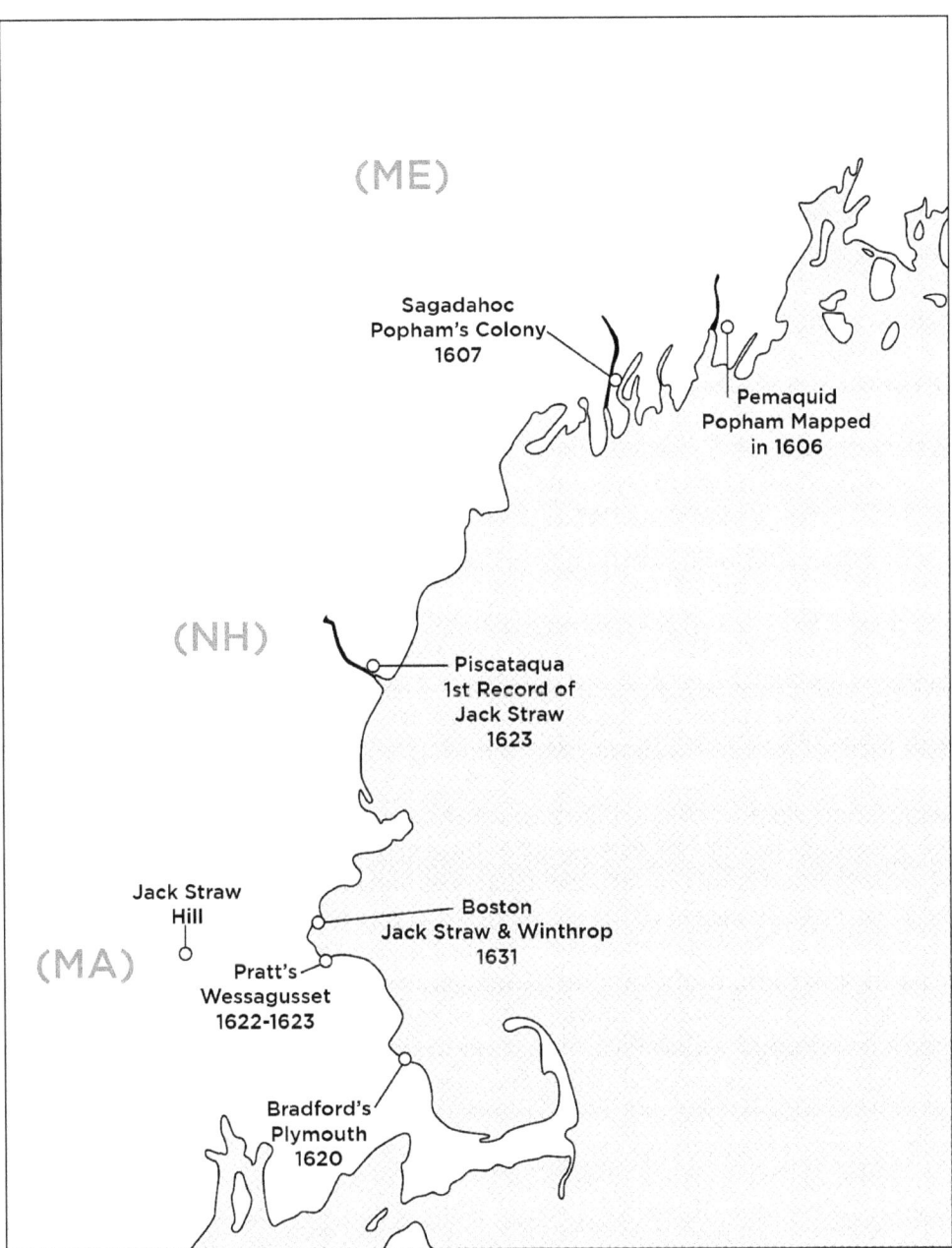

New England settlements referenced in Forbes's "Manteo and Jack Straw" (courtesy Michael Gayle).

of the higher social classes, particularly the nobility, the common rebels were looked upon with disdain. It is likely that the unnamed Englishman who labeled the two Indians "Watt Tylor" and "Jack Straw" considered them dangerous "Salvagis" and viewed them with the same contempt. If this Indian called Jack Straw was Manteo, as Forbes believed, his first appearance in the historical record after 1587, as well as the origin of his new name "Jack Straw," can be traced back to the Piscataqua settlement, at present-day Odiorne Point, New

Hampshire, in the fall of 1623. Jack Straw's Algonquian name was not recorded, and the new name evidently stuck. Pratt's references to a Capt. Doomer and the other Indian being found as a boy on an island "in great distress" are unknown.

Forbes also wrote that early maps and grants in the Massachusetts archives provide proof that various landmarks bearing the name "Jack Straw" existed "many years prior to the first white settlement in that vicinity." He noted as examples the aforementioned "Jack Straw Hill" or "Jack Straw's Hill" or "Jackstraw Hill" as well as "Jackstraw Brook" and "Jack Straw's old line." These locations, Forbes said, have been known in Westborough and Marlborough since the earliest days of their settlement. As mentioned, these conclusions are well borne out by other historical sources that affirm "a previous Indian occupation" of Westborough and Marlborough that were known "before the coming of white settlers."[92] D. Hamilton Hurd, quoted above, wrote that Jackstraw Hill was so well known before the arrival of the first settlers that an early grant designated the location of a certain tract of land to be "in a place called Jack Straw's Hill."[93] Westborough and Marlborough, located about 25 miles west of Boston and two or three miles east of Worcester, were settled in 1633 and 1656 respectively. Boston was settled in 1630. It would appear, then, that Manteo/Jack Straw had to have moved to the area west of Boston at some time after 1623, when he was with Levett and Thompson at Piscataqua, and several more years prior to 1631 when he met with Gov. John Winthrop in Boston. The earliest Indian trail, known as the "Connecticut Road" passed near Jack Straw's Hill, and it would have been this path that the sachem Wahginnacut traveled from the Connecticut River Valley to Boston in 1631. On the way he "secured the services of Jack Straw and Sagamore John, as the former Indian spoke English, and the latter lived between the Charles and Mystic Rivers."[94]

Forbes also supplied a 1737 entry from the diary of Rev. Ebenezer Parkman of Westborough, apparently to demonstrate that Jack Straw was well known and well regarded in the present-day Boston area. Parkman had visited an old Indian named David Monanaow who claimed to be 104 years old. The Indian told him that "the name of Boston was not Shawmut but Shaw-waw-muck." While this is obviously a reference to the Algonquian word first recorded as "Shawmutt," believed to be the name of the area where present-day Boston is located, Forbes did not explain the significance of the entry. He seems to have been hinting that "Shaw" was a corruption of "Straw" and thereby suggesting that Jack Straw's name was associated with the Indian land called Shawmutt which was renamed "Boston" in 1630. Forbes did not expand on this bit of information, perhaps recognizing it for the speculative evidence it was, and simply offered it without comment when he read his paper to the American Antiquarian Society, allowing his listeners to draw their own conclusions.

Forbes did not venture a guess about how long Straw/Manteo had been in Maine or New Hampshire before he first met Levett in 1623, nor does he speculate about Manteo's age other than to say that these events occurred "in his old age." If we can guess that Manteo was about 24 years old in 1588, he would have been living among the Algonquian Abenaki tribe for about three decades before settlers started arriving in present-day Maine and New Hampshire, certainly time enough for him to have "turned Indian again," as Winthrop wrote in his Journal. He could have retained his English language facility through the previously mentioned frequent contacts with English-speaking cod fishermen. By the time he met Levett in 1623 he would have been approaching sixty years old, and when he, John Sagamore, and chief Wahginnacut met with Governor Winthrop in 1631, he would have been well into his sixties. The chronology, at least, seems reasonably possible.

John Sagamore, the Indian who accompanied Jack Straw at the meeting with Governor

Winthrop in 1631, is mentioned a few times in the governor's journal. He and Jack Straw appear to have been well known to the governor, and the references to John Sagamore may be instructive in evaluating Jack Straw's standing among the English as well. John Sagamore lived in a village south of the Merrimack River and was apparently well regarded by the English. He died of smallpox along with most of his villagers on December 5, 1633, just two years after the meeting with Jack Straw and the governor. Winthrop wrote of him:

> He promised (if he recovered) to live with the English and serve their God. He left one son, which he disposed to Mr. Wilson, the pastor of Boston, to be brought up by him. He gave to the governor a good quantity of wanpompeague [wampum], and to divers others of the English he gave gifts.... He died in a persuasion that he should go to the Englishmen's God.[95]

There are no known records of the Indian Jack Straw's death, but based on Forbes's research it may have occurred about 1640, when Manteo would have been in his mid-seventies. Forbes proposed, again using documents in the colonial Massachusetts archives, that Jack Straw—and thus Manteo—had traceable offspring in New England. It was common among the Indians, Forbes said, to use the father's first and last name as the surname for a son or daughter. "It seems probable," he concluded "that Jack Straw used his full name as a surname for his son, William Jackstraw, who naturally passed on that surname to his children." Another source indicates that William Jackstraw also had an Algonquian name, Wanuckhow, and was also known as William Wanuckhow or just Jackstraw. William had two sons, Joseph, whose Indian name is not known, and John, whose Indian name was Apumatquin.[96]

By about 1670 the two generations of Straw/Manteo descendants were living at the village of Magunkook (Magunkaquog, Magunco, et al.) in present-day Ashland, just east of the abovementioned landmarks bearing Jack Straw's name. Magunkook was one of the "praying towns" established by Puritan John Eliot for Indians who converted to Puritan Christianity. According to a 1674 report by colonial magistrate Daniel Gookin, there were eleven families residing at Magunkook "and about fifty-five souls, of whom eight are church members and fifteen baptized." By that time, however, relations between the Indians and the English had seriously deteriorated. In June of the following year the English executed three of the sachem Metacom's Wampanoag Indians who had been found guilty of murdering another Indian, John Sassamon, a "praying Indian" who had converted to Puritanism, and was known to be spying for the English.

The executions sparked the bloody conflict called King Philip's War, named after the sachem Metacom who was known to the English as Philip. Ironically, Metacom was the son of the Wampanoag sachem, Massasoit, who had established an alliance with the Mayflower Pilgrims in 1621 and may have saved them from starvation that winter. Now, more than a half century later, fierce battles ensued throughout New England between the colonial militia and a coalition of several Indian tribes, which included the Jackstraws. In February, 1676, William Jackstraw and his two sons were involved in an assault on the farm of Thomas Eames of Farmington led by the Nipmuc Indian, Netus. Thomas Eames himself was in Boston at the time, but "a party of eleven Indians" burned his house and killed his wife and five of his children. In June, as it was becoming clear that the militia was gaining the upper hand in the conflict, the English issued a proclamation offering clemency to those Indians who turned themselves in. On July 25 a group of nearly 200 Indians gave themselves up to the colonial authorities in Boston. Among these, as Forbes noted, were "the three Jackstraws … with their wives and children."

The three Jackstraws were deposed on August 14 before magistrate Thomas Danforth, with John Speen acting as interpreter. It appears, however, that Danforth had a personal interest in this case because, not only had he lost a son in the war, but he owned the land at Mt. Wayte where the Eames farm was located, and he had persuaded Thomas Eames to move there. William Jackstraw and his two sons were quickly indicted, and the three were convicted on August 18 of "firing Eames his house and murder." On September 5 they petitioned the court for their lives, recounting the terms of their surrender and claiming that, although present, they did not partake in the Eames family massacre, but to no avail. They were hanged on Boston Common, September 21, 1676.[97] Chronologically, Forbes concluded his research into the Manteo/Jackstraw genealogy at this point, and at the end of his paper he iterated his thesis to the American Antiquarian Society with the question, "Does it not seem probable that Manteo and Jack Straw were two names of the same man, and he one of the most famous Indians of the English Colonies in America?"

Of course, as interesting as all this may be, the answer to Forbes's question rests almost entirely on the reference in Gov. Winthrop's journal to Jack Straw as "an Indian which had lived in England and had served Sir Walter Raleigh and was now turned Indian again." A related question would be, "how did Manteo end up in New England?" Forbes was silent on that point other than to make the vague and unsatisfactory suggestion that "A large proportion of the ships of that time sailed direct from England to the West Indies, and then followed the coast north and passed in sight of the island of Croatan, Manteo's home." A more reasonable answer is provided by the proposition mentioned earlier, that Manteo joined the abandoned colonists in their attempt to sail to Newfoundland in the pinnace after John White failed to return in 1588. Perhaps they only made it as far as present-day New Hampshire, where the colonists may have encountered unfriendly Abenaki Indians who had learned that contact with European fishermen seemed always to result in widespread sickness and deaths, the last one a particularly deadly typhus epidemic having occurred just two years earlier in 1586.[98] It is not impossible either, that the same coastal Algonquian Abenakis would have embraced the strange Manteo, who could speak an Algonquian dialect similar to their own as well as the language of the whites.

Forbes was essentially correct in saying, "No writer mentions the visit of any other North American Indian to England and of his serving Raleigh,"[99] but his statement needs to be dissected. In addition to Manteo and Wanchese, there were, in fact, quite a few native Indians who were taken to England between Raleigh's first Roanoke voyage sent in 1584 and his death in 1618. Grenville captured three Indians during his 1586 relief attempt at Roanoke and took one to England with him. And of course there was Towaye, the Indian who accompanied Manteo to England in 1586. Two of Grenville's Indian captives managed to jump overboard and swim to shore. The third was taken to England, was baptized and named "Ralegh in 1588," but died there in 1589. Towaye returned to the Outer Banks with Manteo on the 1587 voyage, and nothing more is known about him.

In the early 1600s a number of Virginia Indians were also known to be in England. A few of these were seen by Londoners in 1603 putting on a rowing demonstration in a canoe on the Thames. How these Indians got to England is uncertain. They may have been captured by Samuel Mace in 1602–03 when he was sent by Raleigh to Virginia to trade with the Indians and acquire information about the 1587 colonists. Mace could have reached the Chesapeake Bay and, if so, it is possible that they were the same Indians who had been captured on the Rappahannock River and about whom Chief Powhatan complained to John Smith in 1607.[100] Raleigh had a keen interest in the Virginia Indians who came to England, but there is no evidence to even suggest that he interacted with these two Indians, and what became of them is unknown. Other Virginia Indians who voluntarily went to England were the Powhatan Indians, Namontack and Machumps, both of whom were passengers on the *Sea Venture* and shipwrecked on Bermuda en route to Jamestown. Namontack is believed to have died at Bermuda, and Machumps made it to Jamestown with the *Sea Venture* colonists and died there later. There was also Uttamatomakkin, who accompanied Pocahontas to England in 1616. He was instructed by Chief Powhatan to count the people in England, and, after Pocahontas died there, he returned to Virginia in 1617.

Perhaps the best candidate to challenge Forbes's Manteo/Jack Straw hypothesis would be one of the five Abenaki Indians abducted by Captain George Waymouth during his exploration of the coast of Maine in 1605. All five of the Abenakis—Tahanedo, Amoret, Manedo, Skicowaros, and Sassacomoit—were taken to England. The plan was apparently to question them about their native geography, teach them some English, and then return them to assist in English colonization efforts in Maine. Manedo and Sassacomoit were on their way back to Maine aboard the *Richard* in 1606, when the ship was attacked by the Spanish and the two Abenakis were imprisoned in Spain. Manedo is believed to have died there. Sassacomoit was eventually released and seems to have been brought again to England a number of years later, but his subsequent whereabouts are unknown. Tahanedo and possibly Amoret returned to Maine with Martin Pring when he mapped the coast in 1606. Tahanedo apparently remained at the coastal village at Pemaquid. Skicowaros sailed to Maine in 1607 with George Popham's colonists, who established what was called the Popham Colony at the mouth of the Sagadahoc (Kennebec) River, but it failed in little over a year.

There are three possible Abenaki Indians, then, who could theoretically dispute Forbes's Manteo thesis: Amoret, Skicowaros, and particularly Tahanedo. All three had traveled to England, had learned to speak at least some English, and—with the possible exception of Amoret—returned to their native Maine. Very little is known about Amoret and, as indicated, his return to Maine is not even certain. Skicowaros is known to have returned to Maine with George Popham, as mentioned, and was at the Sagadahoc River settlement at least for a time, but he seems not to have cooperated with the English. Where he went and what happened to him after the settlement failed and was deserted is not known. More can be said about Tahanedo, a sachem or chief, whose whereabouts are more certain. He was at Pemaquid in present-day Bristol in 1606 and is known to have twice visited the Popham Colony about ten miles to the south in 1607. Seven years later he was also at Pemaquid, where he met John Smith during his exploration of New England in 1614. Smith claimed that Tahanedo successfully encouraged trade between the Abenakis and the English ships that frequented the coast.[101]

It is certainly possible that any of these three Abenakis could have been in the vicinity of Piscataqua when the two Indians were presented to Levett and Thompson in 1623 and one was given the name "Jack Straw." Piscataqua was located at the present-day Maine–New Hampshire border, about seventy miles down the coast from the old failed Popham settlement at Sagadahoc, and about eighty miles from Pemaquid where Tahanedo had been between 1606 and at least 1614. It is also reasonable to conclude that any one of the three could have moved farther south to the Westborough and Marlborough area, where the "Jack Straw" landmarks are known to have existed prior to 1630. As mentioned, each of the three had been to England and had returned to Maine with a degree of English fluency. Any one of the three, especially Tahanedo, would otherwise have been a prime candidate to refute Forbes's Manteo theory, but once again, like the Virginia Indians rowing on the Thames in 1603, there are no known records which could indicate that Raleigh had ever met them. Raleigh, in fact, was imprisoned in the Tower of London when the Abenakis were in England and, although he had many visitors, there is no evidence that the Abenakis were among them.

Raleigh did have contact with a number of native Indians from Guiana in 1595 and 1617, when he made his two voyages there in search of the fabled El Dorado. On those voyages he used native Indians from Guiana who had been in England and had acquired some familiarity with the English language. One of the Indians was Cayoworaco, who had been given to Raleigh by Cayoworaco's chieftain father to take to England, and could loosely be said to have served Sir Walter Raleigh. Another chief named Leonard Ragopo was in England with Raleigh, "to whom hee beareth great affection." There were others, too, who perhaps may have "served" Raleigh in some capacity on a temporary basis, but they all were natives from Guiana in South America who spoke either the Wayampi or Emerillon language. There would have been no practical reason to relocate Guiana natives to New England where they could neither speak Algonquian nor even likely survive in the climate.

The Indian known as Jack Straw "had served Sir Walter Raleigh," according to Winthrop's journal, but that phrase leaves room for interpretation. If by "served" was meant "assisted" or "helped" in a general sense, then any number of the abovementioned Indians who could possibly have provided some information to Raleigh might qualify. It is more likely, however, that "served Sir Walter Raleigh" had a more official connotation when Winthrop wrote his entry in 1631, indicating a formal or contractual relationship of someone who had entered the service of Raleigh. This would not have been the case with Wanchese, for example. Although he was lodged with Manteo at Raleigh's Durham House for seven months and must have assisted Raleigh willingly or otherwise, he was not considered to be officially in Raleigh's service, as were Amadas and Barlowe for example, and especially Hakluyt and Harriot, all of whom advised Raleigh at Durham House. Furthermore, Wanchese quickly disassociated himself from the English and turned against them as soon as he returned to his Roanoac village in 1585.

Nor did Manteo officially serve Raleigh in 1585–86, even though he proved to be a true and reliable asset to Lane and the English. It was only after Manteo's second trip to England in the summer of 1586 that plans were undertaken for him to legitimately enter Raleigh's service. Once the 1587 colony was established at Roanoke, those plans were formally enacted. First Manteo was baptized, the first recorded christening of a native Indian into the Church of England. And then, most importantly, he was officially installed as Lord of Roanoac and Dasamonquepeuc "by the commandment of Sir Walter Raleigh." This ceremony conferred an English title on Manteo, established his realm, and named him as Raleigh's "assignee" as provided for in the royal charter granted to him by the queen. August 13, 1587, marked the date that Manteo officially entered Raleigh's service. That distinction was not shared by any Indian other than Manteo.

It is interesting that Winthrop's entry mentioned that the Indian called Jack Straw "was now turned Indian again." Forbes took note of this, saying, "According to Winthrop, this Indian, Jack Straw, had once served Raleigh, and had doubtless once lived as a civilized Christian, or Winthrop would not have observed that he 'had turned Indian again.'"[102] Forbes's observation, if correct, could be seen as supplying additional support for his thesis that Manteo and the Indian called Jack Straw were one and the same. It is also significant that Winthrop inserted the startling details about Jack Straw as a parenthetical remark, sometimes used to indicate that the information came from another source, or perhaps simply assuming that it was common knowledge in 1631. It is even possible that he was informed about it by Jack Straw himself. Unfortunately, Winthrop said no more about it, leaving future readers to wonder who his source could have been.

A line appears near the end of Forbes's paper, apparently indicating that Manteo/Jack Straw later helped negotiate a treaty between the Indians and colonial governors Winthrop of Massachusetts Bay and Bradford of Plymouth: "A few years later he is employed to negotiate a treaty with the colonies of Massachusetts Bay and Plymouth, is dined by Gov. Winthrop and by Gov. Bradford, and the following year is given a coat worth twelve shillings (paid for out of the Colony Treasury), by order of Governor Winthrop."[103] This sentence stands alone without elaboration or context, but it appears to reference additional events in Winthrop's journal concerning Jack Straw. The only passage that seems to correspond with the Forbes quote involved a meeting that occurred on October 21, 1636. On that day Winthrop met with several Narragansett sachems including Miantuunomoh and two of Canonicus's sons during which terms of peace were agreed to. The chiefs dined with Winthrop and left the next day. On March 21, 1637, Miantuunomoh sent several sachems with "forty league of wampom and a Pequod's hand" to Winthrop, who reciprocated with four coats "of fourteen shillings price."[104]

Although Forbes was attempting to emphasize Jack Straw's importance to the Massachusetts colonies, his name is not mentioned either at the meeting in October or during the exchange of gifts in March. It is possible that Forbes's description of events came from a colonial document other than Winthrop's journal, but he did not reference his source. Miantuunomoh is believed to have been born about 1600, thus eliminating him from the Manteo thesis. Canonicus died in June of 1647 "on Conannicut Island opposite Newport [Rhode Island] at the age of eighty-five years,"[105] making him Manteo's approximate chronological equivalent, but nothing is known about Canonicus before the arrival of the first English settlers, and furthermore there is nothing to indicate that he ever was in England.

In the final analysis Forbes's Manteo hypothesis is fascinating, and, when thoroughly examined, cannot be easily dismissed. As mentioned, the proposed attempt by John White's abandoned colonists to reach Newfoundland in 1588 could provide what Forbes could not satisfactorily explain, a rationale for Manteo's later presence in New England. If the Forbes thesis is accurate, Manteo's story and his progeny did not come to an end at Croatoan or Roanoke Island in the late 16th century, but much later somewhere far to the north in the Province of Massachusetts Bay.

Manteo and The Legend of the Coharie

The other source purported to be related to Manteo post–1588 is a North Carolina oral tradition that has been passed down for generations in Sampson County. Although oral traditions by their nature are not based on document sources such as the 1631 entry in Governor Winthrop's journal examined previously, they nevertheless can often provide useful historical information. This particular oral tradition is interesting not simply because it proposes ancestral connections that reach back to the late 16th century Anglo-Algonquian contact, but because it speaks of Manteo specifically, and makes mention, for the first and only time, of "one of the daughters of Manteo."

There are actually two surviving oral traditions that trace native North Carolina ancestral origins to the Croatoans and John White's 1587 colonists. The better known of the two is an account of a Lumbee oral tradition in Robeson County, which Hamilton McMillan recorded in the mid–1880s and published in 1888. McMillan wrote that he first learned of the Lumbee tribe's connection to the Croatoans and the early English colonists in 1864, when he heard an old Indian named George Lowrie testify that his tribal ancestors included Hatteras (Croatoan) Indians and English colonists from Roanoke. McMillan's subsequent investigations and interviews in Robeson County confirmed that there was indeed a tradition connecting at least a segment of the Lumbee tribe to Manteo's Croatoans and the 1587 colonists. Regarding Manteo himself, however, McMillan wrote, "The name of Manteo is not familiar to them [the Lumbees]. While they have a tradition of their leader or chief who went to England, yet they have preserved no name for him."[106] McMillan's arguments subsequently led to North Carolina's recognition of the Lumbee tribe, initially called "Croatan Indians."

The second narrative, which is the focus here, traces the same ancestral tribal connections of the Coharie tribe, who are closely related to the Lumbees in Robeson, but reside mostly in nearby Sampson County. The Coharie narrative had been handed down orally for many generations in Sampson County until it was finally transcribed about 1950 by Sampson resident Ernest M. Bullard and called "The Legend of the Coharie." What is unusual about this oral tradition, in addition to its references to Manteo, is that it asserts a direct genealogical connection between at least a part of the Coharie tribe and the descendants of colonist George Howe, Jr., and one of Manteo's daughters.

Ernest M. Bullard was a member of the Sampson County Historical Society, which accounts for his interest in local history and explains the many historical details which embellish the legend's narrative. His grandson, W. Stephen Lee, believes his grandfather transcribed "The Legend of the Coharie" at about the time of his retirement in 1950, and that it was published afterwards by the historical society.[107] The legend was reprinted in "Pitch 'n' Tar," a series of publications for an oral history project in Roseboro, North Carolina, in the late 1960s or early 1970s. More recently the account was published in the January 2014 issue of "Huckleberry Historian," the quarterly journal of the Sampson County Historical Society. (The full text of "The Legend of the Coharie" is included in Appendix B.)

The exact origin of "The Legend of the Coharie" is unclear. Ernest Bullard wrote that it was first told to him about 1892, and added that it had been passed down "by word of mouth for more than three hundred years before one word of it was ever put into writing." The legend is not widely known today outside of Sampson County and the Bullard extended family, but it appears to have been passed down orally prior to 1892 in the Hall family line. Ernest Bullard wrote, "on top of a knoll overlooking the lowland of Big Swamp in the western part of what was known at the time (1779) as 'The Territory' of Duplin County [the western part of Duplin County became Sampson County in 1784] there stood a small log cabin belonging to Enoch Hall. According to the legend, Hall was "said to have been a lineal descendant from George Howe of the 'Lost Colony,' the name having been changed from Howe to Haw, then to Hall."[108]

George Howe, it will be recalled, was killed by a group of Pemisapan's former followers shortly after John White and the colonists arrived at Roanoke in July of 1587. His son, George Howe, Jr., was among the colonists and in the legend was purported to be, through marriage to one of Manteo's daughters, the ancestral link to the abovementioned Enoch Hall and the Hall descendants in Sampson County a century later. The narrow emphasis on the Howe-to-Hall transition in the legend makes it likely that the legend was transmitted orally within the Hall family line in North Carolina exclusively at least until 1892, when young Ernest Bullard first heard it. There is a genealogical connection between the Bullards and the Halls which might explain Ernest Bullard's access to the legend. His grandson, W.

Stephen Lee, reports that one of Ernest Bullard's great aunts, Lucy Bullard Hall, was married to Everett Hall, son of Enoch Hall, who himself was the son of another Enoch Hall, apparently the one who lived on the knoll overlooking Big Swamp in 1779. Lucy Bullard Hall died in 1892, the same year the legend was related to Ernest Bullard. It seems likely that young Ernest Bullard first heard the legend from one of his Hall relatives when the Bullard and Hall families assembled for Lucy's funeral.[109]

The first part of "The Legend of the Coharie" tells the story of a mixed remnant of colonists and Croatoans led by Manteo, who had "survived a tremendous tidal wave," and headed west to the mainland from Croatoan in search of arable land, because the tidal wave had "salted the earth where they first settled so that it would not grow corn." The group landed at a location which Bullard concluded must have been in Carteret or Pamlico County, since, as the legend claims, Manteo attempted to guide them up the Neuse River where they hoped to find fertile land. In the meantime, the narrative relates, "many of the colonists grew sick for lack of bread to eat with sea foods and game which were abundant." Before they could find a suitable location along the Neuse, however, they were attacked by a hostile tribe during which several in the group were wounded, forcing them all back to the coastal mainland.

There is much to disassemble in this section of the legend. The first is that the narrative evolves from a single event, a powerful hurricane that impacted Manteo and the 1587 colony. As mentioned earlier, documents in the Spanish colonial records have only recently (2016)—nearly seventy years after the legend was transcribed by Bullard—provided evidence that a powerful hurricane did indeed sweep up the Florida coast and strike present-day North Carolina in September of 1589. The legend actually does not speak of a hurricane per se, but rather of "a tremendous tidal wave," which would have accompanied a hurricane. "Tidal wave" was probably the common term used by Ernest Bullard in 1950 for what is technically called a "storm surge" today, although "tidal wave" may actually be more accurate in this instance, since the most deadly surges happen when they coincide with the lunar high tide.

The details in the legend regarding the aftereffects of the tidal wave are consistent with modern NOAA surge models, which of course did not exist when Bullard transcribed the legend, although the impact of hurricanes was certainly familiar to eastern Carolinians. A considerable storm tide would have "salted the earth" in a vast coastal area, including Manteo's Croatoan, which would have been inundated and contaminated. Tidal surges also result in increased levels of both sodium and chloride, both of which are toxic to crop plants such as corn, the main food source for both the colonists and the native Indians.[110] Depending on rainfall and soil factors, salt levels may gradually reduce to tolerable levels within a year's period of time, but "on soils with high water tables, it may take several years for salt levels to drop to acceptable levels."[111] As mentioned earlier, Indian corn planting was done from April through June so that a corn harvest was available from early summer through October. A September 1589 hurricane and surge would not only have spoiled the fall harvest and the remainder of the summer stores, but also contaminated the soil for at least the next nine months, eliminating the 1590 planting season as well. There is strong evidence, to be discussed further at a later point, that the island of Croatoan was uninhabited when White finally returned to the Outer Banks in August 1590, which is to be expected if the coastal areas were contaminated by the hurricane of September 1589. All things considered, a migration westward "to reach higher land on which they could grow Indian corn" would be a plausible development.

The legend also speaks of a secondary effect of the storm surge and the loss of crops and existing food stores. According to the legend "Many of the colonists grew sick for lack of bread to eat with sea foods and game which were abundant." Both the colonists and native Algonquians were dependent on the abovementioned agricultural cycle. Consequently it is reasonable to conclude that survivors of a hurricane and surge, both colonists and native Croatoans alike, would have had little choice but to abandon the sterile areas on the Outer Banks and seek arable land farther west of the flooded coastal mainland. It also seems conceivable that a sudden dietary change, presumably from mostly grain-based to exclusively shellfish and wild game, could have caused acute gastrointestinal disorders in some colonists.

How much of a hurricane's aftereffects, however plausible, could have been retained in an oral tradition that had supposedly been passed down for centuries is debatable. It is likely that some of the subsequent details had to have been added to supplement the legend as it was passed along orally from one generation to the next. The same can be said of the various historical references, dates, and comments that appear throughout the legend, which could not have been part of the original oral tradition. These historical details are associated with the general narrative, but clearly had been added over time, many probably by Ernest Bullard as historian, to augment the legend and to align the narrative as closely as possible with the historical record.

That being said, the attempt to ascend the Neuse River would have been a logical step for a group of hurricane surge survivors seeking higher arable ground for corn production, and the attack upon them by a hostile tribe is also historically plausible, at least from what is known of the late 16th century tribes. An intrusion into Iroquoian territory by a group of whites and Algonquians would probably not have been received kindly. Bullard's mention of Carteret County as the possible place "where they first settled," and from which they ascended the Neuse, echoes McMillan's account of the Lumbee migration to Robeson County. "After the English colony became incorporated with the [Croatoan] tribe," McMillan wrote, "they began to emigrate westward.... The line of emigration extended westward from what is now Carteret County...."[112]

The next part of "The Legend of the Coharie" speaks of later generations, by which time Manteo has disappeared from the narrative, leaving whatever became of him unmentioned. The role of Manteo's daughter is picked up later. The group supposedly remained intact, migrating slowly southward along the coast until they finally settled east of the Cape Fear River, where they dwelt for what seems to have been at least two generations. Eventually, however, white settlers started arriving at the lower Cape Fear, and the by-now admixed descendants of what Bullard calls "Manteo's tribe" moved farther inland "very much desiring peace and tranquility." Bullard suggested that these white settlers were probably the so-called Clarendon Colony, also known as the "Yeamans Colony," established by English settlers from Barbados in 1664. The Clarendon Colony was actually preceded by two other groups to arrive at the Cape Fear River between 1663 and 1664. In September of 1663, Captain William Hilton sailed from Barbados to examine the suitability of the Cape Fear River for settlement, and it was Hilton's report that led to the establishment of the Clarendon Colony the following year.

Earlier in 1663, however, a group of settlers from Massachusetts had entered the Cape Fear river and established themselves on the south bank about twenty miles from the river's mouth. Relations with the local Indians quickly turned hostile. It is believed that these New Englanders took a number of Indian children and, under the pretense of teaching them the ways of civilization, sent them north to be sold into slavery. When the local Indians learned of this treachery, they attacked the settlement with such resolve that the New Englanders abandoned the area after only three months and sailed back to Massachusetts. If the Bullard legend is to be believed, this event could explain the fearful reaction of "Manteo's tribe" to the English and the reason for migrating farther inland at that time. In that case the legend's "colony of white people" could have been the Massachusetts settlers, and the migration inland would probably have begun prior to the arrival of both Hilton in October of 1663 and the Clarendon Colony in May of 1664.

It is also noteworthy that, according to Captain Hilton's journal, none of the Indians he encountered at the Cape Fear could speak English, and communication had to be accomplished through sign language. Hilton recorded only one word—"bonny"—which a few Indians repeated over and over as an indication of their good intentions. Ethnographer James Mooney regarded this as a "reminiscence of previous contact with Spaniards."[113] If "Manteo's tribe" had remained intact and had been dwelling anywhere in the area of the Cape Fear River, its existence was certainly not known to Hilton, and neither apparently to the Indians whom he encountered. Of course after three generations of migration and assimilation, it is likely that any surviving descendants of the 1587 colonists would by this time have been fundamentally "Indian" in appearance, practice, and language. This is a problematic issue in the legend that will be addressed below.

Following the arrival of white settlers, then, "Manteo's tribe" is said to have migrated farther and farther inland, apparently following the Cape Fear River, until it reached the confluence of the Deep and Haw rivers, tributaries of the Cape Fear. An unknown—but apparently considerable—number of years passed during this extended, gradual migration. What follows the arrival at the Deep and Haw Rivers in the Bullard legend is the first reference to a specific genealogical connection between this group and the original colonists, and here the legend is at its weakest. The present-day "Haw" river, we are told, is actually a corruption of "Howe," which the river was originally named in honor of George Howe III, great grandson of Manteo. Two generations are identified in this portion of the legend. George Howe, Jr. (referred to as George Howe "II" in the original text) is said to have married one of Manteo's daughters. If George Howe II was about twelve years of age in 1587 when his father was killed, a marriage to Manteo's daughter, assuming he had one, could perhaps have taken place about 1595. George Howe III could plausibly have been born as early as 1596 putting him about sixty-seven years old at the time the Massachusetts settlement was attempted in 1663 at the Cape Fear. If, as the legend contends, the "Howe" River was named in his honor, it would suggest that elements of this group still retained English identities and surnames after three quarters of a century, a somewhat unlikely consideration.

Furthermore, the legend's account of the naming of the Haw River is challenged by the historical record. John Lawson made the first documented reference to that river in his *A New Voyage to Carolina*, published in 1709. Lawson wrote, "…with great Difficulty, (by God's assistance) [we] got safe to the North-side of the famous Hau-river, by some called Reatkin; the Indians differing in the Names of Places, according to their several Nations. It is call'd Hau-river, from the Sissipahau Indians, who dwell upon this stream, which is one of the main Branches of Cape-Fair." The Sissipahau, also written as "Saxapahaw," are believed to have been the same tribe spelled "Sauxpa" or "Sauapa," whom the Spanish encountered in 1569 near the Santee River in South Carolina. This tribe had to have migrated to the Haw River long before "Manteo's tribe" could have arrived. It would seem, then, that the legend's "Haw" origin had to have been appropriated to suit the "Haw-Howe" tradition and is probably a convenient embellishment.

The legend continues: The group lived in the "Howe" River section for about fifteen years until a severe drought dried the river and all the springs, forcing them downstream. Eventually they reached what is now Cumberland County, Bullard wrote, where they encountered scattered settlements of Scots-Irish families, who had come to the area about 1730. Actually, immigrants had been arriving to that area from the north, particularly Pennsylvania and Delaware, since 1704, when Parliament offered land bounties to encourage the production of naval stores, i.e., tar, pitch, and turpentine. Nevertheless, the legend continues, "With peace and tranquility still uppermost in their minds, they dispatched two runners, one of which was George Howe IV." If George Howe III was born about 1596, it is difficult to imagine that his son George Howe IV, born perhaps about 1616 and now approaching ninety years of age, could have been sent anywhere as a runner in 1704. In any case the legend continues, the two runners headed east and at last one of them located a good stream, shouting to the other "Co-her-ah," apparently an Anglo-Algonquian invocation from which, according to the legend, the Little and Great Coharie Creeks derived their names. Other sources claim that "coharie" is an Iroquoian word which translates as "driftwood."

To support the legend's genealogical claim that the 1587 colonists were ancestors of many present-day Coharie Indians, Bullard wrote:

> Of the more than eighty surnames of the colonists, considerably more than half are today found in the census roll of Sampson County and more than two-thirds can be found among the peoples of southeastern North Carolina. Of the remaining twenty-five or thirty, names of eight are known to have been changed on the records to names as spelled today. Several others are so similar that it is quite reasonable to conclude that they too may have been changed.[114]

This was the identical argument used by McMillan in 1888 for the Lumbees and both are equally flawed. The relatively high percentages of 1587 colonists' surnames in Robeson and Sampson Counties can easily be attributed to the fact that most of the colonists' English surnames were fairly common and could be found in large numbers in all of North Carolina's counties as well as in many other colonies settled by the English. The fact that the same or a similar surname as that of a lost colonist appears on a census role or other document is hardly proof of a direct lineage spanning more than three centuries.

An even more significant problem with Bullard's and McMillan's surname theory was their assumption that a very large percentage of the original 1587 colonists not only survived, but had (male) children, who themselves survived and had male descendants, and so on for more than 300 years, all the while retaining their English surnames, language, and culture. The high percentage of original colonists' surnames estimated by Bullard to be in southeastern North Carolina—about 85 percent if we do the math—seems even to be contradicted by the legend itself, which leads us to believe that only some of the colonists survived the "tremendous tidal wave." In any case, after two or more generations of native contact exclusively, their descendants would have been virtually indistinguishable from the native Indians, and it is probable that the language and any surnames of the original colonists would by that time have been lost as well.

As for Manteo's name, both Bullard and McMillan suggested that his name may also still be found in certain North Carolina surnames. "It has been reported," Bullard wrote, that some with the surname "Manor" who live in the central western section of Sampson County, and on both sides and between the two Coharie Creeks, "have to a considerable degree preserved their Indian blood and characteristics, and claim to be the direct descendants of Manteo." After his interviews among the Lumbee Indians McMillan wrote of Manteo:

The name Manteo they do not recognize, but are familiar with Mayno, a name very common among them and representing a very quiet, law abiding people.... The nearest approach to the name Manteo is Maino or Mainor. An old woman, whom we interviewed, spoke of their great man as Wonoke. This may be a corruption of Roanoke, for we must remember Manteo was made Lord of Roanoke.[115]

Although the surname theory is seriously flawed, what can be said with certainty is that an oral tradition among the Lumbee and Coharie tribes tracing their ancestry to the 1587 colonists undoubtedly exists. A number of sources have confirmed the existence of that tradition. Coharie tribal member Enoch Emanuel reported the following about 1913 when he was approximately 70 years old: "The mixed race of people living in Sampson County are sure that the statements given to us by our ancestors concerning our origin are true.... We have always been told by our fathers and mothers that we were mixed with the Lost Colony of the Roanoke. We therefore are a mixture of Governor White's colony and the original Indians."[116] Coharie tribal member C.D. Brewington wrote, "There is an abiding tradition among these people that their ancestors were the Lost Colony of Roanoke Island, amalgamated with the Five Civilized Tribes of Eastern North Carolina."[117] Lumbees Adolph Dial and David Eliades described the Lumbee tribe as a community consisting of "remnants both of the 'Lost Colony' and several Indian tribes of which the Hatteras and various Eastern Siouan peoples were the most prominent."[118]

A later in-depth investigation of Coharie oral traditions and lore was conducted by Don A. Grady and published in his 1981 Master of Arts thesis at the University of North Carolina at Chapel Hill. Grady wrote, "Perhaps the most important tradition is that of the tribe's origin. They believe very strongly that they are the descendants of a coastal tribe of Indians and the Lost Colony."[119] And of course there is John Lawson's 1701 report about the Hatteras (Croatoan) Indians:

> A farther Confirmation of this we have from the Hatteras Indians, who either then lived on Ronoack-Island, or much frequented it. These tell us, that several of their ancestors were white People, and could talk in a Book, as we do.... I cannot forbear inserting here, a pleasant story that passes for an uncontested truth amongst the Inhabitants of this Place; which is, that the ship which brought the first Colonies, does often appear amongst them, under sail, in a gallant Posture, which they call sir Walter Raleigh's ship, and the truth of this has been affirm'd to me, by Men of the best Credit in the Country.[120]

The "Legend of the Coharie" consists essentially of two separate, interrelated narratives. The first is the chronological and geographical account about survivors of John White's English colony and a group of Croatoan Indians and their eventual migration into present-day Sampson County as the Coharie tribe. As such it provides a more detailed foundation about the tribe's origins than is found in other oral traditions. How much of that account can be relied upon with confidence is an open question. At its core—the gradual inland migration of a small group of coastal Croatoans and colonists who survived a fierce hurricane and surge—the legend is compatible with both Lumbee and Coharie oral tradition. Details such as a hurricane's "tidal wave"—which have only been recently documented—are also interesting. So, too, are the references to the storm surge salting the earth "so that it would not grow corn," which is consistent with modern scientific studies.[121]

Woven into that broader narrative, however, is the highly questionable attempt to trace the male lineage of George Howe, Jr., son of the English colonist killed at Roanoke on July 28, 1587, and an unnamed daughter of Manteo. The arguments based on the high percentage of matching or similar surnames of lost colonists in 20th century census records are flawed on a number of levels. Other efforts to explain the transition of the specific Howe surname to Haw and Hall are also unconvincing. The legend's version about the naming of the Howe/Haw River, for example, is effectively contradicted by Lawson's account.

And what is to be concluded about Manteo? There is no evidence whatsoever in the Roanoke documents spanning 1584 to 1587 that he had any children at all, or even a wife for that matter. Although the absence of such evidence does not automatically preclude the possibility, it weakens the likelihood that George Howe II could have "married one of the daughters of Manteo." Manteo himself, the legend implies, must have died at some unspecified time and place during the group's migration, but he simply disappears from the legend with not a word said about it. His presence in the legend, however, was not indispensable to the overall Coharie narrative, except perhaps to account for his whereabouts after the hurricane and to supply leadership for the migrating group. Of course, if the previously discussed Forbes account is accurate, then Manteo and a group of 1587 colonists would have been on their way to Newfoundland before the hurricane ever struck. Perhaps the credibility of "The Legend of the Coharie" is best left to Ernest Bullard's own assessment: "Only this much of truth I know to be; I tell the tale as 'twas told to me."[122]

"The fift voyage of M. Iohn White ... in the yeere 1590"

Other than the propositions put forth in "Manteo and Jack Straw" and "The Legend of the Coharie," there is little said about Manteo or his Croatoans for that matter after 1588. There were two events, however, one in 1590 and another in 1609 that could provide evidence to support either the Jack Straw or Coharie thesis, or at least establish that Manteo could not have been at Croatoan at either of those times. His absence from Croatoan in 1590 would be of particular significance because it has long been assumed that the colonists relocated to Croatoan when White failed to return in 1588 and were safely settled there with Manteo in 1590. An examination of the facts will not only challenge that assumption, but also demonstrate that no one, neither the Croatoans nor the colonists, could have been at Croatoan at that time.

On March 20, 1590, after an absence of nearly three years, John White finally sailed from England with Captain Abraham Cooke aboard the *Hopewell* in a belated effort to re-establish contact with his abandoned colony. After several successful privateering encounters with Spanish ships in the Caribbean, Cooke headed northward, as he had promised White, to try to make contact with the colony left at Roanoke in 1587. By August 15th they were anchored off Hatorask, and the next morning White, Cooke, and Edward Spicer set out with a party of men in boats towards Roanoke Island. Encouraged at first by columns of smoke rising from Kenricks Mount to the south of Roanoke, they spent the day investigating the source of the smoke, which turned out to be a naturally caused brushfire. The search at Roanoke would wait until the next day.

On the afternoon of August 17th one of the two boats trying to navigate the inlet at Roanoke overturned, drowning seven of the eleven on board. The remaining men were ready to give up the search at that point, "but in the end by the commandement and perswasion of me and Captaine Cooke," White wrote, "they seemed much more willing."[123] The remaining nineteen men set out in the boats again for Roanoke, but by this time it was getting dark and they were unable to make out the landing place near the old settlement. As they continued toward the north end of the island, they fired off shots, sounded a trumpet, "and called to them friendly; but we had no answere." Virtually all of the attention and interest in White's account of the 1590 voyage has been focused on the events of the next two days, August 18 and 19.

At daybreak on August 18, the very day that would have marked his granddaughter Virginia Dare's third birthday, White, Captain Cooke, and the crewmen searched the island and finally arrived at the deserted settlement near the north end of Roanoke Island where the colony was left three years earlier. They found the "houses taken downe," i.e., disassembled for transport to the new settlement location, and the place "ouergrowen with grasse and weedes." They also looked for the small boats and the pinnace left with the colonists, "but we could perceiue no signe of them." Some of the men found five chests that had been carefully buried by the colonists, three of which…

> … were my owne, and about the place many of my things spoyled and broken, and my bookes torne from the couers, the frames of some of my pictures and Mappes rotten and spoyled with rayne, and my armour almost eaten through with rust; this could bee no other but the deede of the Sauages our enemies at Dasamonqwepeuk, who had watched the departure of our men to Croatoan.[124]

These were the same possessions that White worried would be "pilfered away" by the colonists after he sailed for England in the summer of 1587. At that time, it will be recalled, he had the colonists provide him with a signed and sealed bond guaranteeing the "safe preseruing of all his goods." The most important discoveries made by White were the two carved "CRO" and "CROATOAN" messages left by the colonists directing him to Croatoan. These messages are the only undisputed primary-source evidence we have from the colonists after August 27, 1587.

According to White's account of the 1590 voyage, the only one that exists, he concluded from the carved messages that the colony was permanently settled with Manteo at Croatoan. He wrote that the carved messages were meant "…to signifie the place, where I should find the planters seated," and again that the carvings indicated "the name of the place where they should be seated."[125] He later wrote that "…I greatly ioyed that I had safely found a certaine token of their safe being at Croatoan which is the place where Manteo was borne, and the Sauages of the Iland our friends."[126]

On the following morning, August 19, White and Cooke attempted to "goe for the place at Croatoan, where our planters were."[127] However, according to White's account stormy weather, broken anchor cables, and a shortage of fresh water prevented the *Hopewell* from making the stop at Croatoan. White claimed unconvincingly that Cooke then agreed to sail to the Caribbean, spend the winter there, and then return to Croatoan in the spring of 1591. That idea was soon abandoned, however, and they eventually sailed back to England, arriving on October 24. We are led to believe—and it is still widely accepted today—that, had it not been for the abovementioned mishaps, John White would have made the short trip to Croatoan and been reunited with Manteo and the colonists.

White, of course, had no knowledge of the critical events that had occurred during his three-year absence, namely the violent hurricane that had struck the Carolinas and the previously proposed attempt to reach Newfoundland in the pinnace. His colony had, in fact, already ceased to exist. Nevertheless, despite his insistence that the colonists were safely seated with Manteo at Croatoan, he *must have been* aware that neither Manteo nor his colonists—nobody in fact—could have been at Croatoan at that time. This conclusion is supported, once again, by the details contained in White's own account of the 1590 voyage. As was the case with his version of the 1587 voyage, White's credibility as narrator is doubtful here too. As mentioned, all the interest in this voyage has been focused on August 18 and

19, when White found the carved messages, claimed that the colonists were with Manteo at Croatoan, and then was unable to make the short trip down the coast to find them. Little or no attention has been paid to the important events that occurred between August 9 and August 16, *before* White and the Cooke reached Roanoke Island. As the *Hopewell* and *Moonlight* sailed slowly up the coast towards Roanoke, their arrival was delayed for seven days, during which the ships remained anchored first at Wokokon and then at Croatoan. During that seven-day period there were several opportunities for anyone at or in the vicinity of Croatoan or Wokokon to communicate, either by signal fire, shot, or direct personal contact, with the English. Nothing at all was heard or seen during that entire week.

The first sign that Croatoan and the adjacent islands on the Outer Banks were unoccupied was evident between August 9 and August 12, when the ships anchored for three days at Wokokon. During that time White and some of the English crewmen rowed through the inlet to an island in Pamlico Sound where "we tooke in some fresh water and caught great store of fish in the shallow water." White noted that "Betweene the maine … and that Iland it was but a mile ouer and three or foure foote deepe in most places." If Manteo or any of the Croatoans or colonists had been anywhere in the general area during that three day period, the English presence would have been well known, and there was more than enough time either to contact the offshore ships with a signal fire or to make direct contact with White and the Englishmen while they fished and replenished their water supply at the island in the sound.

On the morning of August 12 the English ships sailed northward from Wokokon and actually anchored for the night at the northern end of Croatoan, just off the shallow inlet there. Anyone on Croatoan at this time would have been immediately aware of ships' sails heading northward on the usual route up the present-day Carolina coast. Signal fires would have been lit and initial contact probably made that same day. No signals of any kind were detected as the English ships sailed slowly along the coast of Croatoan. The inlet where the ships anchored at the north end of Croatoan was the same shallow inlet referred to earlier that was not named on White's map, but was labeled Chacandepeco on later maps and closed during a storm in 1672. They remained at that position through the night and on the following morning, August 13, White and a group of men in smaller boats actually entered the inlet to take depth soundings "ouer this breach." White wrote, "This breach is in 35. degr. and a halfe, and lyeth at the very Northeast point of Croatoan."[128] As noted previously, archaeological findings at the Cape Creek site, just northeast of Buxton, have confirmed that the main village of the Croatoans was located "almost on the shore of the Chacandepeco inlet."[129] White and the crew spent the morning taking a number of depth soundings at this channel where their small boats would have come very close to the Croatoan shoreline. If Manteo or the colonists or any Croatoans at all had been on the island while the English were anchored offshore—or particularly when White and the men were taking sounding within a stone's throw of the shoreline—they would certainly have known about it and contact would have been quickly established. It is difficult to believe that White, who was quite familiar with Croatoan, was not curious enough to seek information about the colonists at Manteo's village, which was located so close to the shallows where the soundings were taken. It is very possible that White did, in fact, actually visit the village at that time and, finding it abandoned, chose to exclude the occurrence from his account, for reasons that will be explained below. By August 16 White, Cooke, and the rest of the crew had to have realized that Croatoan and its environs were completely deserted.

On August 18, therefore, when White found the "Croatoan" messages at Roanoke, he must have been keenly aware that Manteo and the colonists were *not* at Croatoan, despite the assurances he gave in his account. Those assurances were likely inserted afterwards, possibly at Raleigh's insistence or by his own hand, to preserve his royal charter for exploring and colonizing the New World. That charter had been granted to Raleigh by Queen Elizabeth on March 26, 1584, but it clearly stated that it would expire after "sixe yeeres and no more"[130] unless a permanent colony had been established. In order to prevent the charter's automatic expiration in March of 1591, just seven months later, it was imperative that the 1587 colonists were believed to be alive and well and "seated" someplace. White's fabricated assurances that his colony was safely seated with Manteo "at Croatoan" served that purpose.

Although the 1590 voyage failed to locate either Manteo or White's colonists, the account does provide some useful information about what did and did not happen to them. First of all, since it can safely be concluded that they were *not* at Croatoan, despite White's statements to the contrary, the likelihood that they had long since sailed for Newfoundland is further enhanced. Secondly, the complete abandonment of Croatoan by Manteo's tribe is convincing evidence that the previously mentioned powerful 1589 hurricane noted in

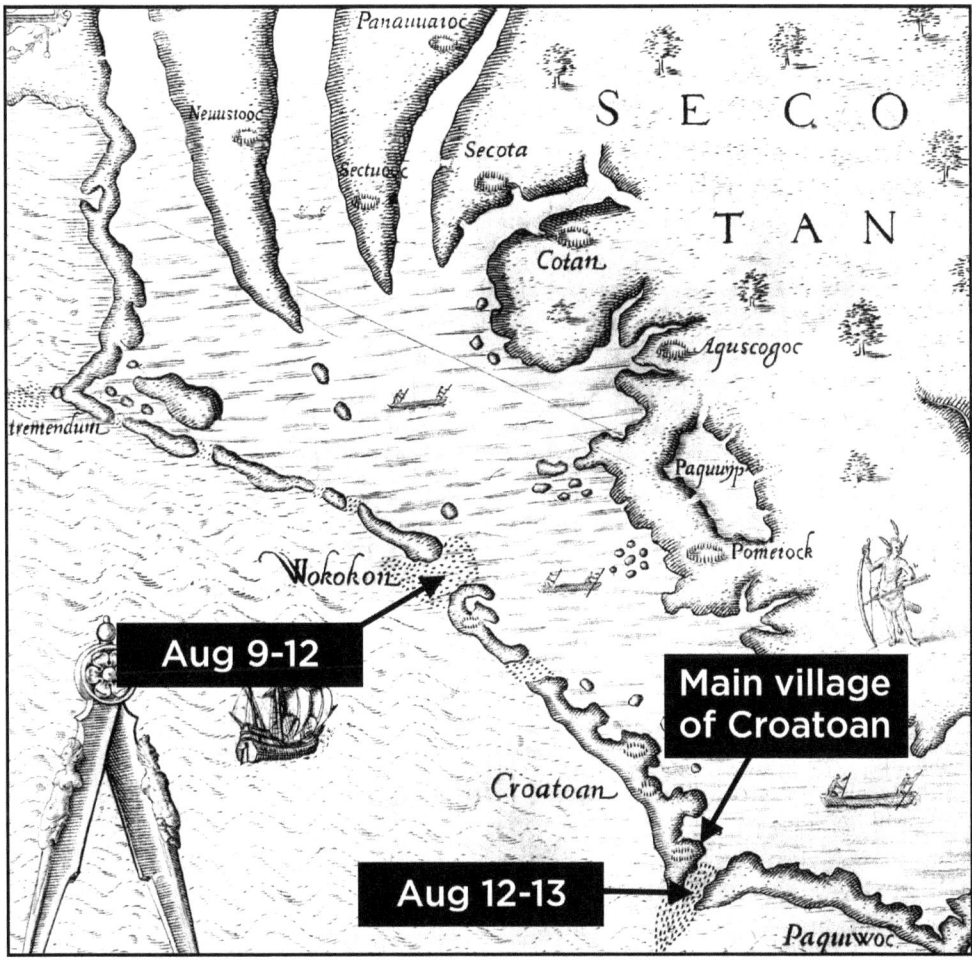

John White's layovers, Aug. 9–13, 1590.

the Spanish colonial documents did, in fact, strike the Carolinas. The accompanying storm surge, it will be recalled, could easily have increased the saline content in the soil to a level that would not allow crop production for a year or more depending on rainfall and soil condition. Ironically, all of this evidence keeps alive the possibilities offered about Manteo's whereabouts both in "The Legend of the Coharie" and "Manteo and Jack Straw." In 1590 Manteo may have been either on the North Carolina mainland to the southwest with survivors of the hurricane, or somewhere near the coast of Maine with the colonists in the pinnace. He was certainly *not* at Croatoan or Roanoke.

There are two further details in White's observations at Roanoke that may provide some insight to the chronology of events in 1588 and the subsequent location of Manteo and the colonists. The first has to do with what can be gleaned about Manteo's and the colonists' whereabouts from White's mention of the pinnace, which, along with a few small ship's boats, was in the possession of the colonists in 1587. White mentioned that he walked from the old settlement at Roanoke "towards the poynt of the Creeke to see if we could find any of their botes or Pinnesse, but we could perceiue no signe of them." Nothing was seen of the pinnace either on August 9, when White and the crewmen went ashore for fresh water and fished off a sandy island west of Wokokon in Pamlico Sound. At that spot White wrote, "betweene the maine[land] and that Iland it was but a mile ouer." And there was no sign of the pinnace between August 12 and 15 when they sailed along the coastline from Croatoan toward Roanoke, during which time they anchored and rowed into the Chacandepeco inlet to take soundings. The fact that the pinnace was nowhere to be found is not conclusive by any means, but it does lend further support to the Newfoundland proposition that Manteo and the colonists had long since used it in an attempt to contact English ships to the north.

The other detail concerns the fact that the chests containing White's possessions "had bene carefully hidden" at the Roanoke settlement by the colonists, but never retrieved. That fact allows for a possible scenario to explain in part the chronology of events following White's departure in 1587. By sometime in March of 1588, as described above, the bulk of the colonists would have been settled at the new site on the mainland to the south preparing for the first planting in April. In the meantime a much smaller group of colonists, Manteo most likely among them, waited for White's return at Roanoke Island where he was expected sometime in the next two or three months. The move to the new mainland settlement location involved multiple trips using the pinnace and the smaller boats in order to transport all of the essential material, equipment, and supplies, including the disassembled dwellings. It would not have been necessary or convenient to transport White's chests or other non-essential items at this point, and so they would have remained with Manteo and the colonists stationed at Roanoke until White's anticipated arrival there in June. At that time his possessions would have been reclaimed, stowed aboard the ships, and transported with the newly arrived colonists and supplies to the mainland settlement.

White failed to return, however, and so Manteo and the group waiting at Roanoke would have abandoned the fort at some point, probably by late summer of 1588, when it became obvious that he would not return that year. Before leaving they buried five chests, "carefully hidden," three of which contained White's possessions. It was probably at that time that they also carved the prearranged messages on the trunk of a nearby tree and on a post at the entrance to the fort directing White to Croatoan, where Manteo and possibly a small contingent of colonists had gone. If White had arrived at Roanoke shortly thereafter, he would have found the messages and sailed on to Croatoan, where he would have been escorted to the new settlement via the Wokokon inlet. His hidden chests at Roanoke could have been retrieved any time afterwards. Of course, White did not return until 1590, by which time Manteo and the colonists were long gone, and his possessions had been unearthed by "no other but the deede of the Sauages our enemies at Dasamonqwepeuk," and left to be "spoyled with rayne."[131]

Manteo's Croatoan Tribe

Croatoan was uninhabited in August 1590, just as it must have been following other severe hurricanes that had struck the Outer Banks previously. According to a 2015 study, Cape Hatteras is one of the most vulnerable locations, with a 15 percent probability of a hurricane strike in any given year.[132] The Hurricane Research Division of the National Oceanic and Atmospheric Administration (NOAA) listed fifty hurricanes that struck North Carolina between 1851 and 2014,[133] averaging one every 3.26 years. Based just on probabilities, it is likely that the Croatoan tribe had occasionally been forced to vacate their island on previous occasions, but they always returned once their fields could be planted again. The tribe undoubtedly reoccupied Croatoan at some point after August of 1590.

There were few recorded voyages to the Outer Banks in later years. In 1602 and 1603 Samuel Mace is known to have been in the area of Cape Fear trading with local Indians, but if he sailed farther north to Croatoan or Roanoke Island there is no record of it. In 1605 an expedition to the coast was led by John Jerome and Bertrand Rocque to search out potentially valuable commodities and medicinal plants. They were instructed to stop specifically at Croatoan, but they never made it that far up the coast. The Spanish captured their ships at St. Helena Sound and, after interrogating Rocque and three others, they learned of their intention to visit Croatoan, where information about the 1587 colonists might be found. Florida Governor Pedro de Ibarra then dispatched Francisco Fernández de Écija to search for the English alleged to be at Croatoan, but Écija seems only to have gotten as far as Cape Fear before turning back to St. Augustine.

By 1608 the Spanish knew that the English had established another colony in "Virginia" (Jamestown), but did not know exactly where, or whether they were settled in more than one location. Consequently, in 1609 Francisco Fernández de Écija was sent once again to find the English. The account of his voyage provides some interesting information about the occupants at Croatoan and Roanoke at that time, and whether or not Manteo could have been at either of those places. Écija was ordered to sail only by day and to search the coast carefully including the islands along the Outer Banks where the English had reportedly been earlier. After passing Cape Fear, Écija disguised his ship's identity by sailing under the "false colors" of a Dutch ship from Amsterdam in order to advance northward unmolested in case English ships might be in the area. On July 20 when he reached what is believed to be Croatoan, Écija witnessed a remarkable occurrence. He first saw "signals made by means of smoke," and then a small group of Indians appeared on the beach and began drumming and shouting to the ship. When the Spanish called back to them, the Indians became fearful and ran back from the beach. They then started playing on what Écija thought were flutes. A similar event occurred on July 23 as the Spanish sailed slowly past Roanoke Island.

The perception and reaction of the Indians at Croatoan and Roanoke Island, when they saw Écija's ship sailing slowly just offshore, are of particular interest. It is not at all likely that the typical Croatoan Indian in 1609 would have been capable of recognizing the "colors" flown by a Dutch ship. Manteo, on the other hand, had sailed across the Atlantic on four occasions: his 1584 trip to England with Amadas and Barlow, his 1585 return with the Grenville/Lane colony, his 1586 voyage to England during Drake's evacuation of Lane's colony, and his 1587 voyage to Roanoke with John White. During these many trans-oceanic voyages, as well as his time spent in England, Manteo would have seen any number of "foreign" vessels, and he probably would have become familiar with the "colors" of many. He certainly was personally familiar the Spanish flag and had heard the Spanish language, having witnessed a number of exchanges and privateering actions against them on his various voyages to and from England. He knew them to be the principal enemies of the English. Manteo would have immediately recognized at least that Écija's ship was *not* English, and surely would have been more cautious about attracting the attention of those on board. The Indians' fearful retreat when the replies came back in Spanish perhaps indicates that they believed the ship *was* English and consequently expected the replies from the men aboard to be in English. It also implies, of course, that at least some of the Indians at Croatoan could still recognize the enunciation of the English language.

The Indians' persistent effort to make contact with the ship after the shouts came back in Spanish suggests that Manteo could not have been present. After fleeing from the shore in fright upon hearing the Spaniards' strange replies, a few Indians tentatively returned, playing what Écija thought were pipes or flutes in a European style.[134] The Spanish did not know what to make of this highly unusual activity, but the Croatoans, probably rather confused themselves, may have been attempting to mimic English tunes and to identify themselves as friends. As mentioned earlier, the same tactic was employed by John White in 1590 when he attempted to announce his arrival at Roanoke: As they rowed towards the island the men "sounded with a trumpet a Call, and afterwardes many familiar English tunes and songs."[135] If Manteo had been at Croatoan when Écija's ship slowly cruised by, he would have realized—certainly as soon as the replies came back from the ship—that it was a Spanish vessel, and any further efforts to contact the ship would have been terminated.

The same sequence of events occurred when Écija's ship passed near Roanoke Island on July 23, and the same conclusions can be drawn. The events that had transpired on July 20 at Croatoan would have been relayed to Roanoke Island well before Écija's ship appeared offshore. If Manteo had been at Roanoke during this time, he would have quickly grasped what had happened at Croatoan as soon as the news reached him. Having been forewarned, Manteo would not have repeated the same determined attempts to contact what he knew to be an enemy Spanish ship. The fact that the identical sequence happened at Roanoke as had occurred at Croatoan three days earlier is a good indication that Manteo could not have been at either location at that time. Whether or not in 1609 Manteo could have been in New England, as Forbes proposed, or somewhere near the Cape Fear River, as the Coharie legend claimed, is an open question, but he was *not* at Croatoan or Roanoke Island in 1590, and he seems *not* to have been at either place in 1609.

What is known about Manteo's Croatoan tribe over the next century is rather limited. Indians were still frequenting Roanoke Island, as the Croatoans had often done, but there were no Indians dwelling there when Francis Yeardley sent a small party southward from Virginia in 1653 to acquire land. Yeardley's men met the "great commander of those parts" who happened to be hunting with his tribesmen on Roanoke Island.[136] The chief treated the Englishmen well and even showed them the remains of Lane's old fort, but he seemed to know little about its history. The purchase of a vast tract of land was subsequently arranged and "possession was solemnly given them by the great commander, and all the great men of the rest of the provinces."[137] Unfortunately the account does not provide any more information about the "great commander" or the tribal identities of "all the great men of the rest of the provinces." It is not likely, however, that the "great commander" could have been a Croatoan; if he had been, he would probably have known more of the history of the fort and the Roanoke Colony, and that a former weroance of his tribe was once Lord of the Roanoacs.

It should be noted that the Croatoans became known as "Hatteras" Indians probably after 1672. As mentioned, the English names for the various tribes were usually derived from the rivers or land features or principal villages where they dwelt. In other instances, such as the Iroquoian tribe spelled "Mongoak" by John White, the name was an Algonquian term and phonetically recorded as such. What they called themselves at that time is unknown. Place names, too, could vary from tribe to tribe, as Lawson commented about "the famous *Hau*-River, by some called *Reatkin*; the *Indians* differing in the Names of Place, according to their several Nations."[138] Hatorask and its various spellings, including the later "Hatteras," was the Algonquian name for the northern part of the island that then extended from Port Ferdinando (the Hatorask inlet near Roanoke Island) south to the Chacandepeco inlet. As illustrated earlier, the island immediately south of the Chacandepeco inlet was Croatoan. After the inlet closed during a storm in 1672, merging the two islands of Hatorask and Croatoan, that entire stretch of the Outer Banks was referred to as Hatteras, and the Indians who dwelt there were afterwards known as Hatteras Indians.[139]

According to findings at the Cape Creek site on present-day Hatteras by archaeologist David Phelps in 1998, Europeans had been periodically interacting with the Croatoan/Hatteras Indians since about 1650. Phelps discovered evidence of mid–17th century European-Indian trade goods which contradicted the widespread belief that the Croatoan/Hatteras Indians had no contact with Europeans between the 1587 Roanoke voyage and the arrival of John Lawson in 1701. Lawson described the Hatteras as "*Civiliz'd* Indians … that wear the *English* Dress,"[140] and the Hatteras Indians told Lawson "that several of their Ancestors were white People, and could talk in a Book, as we do." Lawson went on describe the "gray Eyes being found frequently amongst these *Indians*, and no others" and "their Affinity to the *English*,"[141] all of which he attributed to the Indians' interaction with White's 1587 colonists.

Historian Baylus Brooks, however, suggested the very plausible possibility that it may have been exposure to Europeans during the previous half century, rather than the 1587 colonists, that accounted for the cultural and genetic attributes noted by Lawson. It could also account, Brooks wrote, for "an oft-repeated story of 'Raleigh's ship' [told] to the Indians."[142] The fact that the "Civiliz'd" Hatteras Indians Lawson encountered were wearing English clothing in 1701 seems far more likely to have resulted from the more recent contacts with Englishmen rather than contact with White's colonists 114 years earlier. Brooks correctly pointed out that the late 17th century interactions with English traders does not preclude an earlier connection with White's colonists, but it does imply that the Hatteras were "anglicized" by the more recent contacts. If the English attributes and habits Lawson observed among the Hatteras did not result from contact with White's 1587 colonists, it strengthens the likelihood that they—and Manteo—had long before left the area in their pinnace in an attempt to reach Newfoundland.

By the time Lawson visited the Hatteras Indians in 1701, the Carolina tribes had been devastated by European-introduced diseases. The expansion of white settlements from Jamestown in the latter part of the 17th century brought with it deadly infectious outbreaks which took a heavy toll on the tribes. In 1696–7 a smallpox epidemic swept down from Virginia and devastated the Carolina tribes. According to one source, the Indians in North

Carolina's Coastal Plain numbered approximately 30,000 in 1660, but by about 1700, "rum, small pox, and intertribal warfare had reduced them to no more than 5,000."[143] In 1701 the Hatteras tribe was reported to have just one village called Sandbanks on Hatteras and just sixteen fighting men. Lawson wrote of the effect smallpox and rum had on the Indians in general:

> formerly it destroy'd whole Towns, without leaving one *Indian* alive in the Village.... The Small-Pox and Rum have made such a Destruction amongst them, that, on good grounds, I do believe, there is not the sixth Savage living within two hundred Miles of all our Settlements, as there were fifty Years ago.[144]

The Carolina tribes were further reduced during the Tuscarora War, the bloodiest Indian war in North Carolina history, lasting from 1711 until 1715. By the time it was over, about 2,000 to 3,000 Indians had been enslaved or killed, and, according to at least one historian, "that number could easily be higher."[145] Several tribes, such as the Pamlico, Neuse, Bay or Bear River, and Weetock, disappeared altogether from the historical record. Although the Hatteras Indians remained neutral throughout the war, they did not escape its turmoil. There are only a few references to the Hatteras tribe in the North Carolina colonial records, but it is clear that the Hatteras struggled during and after the Tuscarora War. In late May 1714, the Hatteras sought help from the English military commander, Col. Thomas Boyd, who reported the problem to the Governor's Council. The minutes of the Council for May 29 stated:

> Whereas report has been made to this board that ye Hatteress Indyans have lately made their Escape from ye Enemy Indyans and are now at Coll Boyds house It is ordered By this Board that the afsd Coll Boyd Doe supply the Said Indyans wth Corne for their Subsistance untill they can returne to their owne habitations againe....[146]

The "Enemy Indyans" were probably Machapungas, also known as Mattamuskeets, which would place at least some of the Hatteras Indians at Lake Mattamuskeet prior to their "escape."[147] In any case it is clear that these Hatteras were not at "their owne habitations" on the Outer Banks in 1714 and that they were not faring well at all. In March of the following year the Hatteras made another appeal to the Council, which reported, "Upon Petition of the Hatterass Indyans praying Some Small reliefe from ye Country for their services being reduced to great poverty."[148] Although the Hatteras were still mentioned as a tribe by the Governor's Council in 1731, the new royal governor, George Burrington, wrote that same year, "[of] the Indians here, of late years they are much diminished."[149] Another source claimed that "by 1733 there were only six or eight Indians living at Hatteras and these lived among the English."[150] In May of 1761 the Hatteras were mentioned in a letter written by Alexander Stewart to Philip Bearcroft about his March trip to "Altamuskeet [Mattamuskeet] in Hyde County."

> ... I likewise with pleasure inform the Society, that the few remains of the Altamuskeet, Hatteras & Roanoke Indians ... appeared mostly at the chapel & seemed fond of hearing the *Word* of the true God & of being admitted into the church of our Lord Jesus Christ. 2 men & 3 women & 2 children were baptized by me.[151]

In another letter Stewart wrote, "the remains of the Attamuskeet, Roanoke and Hatteras Indians, live mostly along that coast, mixed with the white inhabitants, many of these attended at the Places of Public Worship, while I was there & behaved with decency & seemed desirous of instruction & offered themselves & their children to me for baptism & after examining some of the adults I accordingly baptized, 6 adult Indians, 6 Boys, 4 Girls & 5 Infants."[152] The handful of remaining named tribal groups were by this time tributaries of North Carolina, and were provided with surveyed reservation tracts, subject to English law and justice. The Hatteras did not receive a reservation until 1759, when they were given a 200-acre tract at the south end of Hatteras Island.[153]

The Hatteras had virtually disappeared by the 1780s, according to Louis Torres, and the last record of them appeared in a 1788 deed from Mary Elks, "Indian of Hatteras Banks," to Nathan Midgett, transferring a tract of land in the old Indian town.[154] The Elks-Midgett transfer probably represented the final sale of the old Hatteras reservation tracts. As mentioned, the Hatteras had only acquired their reservation in 1759, but it had been completely sold off by 1788. The gradual disappearance of the Hatteras and other remaining eastern North Carolina tribes coincided with their selling off of tracts of reservation land, which had for a while preserved tribal identities. As the land was sold off, the former Indian residents "mixed with the white inhabitants," as Stewart noted in his letter. Others may have moved off to locations beyond the edges of white settlements and formed groups and small communities of their own. The few remaining Hatteras Indians on the Outer Banks had become well-acculturated and were dwelling among the English who lived there.

Manteo, North Carolina

On February 3, 1870, the General Assembly of the State of North Carolina ratified an "Act to lay off and establish a New County" by the name of "Dare," celebrating Virginia Dare, the first English child born and baptized in the New World. The new county was "to be formed out of portions of Currituck and Tyrrel[l] and Hyde counties." Manteo was also memorialized in the naming of the new county's seat which was established on Roanoke Island in the area around Shallowbag Bay. The Manteo Post Office opened there in 1873. The tributes to Virginia Dare and Manteo were largely consequences of a renewed interest in the early history of Roanoke Island which had been growing since about 1860, following the appearance of an article in the national publication, *Harper's New Monthly Magazine*, which focused on Roanoke Island and Ralph Lane's old fort. An 1884 congressional proposal to create a monument at the old fort's site failed, but awareness of the Lost Colony and Virginia Dare was resurrected by the creation of the Virginia Dare Memorial Association in 1892. In 1894 the newly formed Roanoke Colony Memorial Association purchased a sixteen acre tract of land which included what was thought to be the old fort site, and in 1896 the group erected a granite tablet dedicated to Raleigh's colonization attempts there as well as the baptism of Manteo and the birth and baptism of Virginia Dare.

The lengthy inscription reads:

> On this site, in July–August, 1585 (O.S.) ['old style'], colonists sent out from England by Sir Walter Raleigh, built a fort, called by them the New Fort in Virginia. These colonists were the first settlers of the English race in America. They returned to England in July, 1586, with Sir Francis Drake. Near this place was born, on the 18th of August, 1587. Virginia Dare. The first child of English parents born in America, daughter of Ananias Dare and Eleanor White, his wife, members of another band of colonists sent out by Sir Walter Raleigh in 1587. On Sunday, August 20, 1587, Virginia Dare was baptized. Manteo, the friendly chief of the Hatteras Indians, had been baptized on the Sunday preceding. These baptisms are the first known celebrations of a Christian sacrament in the territory of the thirteen original United States. [on base] 1896

On February 16, 1899, the General Assembly ratified "An act to incorporate the town of Manteo."[155]

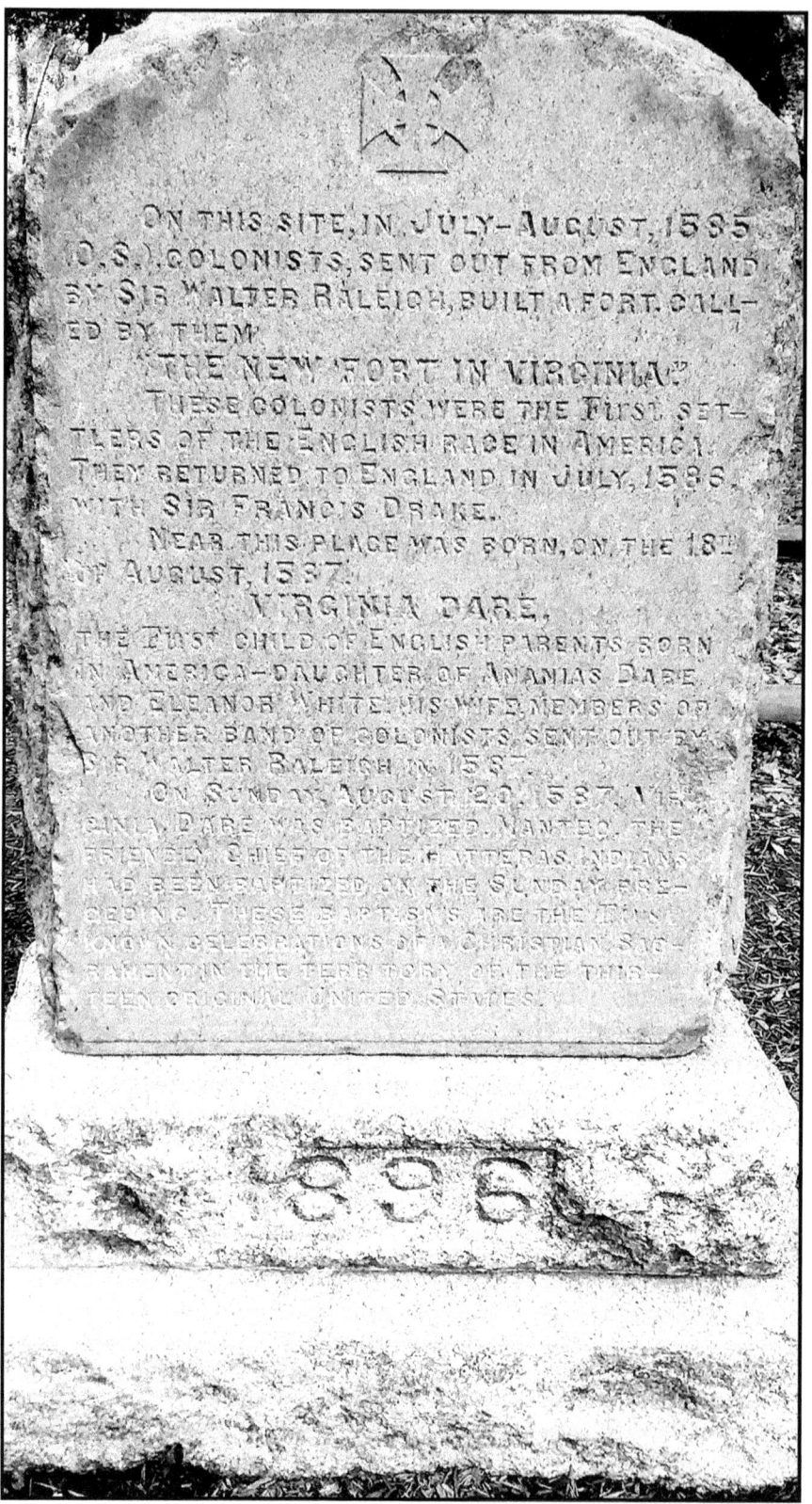

1896 Virginia Dare Memorial on Roanoke Island (photo by author).

> **An act to incorporate the town of Manteo.**
>
> *The General Assembly of North Carolina do enact:*
>
> Incorporation; name of town, subject to all provisions of law.
>
> Section 1. That the town of Manteo, in the county of Dare, be and the same is hereby incorporated by the name of the town of Manteo, and shall be subject to all provisions of law now in force or hereafter enacted relating to incorporated towns and cities, except as herein provided.

1899 Act to Incorporate the town of Manteo on Roanoke Island.

By the late 1920s it had become evident that the key to economic prosperity on the Outer Banks would be tourism. Two of the area's most ardent promoters were conservationist, author, and land developer Frank Stick and noted editor of *The Independent* newspaper, W.O. Saunders. Their efforts were largely responsible for the success of the 1927 bill to create a national monument at Kill Devil Hills on the Outer Banks, the site of the Wright Brothers' first flight. Stick and Saunders were planning a similar promotion at what was called Fort Raleigh on Roanoke Island. Saunders, in fact, was the guiding force behind the creation of the Roanoke Island Historical Association whose goal was a grand celebration at the fort to commemorate the 1587 Lost Colony and the 350th anniversary of the birth of Virginia Dare.

In the decade leading up to the 350th anniversary celebration several bills were introduced by North Carolina congressmen in an attempt to obtain federal funds for the preservation of the Fort Raleigh site, but these ultimately failed. Nevertheless, the Roanoke Colony Memorial Association erected

A 1930 commemorative plaque, with spelling error (photo by author).

a pavilion at Fort Raleigh and continued to sponsor August events commemorating the birth of Virginia Dare. A few years later legislation was finally authorized providing the funds for two pillars with stone tablets which were constructed in 1930, one dedicated to Virginia Dare and the other to Manteo and the 1587 colonists. Unfortunately the stone carver apparently mistook the "D" in "Dasamonguepeuk" for a "P" in his sample and the error remains to this day.

In the early 1930s the Roanoke Island Historical Association and the Roanoke Colony Memorial Association pushed ahead with plans for the Lost Colony's 350th anniversary celebration to be held in the summer of 1937. Playwright Paul Green, a native North Carolinian and winner of the 1927 Pulitzer Prize for his *In Abraham's Bosom*, agreed to write a script for a theatrical production about the Lost Colony. Using funds provided by the New

June 24, 1936 Act authorizing commemorative coin and Dare stamp issued August 18, 1937.

The Waterside Theater (photo by author).

Deal's Works Progress Administration, the Roanoke Island Historic Association contracted with Albert Bell for the design and construction of an outdoor amphitheater aptly called the Waterside Theater at the Fort Raleigh site overlooking Roanoke Sound. Congressman Lindsay Warren, who represented the Outer Banks, proposed the minting of fifty cent coins commemorating Raleigh's 1587 colony and the birth of Virginia Dare. The proposal passed Congress and was signed into law by President Roosevelt in 1936. Warren's efforts were also successful in the issuance of a five cent stamp commemorating the birth of Virginia Dare.

All of these developments had catapulted Roanoke Island and the Lost Colony into the national spotlight, but the biggest news was yet to come: President Roosevelt would arrive at Roanoke Island on August 18, Virginia Dare's 350th birth date, to see the "Lost Colony" play and partake in the celebrations.

August 18, 1937, was an extraordinary day. FDR arrived at Roanoke Island aboard a Coast Guard vessel and then rode to Fort Raleigh in an open car. A huge crowd gathered at the site and listened to his speech in which he compared the hopes and inspirations of the 1587 colonists with the same spirit that would bring the country through the current Great Depression. After his speech the president joined the crowd in a fish fry which was held on the grounds. At the Waterside Theater that evening the president enjoyed Paul Green's play from a platform specially designed and built by Albert Bell to accommodate FDR's vehicle. It was an enormously successful day, and 50,000 people would come to see the "Lost Colony" performance that summer. Fort Raleigh and the Lost Colony had finally graduated to national prominence. Since 1937 the "Croatoan Indian Manteo" has appeared at the Waterside Theater in every performance of what is described as "the nation's premier and longest-running outdoor symphonic drama."

In 1941 the Roanoke Island Historical Association transferred the fort site property to the National Park Service, thus establishing the Fort Raleigh National Historic Site. Fort Raleigh and the Waterside Theatre are both located at the north end of the island. Minutes away is the town of Manteo, now a popular and attractive Outer Banks summer vacation destination with bed and breakfasts, gift and antique shops, and restaurants lining the downtown streets and bordered by a waterfront with museums, a marina, and the Roanoke Marshes Lighthouse. Manteo's historical connections to the Roanoke voyages are visible everywhere. Virtually every thoroughfare in the town recalls a notable late 16th century figure with whom the Croatoan Indian Manteo was at one time acquainted. A partial list of roadways includes Harriot Street, Barlowe Street, Sir Francis Drake Street, George Howe Street, Sir Walter Raleigh Street, Grenville Street, Eleanor Dare Place, Queen Elizabeth Avenue, and Ananias Dare Street.

Street signs in Manteo (photo by author).

Andacon

Andacon was a Roanoac tribesman who was only briefly mentioned in Ralph Lane's *An account of the particularities of the imployments of the English men left in Virginia...*, but he was intended to have played a key role in Pemisapan's carefully coordinated plan to annihilate the English at Roanoke Island in 1586. Andacon was one of Pemisapan's "principall men," perhaps a weroance of some rank himself, and was described as "very lustie [lively, spirited]." Pemisapan's plot was to be launched from the villages of Dasamonquepeuc and Roanoac on June 10, 1586, by a combined force of neighboring tribes, and its initial stage was designed to eliminate the English leadership and "the rest of our better sort." Pemisapan had assigned twenty warriors to Andacon and another Roanoac Indian, Tarraquine, specifically to target Governor Ralph Lane while he slept. Their instructions were to approach Lane's dwelling quietly in the dead of night and set fire to the reeds that covered his roof. As soon as the startled Lane was awakened and rushed out in his nightshirt, the plan was to pounce upon him and "knock out [his] braines." Once the principal Englishmen had been eliminated in like manner, the combined forces of Indians, who would have come over to Roanoke Island from Dasamonquepeuc during the night, could then overwhelm the rest of the colonists.

However, two Indian informants told Lane about Pemisapan's plans, and on June 1, before the tribes were able to assemble, Lane attacked Dasamonquepeuc. Pemisapan and "seuen or eight of his principall Weroances and followers, (not regarding any of the common sort)" were taken by surprise and a number of them were killed outright. Pemisapan was wounded twice and managed to escape into the woods, but he was pursued and beheaded by two of Lane's men. As one of Pemisapan's "principall men," it is very possible that Andacon was at Dasamonquepeuc when Lane attacked, but it is not known whether or not he survived.

Cossine

Like Andacon, Cossine was mentioned just once in Ralph Lane's report of the 1585–6 attempt to establish a colony on Roanoke Island. Cossine was also a Roanoac tribesman and supporter of the weroance, Pemisapan (Wingina), in his efforts to destroy the English. In March of 1586 Cossine was one of three Roanoac Indians—the other two being Tetepano and Eracano—who accompanied Lane's expedition up the Moratuc [Roanoke] River to a place called Chaunis Temoatan where there was said to be a "marueilous and most strange Minerall … they say is [called] Wassador." In the nine months during which the English had occupied Roanoke Island, they were unable to learn anything about the precious metals they so eagerly sought. The report of this "very soft, and pale … mettall" that the Native Indians took "out of a riuer [at] Chaunis Temoatan" was very promising.

It is possible that the story about Chaunis Temoatan was a deception fabricated or exaggerated by Pemisapan and the Chawanoac weroance, Menatonon, to lure Lane and his men far up the river into a trap. In any case, while Lane was preparing his river expedition, Pemisapan arranged for the Moratuc Indians, through whose territory the English would have to pass, to remove their food supplies and vacate their villages along the river. His plan was to prevent Lane and his men from replenishing their provisions as they ascended the river into Mangoak territory, where Chaunis Temoatan was said to be located. As a result Lane and his men would eventually face starvation, at which time the Indians would fall upon the weakened group and massacre them.

Exactly what role Cossine and his two Roanoac companions would have played is not clear. They very possibly could have been sent by Pemisapan to act as guides, who would turn on Lane and join in the attack, after which they would report back to Pemisapan that Lane and the rest of the English expedition had been destroyed. If the plan had succeeded and Lane and his men were killed on the Moratuc River, the remaining Englishmen at Roanoke Island would have been far more vulnerable to an attack by a confederation of tribes organized by Pemisapan. It was only because of the quick reaction of the Croatoan, Manteo, who warned Lane just as the attack was about to be sprung, that the plan was foiled. The Englishmen managed to avoid starvation by killing and cooking the two mastiffs Lane had brought along and then by eating boiled sassafras leaves for the rest of the journey back to Roanoke Island. The unexpected return of Lane's party and the disappointing report by Cossine and his two Indian companions forced Pemisapan, temporarily at least, to postpone his plans for a coordinated attack on the English.

After the death in late April of old Ensenore, who had continually advocated cooperation with the English, Pemisapan revived his plan to destroy the English. On June 1, however, Lane and his men made the surprise appearance at Dasmonqueponk, and immediately launched an attack, killing Pemisapan and a number of leading tribesmen. It is very likely that Cossine would have been with Pemisapan at that time, but it is not known if he was among the casualties.

Ensenore

Ensenore was the former chief weroance of the Roanoac tribe, father and advisor to Granganimeo and Wingina, the current principal weroance when the English arrived. As an elder tribesman Ensenore was highly respected among the Roanoacs and remained a moderating influence over Wingina, who wavered between reluctant tolerance and open hostility towards the English. The image below by Theodor de Bry was titled "An Ageed manne in his winter garment," engraved from a drawing by John White, which was composed during his tour of Pamlico Sound in 1585. Although this is not a drawing of Ensenore himself, it probably offers a fair representation of his general appearance and manner of dress.

The following description by Thomas Harriot accompanied the deBry engraving, which was published in 1590:

"The aged men ... are couered with a large skinne which is tyed vppon their shoulders on one side and hangeth downe beneath their knees wearinge their other arme naked out of the skinne, that they maye bee at more libertie. Those skynnes are Dressed with the hair on, and lyned with other furred skinnes. The yonnge men suffer noe hairr at all to growe vppon their faces but assoone as they growe they put them away, but when thy are come to yeeres they suffer them to growe although to say truthe they come opp verye thinne. They also weare their haire bownde op behynde, and, haue a creste on their heads like the others."[1]

Ensenore is not mentioned in the Roanoke accounts until 1585, and so it is not known whether he had any direct contact with the English during their month

De Bry's engraving of "An Ageed manne in his winter garment."

long anchorage at the Outer Banks in 1584. He undoubtedly had at least heard about the strange visitors from his son, Granganimeo, who was the first named weroance to interact with the Amadas-Barlowe expedition upon their arrival and had established such promising relations. It is very likely that Ensenore was at the village of Roanoac when Barlowe and seven others made an unexpected visit there. Ensenore would have watched in wonder as his daughter-in-law, Granganimeo's wife, "came running out to meete vs very cheerefully and friendly, her husband was not then in the village: some of her people shee commanded to drawe our boate on shore."[2]

The arrival of the English in 1584 was not only the first actual European-Indian contact for the Roanoac tribe, but due to their geographic position on the coastal plain and their isolation from what was called the Great Trading Path farther inland (see *Wingina*), "there was neuer any people apparelled, or white of colour, either seene or heard of amongst these people," a remarkable phenomenon. Concurrent with Ensenore's rule of the Roanoac tribe perhaps two to three decades earlier, there were a number of European explorations and expeditions, particularly by the Spanish, to the north and south, but he knew nothing about them. Isolation from the interchange of stories and oral traditions of the tribes with access to the trading path explains to a great extent the Roanoacs' awe and wonder regarding the seemingly inexplicable "powers" of the English, particularly among the priests and elder tribesmen like Ensenore, whose opinions and advice were highly respected.

The priests, Harriot wrote,

"are well stricken in yeers, and as yt seemeth of more experience then the comon sorte. They weare their heare cutt like a creste, on the topps of their heades as other doe, but the rest are cuttshorte, sauinge those which growe aboue their foreheads in manner of a perriwigge. They also haue somwhat hanginge in their ears. They weare a shorte clocke made of fine hares skinnes quilted with the hayre outwarde. The rest of their bodie is naked. They are notable enchaunters, and for their pleasure they frequent the riuers, to kill with their bowes, and catche wilde ducks, swannes, and other fowles."[3]

One of the "opinion[s] very confidently at this day holden by the wisest amongst them, and of their old men" had to do with what was seen as the uncanny ability of the English to strike down their enemies, or even anyone who may have displeased them, in spite of the fact that they were "100 miles from any of vs."[4]

De Bry's engraving of one of the "Religeous men."

Thomas Harriot recorded the same beliefs among the Roanoacs. "There could at no time happen any strange sicknesse, losses, hurts, or any other crosse vnto them, but that they would impute to vs the cause or meanes thereof, for offending or not pleasing vs." Ensenore was one of those to whom Harriot referred when he wrote that to "the oldest men in the Countrey" this wonder had "neuer happened before, time out of minde." The English, too, ignorant of the infectious diseases they were transmitting and the Indians' lack of natural immunities, were at a loss to explain what Harriot called "this marueilous accident."

> "There was no towne where wee had any subtle deuise practised against vs, wee leauing it vnpunished or not reuenged ... but that within a few dayes after our departure from euery such Towne, the people began to die very fast, and many in short space, in some Townes about twentie, in some fourtie, and in one sixe score, which in trueth was very many in respect of their numbers. This happened in no place that we could learne, but where we had bin, where they vsed some practise against vs, and after such time. The disease also was so strange, that they neither knewe what it was, nor how to cure it.... A thing specially obserued by vs, as also by the naturall inhabitants themselues."[5]

Traditional treatments with wapeih (medicinal clay), winauk (sassafras), and other medicines proved to be useless. So too was the practice of bloodletting, a treatment not usually associated with native Indians, but one clearly used by these Algonquians. Harriot wrote that "Vnder their brests about their bellyes appear certayne spots wheare they vse to let themselues bloode, when they are sicke."[6] The native "Phisitions" performing the bloodletting, "(to excuse their ignorance in curing the disease) would not be ashamed to say, but earnestly make the simple people beleeue, that the strings of blood that they sucked out of the sicke bodies, were the strings wherewithall the inuisible bullets were tied and cast."[7] Bloodletting, incidentally, was also being used at that time in England for most diseases and would continue to be practiced well into the 19th century.

A wide variety of explanations were proposed to account for this amazing and dreadful occurrence. Some thought that the English were able to shoot the disease "out of our pieces, from the place where wee dwelt, and killed the people in any Towne that had offended vs, howe farre distant from vs soeuer it were." Others claimed that it was "the speciall worke of God for our sakes." Since it was well known that "there was no man of ours [the English] knowen to die, or that was specially sicke," many of the Indians concluded that the English may not be men at all, but rather supernatural beings, or at least that their God had bestowed this power upon them. The fact that there were no women among the English led some of the Indians to question whether they were really "borne of women" and therefore were perhaps from an ancient generation "risen againe to immortalitie."[8] Even the tribal conjurers, who were said to converse with devils, and to whom "the inhabitants give great credit vnto their speech," were at a loss to explain this phenomenon.

As the disease continued to take its toll, relations with the English steadily declined. Some came to the conclusion that the English presence should be resisted, and they joined with the principal weroance, Wingina, who was gathering support to resist them. Ensenore's views on the matter, however, kept the opposition in check for the time being. As both a tribal elder and a highly respected former weroance, his guidance carried tremendous weight. He warned all those who sought to oppose the English, including his son Wingina, that their efforts would result in their own destruction. As Lane wrote, "Ensenore ... had often before tolde them ... that wee were the seruants of God, and that wee were not subiect to bee destroyed by them: but contrariwise, that they amongst them that sought our destruction, shoulde finde their owne."[9]

A good part of Ensenore's advice regarding the futility of opposing the English may

De Bry's "The Con[j]uere" wearing "a small black birde aboue one of their ears as a badge of their office."

have been that their presence at Roanoke Island and all that resulted from it were, in his eyes, forewarned by signs in the heavens and were therefore irreversible. Most 16th century societies, including the English, believed that strange astronomical phenomena were warnings of things to come. Ensenore and all the Algonquians had experienced two such recent occurrences. On April 29, 1585, a solar eclipse occurred and was observable from Central America all the way to Canada. At that time Grenville's fleet, with the 1585 colonists aboard, had already departed from the Canary Islands on April 14 (on the Julian calendar) and was crossing the Atlantic en route to Roanoke Island when the solar eclipse occurred. Writing in 1586, Harriot commented on the "Eclipse of the Sunne which we saw the same yeere before in our voyage thitherward." The arrival of the English at Roanoke not very long afterwards may have been seen in some way by the tribal priests and elders as a consequence of the eclipse, or at least associated with it. The Indians certainly observed and were troubled by the eclipse, Harriot was told, "which vnto them appeared very terrible."

Even more ominous was the appearance of a comet in the night sky over Roanoke

Island. Comets had long been considered warnings from God or portents of disaster, and in the late 16th century that belief was shared by both Algonquians and Europeans. In Elizabethan England comets were believed to be divinely sent omens of public disasters such as crop failures, pestilence, bloody battles, the fall of monarchies, and the death of kings[10] ... not very different from Ensenore's belief. Almost exactly a century later, notable Massachusetts minister Increase Mather would publish his *A Discourse Concerning Comets.... Heavens Alarm to the World.... Wherein is Shewed, that Fearful Sights and Signs in Heaven are the Presages of great Calamities at hand*.[11] What was particularly significant about the comet seen by all at Roanoke Island was its timing. "The Comet," Harriot wrote, "began to appear but a fewe dayes before the beginning of the saide sicknesse."[12]

Ensenore's advocacy for cooperation with the English seems not to have been grounded in loyalty or admiration and perhaps not entirely in fear either, but rather in resignation. In spite of the sickness and death around him, he may have resigned himself to what seemed to be the undeniable fact that the suffering was inevitable, preordained by a powerful God whose representatives—the English—could not be opposed. This scenario would help explain his persistent encouragement for cooperation with the English as resentment toward the English was steadily spreading, and even after his own son, Granganimeo, later fell victim to the strange disease.

As mentioned, Lane's account is conspicuously silent about the events that occurred between the fall of 1585 and the beginning of March 1586, during which time relations with the Indians deteriorated and bloody conflicts occurred. It is very possible that those declining relations were initiated by the outbreak of the deadly disease, which the Indians soon determined was connected in some inexplicable way to the English. Since the comet first appeared "a fewe dayes before" the initial outbreak of the disease, the specific date of the 1585 comet's appearance can help determine when "the saide sicknesse" started. That, in turn, may provide a fairly accurate timeline regarding the declining relations during the gap in Lane's account.

Comets generally remain visible for several weeks, appearing to be motionless against the backdrop of the night sky, but they actually move several degrees a day. The Rev. T.J. Hussey listed the 1585 comet in his *Catalog of Comets* as having appeared in October and November,[13] but gave few further details. Fortunately, the 1585 comet had been observed by German astronomer Christoph Rothmann, who took careful notes and later published his *Discourse on the comet of 1585*. Rothmann first noticed the comet faintly in the night sky on October 8 and it was brightly visible thereafter. Except for some intermittent bad weather, he observed the comet nightly until November 10, when "I saw a trace of it ... and on 11 November it had completely disappeared."[14]

Since comets are usually visible simultaneously in Western Europe and the eastern parts of America, it is probably safe to say that the Indians and English at Roanoke Island and the tribes elsewhere must have become aware of the comet by October 9 or 10. According to Harriot the comet appeared "but a fewe dayes before the beginning of the saide sicknesse," and so the initial outbreak of the disease probably occurred about October 13 to 15, 1585, two and a half months after Grenville's fleet anchored at the inlet off Roanoke. During that time period the English were in the process of exploring the area and visiting various villages, in part to learn about the availability of marketable commodities, the possibilities of finding the fabled waterway through North America to Asia, and the potential location of the elusive "gold and siluer" which they constantly sought. It would not have taken the Indians very long to associate these visits by the English with the fact that "within a few dayes after our departure from euery such Towne, the people began to die very fast."[15] That cause and effect connection would have been well established among the neighboring tribes conceivably by mid–November, and it is likely that relations declined shortly thereafter, followed by the number of bloody conflicts hinted at by Harriot and later removed from Lane's account.

On a date that was either unrecorded by Lane or eliminated later when portions of his account were edited, an event occurred that further damaged relations with the English: the death of Granganimeo, Ensenore's son. Granganimeo was personally responsible for the good relations that had been established in 1584, and he remained, like Ensenore, an advocate of friendly cooperation with the English. Neither the date nor the cause of his death was recorded, but it may have happened in late October or early November and very likely resulted from the same infectious disease that had just begun to take a toll among the villages visited by the English. At that early stage the Indians were not only beginning to understand that the strange sickness was somehow caused by the English, but also raising the possibility that it was intentionally directed as a punishment against "the people in any such towne that had offended vs." Granganimeo's death, therefore, presented a logical challenge. If Granganimeo died from such a disease, the responsibility for his death would have to be placed entirely on the English, who alone had the supernatural ability to "make the people to die in that sort as they did, by shooting inuisible bullets into them." Wingina must have drawn that same conclusion because, immediately upon Granganimeo's death, he changed his name to Pemisapan and started to conceive strategies aimed at doing away with the English. Ensenore, of course, must also have been troubled by Granganimeo's death, but he did not waver in his conviction that cooperation with the English was his tribe's only option.

The split between Ensenore and his son Wingina/Pemisapan was clearly demonstrated in March 1586, when Lane embarked on his expedition up the Moratuc River in search of the precious mineral the Indians called "wassador." Pemisapan had sent word to the Moratucs that the intention of the English was to exterminate the Indians and that they should abandon their villages along the river, taking their food supplies with them. With the English deprived of food and slowly weakened by starvation, they would eventually be susceptible to attack by the Mangoaks who dwelt further up the river. During Lane's absence Pemisapan worked diligently to counter Ensenore's belief that the English had supernatural powers and could not be destroyed. He spread the word that the God of the English "was not God, since hee suffered [the English] to sustaine much hunger" and allowed them to be killed by the Mangoak Indians, an outcome he fully expected. Ensenore remained true to his conviction that the English "were the seruants of God, and … were not subiect to bee destroyed by them." On the contrary, he argued, any Indians who resisted the English would be destroyed themselves.

Lane, as it turned out, survived the plot and his safe return to Roanoke enhanced Ensenore's standing while it diminished Pemisapan's for the time being. An appreciative Lane noted that Ensenore was constantly on guard "to saue vs from hurt [and] did not a little asswage all deuises against vs." Pemisapan, who had refused to build weirs for the English and wanted to deny them ground for the coming spring planting, was now forced to comply with Ensenore's wishes. "He cause[d] his men to set vp weares foorthwith for vs," Lane wrote, and "had sowed a good quantitie of ground, so much as had bene sufficient, to haue fed our whole company." This was a great relief to Lane and his men and now, thanks to Ensenore's efforts, things were looking up. There would soon be fish in the weirs, and the first harvest would be ready by late June or early July, by which time fresh supplies would have arrived from England.

Lane's hopes for the future were dashed on April 20, 1586, when old Ensenore died. The English suddenly found themselves without a friendly voice among the Roanoacs as the balance of opinion shifted rapidly to Pemisapan's side. Lane, well aware of the problems the English now faced, wrote, "He [Ensenore] alone had before opposed himselfe in their consultations against all matters proposed against vs, which both the King [Pemisapan] and all the rest of them after Grangemoes death, were very willing to haue preferred." Soon after Ensenore's death Pemisapan and his followers "put their old practises in vse against vs, which were readily imbraced, and all their former deuises against vs, reneued, and new brought in question."

Pemisapan's new "deuise" involved using Ensenore's death as part of a well-crafted scheme designed to destroy the English once and for all. A large gathering of neighboring tribes was to assemble at Dasamonquepeuc in early June. The amassing of such a sizable group of Indians close to Roanoke Island would normally alarm the English, but Pemisapan let it be known that the purpose of this assembly was nothing more than a traditional ritual designed to honor a former weroance of Ensenore's high status. Lane acknowledged that such events were commonly held "to solemnise in their Sauage maner for any great personage dead and should haue bene for Ensenore." During the night, fires were to be lit on Roanoke Island's western shoreline signaling the main force at Dasamonquepeuc to cross over to Roanoke. In the meantime small groups of Indians were assigned to kill Lane and his leading men as they slept, after which the large Indian force would fall upon the remaining English and overpower them. Lane, however, was informed of the plot by Menatonon's son Skiko, whom Lane held prisoner. An unnamed Roanoac Indian, likely one of Ensenore's former followers, also provided Lane with information about the planned attack. Consequently, Lane was able to launch an early surprise attack at Dasamonquepeuc before the Indian forces had a chance to assemble there.

It is fair to say that Ensenore's death set in motion a chain of events that altered the course of English colonial endeavors. For one thing it immediately silenced the one remaining influential voice within the Roanoac tribal community that persistently called for cooperation with the English. Ensenore had successfully countered the growing resentment towards Lane and his men which intensified dramatically after Wingina's earlier transformation to "Pemisapan," symbolizing his opposition to the English. Immediately after Ensenore's death Pemisapan renewed his plans to destroy the English and began assembling a coalition of tribes to annihilate Lane and his men at Roanoke. Of course Lane's preemptive attack on June 1 at Dasamonquepeuc thwarted Pemisapan's plan, killing him in the process, but by this time virtually all of the surrounding tribes had turned against the English. On June 8 Sir Francis Drake's large fleet of 23 ships was sighted off shore, and, despite Drake's offer of additional men, provisions, munitions, equipment, and vessels, Lane decided to abandon the colonial enterprise at Roanoke and return to England with Drake.

Drake's arrival should have insured the continuance of Raleigh's first colonization effort, if not at Roanoke Island, then farther north. Lane had realized by late 1585 that Roanoke was an inadequate location for a growing, permanent colony or military base which would require a better harbor. The inlets near Roanoke were far too shallow or narrow to allow access by vessels any larger than a small pinnace, making it difficult and inefficient to transport supplies and material to and from larger ships which had to remain anchored offshore. Lane had made several complaints about "our bad harborow" and the need for "a better harborough then yet there is." He had sent an expedition north to the Chesepians during the winter and, after it returned with positive reports, he concluded that a better harbor "must be to the Northward." In fact he intended, if all had gone well, to construct a fort there "both for the defence of the harborough, and our shipping also, and would haue reduced our whole habitation from Roanoak and from the harborough and port there (which by proofe is very naught) vnto this other."[16]

Drake was prepared to give Lane everything he needed to reinforce and maintain the existing colony including "barks, pinnesses, and boats; they also by him to be victualled, manned and furnished to my contentation" as well as "some sufficient Masters … to search the coast for some better harborow," which was precisely what Lane claimed he intended to do. In short Drake would have granted "all my other demands whatsoeuer, to the vttermost." When a storm arose on June 13, Drake advised Lane "to deliuer presently vnto him in writing what I would require him to doe for vs; which … he did assure me … shoulde be most willingly performed." Lane conferred with his men, who by then had come to realize that their situation at Roanoke was no longer sustainable. After "considering the case that we stood in, the weaknesse of our company, the small number of the same"—all of which Drake could have remedied—"their whole request was" to evacuate Roanoke Island and return to England.

If Ensenore had not died, it is very possible that his wishes for cooperation with the English would have continued to prevail, particularly if Drake had provided the means for Lane to relocate the Roanoke settlement to a more favorable harbor at the Chesapeake Bay. Their planned departure from Roanoke would probably have been welcome news to Pemisapan, who may have been less inclined to plot their destruction and more disposed to do all that he could to see them vacate his territory. As far as Raleigh was concerned, had Lane relocated the settlement to the Chesapeake and "raised a maine fort" there, as he intended, a firm English foothold would already have existed there as a fortified and safe destination for Raleigh's next colonization venture in 1587. All these possibilities evaporated when Ensenore died, and the English would not establish a permanent settlement at the Chesapeake until two decades later.

Eracano

Eracano was another Roanoac weroance who is nearly forgotten today, but, as Wingina's (Pemisapan's) brother-in-law, he was very likely one of the "Chief mene of Virginia" referred to by Thomas Harriot. He was mentioned by name in Ralph Lane's narrative of the 1585–6 colonization attempt as "his [Wingina's] sisters husband Eracano." Since that was the only reference in the Roanoke narratives to a husband of Wingina's (unnamed) sister, Eracano was almost certainly the Roanoac weroance whose followers bore one of the particular "marks rased on their backs, wherby yt may be knowen what Princes subiects they bee." John White illustrated seven such markings, lettered A to G, and Thomas Harriot supplied the descriptive text for each of them (see the *Wingina* entry). For the following symbol Harriot wrote, "That which hath B. is the marke of Wingino his sisters husband,"[1] indicating that Eracano must have been considered—after Wingina—one of the leading weroances among the Algonquians.

Eracano was one of the three Roanoac Indians, along with Tetepano and Cossine, who were mentioned in Lane's account regarding his expedition up the Moratuc (Roanoke) River in March 1586, in his quest to find the mineral called "wassador" at a place called Chaunis Temoatan. Wassador was probably copper, but since the Indians "call by the name of Wassador euery mettall whatsoeuer,"[2] Lane may have hoped that Chaunis Temoatan might be the source of the elusive gold which the English sought.

Eracano and his two Indian companions were very likely sent by Pemisapan to guide Lane and his men up the Moratuc River as part of his plan to lure the English into a trap. Messengers had already been sent to the Moratuc Indians, who dwelt along the river, that they should abandon their villages and leave no food behind for Lane and his men to

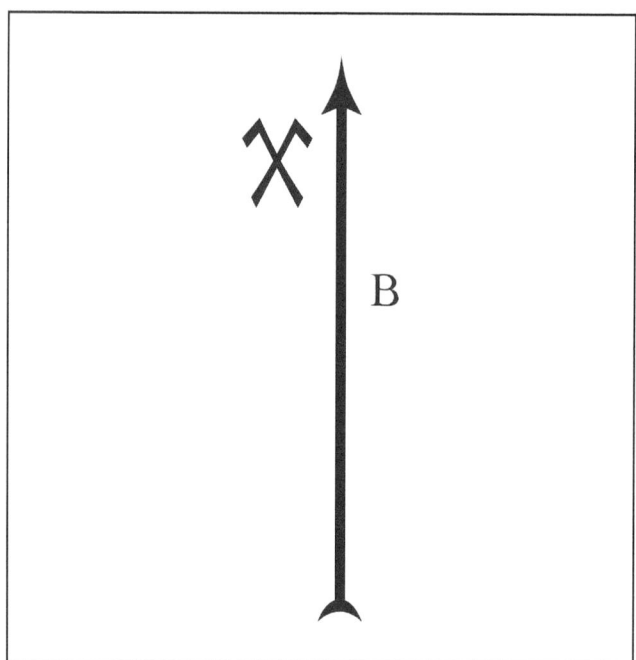

The marking of one of the "Chief mene of Virginia."

find. Pemisapan's plan was to starve the English as they ventured far up the river, where the Mangoak Indians would suddenly fall upon them in their weakened condition. Eracano and the other two Roanoacs most likely intended to abandon the English at that point and join the other Indians in the attack. Once Lane and his men were wiped out, Eracano and his Indian accomplices would have conveyed the news of the successful attack back to Pemisapan, who would then organize a united tribal force to exterminate the rest of the Englishmen at Roanoke. The planned attack on the river failed, however, and the famished Englishmen managed to make it back to Roanoke Island. As a result Pemisapan's plot to destroy the English had to be put on hold for the time being.

Eracano was not mentioned again in any of the accounts, although as an important weroance in his own right he was undoubtedly an essential part of Pemisapan's conspiracy to annihilate the English several months after the Moratuc expedition in March. It is not known whether he was with Pemisapan at Dasamonquepeuc during Ralph Lane's surprise attack on June 1 or what became of him afterwards.

Granganimeo

Granganimeo was an important weroance of the Roanoac tribe, son of the former chief weroance, Ensenore, and younger brother of Wingina, the ruling weroance of the territory that included the villages of Roanoac and Dasamonquepeuc when the English first arrived in 1584. His name was recorded in several of the Roanoke accounts as Grangino, Granganimo, and Grangemoe, and in its various forms translates as "he restrains from ridiculing," according to the noted philologist James Geary. Granganimeo was the first named Algonquian to make contact with the English reconnaissance voyagers led by Philip Amadas and Arthur Barlowe, who were sent by Walter Raleigh on April 27, 1584, to explore the North American coast for potential settlement locations. Granganimeo and his wife, who was unnamed in the accounts, were primarily responsible for establishing the friendly Anglo-Native relations that summer.

On March 25, 1584, Walter Raleigh had been granted Letters Patent by Queen Elizabeth "for the discovering and planting of new lands and Countries,"[1] and he wasted little time. On April 27 he sent Philip Amadas and Arthur Barlowe "with two barkes well furnished with men and victuals" on a reconnaissance voyage to America to find a suitable settlement location. Amadas and Barlowe sailed the conventional route south to the Canary Islands and then across the Atlantic, finally arriving at the islands in the West Indies on June 10th, where, "hauing refreshed our selues with sweet water, and fresh victuall," they continued up the Atlantic coast. On July 13 they landed along the Outer Banks and went ashore to explore the land "stretching it selfe to the West, which after wee found to bee but an Island of twentie miles long, and not above six miles broade."[2]

Three days later first contact with the native inhabitants was initiated by an unidentified Indian, who was paddled in a canoe to a point of land adjacent to the two anchored ships, and he then paced boldly back and forth along the shore in plain sight of the English. Amadas, Barlowe, and a number of other Englishmen rowed to where the Indian stood on the beach, noting that he "neuer [made] any shewe of feare or doubt" and he addressed the strangers about "many things not vnderstood by vs." After this truly first Anglo-Algonquian contact, the English "brought him with his owne good liking, aboord the ships, and gaue him a shirt, a hat and some other things, and made him taste of our wine, and our meat, which he liked very wel."[3] The Indian was given a tour of both ships and then went back to his boat and "fell to fishing," filling his boat in "lesse then halfe an houre," after which he divided his catch into two parts on the beach, one for each of the English ships.

Thomas Harriot, who was with Raleigh's colonization venture the following year, described the Algonquians' various "manner[s] of fishynge in Virginia." One manner, illustrated below, was the use of a complex construction of weirs made of willow reeds "… because they are so strong as also flexible, do serue for that turne very well and sufficiently."[4]

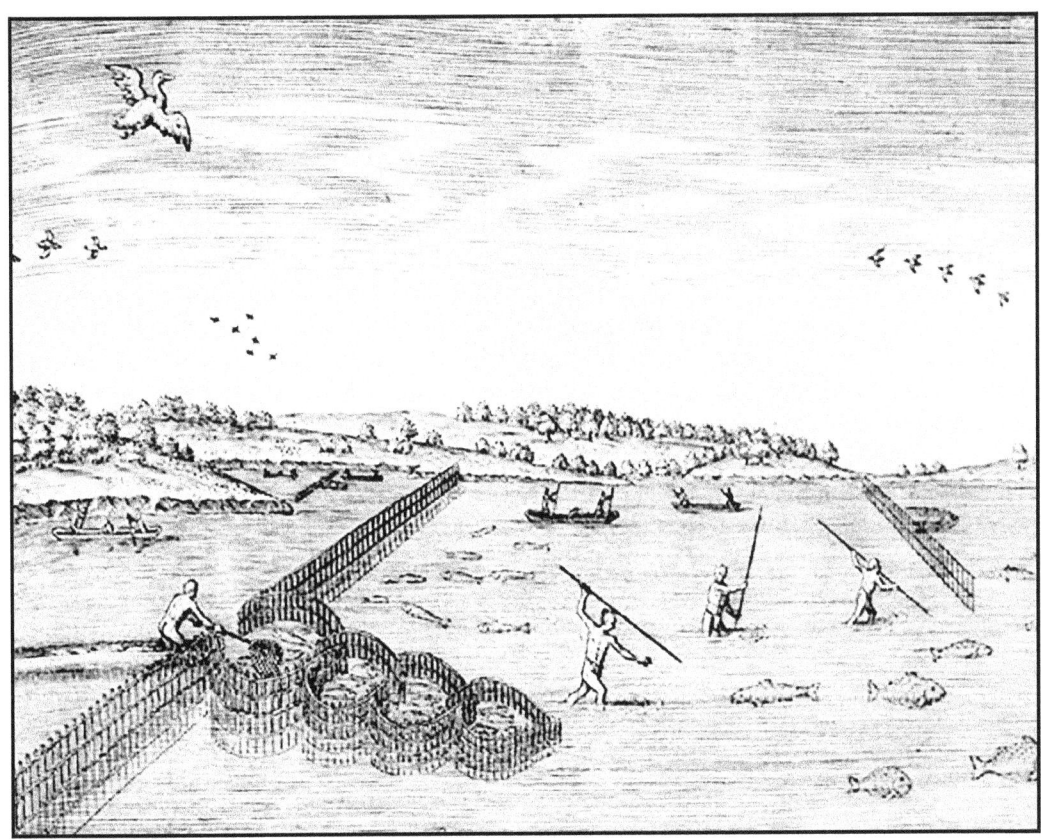

Portion of de Bry's engraving "Their Manner of fishynge in Virginia."

The method involved "settinge opp reedes or twigges in the water, which they soe plant one within a nother, that they growe still narrower, and narrower. Ther was neuer seene amonge vs soe cunninge a way to take fish withal."[5]

In shallow waters a form of spear fishing shown above was used which Harriot considered "more strange ... with poles made sharpe at one ende, by shooting them into the fish after the maner as Irishmen cast dartes; either as they are rowing in their boates or els as they are wading in the shallowes for the purpose."[6] On this first contact occasion the native Algonquian probably speared fish from his boat and "whear as they lacke both yron, and steele," he would have used a "longe Rodd" either sharpened or tipped with "the hollowe tayle of a certaine fishe like to sea crabb in steede of a poynte."[7] It is unfortunate that history has not recorded the name of this resourceful native Indian who was responsible for the very first Anglo-Algonquian contact.

The specific location of this historic contact on the Outer Banks is the subject of some debate. Barlowe wrote that the two ships reached the coast on July 4 and "sayled along the same a hundred and twentie English miles before we could finde any entrance ... the first that appeared vnto vs, we entred" on July 13.[8] Since it is not known where it was along the coast that they sighted land on July 4, the location of the inlet 120 miles to the north cannot be determined by measurement. Chronicler Richard Hakluyt, who published Barlowe's account in 1589, identified the barrier island where the English went ashore as "The Isle of Wokokon." Richard Butler, an Englishman who claimed to have sailed with Philip Amadas on the expedition, also stated in a deposition to the Spanish more than a decade later that the location was Wokokon.[9] The inlet at Wokokon, known today as the Ocracoke Inlet, was the most navigable inlet in 1584 as it still is today and could well have been "the first that appeared vnto vs." As cited above, Barlowe wrote that the island where they landed was "twentie miles long"—a measurement roughly corresponding with Wokokon's length on the White/de Bry map below (an English league being about three miles), originally drawn by John White in 1585–6 and published by Theodor de Bry in 1590. Barlowe also wrote that "wee beheld the Sea on both sides to the North, and to the South, finding no ende any of both ways," a vista that would fit Pamlico Sound from the Wokokon inlet. Furthermore, Barlowe wrote that "my selfe, with seuen more went twentie mile into the Riuer [en route to Roanoke Island] … which Riuer they call Occam … on which standeth a towne called Pomeiock."[10] Although the passage is confusing, if Barlowe meant that "twentie mile" was the distance they traveled from their departure point to Pomeiock, then that would support the Wokokon location, Pomeiock being situated about twenty miles from Wokokon. Also, because they eventually made it to Roanoke Island, Occam was certainly Pamlico Sound, and they must have been traveling north. All of this would seem to support the Wokokon location as the contact site.

The argument against the Wokokon contact location comes from a single line in Barlowe's account where he describes the abovementioned arrival at Roanoke: "The euening following," he wrote, "wee came to an Island which they call Raonoak, *distant from the harbour by which we entered, seuen* leagues"[11] (italics added). Therefore, it is thought, since the scale of leagues on White's map below indicates that the inlet at Wokokon was nearly thirty leagues from Roanoke Island, the actual contact location must have been much closer to Roanoke. Based again on White's scale, however, there was no inlet *seven* leagues from Roanoke. "Trinety harbor" to the north of Roanoke was more than ten leagues away, and turned out to be no more than a shoal.[12] Furthermore this would certainly not have been the first inlet that "appeared vnto vs" as they sailed up the coast. The "Hatorask" inlet (*not* present-day Hatteras), which historian David Quinn believed "with little doubt" was where the first contact took place,[13] was perhaps three leagues, not seven, from Roanoke Island. Also, as mentioned above, Barlowe and his men traveled "twentie mile into the Riuer [Pamlico Sound] … and the euening following, wee came to an Island which they call Raonoak."[14] If the Hatorask inlet had been "the harbour by which we entered" (the first contact point) and Barlowe along with his seven men approached Roanoke Island from that location, they would have arrived there long before they had gone twenty miles, and it would have taken perhaps an hour, not the better part of a day.

It is quite possible that the "seuen leagues" may have been either an error in the original journal or more likely a later transcription error—perhaps "seven leagues" instead of "*twenty*-seven leagues"—made in a copy provided afterwards to Hakluyt. It is also possible that when Barlowe arrived at Roanoke Island "the euening following," he meant on the evening of the *second* day of the journey, after having traveled twenty miles to Pomeiock the previous afternoon. If the trip took the greater part of two days, the "harbour by which we entered" could refer, not to the original anchorage at Wokokon on July 13, but rather to a layover "harbor" or shelter where Barlowe and the seven men must have anchored the skiff for the night en route to Roanoke. It is worth noting, too, that when the English returned the following summer, the commander of the expedition, Richard Grenville, sailed directly to Wokokon, not Hatorask, and spent two weeks exploring the mainland via the Wokokon inlet there.

Wherever this first contact took place on the Outer Banks on July 13, 1584, word of the

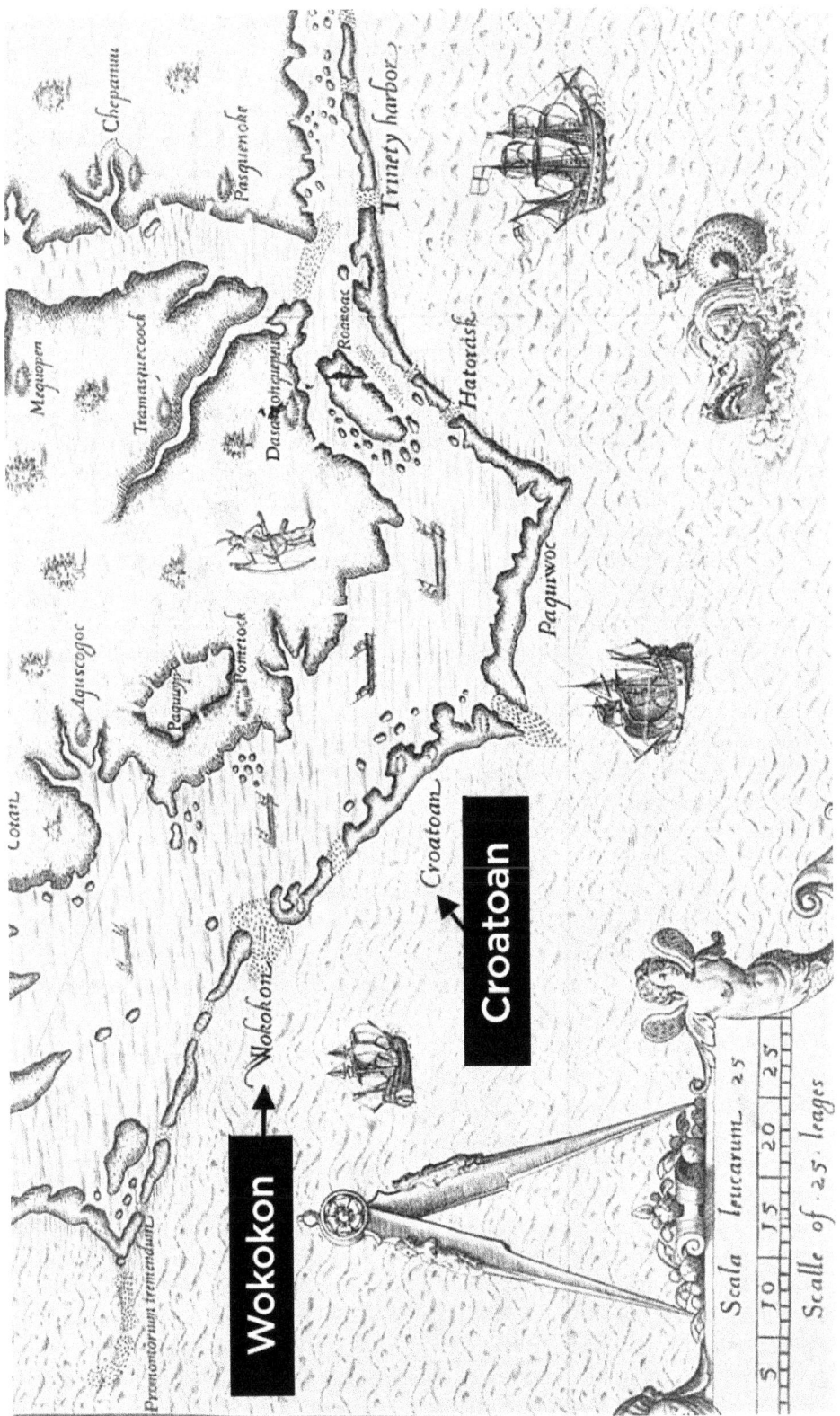

Portion of the White/de Bry map showing the inlets and White's Scale of Leagues.

event was relayed to Granganimeo at his village of Roanoac, and the next day he arrived at the shore accompanied by forty or fifty men, "very handsome and goodly people, and in their behauiour … mannerly and ciuill."[15] A long mat was spread on the sand and Granganimeo seated himself at one end. Four of his servants sat at the other end, and the rest remained standing behind. In Algonquian custom this arrangement had particular significance. By spreading a mat to sit upon, traditionally done at the arrival of a notable leader to the village or territory of a weroance, Granganimeo was acknowledging the high status of these strangers.[16] The presence of servants as well as forty or fifty others marked this as an important public event to be shared and remembered.

The English approached in one of their small boats carrying an assortment of items, and Granganimeo beckoned them to join him on the mat, whereupon he gave a speech welcoming the strangers to his land. During his oration Granganimeo placed his hand on his chest and did the same to the strangers, a traditional sign of peace among Algonquians by which he pledged harmony between their two peoples.[17] He also placed his hand on his forehead and did likewise to the strangers, symbolically expressing that they were of the same mind and were now formally united in a bond of friendship and brotherhood. Although the English could not have entirely understood the significance of everything they were witnessing, Barlowe at least recognized that this was an attempt "to shew wee were all one, smiling and making shewe the best he could of all loue, and familiaritie."

Through sign and gesture the English learned Granganimeo's name and that of his brother, the chief weroance named Wingina, who was at a village inland recovering from wounds he had received in an ongoing battle with a hostile tribe. Granganimeo learned that these strangers were called "English" and that they had come from far across the eastern waters where the sun rose. Still, communication would have been quite challenging at best. It was probably during this initial "conversation" that Granganimeo made reference to something that sounded like "Wingandacoa" to the English, who mistakenly concluded that the country was called "Wingandacoa" after its ruling weroance, Wingina. In actuality the phrase was the Algonquian's observation regarding the Englishmen's attire which meant, "You have good clothes." Although the misunderstanding was probably discovered several months later in England by Thomas Harriot, it would not be corrected in print until Sir Walter Raleigh made a note of it in his *History of the World*, published thirty years later. Writing of his attempt "to inhabit Virginia," he wrote, "When some of my people asked the name of that Countrie, one of the Saluages answered *Wingandacon*, which is as much to say, as, you weare good clothes, or gay clothes."[18]

Granganimeo received many gifts from the English and he thanked them heartily. The English afterwards gave a few gifts to the Indians who sat at the other end of the mat, but Granganimeo immediately stood and retrieved those things, which he then placed in his own basket. He attempted to explain to the somewhat confused English that these other Indians were servants and that tribal conventions and etiquette demanded that all such gifts be delivered solely to him.[19]

Trading began in earnest a day or two later, and the Indians found that the English had many things that were greatly desired. Granganimeo especially prized "a bright tinne dish … which hee presently tooke vp and clapt it before his breast, and after made a hole in the brimme thereof and hung it about his necke, making signes that it would defende him against his enemies arrows."[20] According to historian Karen Kupperman, however, the English may have misinterpreted this behavior, since important weroances hung plates of copper from their necks simply as gorgets to indicate their high status.[21] Granganimeo traded twenty pelts for the platter and a copper kettle fetched even more. Also of great interest were the English hatchets and knives for which the Indians eagerly traded. The most desirable of all items were the swords which the English wore at their sides, but they would not part with them for any price, even for the box of pearls which Granganimeo offered.

Relations continued to flourish over the next several days and Granganimeo eventually boarded the English ships and sampled their meat, bread, and wine, which he "liked exceedingly." On his next visit to the ships Granganimeo was accompanied by his daughter and several other children, along with his wife, who wore a band of white coral about her forehead and long strings of pearls from her ears. Granganimeo wore a copper plate upon his head, another sign of his high status. Granganimeo's wife came to the shore several times afterwards with an entourage of forty or fifty women, but only allowed her two daughters and a nurse and a few others to board the English ships. Granganimeo's wife is unfortunately not named in the account, although she would play an important role a few days later when Barlowe and seven of his men arrived unexpectedly at her village on Roanoke Island. She was described by Barlowe as being

> very well fauoured, of meane stature, and very bashfull: shee had on her backe a long cloake of leather, with the furre side next to her body, and before her a piece of the same: about her forehead shee had a bande of white Corall, and so had her husband many times: in her eares shee had bracelets of pearles hanging downe to her middle ... and those were of the bignes of good pease.[22]

Word of these exchanges spread quickly among the surrounding villages and soon people from near and far came bearing skins and coral and many other things to trade with the English. During all of this Granganimeo kept strict order and control over the activities from shore, even lighting signal fires along the beach to inform the English of the number of Indian boats he would allow to continue on to the ships, one fire for each boat. When Granganimeo himself visited the ships, only he was permitted to trade unless there were other weroances there who also wore pieces of copper on their heads. Granganimeo became a trustworthy partner in these exchanges and sometimes the English even gave him merchandise on his promise alone to bring his trade goods later, a trust he never once violated. In addition he often sent the English a freshly killed deer, as well as rabbits and fish, and many excellent fruits and also corn from their first harvest of the year.

Barlowe was confident enough in the friendly behavior of Granganimeo and the neighboring Indians that he embarked on an exploratory expedition up the River Occam, which was Pamlico Sound as noted, in an oared boat with seven others. On the following evening they "came to an Island which they call Raonoak" where Granganimeo dwelt. As they rowed northward they came to a village comprised of nine cedar dwellings and surrounded by a protective barrier of sharpened tree limbs and narrow trunks. Granganimeo was absent at that time, probably supervising trade with the English or possibly visiting his brother, Wingina, with the latest news about the successful relations and trade he had established.

It was raining when Granganimeo's wife saw the English approach unexpectedly, and she ran forward and greeted them warmly. She ordered some of her people to pull the boat ashore and to take the oars to her house so they would be safe. Others were commanded to carry the English on their backs to dry ground, and then she escorted them to her house, where she exhibited extraordinary hospitality and friendship: As the English sat by a great fire, she took their clothes and washed them, while other women removed the men's stockings and bathed their feet with warm water. Granganimeo's wife took great care to see that all this was done properly and that food was prepared for her guests. Once the clothes were dried and the Englishmen dressed, they were escorted to another room and provided a meal of venison, fish, and a variety of fruits and "were entertained with all loue and kindnesse, and with as much bountie (after their maner) as they could possibly deuise."

Although the following engraving of "A cheiff Ladye" by de Bry does not represent Granganimeo's wife, Harriot wrote that the appearance and attire of the "ladye" in this depiction "differeth but litle from the attyre of those which lyue in Roanaac," such as Granganimeo's wife.

Harriot's description continued:

De Bry's engraving of "A cheiff Ladye."

"...they weare their haire trussed opp in a knott ... and haue their skinnes pownced [painted or tattooed] in the same manner, yet they wear a chaine of great pearles, or beades of copper, or smoothe bones 5. or 6. fold obout their necks, bearinge one arme in the same, in the other hand they carye a gourde full of some kinde of pleasant liquor. They tye deers skinne doubled about them crochinge hygher about their breasts, which hange downe before almost to their knees, and are almost altogither naked behinde.²³

During the meal an incident occurred which might have had unintended consequences were it not for the quick action of Granganimeo's wife: A few Indians, apparently returning from hunting, entered the village carrying their bows and arrows. When the English saw them, they became nervous and started to reach for their weapons. As soon as Granganimeo's wife noticed their reaction, she immediately sent some of her men out to disarm the Indians, break their bows and arrows, and physically drive the likely confused Indians from the village.

As evening approached, Granganimeo's wife attempted to persuade the English to stay the night in the comfort of her village, but as Barlowe wrote, "because wee were fewe men, and if wee had miscaried, the voyage had bene in very great danger, wee durst not adventure [risk] any thing." Nevertheless, she went to extraordinary lengths to reassure and assist the Englishmen, delivering meals to them in their boat as well as mats to cover and protect them from the rain. She was "much grieued" that the English decided to spend the night anchored "a prettie distance from the shoare," and she arranged for a number of men and thirty women to sit through the night on the shore to ensure the safety of the Englishmen. Barlowe concluded this episode by saying that there was really no cause for concern "for a more kinde and louing people there can not be found in the worlde."[24]

In about mid–August "we resolued to leaue the countrey," Barlowe wrote, "and to apply ourselues to returne for England, which we did accordingly." After promising to return the following year, Amadas and Barlowe set sail with two Algonquians aboard, the Croatoan Indian named Manteo and a Roanoac Indian named Wanchese. As the ships sailed from sight, Granganimeo and his wife must have been quite pleased with the results of their efforts to befriend the English and with the prospects for a continued beneficial relationship upon their return. Neither Granganimeo nor his wife could have understood, however, that the English had not only formally claimed the territory they thought was "Wingandacoa" and taken "possession of the same, in the right of the Queenes most excellent Maiestie," but that they intended to colonize it. The two ships and all aboard "arriued safely in the West of England about the middest of September."[25]

Preparations for the subsequent 1585 colonization voyage were well under way even before Amadas and Barlowe reached England. Chronicler Richard Hakluyt had been busy with his *A Discourse of Western Planting*, written at Raleigh's request to promote the upcoming colonization venture and to gain the financial support of influential investors. The *Discourse* was intended especially to convince Queen Elizabeth of the benefits to be derived from colonization in America, and she, along with her principal Secretary of State, Francis Walsingham, eventually supplied two ships for Raleigh's enterprise. When Amadas and Barlowe arrived in September with two native Indians and such glowing reports about the newly discovered land and its friendly inhabitants, little or no doubt remained about the potential rewards to be gained by investing or participating directly in Raleigh's upcoming venture.

The fleet that left England for the return trip to Roanoke Island on April 9, 1585, was strikingly different from the small two-vessel reconnaissance led by Amadas and Barlowe the previous year. This fleet consisted of seven ships, and it transported mostly soldiers and equipment for the purpose of establishing a permanent military colony from which privateering ventures could be launched and refitted and from which exploratory expeditions could be sent inland in search of the precious metals the English hoped to find. The fleet was commanded by Raleigh's cousin, Sir Richard Grenville, and the new colony would be governed by Ralph Lane, a soldier and expert in the construction of fortifications. As was the case with the 1584 voyage, Raleigh himself did not sail with this fleet either, having been prohibited by the queen herself, who insisted that her favorite courtier remain close by her side.

Shortly after the fleet arrived at Wokokon on June 26, Grenville sent word ahead to Roanoke Island to announce the arrival of the English, but he spent until July 18 exploring Pamlico Sound and visiting a number of Indian villages. The fleet finally anchored at Port Ferdinando, the inlet near Roanoke also called Hatorask, on July 27 and two days later Granganimeo met with the leading Englishmen aboard the flagship *Tyger* accompanied by Manteo, the Croatoan Indian who had returned from England with the fleet. There are no further details known about this meeting, but it is probable that arrangements were made for a separate settlement site for the English to be located towards the northern end of Roanoke Island. For Granganimeo the long-anticipated return of the English must have been diminished by the reality of what he heard of an incident that had occurred nearly two weeks earlier. One of the Secotan villages visited by Grenville during his tour of Pamlico

Sound was Aquascogoc, where the English asserted that a silver cup was stolen by "one of the Sauages." A group of Englishmen returned to Aquascogoc three days later to demand the cup, and when it was not produced they "burnt, and spoyled their corne, and Towne, all the people being fled."[26] This excessive reprisal must have been particularly troubling to Granganimeo, when he learned that the group responsible for the atrocity at Aquascogoc was led by Philip Amadas, one of the two Englishmen with whom he had established such good relations the previous year.

There were noticeable differences between these newly arrived Englishmen and those with whom Granganimeo had interacted so favorably last summer. It would have been immediately obvious, of course, that these men were not only more numerous than the Amadas and Barlowe group, but that they were almost exclusively well-armed and disciplined soldiers. Equally worrisome was the fact that the English leaders had ignored the ceremonial rituals of arriving guests, who were expected to present themselves formally to the principal weroance at Roanoac, Granganimeo's brother Wingina. Instead, Grenville had spent a week visiting other villages in Pamlico Sound to the south, and after finally anchoring at the Hatorask inlet off Roanoke Island on July 27, "we rested" for two days, as the unidentified narrator of the Grenville voyage wrote. The first official meeting between the leading Englishmen and the Roanoac Indians was held on July 29, but it was orchestrated and hosted by Grenville aboard the flagship *Tyger*. Wingina, the chief weroance of Roanoac, was notably absent. The early warning signs were unmistakable. These Englishmen were far more assertive and imposing than the men of the Amadas-Barlowe expedition, who had acted with deference toward Granganimeo and his wife. Finally, their actions at Aquascogoc, by now well-known among the tribes, left the clear impression that relations with the English would be based as much on fear as on friendship.

Grenville departed for England on August 25, leaving Ralph Lane and 107 other colonists at Roanoke Island, where they rapidly constructed a fort and settlement buildings and spent the remaining summer and fall exploring the surrounding areas particularly to the north and west. Although Lane wrote of the Indians in early September that "the people naturally are most courteous," attitudes among the Indians toward the English were divided. Already unsettled by the incident at Aquascogoc, relations deteriorated further during this time, particularly as the English became increasingly reliant on their Indian neighbors for food. Among the influential weroances, Granganimeo and especially his father Ensenor continued to promote a policy of cooperation and amity towards the English, as did Manteo, the Croatoan Indian who now dressed like an Englishman and could speak in their tongue. On the other side were the principal weroance, Wingina, who was always wary of the English newcomers, and Wanchese, the Roanoac Indian who had been to England but turned against the English shortly after his return.

As attitudes toward the English worsened, another phenomenon was causing discord in a number of Indian villages. Wherever the Englishmen visited, large numbers of Indians soon began to sicken and die, "in some Townes about twentie, in some fourtie, and in one sixe score [120], which in trueth was very many in respect of their numbers."[27] The native Indians had no way of knowing about the communicable viruses the English carried with them to the New World, some as deadly as smallpox or even measles and others as common as influenza, all of which the tribes had no immunities against. "The disease also was so strange," Harriot wrote, "that they neither knewe what it was, nor how to cure it, the like by report of the oldest men in the Countrey neuer happened before." Ralph Lane wrote that there was "an opinion very confidently at this day holden by the wisest amongst them" that the English had powers to strike down Indians "by sicknesse" even those "being 100. miles from any of vs."[28]

Lane's account is otherwise silent on the events that occurred between the fall of 1585 and late February of 1586, but there are indications that English relations with the Roanoacs and the surrounding tribes had deteriorated rapidly during that time period. Harriot wrote elusively about the English "slaying some of the people in some Townes … towards the ende of the yeere," but supplied no details. It is fair to conclude, however, that the English had been involved in fatal confrontations with Indians in a number of villages other than Roanoac, and it is very possible that those clashes were related to the deadly sickness that the Indians correctly blamed on the English. The gap in Lane's account can probably be attributed to later editing by Raleigh or his friend Hakluyt in order to keep the true state of Indian relations concealed from prospective colonists and investors.

It was almost certainly one of these deadly diseases that claimed the life of Granganimeo. Although Lane's account did not mention the date or the circumstances of his death, it may have occurred as early as November, not very long after the outbreak of the sickness (see the *Ensenore* entry). Granganimeo's death had far-reaching consequences for both the Indians and the English. He alone had been primarily responsible for the positive Anglo-Indian relations established in 1584, and he continued to advocate for cooperation with the English even as tensions rose in 1585. With his passing the English lost an important ally among the Roanoac tribe, leaving only old Ensenore and his followers, who advocated friendship in large part because they believed the English possessed supernatural powers. The most significant and immediate consequence of Granganimeo's death, however, was the effect that it had on his older brother and principle weroance, Wingina. Upon Granganimeo's death Wingina changed his name to Pemisapan and initiated a series of events that would have deadly consequences and ultimately contribute to the abandonment of the Roanoke colony.

Menatoan

Menatoan (not to be confused with the Chawanoac weroance *Menatonan*) was a Croatoan weroance who was nearly killed accidentally, along with his wife and child, during Raleigh's second colonization attempt. On July 28, 1587, shortly after the arrival of the second colony, a colonist named George Howe wandered from the settlement and was killed by Indians from Dasamonquepeuc. A few days later, in an attempt to restore peaceful relations, the new governor John White sent an offering of peace to the weroances at Pomeiock, Aquascogoc, Secota, and Dasamonquepeuc. On August 9, after a week had passed with no reply to his overtures, White's made an ill-advised attack on what he thought was a gathering of hostile Indians at Dasamonquepeuc. Guided by Manteo, White and his force were able to approach Dasamonquepeuc stealthily during the night and fall upon a group of Indians sitting around the fire. Unfortunately, these Indians were friendly Croatoans, Manteo's people. They had occupied Dasamonquepeuc after the Indians responsible for killing George Howe, fearing just such a retaliatory attack, had fled farther inland. At least one Croatoan was instantly shot "through the bodie with a bullet," and Menatoan's wife would have been slain as well, had not one of the attackers noticed the child she carried on her back. The English finally realized their mistake and terminated the assault. The number of Croatoan casualties was not stated.

White's unfortunate attack at Dasamonquepeuc was particularly grievous because this was the second time such a mistake had occurred. Furthermore, about a week earlier these same Croatoans had earnestly requested that the English provide them with "some token or badge … whereby we might know them to be our friends, when we met them any where out of the Towne or Island."[1] The request for badges was specifically made to avoid the recurrence of Lane's attack at Dasamonquepeuc the previous year, when Croatoans had been accidentally targeted. The Croatoans even "shewed vs one [of their tribesmen injured in Lane's assault] which at that very instant lay lame, and had lien of that hurt euer since."

Manteo had guided White and his men to Dasamonquepeuc and, although he did not participate in the assault, was deeply troubled by the mistaken attack on his own people. It is a near certainty that he had warned White that his Croatoan people often visited Dasamonquepeuc, just as he had warned Ralph Lane the previous year before a few Croatoans were injured in the attack on Pemisapan and his followers. After White's imprudent attack was halted, the English "tooke Menatoan his wife, with the yong child, and the other Sauages with vs ouer the water to Roanoak,"[2] and Menatoan was not mentioned again in any of the accounts.

Menatonon

Menatonon was the principal weroance of the powerful Chawanoac tribe who dwelt in villages mainly along the Chowan River and part of the Meherrin River in present-day Chowan, Bertie, Hertford, and Gates Counties. His name is usually said to mean "One who listens well, alert," which parallels Algonquian linguistic expert James Geary's literal translation: "He listens carefully to someone (something) he sees."[1] Menatonon ruled over the "iurisdiction of Chawanook," and, despite being physically disabled, he was widely esteemed for his wisdom and influence and was respected by both Indians and English alike. Lane wrote of Menatonon in his account of the 1585–6 colonization attempt, "The king of the sayd Prouince is called Menatonon, a man impotent in his lims, but otherwise for a Sauage, a very graue and wise man, and of a very singular good discourse in matters concerning the state, not onely of his owne Countrey, and the disposition of his owne men, but also of his neighbours round about him as well farre as neere, and of the commodities that eache Countrey yeeldeth."[2]

Menatonon's main village was referred to by the English as "The towne of Chawanook," following the common English practice of naming principal Indian villages after the name of the tribe that inhabited the area. Lane claimed that "the Towne it selfe is able to put 700. fighting men into the fielde, besides the force of the Prouince it selfe,"[3] although that number may have been either a transcription error or an exaggeration on Lane's part. Harriot, who was with Lane on the 1585–6 colonization venture, gave a much more realistic assessment. He wrote in his *A Briefe and true report*, "the greatest Wiroans that yet wee had dealing with"—generally believed to be Menatonon—"had but eighteene townes in his gouernment, and able to make not aboue seuen or eight hundred fighting men at the most."[4] If Menatonon's "eighteene townes" could field a total of 700–800 warriors, it would put the average number of fighting men per town at between 39 and 44, a more reasonable count. It should be noted, though, that Harriot's "report" was written largely at Raleigh's behest to counter the stories being circulated by some of Lane's returning men about the hostile Indians they encountered. Some of Lane's men, Harriot wrote, "haue maliciously not onely spoken ill of their Gouernours, but for their sakes slandered the countrey it selfe."[5] It would have been in his friend Raleigh's best interests for Harriot to downplay the strength of the Chawanoacs' military prowess.

The affiliation of a few of the villages along the Chowan River is not certain, especially those located on the east bank. Anthropologist John Swanton named five "Chowanoc" villages: Maraton ("Waratan" on the de Bry map) and Catoking on the east bank of the Chowan River, Ohanoak and Metocaum on the west, and Ramushonok (Ramusouuoq) between the Meherrin and Chowan Rivers.[6] Those five villages, as well as another village called Tandaquomuc, which may or may not have been part of Menatonon's domain, are shown on the

1590 White/de Bry map below. There must have been many other smaller villages located on the Chowan River's tributaries, particularly if Harriot's count of 18 villages was accurate.

Menatonon's main "towne of Chawanook" was not shown on the White/de Bry map, perhaps leading some 20th century authors to conclude that Chawanoac was probably the village called Waratan by the Indians, and misspelled "Maraton" by Swanton and "Mavaton" by Dr. Richard Dillard in the citation below. In 1906 Dillard wrote,

> One of the largest and most remarkable Indian mounds in eastern North Carolina is located at Bandon on the Chowan, evidently the site of the ancient town of the Chowanokes which Grenville's party visited in 1585, and was called Mavaton [Waratan].... The mound extends along the river bank five or six hundred yards, is sixty yards wide and five feet deep, covered with about a foot of sand and soil. It is composed almost exclusively of mussel shells taken from the river, pieces of pottery, ashes, arrow heads and human bones....[7]

The fact that it was Lane's party, not Grenville's, who visited the Chawanoacs, and that it occurred in 1586, not 1585, is problematic, as are a few other details in Dillard's twenty-three page account. Nevertheless, Dillard's hypotheses seemed plausible at the time and North Carolina historian Samuel A'Court Ashe later included this and other excerpts from Dillard's commentary in his *History of North Carolina 1584–1783*.[8]

A number of archaeological surveys were conducted in the 1970s and 1980s by the

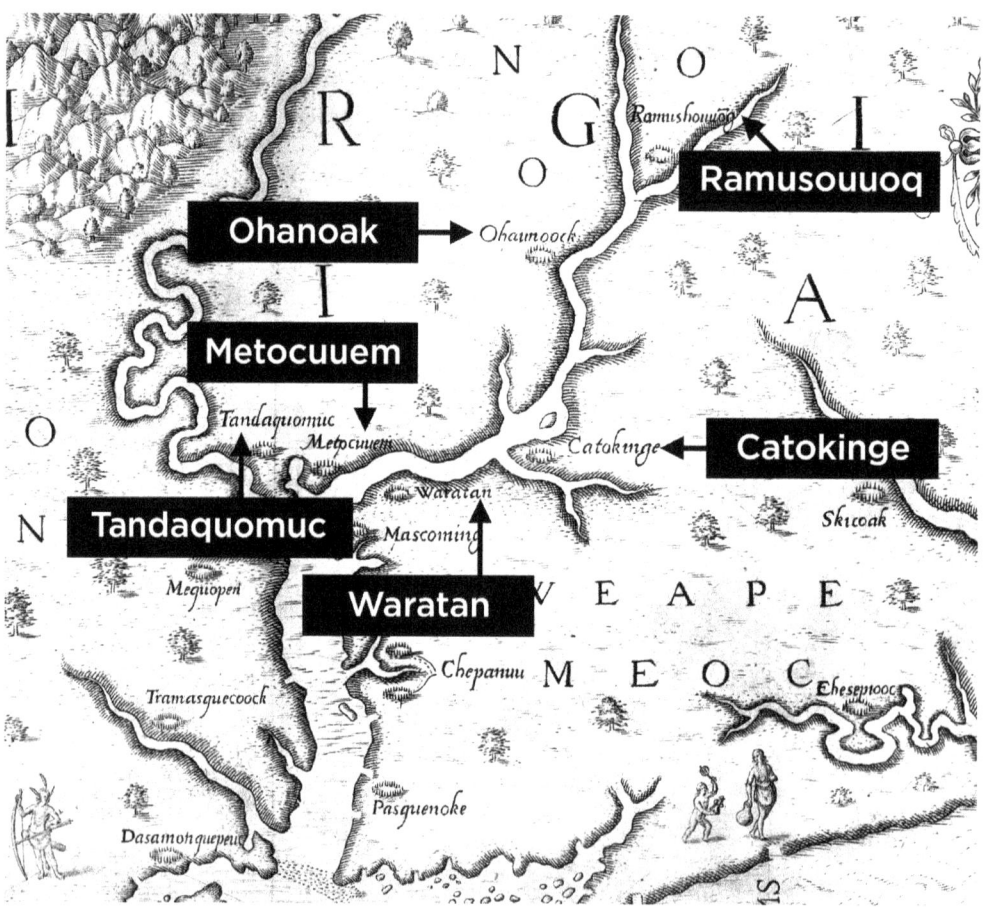

Some of the villages attributed to the Chawanoac tribe.

University of North Carolina at Chapel Hill and East Carolina University focusing on the areas bordering the Chowan River with the expressed goal of identifying "specific archaeological sites as historically known localities." One of the most notable results of the many recorded sites was the "possible location of 'Chowanoak' (31HF20) the capital town of the Chowan Chiefdom first visited in the 1580s by Ralph Lane."[9] Archaeologist David Phelps, then of East Carolina University, wrote, "The archaeological site of Chowanoke is located on the western bank of the Chowan River in Hertford County along a series of high bluffs that extend for approximately one mile along the river."[10] At the mouth of the Chowan River, Ralph Lane had explained, "we enter into the ... iurisdiction of Chawanook: There the Riuer beginneth to straighten vntil it come to [the town of] Chawanook, and then [the river] groweth to be as narrow as the Thames betweene Westminster and Lambeth."[11] That description, Phelps noted, corresponds exactly to the present-day bluffs where the Chowan River narrows below the mouth of Goose Creek. The actual town of Chawanoac may have been comprised of a "central core" containing Menatonon's house and those of the "nobility and the temples or other public buildings ... with commoners' residences dispersed along the shore."[12] If the boundaries of Menatonon's town of Chawanoac were not clearly defined and instead stretched nearly 1,800 yards along the river, as Phelps's excavations indicated, that might account for the lack of a precise notation on the White/de Bry map. The location of Chawanoac was, however, indicated on *La Virginea Pars* map drawn by White in 1585, and it appears to correlate with the area excavated by Phelps.

The first mention of Menatonon appeared in Arthur Barlowe's account of the reconnaissance voyage sent out on April 27, 1584, by Walter Raleigh "to discouer, search, finde out, and view such remote, heathen and barbarous lands, countreis, and territories."[13] Barlowe and the English learned from their contact with the coastal Indians at the Outer Banks, probably near the Wokokon inlet, of "another riuer, called Nomopana [the Chowan], on the one side whereof standeth a great towne called Chawanook ... and another king, whom they call Menatonon."

Other than a lengthy excursion northward "to the Chesepians," Lane's account is unfortunately silent about English activities in the fall and winter of 1585–6. It is possible that a group was also sent on an exploratory mission westward across Albemarle Sound at about that time, but Lane's first personal encounter with Menatonon seems to have occurred in early March of 1586. By that time relations with the Indians at Roanoac and other surrounding villages had deteriorated significantly, and the Roanoac weroance Wingina, who had by now changed his name to Pemisapan, was in the process of organizing a great tribal "confederacie ... to the number of three thousand bowes, preparing to come vpon vs at Roanoak." When Lane and his men made an unexpected appearance at Menatonon's main village of Chawanoac, they interrupted a gathering of "Choanists," "Mangoaks," and "Moratoks" who had assembled there, according to Lane, as part of Pemisapan's conspiracy.

Lane and his group of about fifty men managed to break up the assembly, seize the crippled Menatonon, and put him in "an handlocke." "When I had him prisoner with me, for two dayes that we were together," Lane wrote, "he gaue mee more vnderstanding and light of the Countrey then I had receiued by all the searches and Sauages that before I or any of my companie had had conference with." Menatonon told Lane that a journey of three days up the Chowan River and then four days more overland would bring him "to a certaine kings country" with a deep bay (the Chesapeake), where a "greate quantitie of Pearle" could be found. This king, Lane learned, had visited Menatonon "two yeeres before" and brought black pearls with him to trade.

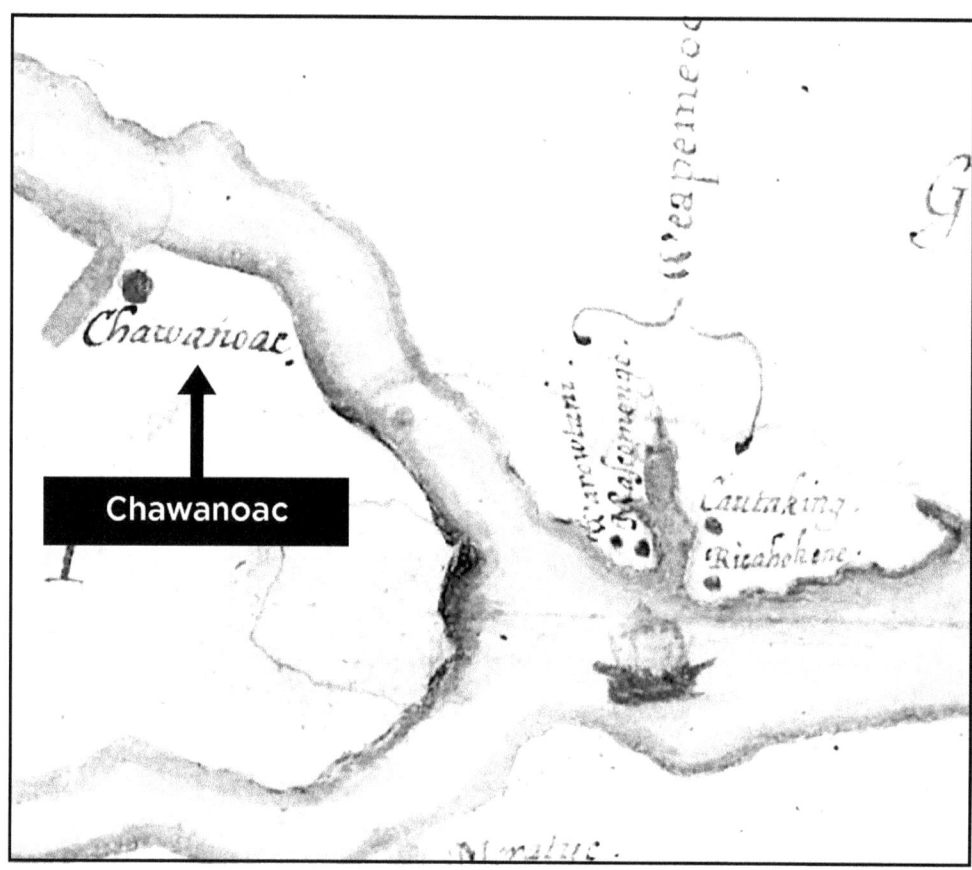

Portion of White's *La Virginea Pars* map showing the location of Chawanoac.

Since Menatonon's province was bordered to the north by the Virginia Algonquians, it is often concluded that the visiting king must have been Wahunsunacock, who would be known to the English two decades later as Chief Powhatan. John Smith estimated that Wahunsunacock's age was "neare 60" in 1607, so he would have been perhaps in his mid to late thirties if and when he visited Menatonon in 1584. It is true that Chief Powhatan eventually expanded his chiefdom to include more than thirty tribes by the time the Jamestown colonists arrived in 1607, but at the time he is said to have visited Menatonon in 1584, he most likely could not have ruled over many more than the six he had originally inherited. Furthermore the Chesepians, who dwelt at the Chesapeake Bay at that time, were an independent tribe east of Powhatan's domain. It was not until 1607, after Powhatan had expanded his chiefdom, that he was able to subjugate the Chesepians. If the chief of the Chesepian tribe visited Menatonon in 1584, that chief could not have been Wahunsunacock.

In any case, Lane was so enticed by Menatonon's relation of a deep water port to the north that he envisioned building "a maine fort [there], both for the defence of the harborough, and our shipping also, and would haue reduced our whole habitation from Roanoak and from the harborough and port there (which by proofe is very naught)."[14] It would not be until almost two decades later, however, that Menatonon's promise of a deep water harbor at a bay to the north would be fulfilled, when the Jamestown settlers arrived at the Chesapeake Bay in 1607.

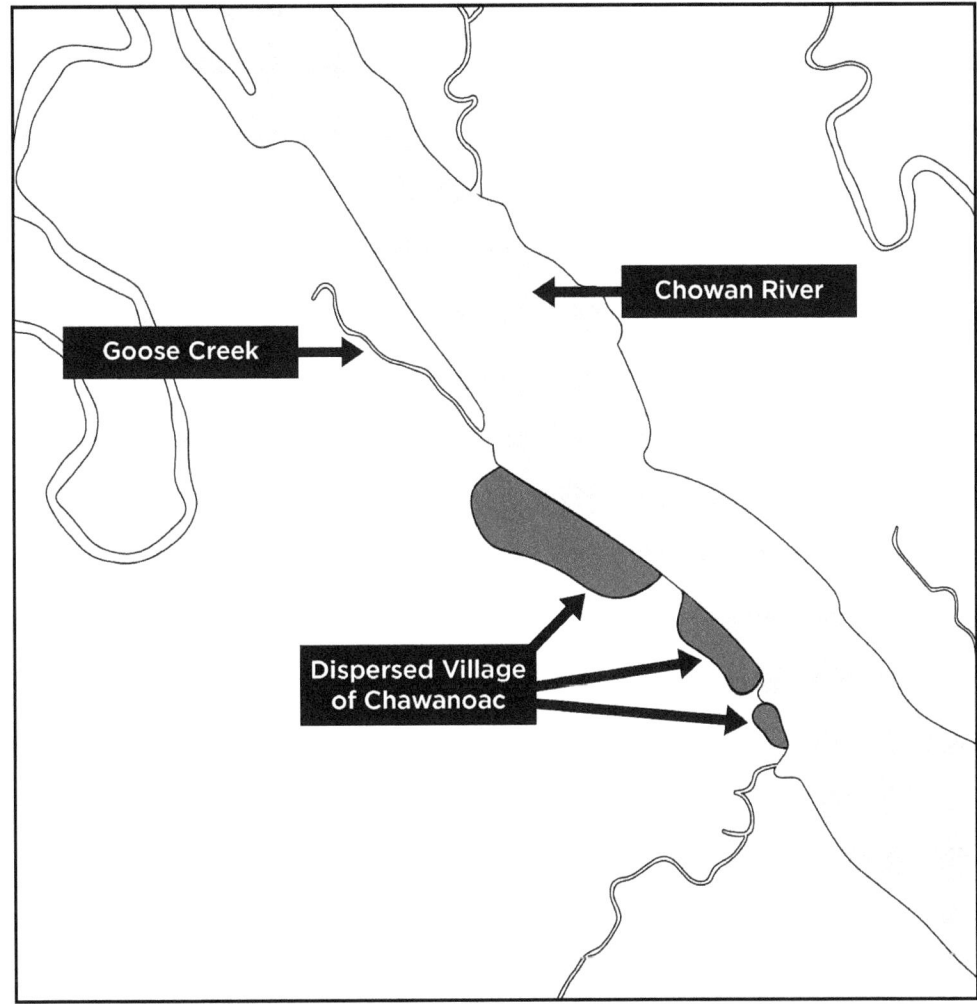

Location of the dispersed Town of Chawanoac based on Phelps's notes (courtesy Michael Gayle).

What attracted Lane's immediate attention was Menatonon's description of the "Country of Chaunis Temoatan." It was located some distance up the Moratuc River, where Menatonon reported there was a famous mine well known to the Chawanoacs, the Moratuks, the Mangoaks, and all the mainland tribes to the west. The mineral found there was called "Wassador ... which is copper, but they call by the name of Wassador euery mettall whatsoeuer." The description Menatonon provided to Lane was that the wassador at "Chaunis Temoatan is very soft, and pale," and probably raised the possibility that it could be gold. Lane must have pressed Menatonon about the method used by the Indians at Chaunis Temoatan to find and process the wassador, and the details Lane learned could only have raised his hopes that the wassador was indeed gold:

> ... they say that they take the saide mettall out of a riuer that falleth very swift from the rockes and hils, and they take it in shallow water: the maner is this. They take a great bowle by their description as great as one of our targets [shields], and wrappe a skinne ouer the hollow parte thereof, leauing one part open to receiue in the minerall: that done, they watch the comming downe of the current, and the change of the colour of the water, and then suddenly chop downe the said bowle with the skinne, and

receiue into the same as much oare as will come in, which is euer as much as their bowle will holde, which presently they cast into a fire, and foorthwith it melteth, and doeth yeeld in fiue parts at the first melting, two parts of mettall for three partes of oare. Of this mettall the Mangoaks haue so great store, by report of all the Sauages adioyning, that they beautify their houses with greate plates of the same.[15]

The possibility of finding precious metals in the New World, as the Spanish had already done, was one of the more alluring incentives for English investors and colonists, and Lane wasted no time preparing to find Chaunis Temoatan. One might wonder whether the shrewd Menatonon may have told the story about Chaunis Temoatan to gratify Lane's desire for riches and lure him into what turned out to be a trap on the Moratuc River. The assembly that Lane disrupted was, by his own account, part of a plan to organize a "confederacie" of tribes for the purpose of destroying the English. The plot to annihilate the English on the Moratuc River had to have originated *after* Menatonon enticed Lane with the story of the possible riches to be had at Chaunis Temoatan and was probably arranged by Pemisapan. The plot was fairly involved, requiring the cooperation of all the villages along the Moratuc, as well as the Mangoaks, and it was put in place in a remarkably short amount of time. Lane held Menatonon prisoner for two days, during which the chief told him about Chaunis Temoatan, which in turn prompted Lane's venture up the Moratuc River. The plot was already in place by the time Lane departed.

Lane freed Menatonon—only after receiving a ransom—but in his place took "yong Skiko, the King of Chawanooks sonne of my prisoner." Menatonon's son Skiko was quickly put aboard the pinnace and sent in chains back to Roanoke. In the meantime Lane set out to find Chaunis Temoatan up the Moratuc River in two double wherries and forty men. They carried with them just enough provisions to reach the Moratuc villages, where they planned to acquire food for the rest of the journey.

The plan to destroy the English on the Moratuc almost worked. The Indians dwelling along the river had all agreed to vacate their villages, taking their corn supplies with them, as the English boats advanced upriver. When the provisions eventually ran out and Lane and his men "were like to be starued," an assault on the boats by Indians hiding on an embankment was only prevented by the quick action of Manteo, who was in the boat with Lane. The English managed to make it back to the Weapemeoc village of Chipanum, but not before killing and eating Lane's two mastiff dogs and consuming sassafras leaves. They found Chipanum deserted too, "but their weares did yeeld vs some fish, as God was pleased not vtterly to suffer vs to be lost: for some of our company … were farre spent."[16] The next morning, Easter Monday, Lane and his men arrived back at Roanoke Island.

A few days later Menatonon tried to gain the release of Skiko, "his sonne that he best loued," by sending a messenger to Roanoke with a gift of pearls for Lane, but he refused to free his prisoner. In an extraordinarily unusual development, Menatonon ordered Okisko, the chief weroance of Weapemeoc, to yield himself as servant "to the great Weroanza of England," Queen Elizabeth, "and after her to Sir Walter Raleigh." To confirm the pledge, 24 "of his principallest men" from Weapemeoc were sent to Lane at Roanoke "to let mee knowe that from that time forwarde, hee, and his successours" acknowledged the Queen of England as their absolute sovereign. Menatonon's concern about his son's safety was well founded, since, as Lane wrote, "the King Menatonon his sonne [was] my prisoner, who hauing once attempted to run away, I laid him in the bylboes [leg irons chained to the floor], threatening to cut off his head." Lane welcomed the pledge of loyalty by the Weapemeocs, but he did not release Menatonon's son.

As cooperation with the English continued to evaporate, especially after the death of the former Roanoac weroance, Ensenore, Lane considered trying to enlist Menatonon as an ally. It was never attempted, however, because of the more pressing need to deal with the growing conspiracy of Pemisapan. The rest of Lane's account tells of the imminent assault on the English, Lane's surprise attack at Dasamonquepeuc resulting in the death of Pemisapan, and the evacuation of the Roanoke colony on June 19 after the unexpected arrival of Sir Francis Drake's fleet. According to a later report three Englishmen were inadvertently left behind in the rush to leave Roanoke Island. It has been suggested that the three men may have been en route to Chawanoac on an errand to return Menatonon's son, but it is not even certain that the report about the three being left behind is accurate. What is certain is that neither Menatonon nor his son was mentioned again in the Roanoke accounts.

In 1907 a brief but mistaken passage about Menatonon written by Dr. Cyrus Thomas of the Bureau of American Ethnology appeared in the *Handbook of American Indians*. At the end of an article about Menatonon Thomas wrote, "It is probable that he [Menatonon] died soon after Lane's visit [to Chawanoac in March, 1586], as John White, who was in the country two years later, mentions his wife and child as belonging to Croat[o]an, but says nothing of him."[17] Thomas's erroneous conclusion, however, was based on his misreading of a similar name in White's 1587 account referring to his ill-advised attack at Dasamonquepeuc. During the assault a Croatoan weroance named Menatoan, along with his wife and child were nearly killed by mistake (see the previous *Menatoan* entry).

Nothing else is known about Menatonon or his Chawanoac tribe for the next two decades following Lane's evacuation of Roanoke with Drake on June 19, 1586. In 1587 Raleigh's next colonization attempt was diverted from the intended location at the Chesapeake Bay to Roanoke Island once again, but there is no mention of Menatonon or the Chawanoac tribe in the 1587 account. It has been theorized, however, that the 1587 colonists—who disappeared from the historical record in August of the same year—may have relocated to Chawanoac, since Menatonon had cooperated with Lane the previous year.

There are a number of problems, though, with that hypothesis. As mentioned, it had become obvious in 1585–6 that the inlet to Roanoke Island was not adequate and that future colonization efforts would have to focus on a location with a far better harbor. The Chawanoac location was even more inaccessible, since it would have been necessary to use the same Hatorask inlet at Roanoke in order to reach it. The Hatorask inlet was located just south of Roanoke Island, which would have required navigating some fifteen miles of shallows surrounding the island just to reach the entrance to Albemarle Sound. And then from there everything still had to be ferried fifty to sixty miles farther westward across a narrow channel in the sound and up the Chowan River, a lengthy effort requiring multiple trips and an inordinate amount of time. It would have made little sense for the colonists, who depended upon routine re-supply for their survival as a viable English colony, to select a mainland settlement location that would make those scheduled resupply deliveries logistically unfeasible.

Furthermore, finding refuge and sustenance with the Chawanoac tribe would not have been as promising a prospect as has been suggested. Like all other tribes, the Chawanoacs had to depend upon their own food stores for sustenance through the winter. It does not seem at all likely that the Chawanoacs would have been willing or able to provide the colony with food through the winter, since well over 100 additional people would have placed an impossible burden on the tribe's food stores, which always ran low in the winter. Moreover, as mentioned previously, the so called "cooperation" Lane had received from Menatonon was not offered out of friendship towards the English, but only as a result of coercion and threats *by* the English. Lane had seized Menatonon and released him after two days, but only after he had received a "ransome agreed for." Lane then unexpectedly seized his son Skiko and compelled Menatonon's cooperation because, as noted, Lane kept his son chained to the floor at Roanoke Island and threatened to behead him. It is highly unlikely that Menatonon would have wanted anything to do with another colony of English people. And then, of course, there were the messages the 1587 colonists themselves left at the Roanoke fort. The "CRO" and "CROATOAN" inscriptions were obviously intended to direct White to Croatoan upon his anticipated return in 1588. Croatoan, however, was about 50 miles south of Roanoke Island. It would have made no sense whatsoever to send White some 50 miles south if the colony had actually settled among Menatonon's Chawanoac tribe at the western end of Albemarle Sound and well over 100 miles from Croatoan.

Like all the other Carolina Algonquians, there is little or nothing known about the Chawanoac tribe for more than a half century afterwards. There is one reference to "Chawanoac," however, in John Smith's *Generall Historie of Virginia*. In early 1607 Smith told the weroance at the village of Warraskoyack on the Pagan River near present-day Smithfield, Virginia, that he required "guides to *Chawwonock*, for he would send a present to that King, to bind him his friend."[18] The Jamestown colonists had been instructed to learn what they could about the 1587 "lost" colonists, and that was one of Smith's purposes for the expedition to Chawanoac, the other being to look for "silke Grasse," a commodity used for making cordage. Michael Sickelmore and two Indian guides were sent out in January of 1608. When Sickelmore eventually returned, he reported that he could learn nothing about the colonists and that "the riuer he saw was not great, the people few, the countrey most over growne with pynes, where there did grow here and there straglingly *Pemminaw*, we call silke grasse."[19] This desolate picture hardly fits the description of the once numerous and dominant Chawanoac tribe or the rich land and thriving villages along the Chowan River where they dwelt. It is likely that Sicklemore never reached the Chowan River, perhaps only getting as far as the Blackwater River which joins the Nottaway River to form the Chowan River near the present-day Virginia–North Carolina border.

In early 1622 Virginia Secretary John Pory made what was probably the first excursion from Jamestown to the Chowan River. Only second-hand reports of his expedition have survived, but he apparently met and traded with the Indians living along the Chowan, some of whom would have been of an age to remember Menatonon. From what is known, Pory was impressed with both the settlement possibilities of the Chowan River area and the friendliness of the Indians he met, who were anxious to establish trade with the English. It is said that he was given a piece of copper by one of the Chawanoac weroances. The earliest mention of Pory's expedition in the colonial records included the following entry titled "obseruations of Master John Pory Secretarie of Virginia in his trauels 1622," and stated: "In February also he trauelled to the South River Chawonock some sixtie miles ouer land which he found to be a uery fruitful and pleasant Country, yielding two haruests in a yeere and found much of the silke grasse formerly spoken of, [He] was kindly vsed by the people and so returned."[20]

The lure of rich land east of the Chowan River and the commercial potential of the nearby pine forests for the production of tar, pitch, and turpentine, would eventually draw settlers south from Virginia, and in 1663 the Province of Carolina was established. The earliest colonial documents are unclear about the first settlement date but state, "The first permanent white settlement in North Carolina was made, it may be safely said, to the eastward of the Chowan River, extending in time down to and along Albemarle Sound." As these settlers moved steadily down from Virginia, however, the Algonquian tribes dwelling from just west of the Chowan River to the Outer Banks saw their land and hunting grounds encroached upon. The largest and still most powerful of these tribes was the Chawanoacs, and by the 1660s armed conflicts between the settlers and the Indians on both sides of the Chowan River were occurring with regularity. In 1676 the Chawanoacs became embroiled in the insurrection known as Bacon's Rebellion, which was crushed in 1677, resulting in the defeat of the Chawanoacs and marking the end of the tribe's independence. With the subjugation of the Chawanoacs all the tribes to the immediate north of Albemarle Sound became tributaries of Carolina and no longer posed a threat to the settlers.[21] The Chawanoacs were relocated to a twelve square mile reservation at Bennett's Creek.

By the end of the Tuscarara War in 1715 a number of smaller tribes had disappeared and the handful that remained became, like the Chawanoacs before them, tributaries of what was now the separate colony of North Carolina, and were provided with tracts of surveyed reservation land. The gradual disappearance of these remaining tribes coincided with their selling off of reservation land, which for the Chawanoacs started in 1733, when the leading chief or "king" started selling parcels to nearby settlers. By 1755 the once powerful and numerous Chawanoac tribe ruled by Menatonon was reduced to just five adults, two men and three women, along with their children, living in the Chowan Precinct, and "ill-used by their neighbors."[22]

Okisko

Okisko (also spelled Okisco) was the principal weroance of the Weapemeoc tribe whose villages were located north of Albemarle Sound mostly in the southern portions of present-day Currituck, Camden, Pasquotank, Perquimans, and Chowan Counties. They may also have had seasonal or temporary encampments farther upriver and on the Outer Banks. It is very possible that the group referred to as "Weapemeoc" by the 1585–6 English colonists actually included a number of smaller sub-tribes, each of which exercised a degree of autonomy. In later years "Weapemeoc" was contracted to "Yeopim" and included the Pasquotank, Perquimans, and Poteskeet tribes. According to Algonquian philologist James Geary, Okisko's name may indicate from the Algonquian that "he used white paint and sat on the south side at ceremonial gatherings."[1]

The Weapemeocs were first encountered by the English in early August 1585, when Philip Amadas was sent to explore Albemarle Sound, where he spent at least two or three weeks at various Weapemeoc and Chawanoac villages. It was during this exploratory voyage that the English learned about Okisko, "the king of Weopomeiok." Neither Grenville's nor Lane's account provided any further details about Amadas's Weapemeoc expedition, but some remarks came to light in a Spanish source, in the form of a sometimes confused deposition given more than a decade later by Richard Butler, a prisoner of the Spanish who claimed to have been part of both the 1584 reconnaissance voyage and the 1585 voyage to Roanoke Island. According to Butler this expedition to Weapemeoc encountered hostile Indians, twenty of whom were killed and a number captured.[2] Butler's name, however, does not appear among "the names of those as well Gentlemen as others, that remained one whole yeere in Virginia, vnder the Gouernement of Master Ralph Lane," but he could have been one of Grenville's men who returned to England with him at the end of August. Given Amadas's temperament and his impulsive and excessive reaction at Aquascogoc, it is not beyond the realm of possibility that he could have once again responded to the slightest provocation from the Weapemeocs with deadly results. On the other hand Butler also claimed that the Weapemeocs were enemies of the Roanoacs, but that was certainly not the case in 1586, when the Roanoac weroance, Pemisapan, formed an alliance that included the Weapemeocs to defeat the English. Furthermore Butler's deposition was taken many years later in 1596, by which time his geographic references and recollections may have been mistaken. Quinn was probably close to the mark when he wrote, "Richard Butler … is not to be relied on but cannot wholly be ignored."[3]

Lane wrote that Okisko had "vnder [his] iurisdiction" the waterside villages of Pasquenoke, Chepanoc, Weapemeoc, Muscamunge, and Metackwem. Estimates of the total population of the Weapemeoc tribe in 1585 have sometimes been exaggerated, due in part to a misreading of a line in Lane's account. For example, ethnologist Maurice Mook wrote that

"The reference [Lane's] to the possibility of drawing upon 700 or 800 warriors from Weapemeoc territory suggests a total tribal population of at least 2,500."[4] Ethnologists typically apply a multiplier averaging about 3.5 to the number of "bowes" or fighting men in order to estimate a tribe's total population, giving Mook his minimum approximation of 2,500. The line in Lane's account, however, refers to the number of warriors the Weapemeocs and Mangoaks *combined* were able to put in the field: "Okisko king of Weopomeiok with the Mandoage [Mangoaks] should bee mooued, and with great quantitie of copper intertained to the number of 7. or 8. hundreth bowes, to enterprise the matter thus to be ordered."[5] The passage contains Lane's estimation of the number of warriors those two tribes combined would be able to assemble against the English in a plot that was later organized by the weroance, Pemisapan. The Mangoaks were a completely separate tribe dwelling a considerable distance up the Moratuc River and far removed from Weapemeoc territory. A more accurate estimation of the total Weapemeoc tribal population in 1585–6, then, would be closer to 1,300, or half of Mook's estimate.

Lane referred to the Weapemeoc village of Pasquenoke as "the womans town," the reference to which is not known. Geary translated "Pasquenoke" as "where the current divides," and claimed that the "suggestion of 'women's village' is not [a] tenable" translation. Lane's reference, then, could simply mean that Pasquenoke was governed by a queen or weroansqua, just as another weroansqua, Manteo's mother, likely ruled Croatoan at that time on the Outer Banks to the south. The village of Weapemeoc was possibly located at the mouth of the Perquimans River,[6] or possibly a few miles west, near the mouth of Yeopim River.[7]

In either case the village of Weapemeoc was undoubtedly the principal seat of the tribe and was where Okisko resided. It was not shown either on White's 1585 *La Virginea Pars* map or on the 1590 White/de Bry engraved map possibly because, like the village of Chawanoac, it was a dispersed village, having Okisko's residence and other important structures centrally located and the lesser dwellings spread out on either side along the shoreline. "From Muscamunge," Lane wrote, "we enter into the Riuer [Chowan] and [the] iurisdiction of Chawanook." The village of Metackwem was shown on the White/de Bry map spelled "Metocuuem," but it was placed between the Chowan and Moratuc Rivers, making it most likely a Chawanoac rather than a Weapemeoc village. This would seem to be supported by Lane's observation that Muscamunge, not Metackwem, was the last Weapemeoc village westward before entering Chawanoac territory. It is also possible that de Bry's labeling of Metocuuem at that location was merely an error.

The placement of various villages and territories on the White/de Bry map cannot always be relied upon, in fact, and that is particularly noticeable in regard to the Weapemeoc villages. It is interesting, for example, to compare the locations of the villages in the area labeled "Weapemeoc" on White's *La Virginea Pars* map with those on the White/de Bry engraving. The *Virginea Pars* map is White's original watercolor from 1585–6, which Quinn considered "the major contemporary authority on the configuration of the coastline, on the nomenclature and spelling of place-names, and on the location of villages."[8] The White/de Bry map was engraved later by Theodor de Bry from a modified version—which has not survived—of White's *La Virginea Pars* map. De Bry, perhaps more interested in the overall artistic composition and conventional expectations, may have paid less attention to certain details on his engraving, such as the precise geographic location of certain villages. "Where the maps conflict," Quinn wrote, "preference should probably be given to the White original."[9]

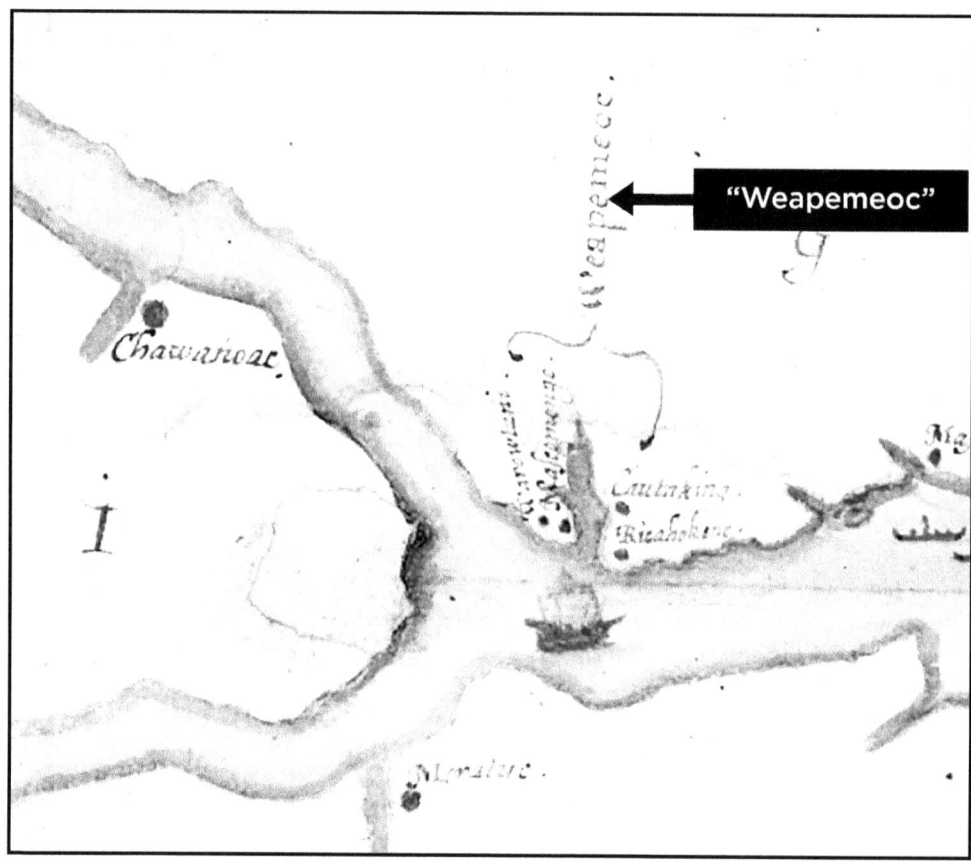

"Weapemeoc" on the *Virginea Pars* map comprising Cautaking, Ricahokene, Mascomenge, and Warowtani.

On the relevant portion of White's *La Virginea Pars* map above, Weapemeoc is a small area confined to four bracketed villages called Cautaking, Ricahokene, Mascomenge, and Warowtani, all of which are situated on either side of what appears to be the Perquimans River.

On de Bry's engraved map the territory labeled "Weapemeoc" comprises an exaggerated area extending northward (to the right) well into the territory of the Chesepian tribe. On the west it infringes on the territory of the powerful Chawanoacs who dwelt on both sides of the Chowan River. The Weapemeoc villages contained within that vast area are Pasquenoke, Chepanuu, Mascoming, Waratan, and Catokinge. Three of these—Mascoming, Waratan, and Catokinge—were undoubtedly Weapemeoc villages as they also appear on the *Virginea Pars* map (spelled "Mascomenge," "Warowtani," and "Cautaking"). Their locations, however, have been completely altered by de Bry. While Mascoming's location is probably not too far off, Warowtani and Cautaking are placed far up the Chowan River and deep into Chawanoac territory.

It seems fairly clear, then, that Okisko's Weapemeoc territory, while probably never well understood by the English in 1585–6, was somewhat inflated by de Bry, particularly to the north and west. The undeveloped depiction of the river mouths along the north shore of Albemarle Sound on both maps indicates that the English did not explore the present-day North, Pasquotank, and Little Rivers at all, and knew little or nothing of the vast territory

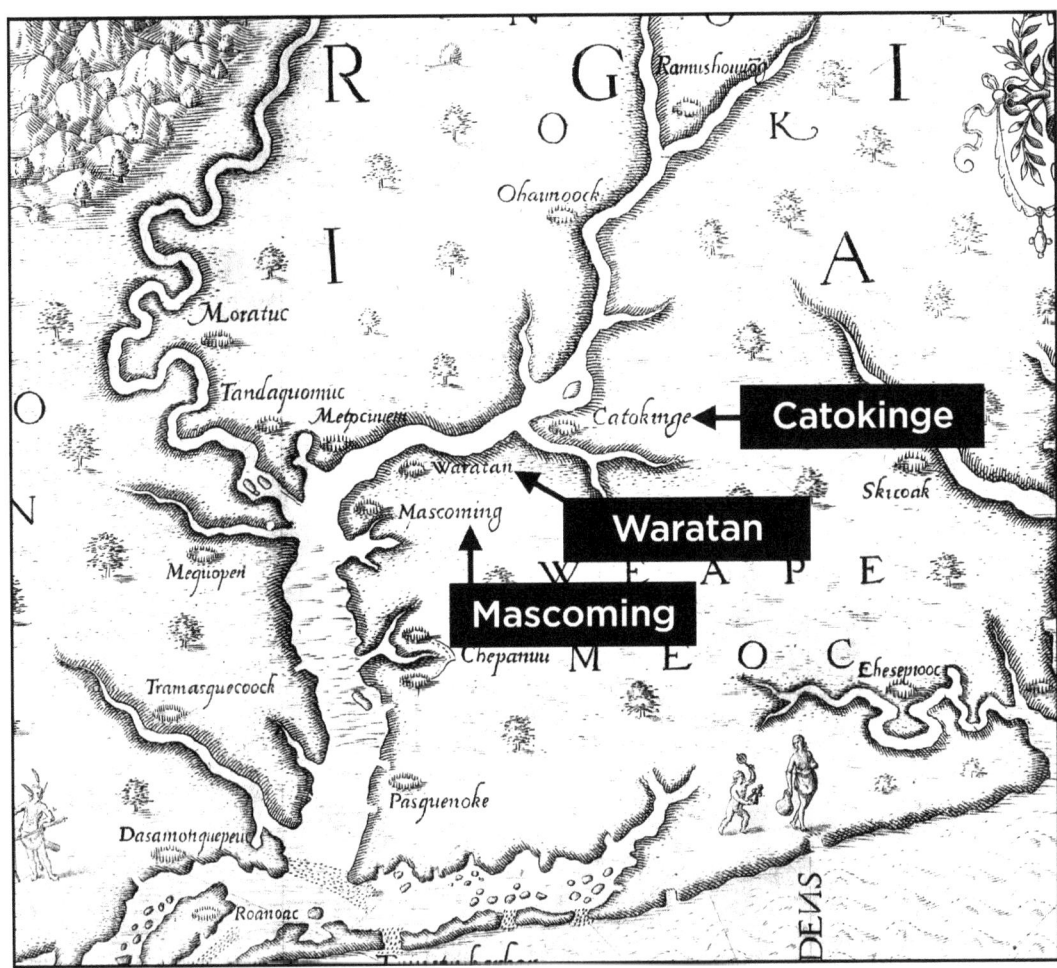

Portion of de Bry's map with misplaced Weapemeoc villages.

labeled "Weapemeoc." De Bry's map also gives the erroneous impression that "Skicoak" and "Chesepioock," two large villages in the "Territorie of the Chesepians," were in Weapemeoc territory.

Lane's account is conspicuously deficient in recounting the months that followed the Amadas exploration of Albemarle Sound in August of 1585, when the English first made contact with Okisko and the Weapemeocs. By the time his narrative picks up again in March of 1586, relations between the English and almost all the surrounding tribes had dramatically deteriorated. As mentioned, the occurrences of hostilities and conflicts with the Indians that had taken place in the fall and winter of 1585–6 were most likely removed from Lane's narrative so that Raleigh's future recruitment efforts would not be adversely affected. When Lane's account resumed in early March of 1586, Wingina had already changed his name to Pemisapan upon the death of his brother Granganimeo, and he was in the process of organizing a great coalition of tribes for the purpose of destroying the English. Menatonon's Chawanoacs and Okisko's Weapemeocs were part of that coalition, at least up to March, when Lane's actions at Chawanoac complicated matters.

In early March 1586, Lane made his unexpected visit to the village of Chawanoac, where an assembly of representatives from the Moratuc, Mangoak, and Weapemeoc tribes had gathered to make preparations for Pemisapan's plan to unite the tribes against the English. Lane and a force of about fifty men dispersed the meeting and apprehended the Chawanoac weroance, Menatonon, holding him prisoner "for two dayes." It was during those two days of captivity that Menatonon told Lane about a place called Chaunis Temoatan far up the Moratuc River where a precious mineral called "wassador" could be found. "A ransome [was] agreed for" the release of Menatonon, but much to his dismay Lane then took "yong Skiko, the King of Chawanooks sonne of my prisoner." Lane sent Skiko back to Roanoke Island to be imprisoned there, while he and about forty of his men proceeded up the Moratuc in search of Chaunis Temoatan. In the meantime Pemisapan arranged with the Moratuc tribe, who dwelt along the river, to remove themselves and their food supplies from their villages as the English ascended the river. According to Pemisapan's plan, the English would be unable to replenish their dwindling provisions and would eventually be faced with starvation. By the time they reached Mangoak territory, the English would be easy prey for the Indians who waited to ambush them.

Pemisapan's plan ultimately failed. Lane and his men barely made it back down the river, only after subsisting on boiled sassafras leaves and the two English mastiffs Lane had brought along. As they neared the mouth of the Moratuc River, a storm delayed their progress for a day, and as soon as it passed they entered Albemarle Sound. Lane immediately headed for Okisko's villages expecting that the Weapemeocs would provide much needed sustenance, but he found that the villages had also been deserted and their food stores removed, persuasive evidence that Okisko had also been part of Pemisapan's plan at least as early as March. At the abandoned Weapemeoc village of Chepanoc, however, Lane and his men were fortunate to find some fish in the weirs and were able to reach Roanoke Island the next morning.

The safe return of Lane's expedition put a temporary halt to Pemisapan's plan to unite a great coalition of tribes to destroy the English. In fact it actually restrained Menatonon and, as a result, Okisko from any further active participation. Okisko, it seems, was in some manner subordinate to Menatonon, the chief weroance of the powerful Chawanoac tribe at this time. A few days after Lane's safe return to Roanoke Island, a messenger came from Menatonon accompanied by twenty-four of Okisko's "principallest men." In what was apparently a remarkable attempt to obtain his son's release, Menatonon had "commaunded Okisko King of Weopomiok, to yeelde himselfe seruant, and homager, to the great Weroanza [Queen Elizabeth] of England, and after her to Sir Walter Raleigh."[10] Although Okisko did not appear in person, he sent his 24 representatives, Lane wrote, "to let mee knowe that from that time forwarde, hee, and his successours were to acknowledge her Maiestie their onely Soueraigne, and next vnto her, as is aforesayd."[11]

After the death on April 20 of old Ensenore, Pemisapan resumed his plans to consolidate the tribes against the English. He moved his base of operations to Dasamonquepeuc on the mainland, and commanded that the Indians deny all requests for food to the English at Roanoke. Pemisapan also sent messengers to the Mangoaks and—interestingly—to Okisko's Weapemeocs as well, to begin preparations to assemble at Dasamonquepeuc at a day to be determined for the annihilation of the English. As mentioned above, according to Lane the Mangoaks and Weapemeocs combined would be able to assemble "the number of 7. or 8. hundreth bowes, to enterprise the matter thus to be ordered [Pemisapan's coalition]." If half that number were to be assigned to Okisko's Weapemeocs, it would suggest a fighting force of about 375 warriors.

Lane claimed that at about this time he tried...

> to haue relied my selfe with Menatonon, and the Chaonists, who in trueth as they are more valiant people and in greater number then the rest, so are they more faithfull in their promises, and since my late being there had giuen many tokens of earnest desire they had to ioyne in perfect league with vs, and therefore were greatly offended with Pemisapan and Weopomeiok [Okisko] for making him beleeue such tales of vs.[12]

Lane's remarks regarding Menatonon are rather disingenuous. While it is true that Menatonon sent Lane a "certaine pearle for a present," forced Okisko to pledge fidelity to Queen Elizabeth, and may have paid lip service to Lane, none of this was done out of affection for the English or an "earnest desire" to join them. Menatonon had but one purpose in mind, and all his efforts were aimed at achieving that goal: the safe return of his son, Skiko, whom Lane had threatened at one point "to cut off his head."

It may seem odd that Pemisapan would send word to the Weapemeocs to join his coalition, particularly after Okisko had vowed his allegiance to Queen Elizabeth. In reality, however, it seems that Okisko's pledge was a personal one which applied only to him "and his successours" and possibly as well to the 24 representatives he had sent to Lane. Okisko's promise had apparently imposed no obligation on the rest of the Weapemeoc tribe, who retained a hostile stance toward the English and a willingness to join Pemisapan. Such a dichotomy between a principal weroance and a large segment of his tribe was unusual, but not entirely unheard of. By March of 1586, for example, there had been considerable opposition by a portion of the Roanoac tribe to Pemisapan's call for the elimination of the English. Nevertheless, Pemisapan's influence and authority was far more extensive and recognized than Okisko's, who may have been somewhat undermined by his compliant relationship with Menatonon, the reasons for which are not known.

It is far more likely, though, that the somewhat limited extent of Okisko's authority was a factor of Weapemeoc tribal organization, and not due to a specific event or a personal setback or conflict with Menatonon. As mentioned, unlike other Algonquian tribal groups such as perhaps the Chawanoacs and certainly the later Powhatan confederacy ruled by Wahunsunacock, the Weapemeoc tribe probably consisted of a loose alliance of villages each of which exercised a certain degree of autonomy. In such a case Okisko may have been the foremost weroance among the various villages of the Weapemeoc, but could not exercise complete control over them. This would go a long way in explaining why the majority of Weapemeocs were not bound by Okisko's pledge, and why many chose to join Pemisapan's coalition.

Pemisapan's efforts to form a coalition of tribes to fall upon and destroy the English may have succeeded, were it not for the fact that his plans were covertly divulged to Lane. In the end Lane averted Pemisapan's assault by launching a preemptive attack at Dasamonquepeuc before the coalition had assembled, during which Pemisapan and a number of his principal followers were killed. At the time, the majority of Weapemeocs were making final preparations to cross Albemarle Sound and merge with Pemisapan's coalition, under the guise of paying their respects to Ensenore. As for Okisko, he remained true to his pledge and would not join the coalition. He "did immediatly retire himselfe" with his followers further into the mainland, and there he and his Weapemeoc tribe disappear from the historical record.

Nothing is known about Okisko's successor or the plight of the Weapemeoc tribe until the middle of the 17th century, when settlers, trappers, and traders began venturing southward from Virginia. As this influx progressed, the name of the Weapemeoc tribe was recorded in the early documents as "Yeopim" or "Yawpin" or other phonetically similar variants as the new Virginia settlers elided the Algonquian "-eoc" suffix. In 1660 early settler Nathaniel Batts purchased land on the west bank of the Pasquotank River from "King" Kiscutanewh of the Yeopim Indians. Although nothing is known of the tribe prior to the migrations of settlers such as Batts, the naming of the rivers and the early Albemarle precincts support the proposition that the Weapemeoc tribe had consisted of semi-autonomous sub-tribes, certainly predating the arrival of the settlers in the mid–17th century and possibly dating back seventy years to the Roanoke voyages. The Yeopim, Pasquotank, and Perquimans Rivers and Currituck Sound were all named after the tribes found inhabiting those areas, as were the Albemarle precincts of Currituck, Pasquotank, and Perquimans.

By the early eighteenth century just two of these sub-tribes seem to have retained separate identities, the Yeopim and the Poteskeet.[13] Pressured by the continuing encroachment of settlers from the north, the Poteskeet, now tributaries of North Carolina, began selling off parcels of land and eventually merged with the Yeopim. In 1731 Governor George Burrington listed only twenty "Pottaskite" families remaining in North Carolina.[14] The Yeopim, in the meantime, also tributaries of North Carolina, were assigned a sixteen-square-mile reservation on the North River in the Currituck Precinct. Like the Poteskeet, the Yeopim began selling off parcels of land in 1724 and by mid-century the last vestiges of the Yeopim tribe disappeared from the historical record. The site of the former Yeopim reservation continued to appear on colonial maps such as Edward Moseley's 1733 "New and Correct Map of the Province of North Carolina" as "Yawpim," and that location is still known as "Indiantown" today.

Osacan

Osacan (also spelled Osocon) was one of the leading Roanoac Indians, a weroance in his own right, and one of Pemisapan's principal lieutenants and accomplices in the plot to destroy the English. In March of 1586, when it was mistakenly thought that Lane's expedition had been wiped out on the Moratuc River, Osacan participated in Pemisapan's plan to starve the remaining Englishmen at Roanoke Island by denying them corn and by refusing to build weirs for them. Lane specifically mentioned Osacan by name as one of the "great enemies about Pemisapan" who had become a committed foe of the English after the deaths of his brother Granganimeo, probably in the fall of 1585, and his father Ensenore in April 1586. Osacon subsequently assisted Pemisapan in his plan to unite a great coalition of tribes for the purpose of annihilating the English.

Osacan was apparently involved in an attempt to free the young Chawanoac Indian, Skiko, from captivity by the English at the Roanoke fort. The Chawanoacs were allied with Pemisapan, but their active participation in the plan to destroy the English was effectively prevented because Lane had imprisoned Menatonon's "best beloued sonne," Skiko, at Roanoke, where he "laid him in the bylboes [leg irons], and once threatened to cut off his head after he attempted to escape. A number of Pemisapan's followers visited Skiko and, assuming that he supported the alliance against the English, kept him informed about their progress. Osacan was probably one of these, and on May 31, 1586, the night before Lane's preemptive attack against Pemisapan at Dasamonquepeuc, Osacan attempted to free Skiko. Lane wrote that "Osocon … was conueying away my prisoner, whom I had there present tied in an hand-locke." It is not clear, though, whether Osacan actually managed to free Skiko or whether they were caught in the process. What is certain is that Lane used that story as a ruse to approach Pemisapan at Dasamonquepeuc and put him off guard, pretending that he and his men were there to complain about Osacan's actions at Roanoke the night before. When everyone was in place, Lane "gaue the watch-word agreed vpon," and the assault commenced, during which Pemisapan and a number of his followers were killed.

Whether or not Osacan was successful in his attempt to free Skiko on the night of May 31, the two must have been on Roanoke Island when Lane attacked Dasamonquepeuc on the following morning of June 1. As part of Lane's plan to surprise Pemisapan, the English had forcibly and successfully guarded the shoreline, preventing any Indians from leaving Roanoke Island for Dasamonquepeuc the night before the attack. Consequently, it is a virtual certainty that Osacan could not have been killed or injured during Lane's assault at Dasamonquepeuc the next day. Assuming he was not captured or killed at Roanoke afterwards, he very likely would have joined with Wanchese and Pemisapan's former followers at Dasamonquepeuc. As one of the few surviving Roanoac weroances, Osacan may well have assumed a leadership role there, and as such he probably would have been involved in the decision to evacuate Dasamonquepeuc after the killing of colonist George Howe on July 28, 1587. At that time all the former supporters of Pemisapan left Dasamonquepeuc and withdrew farther inland.

Pemisapan

Pemisapan was the name taken by the Roanoac weroance, Wingina, after the death of his brother, Granganimeo, probably in November of 1585. The name "Pemisapan" is said to translate from the Algonquian as "a wolf who watches from a distance." (See the *Wingina* entry.)

Piemacum

Piemacum was the principal weroance of the Pomouik tribe—later to be known as the Pamlico Indians—who dwelt in the territory between the Pamlico and Neuse Rivers in present-day Beaufort and Pamlico Counties. The name "Piemacum" is believed to be a combination of two Algonquian forms meaning "to twist" or "throw around" plus "a body of water," suggesting that his name could be translated as "he who churns up the water."[1] Piemacum is identified in Barlowe's account of the 1584 reconnaissance voyage as the king "of a countrey called Pomouik." Piemacum's people were referred to by the same name, "Pomouiks," and his main village was written as "Panauuaioc" on the 1590 White/de Bry engraved map, spelled "Pananuaioc" by Hakluyt in 1589, and was written as "Pananaioc," "Pananiock," and "Panawicke" two decades later by the Jamestown chroniclers.[2] All of these were late 16th and early 17th century spelling variations for the same principal town within the territory ruled by Piemacum and located south of the Pamlico River.

The multiple spelling variations are responsible for a number of significant errors in later published historical texts whose authors have confused Piemacum's village—as noted above, spelled "Panauuaioc," "Pananuaioc," "Pananaioc," "Pananiock," and "Panawicke"—with the Secotan village of "Pomeiock," which had entirely different tribal allegiances and was located a considerable distance to the northeast of Piemacum's realm. An early example of such confusion appeared in a 1907 publication by Hamilton McMillan, who wrote, "The name Pananiock is variously spelled. On DeBry's map of Lane's expedition it is spelled Pomeiock and located between Lake Paquipe or Mattamuskeet and Pamlico Sound and in the present county of Hyde."[3] Virginia scholar Lyon Gardiner Tyler, editor of the *Narratives of Early Virginia*, correctly noted in 1907—the same year that McMillan's erroneous statement was published—that Panawicke/Pananiock was "The Panauuaioc of Hakluyt and of DeBry's map."[4]

The confusion over these names has persisted since McMillan's error in 1907, even in otherwise reliable sources, which include such statements as "His [Wingina's] enemy, Piemacum, ruled from Pomeioc"[5]; "Piemacum, the leading weroance at Pomeiooc"[6]; "Pomeiooc (as scholars now spell it) was a palisaded town in the Outer Banks whose *weroance*, or chief, was Piemacum"[7]; and "The next day they arrived at Pomeiooc, home of the weroance Piemacum."[8] As noted, however, Pananaioc—with its spelling variations—was a completely different and distant village from Pomeiock and had opposing affiliations. As shown on the map below, "Pananaioc" was the early 16th century spelling used by Jamestown's John Smith for the village of the Pomouik tribe, which had been ruled by Piemacum in 1584, and located in present-day Beaufort County. "Pomeiock" was located far to the northeast in present-day Hyde County (north is to the right).

On the more familiar 1590 de Bry engraving of John White's map (p. 134), Piemacum's

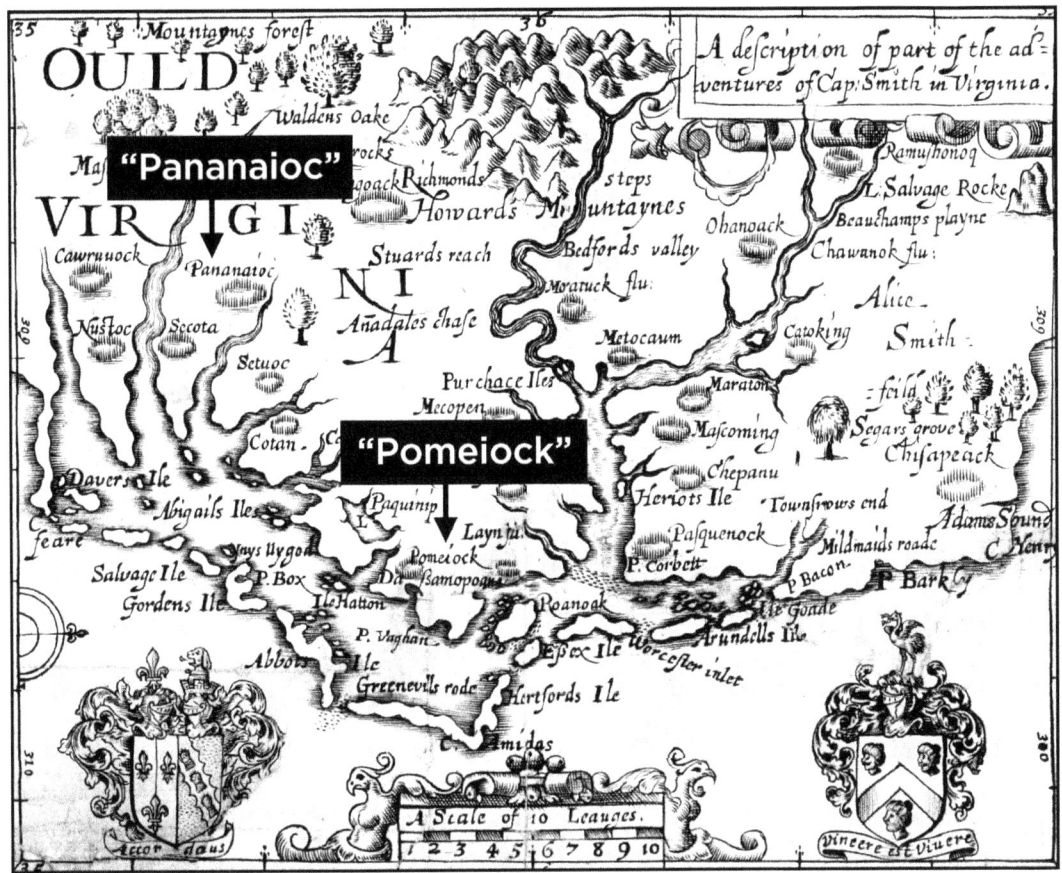

John Smith's 1624 map of "Ould Virginia" showing the locations of Pananaioc and Pomeiock.

village was written as "Panauuaioc" and, as Barlowe wrote, "the countrey called Pomouik, belong[ed] to another king whom they call Piamacum."[9] His people were the Pomouik tribe, and his main village of Pananaioc—with its spelling variations—was located somewhere south of the Pamlico River on the White/de Bry map. Pomeiock was a distant Secotan village near present-day Lake Mattamuskeet in Hyde County. In all the villages located in the large area labeled "Secotan"—including Pomeiock—"there remaineth a mortall malice … for many iniuries and slaughters done vpon them by this Piemacum."

The greater problem with confusing these two villages is the impact that it could have, or has had, on the specific portion of the historical record dealing with the Anglo-Algonquian contact period. It has resulted, for example, in misunderstandings concerning the English activities in Pamlico Sound during Sir Richard Grenville's weeklong excursion from July 11 to July 18, 1585. In the case of Piemacum such errors distort his historical role, incorrectly portraying him as the weroance of a distant Secotan village hostile to his own Pomouik tribe, and leading to the erroneous assumption that Piemacum interacted with Grenville and his men when they visited Pomeiock on July 12. John White visited and sketched the village of Pomeiock on July 12 during Grenville's excursion, *not* the Pomouik village of Panauuaiock. Likewise, neither White nor any of Grenville's party ever met Piamacum, as is sometimes mistakenly claimed, nor did they ever visited his Pomouik village of Panauuaiock.

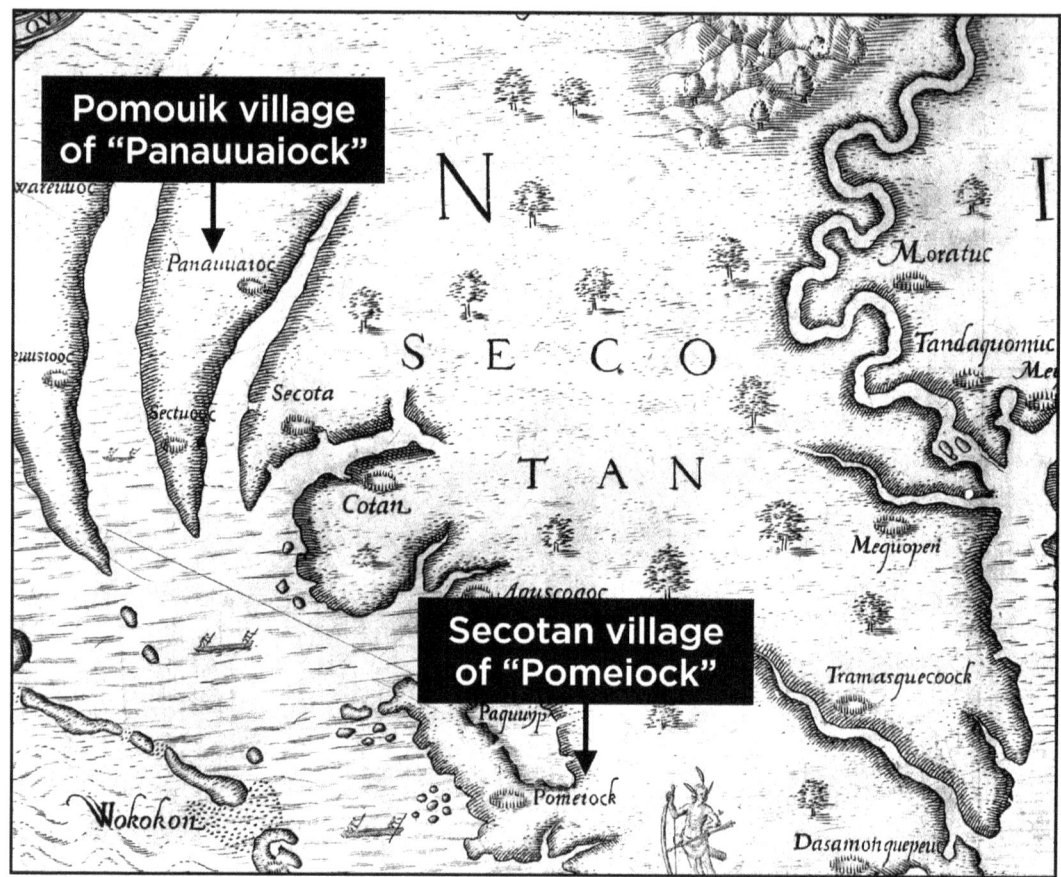

Portion of the 1590 de Bry map showing locations of Piemacum's village of Panauuaiock and the village of Pomeiock.

Piemacum's Pomouik tribe was geographically unique in that it represented the extreme southernmost extension of the Algonquian language group.[10] Anthropologist Frank Speck, specialist in the Algonquian and Iroquoian peoples, wrote that the Carolina Algonquians were comparatively recent intruders into the region and formed the last offshoot of the general Algonquian migration southward from Canada along the Atlantic Coast.[11] Because of their southernmost geographic location in the area between the Pamlico and Neuse Rivers, the Algonquian Pomouiks bordered directly on Iroquoian territory perhaps to their south and definitely to their west. To the immediate south were the Neusiok, who dwelt on the south side of the lower Neuse River in present-day Carteret and Craven Counties. The language affiliation of the Neusiok tribe has not been definitively identified. It was once thought that the Neusioks were Algonquian, although ethnologists now generally hold that they were Iroquoian. To the immediate west of the Pomouiks were the Iroquoian Tuscarora, known to the English as Mangoaks, who occupied the upper Neuse River at that time and were frequently at war with the tribes closer to the coast.

It was perhaps due to this close proximity to Iroquoian groups, and the inevitable interactions that must have occurred, that a mutually cooperative alliance eventually formed between the Pomouiks and their Iroquoian neighbors. What is known for certain is that by 1584 Piemacum was "in league with the next king adioyning towards the setting of the

Sunne, and the countrey Newsiok, situate vpon a goodly riuer called Neus."[12] It is known, too, that Piemacum had been involved in a "mortall warre" with Wingina and the Secotans for a number of years prior to the arrival of the English in 1584, and, as mentioned above, that "there remaineth a mortall malice in the Secotanes, for many iniuries and slaughters done vpon them by this Piemacum." The worst of these "iniuries and slaughters" had occurred just two years earlier. As it was related to the English, it seems that a peace had been arranged between Piemacum and the "Lord of Secotan." To celebrate the event Piemacum "inuited diuers men, and thirtie women of the best of his countrey to their towne to a feast: and when they were altogether merry, and praying before their Idol, the captaine or Lord of the town came suddenly vpon them, and slewe them euery one, reseruing the women and children,"[13] as was the custom in intertribal warfare.

Although Piemacum is not mentioned in the subsequent accounts of Raleigh's colonization attempts, he may have played an important role during the selection of a relocation site on the mainland for John Whte's 1587 colonists. It will be recalled that the 1587 colonists had originally intended to settle to the north of Roanoke Island at the Chesapeake Bay, but—as has been proposed—the plan had to be aborted when the English learned that the Spanish knew about their intentions and were actively searching for them at the Chesapeake.[14] As a result the colonists landed instead at the familiar Roanoke Island, the site of the 1585–6 settlement attempt, and they wintered there while considering alternative settlement locations. The old settlement structures and fort were located there, and, most importantly, Roanoke was situated inside the barrier island chain and was shielded from Spanish ships patrolling the coast.

The stay at Roanoke Island was intended to be temporary, while a permanent settlement location could be found and prepared on the mainland. The colonists repaired the old settlement buildings at Roanoke, fortified and enclosed them with a strong palisade, and spent the winter there. At the same time the colonists, no doubt with the help of the Croatoan Indian Manteo, explored the mainland for a good settlement site, which had to be readily accessible by way of a navigable inlet for John White's return with supplies and additional colonists, as well as for future resupply and commerce with England. Their survival as a viable colony depended upon their anticipated regular contact with supply ships from England. Obviously this could only be accomplished if their mainland settlement location was accessible for re-supply. Accessibility to a settlement site on the mainland depended entirely on its proximity to one of the inlets along the barrier islands. Once the Chesapeake location had been eliminated, the deepest and most stable inlet to be found on the Outer Banks was at Wokokon, present-day Ocracoke. All the other existing inlets along the coast were too shallow to allow access to the sounds in anything but small vessels, a problem which the English had experienced since the first colonization attempt in 1585. Present-day Pamlico or southern Beaufort County, the territory of Piemacum, is directly west of the Ocracoke Inlet and may have been a logical geographic choice for the new settlement location.

The dramatic shift in Anglo-Indian relations between 1584 and 1587 may also have contributed to the selection of Pomouik as a mainland settlement site. During the span of the Roanoke voyages the English had the most frequent contact with the Secotan tribal group, whose large territory extended from Albemarle Sound to the border of Piemacum's domain near the Pamlico River. The cordial reception extended by the Secotans to the Amadas-Barlowe expedition in 1584 appeared to foreshadow a mutually beneficial alliance in the years to come. The English were seen by the Secotans as not only a source of valuable trade goods, but also as a potentially powerful ally. It was even hoped at the time that the

English might be "perswaded ... to surprize Piemacum [in] his towne, [and] that there will be found in it great store of commodities."

By 1587, however, the earlier promise of a beneficial relationship between the Secotans and the English had been completely shattered. The 1585–6 colonization attempt at Roanoke Island was marked by escalating hostilities, which ultimately led to Pemisapan's conspiracy against the English, Lane's surprise attack at Dasamonquepeuc, the beheading of Pemisapan, and the evacuation of Roanoke by the English in 1586. The contingent of men stationed by Grenville at Roanoke shortly thereafter was attacked and driven from the island by a combined force of Secotans from the villages of Aquascogoc, Secota, and Dasamonquepeuc. On August 1, 1587, not long after White's colony arrived at Roanoke Island, colonist George Howe was killed by a group of Pemisapan's former followers. By that time the Secotans were dedicated foes of the English. It would have been inconceivable, therefore, for the English to consider establishing a new mainland settlement anywhere on the Secotan mainland. Consequently, once that large hostile region was eliminated as a possible settlement location, a viable option could have been the area south of the Pamlico River where Piemacum and the Pomouiks dwelt. As noted, Pomouik had the added geographic benefit of being close to the most accessible inlet along the Outer Banks: Wokokon.

Little is known with certainty about the activities of Piemacum and the Pomouiks other than the fact that they had already been engaged in that "mortall warre" with Wingina and the Secotan tribes for a number of years prior to the arrival of the English in 1584. By 1587, though, a virtual state of war now existed between the Secotans and the English. The only trusted allies the English could rely upon at that time were Manteo and his small tribe at Croatoan on the Outer Banks, where, White wrote, "is the place where Manteo was borne, and the Sauages of the Iland our friends." Manteo, in fact, would have been an essential asset during the discussions about a mainland settlement site, and he undoubtedly acted as guide and emissary as they explored potential locations. Because the Croatoans dwelt farther to the south on the Outer Banks, they very likely would have had some affiliation with their coastal neighbors. One of these neighboring tribes was the Coree, who are believed to have been related to the Neusioks, who in turn are known to have been allied with Piemacum and his Pomouiks against the Secotans. Consequently, by 1587 the opportunity may have existed for a beneficial partnership among those four tribes *and* the colonists. The Neusioks, Pomouiks, Corees, Croatoans, and the 1587 colonists all would have shared a common enemy: the hostile Secotan tribes north of the Pamlico River.

It seems possible, then, that with the help of Manteo an arrangement could have been made with Piemacum for the colony to settle somewhere on the Pomouik peninsula between the Pamlico and Neuse Rivers. Geographically that area would have been uniquely positioned to satisfy the colonists' concerns in 1587–8. It was sheltered from Spanish ships patrolling the coastline, and also separated from the hostile Secotan tribes to the north. Equally important, it was accessible for future re-supply via the Wokokon inlet, the only proven navigable channel into Pamlico Sound. We know that the colonists dismantled their dwellings at Roanoke and transported them for reassembly at the new settlement. The relocation probably took place in stages, and it very likely was accomplished by March of 1588 in time for the first planting in April. Before the final departure from Roanoke Island, the colonists left carved messages behind directing White to Croatoan upon his expected return in the early summer with fresh supplies and additional colonists. From there they would have been escorted through the Wokokon inlet to the new settlement on the mainland.

There is some documentary evidence, recorded two decades later, supporting the proposition that the 1587 colonists may have relocated to Piemacum's Pomouik territory. In 1607 the Jamestown leaders were instructed to learn what they could about the "lost" 1587 colonists whose whereabouts were unknown after they departed from Roanoke Island. Captain John Smith inquired about this among the Powhatan Indians, who told him what their oral tradition recalled of "clothed men." In his *A True Relation*, published in 1608, Smith wrote that "We had agreed with the king of Paspahegh [Wowinchopunck] to conduct two of our men to a place called Panawicke beyond Roanoke, where he reported many men to be apparelled."[15] A similar reference was repeated in a notation on a 1607–8 rough and geographically confusing drawing of the mainland (called the Zúñiga Map after the Spanish ambassador who obtained possession of it) next to the location marked "Pananiock." The notation read, "here the King of Paspahegh reported our men to be and wants to go." The map was probably drawn by Jamestown colonist John Martin and demonstrates how unfamiliar the 1607 colonists were with the territory south of Jamestown.

Another notation written next to a location called "Warraskoyack" on the map read, "here [the king of] Paspahegh and 2 of our own men landed to go to Pananiock." Warraskoyack was a village bordering the lower James River where the planned expedition to Pananiock/Panawicke was supposed to have commenced. There can be no doubt that these were references to the principal town located in the territory of the Pomouik between the Pamlico and Neuse Rivers, and ruled by Piemacum during the Roanoke voyages. John Smith's own map of "Ould Virginia," published in his 1624 *Generall Historie* (shown earlier), accurately placed Pananaioc at that location. As mentioned, it has been firmly established that Pananiock, Panawicke, Pananaioc, Panauuaioc, and Pananuaioc were all spelling variations of Piemacum's main village.

Unfortunately, the planned trip to Pananiock was never completed. All that is known is what Smith wrote about Wowinchopunck, the king or leading weroance of the Paspahegh, that he, "playing the villaine, and deluding us for rewards, returned within three or foure dayes after, without going further," and Panawicke/Pananiock was not mentioned again. Relations with Wowinchopunck and his Paspahegh tribe had been strained since the English first arrived in May of 1607. The English had established their new colony of Jamestown in Paspahegh territory, and this was considered by Wowinchopunck to be a blatant encroachment upon his domain. Two weeks after the English arrived the Paspahegh

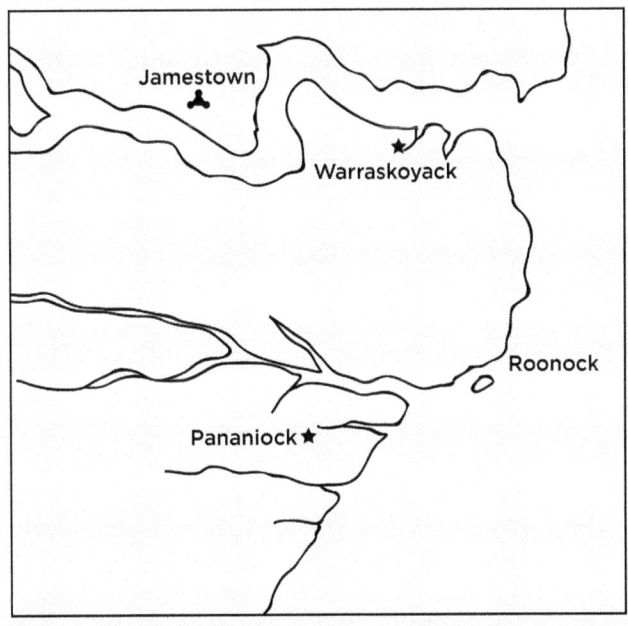

Author's rendition of the portion of the Zúñiga Map showing the relative locations of Jamestown, "Roonock" (Roanoke Island), Pananiock, and Warraskoyack).

attacked Jamestown, but were repulsed. Later Smith traded for corn on several occasions with the Paspahegh, but their dealings were always marked with suspicion, and he considered them a "churlish and trecherous nation." Smith also learned from other surrounding tribes "that [the] Paspahegh … did hate us, and intended some mischief." Smith probably dismissed the entire report about "apparalled" men at Pananiock as nothing more than a ploy conceived by the villainous Wowinchopunck for no other reason than to obtain "rewards" from the English. It is also possible, though, that Wowinchopunck realized it would be unwise and dangerous to risk contact by the Jamestown colonists with other troublesome Englishmen to the south.

Of course by early 1608 when John Smith was recording the information about the men "apparalled" at Pananiock, the colonists had been missing for two decades. Assuming Wowinchopunck's information was accurate, it was certainly not current, and may have recalled events from 1588, when the colonists occupied their new settlement to the south of Roanoke. All that can probably be concluded is that English colonists may have been at Pananiock twenty years earlier, when Piemacum ruled, but one can only speculate about whether or not any signs of the colonists would have remained there in 1608. What can be said with confidence is that—other than the English who were involved in the Roanoke voyages—there were no Europeans on the mainland bordering Pamlico Sound from 1584 to 1608, when Smith's *A True Relation* and the Zúñiga Map were composed. The failure to complete the trip to Pananiock may not only have been a missed opportunity to learn about the missing colonists, but also to shed some light on the elusive activities and history of the tribes surrounding Pamlico Sound after 1587, the Pomouiks in particular.

Much of that obscurity results from the fact that the area south of the Pamlico River remained largely unknown and unexplored for a century after the Roanoke voyages. Settlement did not begin at the upper reaches of the Pamlico River until more than 100 years after John White's last voyage to Roanoke Island in 1590, and it was not until the early 1700s that settlement started in present-day Beaufort and Pamlico counties, traditional lands of the Pomouiks who were once ruled by Piemacum. Nothing else in known about Piemacum or his successors, but later documents recorded the condition and decline of Piemacum's once formidable Pomouik tribe.

In 1696–97 a smallpox epidemic spread rapidly from Virginia and decimated a number of Carolina tribes, one of those being the Pomouiks, who by this time were called the Pemlicoes or Pampticoughs. English colonial Governor John Archdale wrote, "When I was in the North about eleven Years since [1696], I was told then of a great Mortality that fell upon the Pemlicoe Indians."[16] Explorer John Lawson reported that by 1700 the "Pampticough Indians" had been reduced to just fifteen fighting men and lived in one village on an island in the "Pampticough River." In 1711, the remaining Pamlicos joined the Tuscaroras and several other tribes in a surprise attack on the encroaching North Carolina settlements and initiated what would afterwards be called the Tuscarora War, the bloodiest Indian war in North Carolina history. By the time it was over four years later, thousands of Indians had been killed and a few tribes—including the Pamlicos—disappeared from the historical record.

Piemacum's name briefly survived in the historical record, but only in summaries of the 1584 Amadas-Barlowe expedition, such as was included in John Smith's 1624 *Generall Historie of Virginia*, in which the Pomouik chief's name is spelled "Piamacum" and "Pieneacum." Although Piemacum's name has otherwise faded from history, his tribe's name endures in the Pamlico River and Pamlico Sound into which it flows, as well as the later formation of Pamlico County, carved out of Craven and Beaufort Counties in 1872.

Pooneno

Pooneno, also spelled Pooneho, was a weroance mentioned only briefly in one of the Roanoke accounts, that of Arthur Barlowe's narrative of the reconnaissance voyage sent out by Raleigh in 1584. Pooneno appears in the following somewhat confused description of what Barlowe understood from the Indians about the geography, villages, and "Lords" on the mainland beyond the Outer Banks:

> "Beyond this Island [Roanoke] there is the maine lande, and ouer against this Island falleth into this spacious water, the great riuer called Occam [Pamlico Sound] by the inhabitants on which standeth a towne called Pomeiock; and six dayes journey from the same is situate their greatest citie, called Skicoak, which this people affirme to be very greate: but the Sauages were neuer at it, only they speake of it by the report of their fathers and other men, whom they have heard affirme it to bee aboue one houres iourney about.
> Into this riuer falleth another great riuer, called Cipo [possibly the Pamlico or Neuse River], in which there is found great store of Muskles in which there are pearles: likewise there descendeth into this Occam, another riuer, called Nomopana [either the Chowan River or Albemarle Sound or both combined], on the one side whereof standeth a great towne called Chawanook, and the Lord of that towne and countrey is called Pooneno: this Pooneho is not subject to the king of Wingandacoa [Wingina], but is a free Lord: beyond this country is there another king, whom they call Menatonon, and these three kings are in league with each other."[1]

Barlowe misunderstood some of the information he was told, particularly regarding the names of the three lords or weroances who were "in league with each other." The chief weroance of the Chawanoac tribe that dwelt along the Chowan River was Menatonon, not Pooneno. The weroance of Weapemeoc to the east of Menatonon's territory was Okisko. The king of "Wingandacoa," which Barlowe also mistakenly thought was the name of the territory south of Roanoke Island, was Wingina. Pooneno, then, was most likely the chief weroance of the Moratucs, whose villages were located along the Moratuc (present-day Roanoke) River. Pooneno, Wingina, and Menatonon, consequently, were probably the "three kings ... in league with each other." The map below shows the locations of the principal village where each of these three weroances dwelt (north is to the right).

Very little was known about the Moratucs until 1943, when anthropologist Maurice A. Mook published a paper describing them as a separate and distinct Algonquian tribe.[2] Mook not only identified their linguistic affiliation as Algonquian, but also corrected errors made by ethnographer James Mooney in 1907 about the location of the tribe on the Roanoke River and its affiliations. Based apparently on an erroneous line in John Smith's 1624 *Generall Historie*, Mooney had written, "They [the Moratucs] ... refused to hold intercourse with the English."[3] Mooney's statement, however, is contradicted by Ralph Lane's first-hand account, which refers to the Moratucs as a tribe "with whom before wee were entred into a

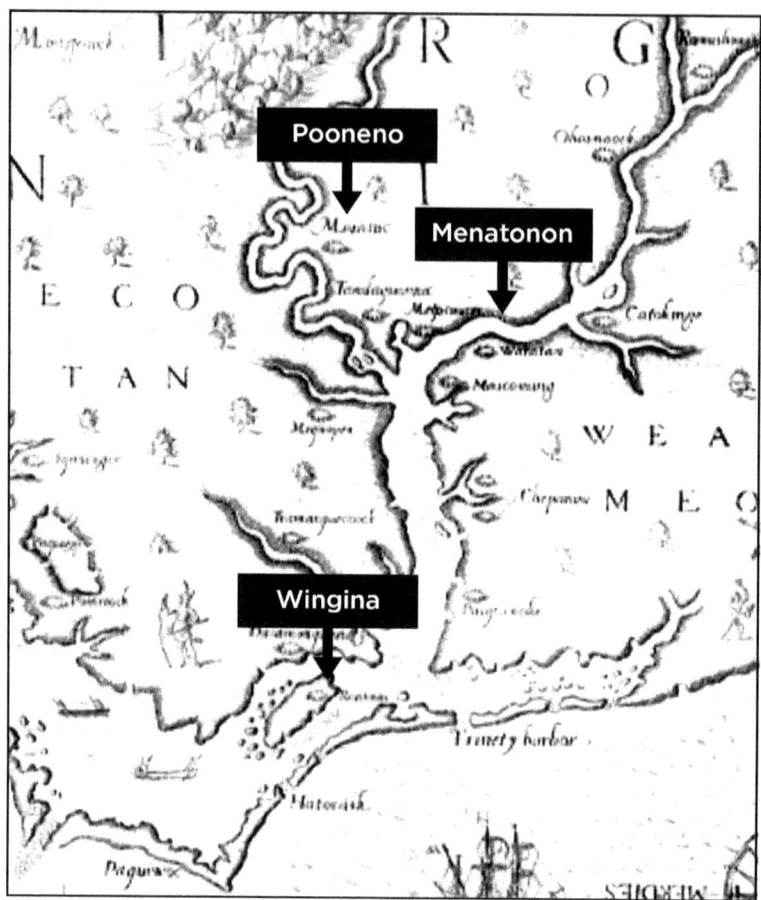

Locations of Pooneno's, Menatonon's, and Wingina's main villages.

league, and they had euer dealt kindly with vs." Of course, that had been in 1585, before friendly relations with the English had widely deteriorated.

Although Pooneno was not mentioned again by name in the Roanoke accounts, the Moratuc weroance would play a role in the later attempt to defeat Governor Ralph Lane and the English colonists who had settled on Roanoke Island in the summer of 1585. By 1586, after relations with the English had deteriorated dramatically, Wingina changed his name to Pemisapan and was in the process of assembling a coalition of tribes to destroy the English. An early opportunity came in March when Lane and about forty Englishmen attempted to ascend the Moratuc River through Pooneno's territory in search of a place called Chaunis Temoatan. The Moratuc chief agreed to have his tribesmen abandon their villages along the river, taking their food stores with them, and thus prevent Lane and his men from resupplying their dwindling provisions. In a few days the English would be nearly starved and sufficiently weakened so that by the time they had traveled far up the river, they could be massacred in a surprise attack. Although the plot initially worked as planned, the anglicized Croatoan Indian, Manteo, recognized that an ambush was imminent and warned the English off in time. Pooneno and his Moratucs apparently remained part of Pemisapan's coordinated alliance preparing to destroy the English in June, but after Pemisapan's death and Lane's departure from Roanoke Island, the Moratucs were not mentioned again in the Roanoke accounts.

"Raleigh"

"A Wynganditoian" Indian named "Raleigh" was listed in the parish register in Bideford, England, as having been baptized there on March 27, 1588. He almost certainly must have been the same Indian whom Grenville abducted in late June or early July of 1586, when he made his belated return to Roanoke Island with the supplies for Lane's colony. Grenville discovered that the fort and settlement at Roanoke were deserted—Lane had departed with Drake about two weeks earlier—and he spent some time searching the area for them. In the process Grenville found three Indians, their tribal affiliations unknown, whom he tried to take aboard his ship, but two jumped overboard and escaped. The third was taken back to Bideford, Grenville's home, where he apparently remained and may have become part of Grenville's household.

It is interesting to note that two other Indians were already in London when Grenville returned to England with "Raleigh" on December 26, 1586. These two were Manteo and Towaye, who was most likely one of Manteo's Croatoan tribesmen. They had come to England with Lane when he evacuated Roanoke. Although Bideford is located in southwest England nearly 200 miles from London, there is a slight possibility that the Indian "Raleigh" could have seen or even interacted with the two Croatoans at some point. Grenville is known to have been in London shortly after his return for the specific purpose of recruiting prospective colonists for Sir Walter Raleigh's next venture.[1] It is not impossible that Grenville could have used the Indian "Raleigh" for promotional purposes in that recruitment process, just as Raleigh had done with Manteo and Wanchese prior to the 1585 colonization attempt.

In any case the same "Raleigh" who was baptized at Bideford in 1588 was also named on the parish list of "Burynges" in 1589: "Rawly A man of Wynganditoia the vii day of Aprile sepultus fuit [was buried]."[2]

Skiko

Skiko (also spelled Skyco) was the young son of Menatonon, the principal weroance of the powerful Chawanoac tribe that dwelt along the Chowan River. At some point before the arrival of the English, Skiko had been held prisoner for a time by the Mangoaks (also spelled Mangoags, Mandoags), an Iroquoian tribe dwelling farther inland to the west of the Chawanoacs. "Mangoaks" was a term used by the Algonquians to refer to that tribe, and the name is believed to translate as "rattlesnakes."[1] Skiko would also spend several months in 1586 as a prisoner of the English at Roanoke Island, and his captivity there directly affected intertribal alliances and Anglo-Indian relations.

Skiko was first mentioned by name in Ralph Lane's account of the 1585–6 colonization attempt, when Lane made a surprise visit at Chawanoac in early March of 1586 and interrupted an assembly of weroances being conducted by Menatonon. By that time relations with the English had seriously deteriorated, and the Roanoac weroance, Pemisapan, was in the process of organizing a coalition of tribes to eliminate them. The purpose of Menatonon's assembly, it seems, was to coordinate plans among the various tribal weroances who were "preparing to come vpon vs at Roanoak." Lane and his men scattered the assembly and took Menatonon prisoner.

During his two days of captivity the Chawanoac weroance provided Lane with information about potential sources of the valuable material sought after by the English. One of these was located a good distance to the northeast, where the weroance "had so greate quantitie of Pearle … that it is a wonder to see."[2] Another was a place called Chaunis Temoatan, where a precious metal called wassador could be found. "Of this mettall the Mangoaks haue so great store," Menatonon told Lane, "that they beautify their houses with greate plates of the same." This report was verified by Skiko "who also him selfe had bene prisoner with the Mangoaks, and set downe all the particularities to me before mentioned." Chaunis Temoatan was located in Mangoak territory, Lane was told, which could be reached by boat up the Moratuc River. One can only wonder whether these stories were intentionally embellished by Menatonon and Skiko to lure Lane and his men away from Chawanoac, particularly in light of what happened during Lane's subsequent expedition.

After receiving "a ransome agreed for," Lane released Menatonon and prepared two boats to ascend the Moratuc with forty men in search of Chaunis Temoatan. Unexpectedly, however, Lane seized Skiko and sent him aboard the pinnace back to Roanoke Island, where he was imprisoned. In the meantime Lane proceeded up the Moratuc and nearly fell victim to a plot arranged by Pemisapan, whereby the Moratucs would deny them food along the way until they or the Mangoaks finally fell upon the weakened group of Englishmen. The attack was averted and Lane's half-starved troop managed to make it back to Roanoke on April 4.

Lane's surprising survival caused Pemisapan to temporarily suspend his plans to destroy the English, and Skiko's imprisonment prevented Menatonon from participating in any action that might further endanger "his best beloued sonne." Just a few days later Menatonon sent an emissary to Lane, accompanied by twenty-four important Weapemeocs, to check on Skiko's condition and to give Lane a gift of pearls. Lane considered the pearls an attempt "for the ransome of his sonne, and therefore I refused them." The emissary then informed Lane that Menatonon—in an apparently desperate attempt to safeguard is son—had commanded Okisko, the Weapemeoc weroance, "to yeelde himselfe seruant" to Queen Elizabeth and to Raleigh. The 24 Weapemeocs were also prepared to pledge their loyalty as well "from that time forwarde."

This exceptional move on Menatonon's part, however, did nothing to persuade Lane to release Skiko. It may, in fact, have prompted Skiko's attempted escape. Although Lane did not specify the timeframe, he wrote that Skiko, "who hauing once attempted to run away, I laid him in the bylboes [leg irons], threatening to cut off his head." It was only through the request of Pemisapan, who naturally assumed Skiko was his ally against the English, that Lane was dissuaded from carrying out his threat. Historian David Quinn thought that Skiko was probably allowed to visit Pemisapan's camp "on parole,"[3] but that seems very unlikely. Lane was well aware of the high value of his hostage and the restraint it placed on Menatonon. Having already chained Skiko to the floor of his cell and threatened to execute him for attempting to escape, it does not seem remotely possible that Lane would then risk having Skiko wandering about "on parole."

It is clear that Skiko was visited occasionally by various Indians, including Pemisapan and his followers, who kept him abreast of developments in the plan to rid the land of the English. It also seems that during the course of his more than three month captivity the young Skiko was befriended by a number of the Englishmen, with whom he was soon able to communicate to some extent, and who, as Lane wrote, "made much of him." This relationship worked in Lane's favor, particularly after April 20, when old Ensenore died and Pemisapan renewed his plan to assemble a coalition of tribal forces to destroy the English. By late May the details of Pemisapan's plan had been finalized, and the assault on the English at Roanoke "was appointed the 10. of June." The plan, however, "was reueiled vnto me [Lane]" by Skiko and also by one of the Roanoac Indians.

On June 1 Lane and an armed group of men made an unexpected visit to Pemisapan at Dasamonquepeuc. The reason for the visit, Lane pretended, was to complain to him about one of his weroances, Osacan, "who the night past was conueying away my prisoner [Skiko], whom I had there present tied in an hand-locke." Lane clearly used this claim as an excuse to gain access to Pemisapan's camp, but it is not known whether or not the attempt to free Skiko the previous night was successful. In any case as soon as Lane and his men approached the camp, they launched an attack, killing Pemisapan and a number of other weroances.

Nothing else is known about Skiko. A week later Sir Francis Drake's large fleet was sighted at sea approaching the inlet at Roanoke. Given the current state of affairs at Roanoke and the fact that the future of the colony was in doubt, Lane decided to evacuate the island and return to England with Drake. In their haste to leave, a storm arose and three men were apparently left behind. It has been speculated that these three had possibly been assigned to return Skiko to Chawanoac,[4] but there is nothing in the texts to support that assumption. Decades later English settlers from Jamestown began to explore the area to the south in search of useful and marketable commodities such as "silke grasse," which was used to make cordage and rope, particularly for ships' rigging. The first verifiable contact with Chawanoac Indians by the Jamestown colonists was made in 1622 by John Pory, who ventured to the Chowan River where he traded with the Chawanoac Indians and was given a gift of copper by one of the weroances. Assuming young Skiko was about fifteen in 1586, when he was Lane's prisoner at Roanoke Island, he could hypothetically have been one of the Chawanoac weroances with whom Pory interacted in 1622.

Tarraquine

Tarraquine was the Roanoac Indian whose name was transcribed in Hakluyt's publication of Lane's account as "Tanaquiny." His name is believed to translate from the Algonquian as "sharp, pointed, or dangerous."[1] Tarraquine/Tanaquiny had attained some degree of status, possibly that of a lesser tribal weroance, and he was certainly a trusted associate of Wingina/Pemisapan, whom he strongly supported. Lane specifically referred to him as one "of our great enemies" along with Osacan and Wanchese. Tarraquine/Tanaquiny had been a leading proponent of Pemisapan's earlier plan to deny food to the English at Roanoke Island, and after the death of Ensenore on April 20, 1586, he became a major participant in Pemisapan's ambitious plot to unite the surrounding tribes against the English.

Tarraquine was mentioned as one of Pemisapan's "principall men," who, along with Andacon, was to have a specific and critical assignment in Pemisapan's strategy to annihilate the English in June of 1586. Tarraquine and Andacon were to lead a group of twenty Indians in the initial phase of the attack on the English at Roanoke. Pemisapan's plan called for the quick elimination of the leading Englishmen, and Lane was to be the first target. Tarraquine was to set Lane's reed roof afire in the middle of the night and then immediately kill him as he fled unarmed from his burning house. The plan never came to fruition, however, because Pemisapan's scheme was divulged to Lane, who launched a surprise attack at Dasamonquepeuc on June 1, killing Pemisapan and many of his followers. It is not known if Tarraquine was with Pemisapan at Dasamonquepeuc when Lane attacked, and if so, whether or not he survived.

Tetepano

Tetepano was one of three Roanoac Indians, including Cossine and Eracano, who joined Lane's expedition up the Moratuc [Roanoke] River in March of 1586 on his search for the precious metal the Indians called "wassador." These three were probably selected by Pemisapan, at least overtly to act as guides for the expedition, but they may well have been covertly sent as part of his plan to entrap and eliminate the Englishmen as they ascended the river. Pemisapan had arranged with the Moratuc weroance to remove their food supplies and abandon their villages as the expedition wound its way up the river toward

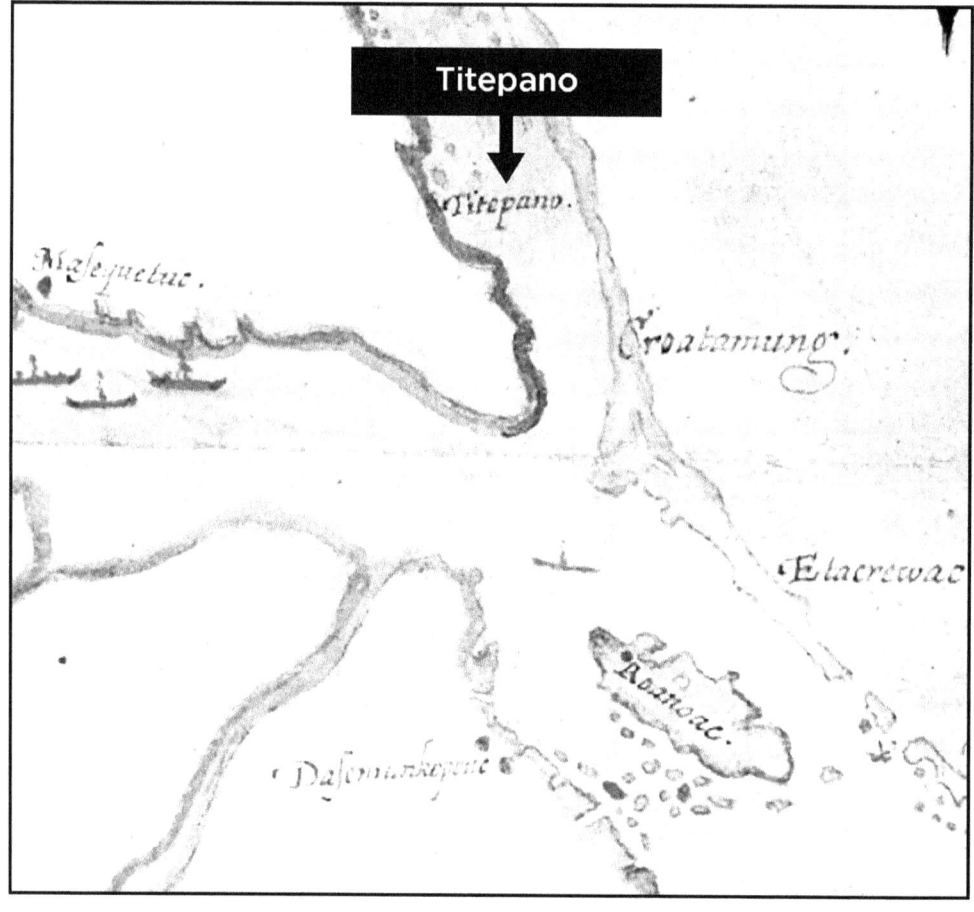

Portion of John White's *La Virginea Pars* map showing "Titepano."

Mangoak territory. Accordingly, when Lane and his men had been weakened by starvation, they would then be easy prey for the Mangoaks waiting to attack them. Lane and his men avoided the ambush, thanks only to the quick actions by Manteo. Lane's safe return was a great disappointment to Pemisapan, whose plans to unite a coalition of tribes against the English now had to be delayed.

Tetepano's name is said to translate from the Algonquian as "whirling around" or "whirlwind."[1] The very close Algonquian word "Titepano" was used on John White's *La Virginea Pars* map to label present-day Currituck Sound. Algonquian language philologist James Geary was confident that the word could apply to currents in a body of water, in which case the Algonquian meaning would be "there is a swirling current," or "it swirls around."[2]

As one of Pemisapan's principal followers, it is certainly likely that Tetepano was with him at Dasamonquepeuc while preparations were being made to fall upon the English at Roanoke on June 10 with a combined force of warriors. Consequently, Tetepano may have been one of the "principall Weroances and followers" who were there with Pemisapan on June 1, when Lane launched his surprise attack. Pemisapan and a number of others were killed on that day, but it is not known if Tetepano was among them.

Towaye

Towaye was an Algonquian Indian whose tribal affiliation was not noted, but he was very likely a Croatoan, one of Manteo's tribesmen. He was only mentioned once in the Roanoke accounts, at the end of a list of "The names of all the men, women and children, which safely arriued in Virginia, and remained to inhabite there." This was the listing of those who had voyaged from England in 1587 to establish a colony under the governorship of John White. At the very end of that list Towaye was named as one of the two (Manteo being the other) "Sauages that were in England and returned home into Virginia with them."[1] According to James Geary, the name "Towaye" may possibly translate from the Algonquian, oddly, as "the one who injures trees."[2]

There was no explanation of how Towaye got to England in the first place, but he must have accompanied Manteo and the departing colonists when Lane evacuated Roanoke on June 19, 1586, and sailed to England with Drake's fleet. Therefore, Towaye would have spent nearly ten months in London lodged with Manteo at Raleigh's Durham House on the Thames River. During that time he certainly interacted often with Harriot, who also lodged at Durham House, and to a lesser extent with other notable visitors and lodgers who occasionally stopped there. He also would have been present when Raleigh was developing his plans for the next colonization venture.

It is possible, as some have suggested, that Towaye accompanied Manteo to be his servant aboard ship and in England. It is also possible, however, that Towaye was selected by Manteo for a more meaningful station: to be his protégé or assistant in the 1587 colonization venture. Because Manteo was highly regarded by Lane and the English during the 1585–6 colonization attempt at Roanoke, particularly in the latter months of the enterprise, he was probably assured by Lane, Harriot, and the other leading Englishmen that he would have an enhanced role in Raleigh's future plans. It would have been sensible for Manteo to consider an assistant at that point, and he may well have selected Towaye for that position, encouraging him to sail to England in preparation. In any case, all that is known for certain is that Towaye returned to "Virginia" with Manteo in July of 1587, and nothing was heard about him afterwards.

Wanchese

Wanchese was a Roanoac Indian who, along with Manteo, sailed to England with the return voyage of the Amadas-Barlowe reconnaissance expedition in the summer of 1584. While in England he and Manteo learned English under the tutelage of Thomas Harriot, and in June 1585, they returned to their homeland aboard the *Tyger*, the flagship of Grenville's fleet sent to establish Raleigh's first colony in America. Wanchese turned against the English shortly thereafter and was a trusted associate and follower of Wingina, the principal weroance of Roanoac and Dasamonquepeuc at that time. Wanchese remained an influential opponent of the English throughout most of 1585–6, and he became a prominent adversary after the arrival of the second colony in 1587. The name "Wanchese" is said to translate from the Algonquian as "flies out" or "flying out."[1]

Any examination of Wanchese and his role in the Roanoke voyages must ultimately confront the following question: Why did he, unlike Manteo, reject the English and turn against them upon his return to Roanoke Island in the summer of 1585? Part of the answer probably lies in his reason for going to England in the first place. When the Amadas-Barlowe reconnaissance voyagers arrived at the Outer Banks on July 13, 1584, the principal weroance, Wingina, was days away recuperating from wounds he had received in his "mortall warre" with Piemacum and his allies far to the southwest. News about the arrival of the bearded strangers was relayed by messenger to Wingina, whose brother Granganimeo, in the meantime, was in the process of establishing initial contact with the English.

The reports sent to Wingina were cautiously optimistic. Although these English were strangely attired and could not be understood very well, they appeared to be friendly and they certainly had many desirable goods to trade, a sample of which was very likely taken to Wingina. Of particular interest were "our hatchets, and axes, and kniues," Barlowe wrote, "and [the Indians] would haue giuen any thing for swordes: but wee would not depart with any." The English also possessed another kind of strange and powerful weapon, which both frightened and astonished the Indians when it was first demonstrated. "Hauing discharged our harquebuz-shot [matchlock arquebus], such a flocke of Cranes (the most part white) arose vnder vs, with such a cry redoubled by many ecchoes, as if an armie of men had showted all together."[2]

Wingina must have been fascinated by the reports from home being relayed to him, and he would have wondered whether these English could be potentially powerful allies in the war presently being waged against his enemy Piemacum. Both Manteo and Wanchese, in fact, would later try to "perswade vs to surprize Piemacum his towne, hauing promised and assured vs, that there will be found in it great store of commodities." On the other hand nothing was really known about the strangers, neither where they had come from nor what their intentions were. All of this must have weighed heavily on Wingina, who had to rely on intermediaries for information and was helpless to evaluate the English first-hand. As Wingina's trusted fellow tribesman, Wanchese may very well have been one of the warriors fighting with him in the war against Piemacum, and, if so, he too would not have had any direct contact with the English initially. In any case, it stands to reason that someone like Wanchese would have been Wingina's likely choice to be a delegate, sent to England to learn about these people. In that role Wanchese's reason for making the dangerous trip was to act as Wingina's agent: to estimate the numbers of the English, evaluate their strengths and weaknesses, learn what the English intended to do upon their return, and report those findings back to Wingina.

Manteo's reasons for making the trip were completely different. He experienced the arrival of the English in person and may have been among the first Indians to interact with them. He too was fascinated with the strange powers the English seemed to possess, but saw the daring trip to England as an opportunity to acquire those seemingly supernatural capabilities, to harness this spiritual force known to the Algonquians as "manitou" and return to Croatoan in some way transformed. The name Manteo itself is believed to be associated with "manitou" and, as proposed, may have been adopted just prior to the trip, reflecting the spiritual and transitional nature of his journey. This would explain the remarkable cultural change Manteo would subsequently undergo. It would also help explain the markedly different attitudes towards the English displayed by Manteo and Wanchese upon their return from England.

Wanchese arrived in England in mid–September 1584, and was undoubtedly amazed when he first saw the city of London, a sprawling metropolis with a population that would reach 200,000 within the next decade. By contrast, his home village of Roanoac contained nine dwellings.

Wanchese was lodged with Manteo at Raleigh's spacious Durham House on the Thames River in London (a considerable distance beyond the left edge of the following map), and within a week or two they had exchanged their native attire for English brown taffeta clothing. It was there at Durham House that they worked with Harriot on learning each other's language, and where Harriot, also a resident at Durham House, was constructing an Algonquian phonetic alphabet. Wanchese and Manteo also interacted with many of London's leading luminaries who visited Raleigh and Harriot at Durham House, and Harriot in particular very likely used those occasions to demonstrate the progress being made in the Algonquians' language studies. Both Wanchese and Manteo evidently had achieved a reasonable degree of fluency in the English language during their stay in London, as is evident from the testimony of a Spaniard who saw them aboard Grenville's ship on their return to the Outer Banks in 1585. The Spaniard reported that "they [Grenville and his men] were accompanied by two tall Indians, whom they treated well, and who spoke English."[3]

During their seven month stay in London, Raleigh escorted Wanchese and Manteo around the city, where they were quite a sensation, and he did not miss the opportunity to use them for propaganda purposes whenever possible to entice potential investors for his upcoming colonization venture. The two Indians could verify, perhaps with Harriot's linguistic assistance, the abundant and profitable commodities said to be found in America. For those who required a more spiritual motivation, the two Algonquians, now dressed in English clothing and able to speak some English, were living proof of how easy it would be, as Hakluyt wrote, to "distill into their [the Indians'] purged minds the sweet and lively lines of the gospel."[4]

From all that is known of their entire sojourn in London, Wanchese and Manteo shared

Part of London proper from the *Civitas Londinium* map, composed about the time Wanchese was in England.

the same experiences and events, witnessed the same spectacles, met and conversed with the same people, and toured the same grand palaces of London. On one special occasion they were both formally presented at Queen Elizabeth's Court with all its royal splendor on display. It is barely possible that they may have had a brief look at London's seedier side, too, the noisy, crowded streets as well as the poverty and filth. The point to be made is that they both saw and experienced London together, and yet their reactions to it all were totally different. Again, much of that difference was probably due to their abovementioned differing approaches and expectations for the voyage to England.

A number of other assumptions have been offered, however, to account for the fact that Wanchese turned against the English. One suggestion was that Raleigh and the English had treated him poorly in London, with less favor or preference than Manteo.[5] Another was that "Wanchese came to view them [the English] as captors," and that "he evinced no interest in learning English and showed even less desire to stay in London."[6] Although specific references to the two Indians are scarce in the existing records, there is nothing whatsoever to support either of those suggestions. All the references that do exist, speak of Wanchese and Manteo as equals, making no distinctions or judgements at all. Barlowe and Amadas "both noted" that the intelligence supplied by "these two [Wanchese and Manteo]" was of equally high value, and, addressing his account to Raleigh later, Barlowe pointed out that "you [Raleigh]" similarly regarded the information provided "since by these men, which we brought home." Later Hakluyt added a notation to the account, simply indicating that Barlowe "brought home also two of the Sauages being lustie [strong, robust] men, whose names were Wanchese and Manteo." When Grenville stopped at Puerto Rico on his way to Roanoke Island in June of 1585, a Spaniard noticed "two well-attired Indians aboard. Finally, as cited above, another Spanish observer reported that the two Indians were "treated well" by the English on their trip back to Roanoke.

The Spaniard's observation—that both Wanchese and Manteo were well treated—was probably an accurate reflection of the manner in which the two were regarded by the English throughout their stay in London and as late as June 1585, just a month before Grenville's fleet arrived at Wokokon. Of course, Wanchese's estimation of the English differed radically from Manteo's by this time, but, as stated, that was more likely because his mission was to convey the strength and potential threat of the English, which he apparently found formidable, to his weroance, Wingina, at Roanoac. It would also indicate that, for obvious practical reasons, he had concealed his true feelings and conclusions about the English, and that they were completely unaware of the negative nature of the information he would later relay to Wingina. It seems fair to say that while Manteo embraced his association with the English as a great opportunity for his and his tribe's future, Wanchese was wary of the English and saw their behavior and advanced capabilities as threats to the well-being of his Roanoac people.

Grenville anchored at Wokokon on June 24, and on July 3 he "sent word of our arriuing at Wocokon, to Wingina at Roanoak." It was very possibly Wanchese who delivered the news of their arrival, and he would have spent a good deal of time afterwards describing his experiences in London and providing Wingina with a detailed assessment of what he had learned about the English. Grenville, in the meantime, remained at Wokokon preparing to tour Pamlico Sound with forty of his leading men. One of the stops on this week long tour was at the village of Aquascogoc, where the theft of a silver cup prompted the English to burn the village and destroy their corn harvest. That incident occurred on July 16, eleven days before Grenville anchored at Hatorask off Roanoke Island on July 27. In the interim, word of the alarming event at Aquascogoc most certainly reached Wingina at his Roanoac village, and it would have confirmed Wanchese's ominous warnings about what might be expected from these dangerous English people.

The first overt sign of Wanchese's rejection of the English probably occurred on July 29 when neither he nor Wingina showed up for Grenville's first formal meeting aboard the flagship *Tyger*. Although Wingina's absence was likely due in part to Grenville's disrespectful failure to abide by Indian protocol regarding the arrival of high-ranking visitors (see the *Wingina* entry), the fact that both Wingina and Wanchese avoided the meeting is notable. From the English perspective, a good part of the reason for taking Wanchese and Manteo to England was so that they could be taught English and be their interpreters when they returned. Wanchese's and Wingina's absence had to have been intentional, leaving only Manteo to translate, and Granganimeo to act in Wingina's behalf. We also know from the June Spanish report that both Wanchese and Manteo were "well-attired" in English clothing when they arrived at the Outer Banks, and it is possible that Wanchese had already exchanged his English attire for traditional tribal dress by the time this meeting took place.

Wanchese was not mentioned again in the Roanoke accounts until the end of April 1586, by which time Wingina had changed his name to Pemisapan and was organizing a tribal coalition to destroy the English. Governor Ralph Lane noted in his account that "certaine of our great enemies.... Wanchese most principally, were in hand againe to put their old practises in vse against vs, which were readily imbraced, and all their former deuises against vs, reneued, and new brought in question."⁷ It is clear that attitudes toward the English had turned decisively negative over the preceding months, that a number of plots against the English had already been attempted, and that Wanchese was now a leading figure in the opposition against them. His first-hand experience and knowledge about the English would have been a valuable asset to Pemisapan in planning their defeat.

The plan put together by Pemisapan, possibly with Wanchese's input, was well thought out. A large force consisting of warriors from the surrounding areas was to assemble at Dasamonquepeuc under the pretense of honoring old Ensenore, the former Roanoac weroance who had recently died. On the night of June 10 a small but select group of Indians stationed at Roanoke Island was to set fire to Lane's and other leading Englishmen's dwellings and kill them as they ran from the burning structures without their weapons. In the meantime the main force of warriors would have already been alerted by signal fires to cross over from Dasamonquepeuc to Roanoke, where they would strike the main body of confused and leaderless Englishmen and annihilate them. Pemisapan's plan, however, was divulged to Lane in late May by two Indians. Consequently, on June 1 Lane and his men launched a surprise attack at Dasamonquepeuc before the coalition of warriors had time to assemble, and Pemisapan and many of his weroances and followers were killed. A week later Sir Francis Drake arrived with a large fleet, and Lane decided to evacuate Roanoke. Wanchese's whereabouts at the time of Lane's attack are not known, but, since he was mentioned specifically by John White the following year as one who "kept companie" with "the remnant of Wingin[a]s men dwelling then [1587] at Dasamonquepeuc," he certainly survived.

We know nothing about Pemisapan's successor or the ruling structure of the Roanoac tribe after Lane's attack. Pemisapan's brother, Granganimeo, had already died and no other siblings were mentioned. It stands to reason that Wanchese would have emerged as a leader of some importance, although perhaps not as the principal weroance whose title was normally passed down through familial lines. As mentioned, Lane referred to Wanchese specifically as one of his "great enemies," and John White later considered him to be a leading figure among the hostile Indians at Dasamonquepeuc. Because Wanchese had remained a primary adversary of the English after Pemisapan's death, he most likely had a hand, either directly or indirectly, in three subsequent events involving English activities at Roanoke Island.

The first of these was an attack on a contingent of Englishmen, who were left at Roanoke about two weeks after Lane departed with Drake. In early July of 1586 Grenville arrived at the Hatorask inlet with the supplies that had been expected two months earlier. Finding Roanoke deserted, he returned to England, but not before leaving a small company of fifteen men well-provisioned at the previous settlement location in order to retain territorial possession for Raleigh. By this time the old Roanoac Indian village had been vacated and the remnant of Pemisapan's former followers, along with Wanchese, now dwelt at Dasamonquepeuc. The fifteen-man contingent of Englishmen at Roanoke did not go unnoticed by Wanchese and the Indians, who watched them carefully while a plan of attack was devised, presumably with Wanchese taking the lead in developing the strategy. A force of thirty warriors drawn from the villages of Aquasogoc, Secota, and of course Dasamonquepeuc, stealthily approached the English settlement. It is not known whether Wanchese actually participated in the attack, although he may well have done so, since he was the only named Indian who "kept companie" with those at Dasamonquepeuc. He certainly would have at least been engaged in organizing the strategy involved in the assault.

At the time of the attack, four of the Englishmen were off digging oysters, leaving the remaining eleven at their compound. While most of the Indians hid in the nearby woods, two of them, appearing to be unarmed, approached the English dwellings "calling to them by friendly signes" and asking that "two of their chiefest men should come vnarmed to speake" with them. As soon as the men approached, one of the Indians embraced the nearest Englishman while the other quickly drew a wooden club from beneath his mantle and "strooke him on the heade and slew him." The twenty-eight other Indians immediately emerged from hiding and showered the Englishmen with arrows, killing one of them outright and wounding several others. The surviving Englishmen retreated to the shoreline and managed to escape in a boat. After picking up the four who were gathering oysters, they rowed off and were not heard of again. The attack and routing of the Englishmen at Roanoke would have been seen as a great Indian triumph, almost certainly their first complete victory against the English in battle.

The second event involving Wanchese occurred less than a year later when Raleigh made his last effort to colonize what was by now called "Virginia." On May 8, 1587, three ships and a group of about 117 colonists under the leadership of John White departed from Plymouth. As opposed to Lane's colony, which was made up of essentially military men, this time the colonists included men, women, and children, who were intended to establish a self-sustaining agricultural colony that would not have to depend on the Indians for food. The new colony was expected to be established at the Chesapeake Bay, where there was a good deep-water harbor, but the plans were changed and the colonists were re-routed to Roanoke Island on July 22,[8] where they repaired the dwellings at the old settlement and prepared to spend the winter.

Less than a week later one of the colonists, George Howe, was attacked by a small group of Indians from Dasamonquepeuc who were spying on the newly arrived English colonists. Unlike the attack at the Roanoke settlement the previous year, which was probably planned and organized by Wanchese, this one was spontaneous. The unfortunate Howe had wandered a mile or two from the settlement to catch crabs and became a target of opportunity. The Indians "gaue him sixteen wounds with their arrowes: and after they had slaine him with their woodden swords, they beat his head in pieces, and fled ouer the water to the maine." The incident tells us something of the mindset of both the Indians and English colonists in the summer of 1587. First, it obviously demonstrates the level of resentment and hostility that still remained among the Indians towards the English since Lane's departure. It also demonstrates how unprepared and unaware the new colonists were about the state of Anglo-Indian relations. As mentioned, Raleigh and his backers made a concerted effort to conceal from prospective investors and colonists the bloody conflicts that had occurred in the winter of 1585–6 and the actual state of hostilities that existed when Lane departed.

Soon after the Indians responsible for killing Howe returned to Dasamonquepeuc, Wanchese and the rest of the Indians there decided to withdraw, for the time being, farther into the mainland. Perhaps remembering Lane's surprise attack the previous year, they feared a similar reprisal from the new colonists. Those fears were justified a week or so later, when White made an ill-advised night assault at Dasamonquepeuc on what he thought was Wanchese's band of Indians. The unintended victims, however, were friendly Croatoans who had occupied the village after Wanchese and the Indians left.

The last historical reference potentially involving Wanchese was a minor one, probably occurring in the fall of 1588, after the colonists left Roanoke Island for their new settlement somewhere on the mainland, and it had to do with John White's "stuffe and goods" left behind. On August 27, 1587, White sailed for England to acquire supplies and additional colonists and expected to return to Roanoke the following summer. Before leaving he had his principal colonists sign a pledge guaranteeing that his belongings would not be spoiled or "pilfered away" during his absence. In the meantime the colonists, with the help of Manteo, searched the mainland for a suitable relocation site. When the relocation process was nearly completed, probably in March of 1588, the colonists buried five chests filled with non-essential items at the Roanoke settlement, which were to be recovered later. Three of these chests contained White's "stuffe and goods," the possessions which he had left behind.

It was probably shortly after Roanoke was evacuated that Wanchese and his Indian associates, who had by now returned to Dasamonquepeuc, searched the abandoned settlement and located the buried chests, salvaging what useful items they could find. It is very likely that Wanchese was among these Indians, particularly given his previous stay in London and his knowledge about English goods and merchandise. When White finally managed to return to Roanoke Island in 1590, he found the old fort and settlement deserted, and what was left of his possessions had been ruined, as he wrote, by "the Sauages our enemies

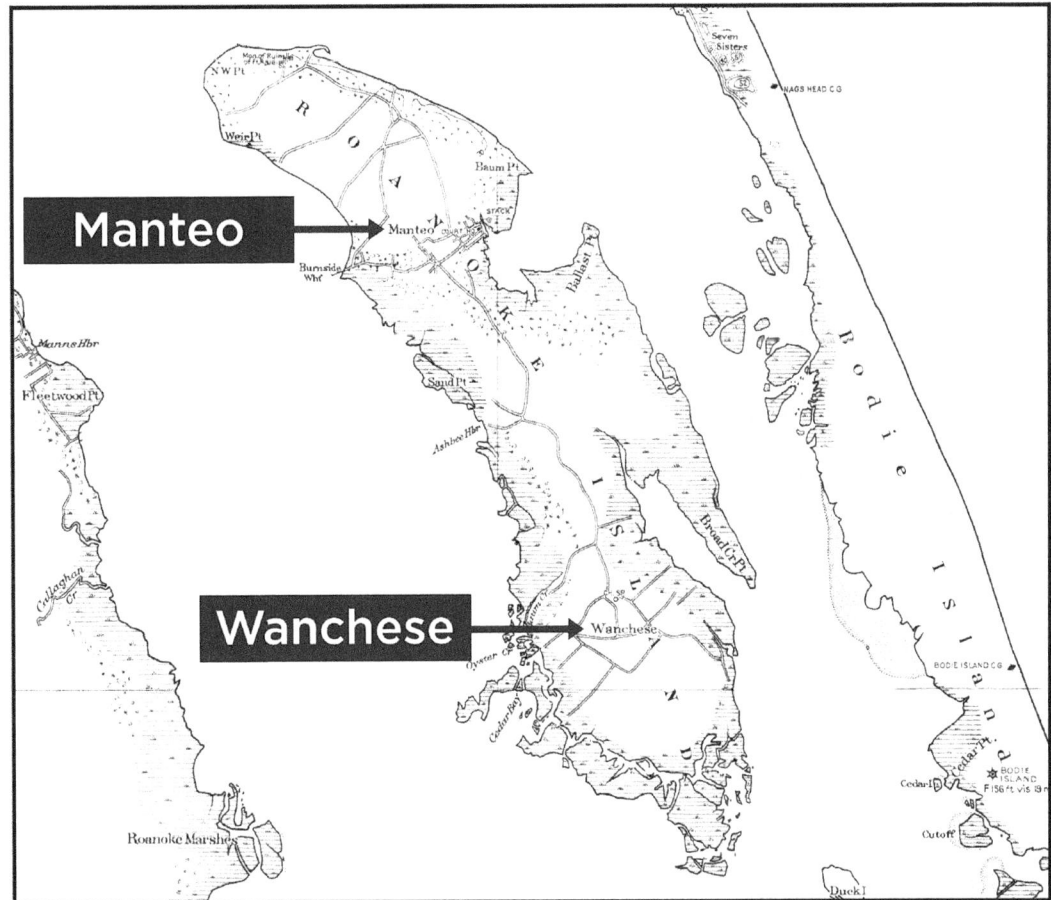

1923 U.S. Coast and Geodetic Survey map of Roanoke Island showing Manteo and Wanchese.

at Dasamongwepeuk." No doubt Wanchese was foremost in his mind. It is not known how long Wanchese remained in the area of Roanoke Island and Dasamonquepeuc afterwards, and he subsequently disappeared from the historical record.

His name is recalled today in the community of Wanchese, North Carolina, which comprises the lower third of Roanoke Island. Archaeological evidence indicates that the Indians had seasonal encampments at that location, where they came in the spring and fall to fish and gather oysters. In the historical period, the area was first settled in the latter part of the 17th century and eventually "the lower end" of the island, as it was called, developed into an important commercial fishing location.[9] Dare County had been created in 1870 and its county seat on Roanoke Island was named after the Croatoan, Manteo. At "the lower end" of the island a post office was eventually opened in 1886 to serve the local fisherman there. That post office and its surrounding community were named after Wanchese. With Manteo to the north and Wanchese on the opposite end of Roanoke Island, they are fitting reminders of the two Algonquians who once traveled to England together and afterwards went their separate ways.

Wingina

"Wingina, King of Wingandacoa"

Wingina was the principal weroance or ruler of the Roanoac tribe, although his influence probably extended well beyond Roanoke Island and the village of Dasamonquepeuc on the mainland, where he sometimes dwelt. Wingina did not attain the dominant status of "mamanatowick," an Algonquian term later used to describe the paramount chief Wahunsonacock, referred to by the English as Powhatan. Wahunsonacock's sovereignty extended to nearly all the Algonquian tribal groups in present-day Virginia by the time the Jamestown settlement was established. Yet Wingina was certainly an important weroance who exerted varying degrees of control and influence over the tidewater region from Albemarle Sound to approximately the Pamlico River. Although his direct contact with the English spanned less than a year—from July of 1585 until June 1, 1586—Wingina's role during that relatively short period had a far greater impact on the outcome of Raleigh's colonization plans than any other native Algonquian. Clever and resourceful, Wingina had, at best, a tenuous relationship with the English in 1585 and eventually conceived and organized the opposition against them in 1586.

The image below, drawn by John White in 1585 and then engraved and published by Theodor de Bry in 1590, was titled "A cheiff Lorde of Roanoac" and is almost certainly that of Wingina himself. As such it represents the only one of White's drawings to which the name of a specific Algonquian can be attributed with a degree of confidence. It is interesting to note that Wingina would have been frequently seen with his arms appropriately folded, as they are in the illustration, since only chief weroances walked about or talked with other weroances in that manner as a "signe of [their] wisdome."

Harriot's text, which accompanied this illustration, described his appearance and manner of dress:

> The cheefe men of the yland and towne of Roanoac reace the haire of their crounes of theyr heades cutt like a cokes cōbe [Coxcomb or cock's comb], as the other doe. The rest they wear loge [long] as woemen and truss them opp in a knott in the nape of their necks. They hange pearles stringe oppon a threed att their eares, and weare bracelets on their armes of pearles, or small beades of copper or of smoothe bone called minsal, nether paintinge nor powncings [tattooing] of them selues, but in token of authoritye, and honor, they wear a chaine of great pearles, or copper beades or smoothe bones abowt their necks, and a plate of copper hinge vpon a stringe, from the nauel vnto the midds of their thighes. They couer themselues before and behynde as the woemē doe with a deers skynne handsomley dressed, and fringed, More ouer they fold their armes together as they walke, or as they talke one wjth another in signe of wisdome. The yle of Roanoac is verye pleisant, ond hath plaintie of fishe by reason of the Water that enuironeth the same.[1]

De Bry's engraving of "A cheiff Lorde of Roanoac," probably Wingina.

Harriot called present-day Roanoke Island "Roanoac," which was also the name of the tribe that dwelt there and at Dasamonquepeuc on the mainland. It was also the name applied to Wingina's principal village from 1584 onwards, following the usual English custom of naming main villages after the tribe that inhabited the area. "Roanoac" is said to translate from the Algonquian as "northern people,"[2] which, some say, may have been derived from the location of Wingina's village somewhere towards the north end of the island. It is very possible, though, that the word was a much older reference to the early Algonquian migration from the north to present-day North Carolina. Arthur Barlowe, who visited Roanoke Island in 1584, placed the village "at the north end thereof" and wrote that it contained "nine houses, built of Cedar, and fortified round about with sharpe trees, to keepe out their enemies, and the entrance into it made like a turne pike very artificially."[3] Dasamonquepeuc, Wingina's alternate village residence, was located directly across present-day Croatan Sound from Roanoke Island at or near Manns Harbor. Algonquian philologist James Geary wrote that "Dasamonquepeuc" translates from the Algonquian as "where there is an extended land separated by water,"[4] which is an apt description for a mainland extension of Wingina's principal village on Roanoke Island.

According to Arthur Barlowe's 1584 account Wingina was "in league" with two other tribes to the west and northwest of Roanoke Island. One of these was the formidable Chawanoac tribe, led by the weroance Menatonon. The second was probably the Moratucs, first identified as a separate and distinct Algonquian tribe by anthropologist Maurice A. Mook in

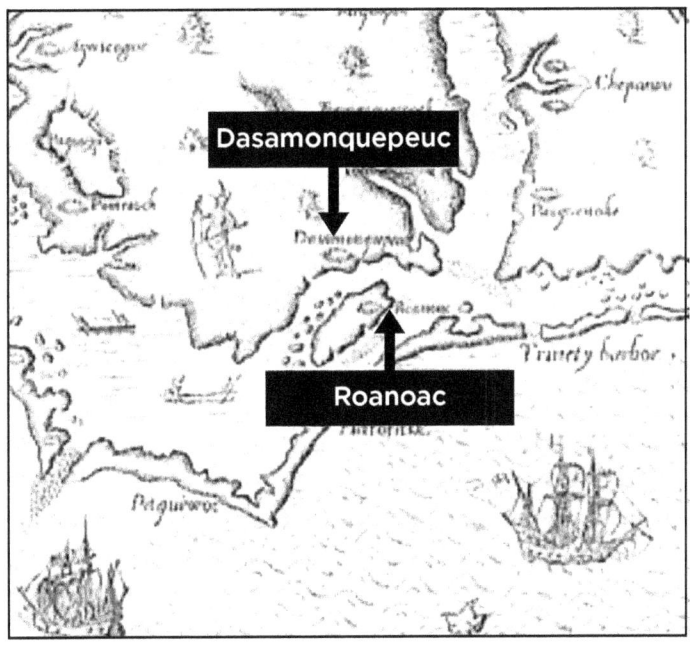

The villages of Roanoac and Dasamonquepeuc.

1943.[5] The Moratuc tribe, once again named after the area or geographical feature where they resided, dwelt along the Moratuc (Roanoke) River to the west of Albemarle Sound. It is also possible that the second tribe allied with Wingina may have been the Weapemeocs, who lived just north of Albemarle Sound, although they seemed to have been under the influence of Menatonon. The position of Wingina's village of Roanoac not far from the north end of the island allowed him easy access to Albemarle Sound and the tribes bordering it. In the final months of the first colony's existence Wingina was quite successful in uniting those distant tribes against the English. As events unfolded in 1586, for example, Wingina's plan to eliminate the English reached far to the west, where the Moratucs and the Mangoaks nearly entrapped Lane and his men, who had ventured well up the Moratuc River. At that point, Lane wrote, "wee were then 160. miles from home [Roanoke Island]," although that estimation may have been exaggerated.

Wingina's name is believed to be a shortened form of "winginam" meaning "he approves" or "is pleased with."[6] His name may also be related to an Algonquian cognate "wingan" meaning "good" as found in several words later recorded by William Strachey at Jamestown. Strachey compiled an extensive list of Algonquian words and phrases which included "wingan" meaning "good," "winganouse" meaning "very good," and "wingganapo" meaning "my beloved or good friend."[7] The same cognate can be found in "Wingandacoa," a term first used by the English in 1584. Barlowe referred to Wingina as "king of Wingandacoa" and concluded perhaps logically, but erroneously, that it was the Algonquian name for the mainland territory presumed to be ruled by Wingina. The Wingandacoa translation error was not corrected in print until many years later when Raleigh wrote that it actually was a complimentary phrase spoken by the coastal Algonquians to the newly-arrived English meaning, "You have good clothes."[8]

The confusion over what to call the newly discovered land was not easily or uniformly resolved. The area misidentified as Wingandacoa in 1584 was later referred to as "Ossomocomuck alias Wyngandacoia" in Raleigh's 1587 Grant of Arms. By 1589 the phrase "Assamacomock alias Wingandacoia alias Virginia" was used to refer to the "sayde countrie." The earliest use of "Virginia" seems to be on Raleigh's 1584 seal naming him Governor of Virginia,[9] which probably marked the approximate time Queen Elizabeth gave permission to use her royal sobriquet, "The Virgin Queen." Yet in December of that same year a bill in the House of Commons mentioned "that he [Raleigh] hath already discovered a place called Windaganroza."[10] Eventually Raleigh's broad American territories were commonly called Virginia, and in the 17th century John Smith referred to Raleigh's previous English holdings to the south of Jamestown as "Olde Virginia."

By whatever name the new land was called, however, it is clear that it was originally understood to stretch from Roanoke Island to the "towne called Sequotan ... the Southernmost towne of Wingandacoa," and that its "king is called Wingina."[11] It is also worth noting that neither Manteo nor Wanchese apparently ever felt the need to correct that understanding after they had acquired a basic fluency in English through their work with Thomas Harriot. More than twenty years later at Jamestown, William Strachey iterated that "Secota was the last town southwardly of the bounds of Wingandacoa."[12] There can be little doubt that Wingina's realm was believed to encompass much of the broad mainland west of Pamlico Sound. Strachey described what we call the Outer Banks today as "a tract of islands two hundred miles in length, adjoining to the ocean sea, and between the islands two or three entraunces." Beyond them, he wrote, was "the continent the Indians call Wingandacoa ... [and] the chief king's name, governing at that time, they fownde to be Wingina." It is evident that to the late 16th and early 17th century English chroniclers, at least, Wingina's realm was believed to have extended a considerable distance to the south and southwest of both the villages of Roanoac and Dasamonquepeuc.

Although Barlowe was mistaken about the actual translation of the Algonquian phrase "Wingandacoa," it is unlikely that he could have misunderstood either the extent of the territorial realm or who ruled it. It should be noted that the final draft of his account was written in England towards the end of 1584 with input from the two Algonquians, Manteo and Wanchese, who were learning English at Raleigh's Durham House. Harriot, also a resident at Durham House, was working with the two Indians to construct an Algonquian phonetic alphabet. By December of 1584 the two Indians "brought home into this our Realme of England" were providing valuable information about "a Land called Wyngandacoia."[13] Historian David Quinn, who held that Wingina's authority extended no farther than Roanoac and Dasamonquepeuc, brushed aside the references to his larger realm, writing that those references must be ascribed "to Indian boasting."[14]

Anthropologist Maurice Mook maintained that Wingina's rule extended far to the south of Roanoac and Dasamonquepeuc. He wrote, "Wingandacoa is usually identified with Secotan, and most of the Indians whom he [Barlowe] mentioned by name—Wingina, the chief, Granganimo, his brother, Wanchese and Manteo, the natives whom he took to England with him—were inhabitants of this area."[15] Mook concluded that the large area misunderstood by the English as "Wingandacoa" was actually Secotan. Since several tribes south of the Pamlico River "have mortall warre with Wingina," as Manteo and Wanchese reported, then it follows that Wingina must have exerted some authority over the large area extending from his principal village of Roanoac to the Pamlico River, which appears to have been the approximate "front line" in that "mortall warre."

Quinn claimed that the abovementioned reference to the "mortall war" Wingina had

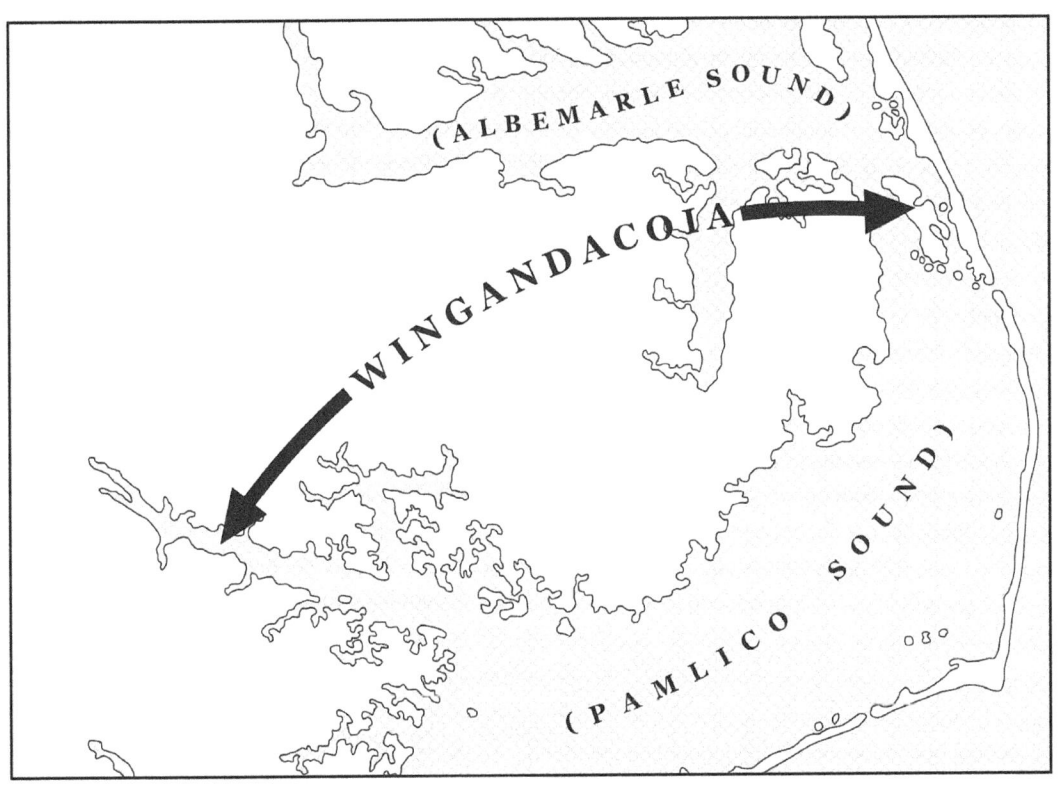

Early understanding of "Wingandacoia" (courtesy Michael Gayle).

with tribes south of the Pamlico River must have been a misprint, "a mistake," he wrote, "possibly by the printer."[16] Again, this conclusion was based on his opinion that Wingina was essentially a local weroance whose authority was limited only to Roanoac and Dasamonquepeuc. Despite the textual evidence to the contrary, that opinion has more recently been cited to support the contention that "the Secotans and the Roanoacs were bitter adversaries," and that "Wingina of the Roanoacs had been shotte in two places through the bodye, and once cleane through the thigh' a year earlier by the Secotans who 'maintaine[d] a deadlie and terrible warre' with the Roanoacs."[17] There is nothing at all in Barlowe's account to suggest that the Secotans and Roanoacs were bitter adversaries or that Wingina had been wounded by the Secotans. On the contrary, that contention is directly opposed by the actual passages in Barlowe's text, which Quinn decided must be due either to "Indian boasting" or printing errors.

Fortunately, the details of that "mortall warre" and Wingina's role in it were provided by two primary Algonquian sources, namely "these men which we haue brought with vs to England [Manteo and Wanchese]." The two native Algonquians "haue giuen vs to vnderstand," Barlowe wrote later, that there had been a "mortall warre" waged with the weroance named Piemacum, who ruled the land of Pomouik or Pananuaioc (not to be confused, as noted, with the Secotan village of Pomeiock near present-day Lake Mattamuskeet). The Pomouiks, a separate Algonquian tribe, would later be known as the Pamlico Indians, whose name is retained today in the present-day county and adjacent river and sound where they dwelt. Piemacum controlled much of the territory between the Pamlico and Neuse Rivers and was in league with "the next king adioyning towards the setting of the Sunne." That tribe to the west was not mentioned by name, but it was most likely the tribe known to the Roanoke voyagers as Mangoaks and later as Tuscaroras. Mook raised the possibility that "tribal distribution in this area suggests they [the tribe to the west] may have been the Woccon, a tribe of Siouan speech,"[18] but that is uncertain. Piemacum was also allied with the chief weroance of the Neusioks, who dwelt just to the southeast of the Pomouiks in the territory near the mouth of the Neuse River. "These kings," Barlowe wrote in 1584, "haue mortall warre with Wingina king of Wingandacoa."

It is clear from Barlowe's account, then, that when the English arrived in 1584, the "mortall warre" against Piemacum and his allies was being waged by Wingina and his allies. It follows that the villages in the area labeled "Secotan" on the later White/de Bry map had either come under Wingina's direct authority, or at least were firmly allied with him in the war against the specific, common enemy named Piemacum, who dwelt a number of days to the southwest of Roanoac and Dasamonquepeuc. It is certainly possible that the Secotan villages would have retained a degree of autonomy in times of peace, but would have united under the authority of a recognized and respected leader against a common enemy like Piemacum.

There is evidence in an illustration from Harriot's *Briefe and true report* that would lend support to the contention that Wingina had attained that authoritative status. The 1590 White/de Bry engraving below, titled "The Marckes of sundrye of the Chief mene of Virginia," illustrates by letter designations the various markings worn on the backs of warriors to indicate "what Princes subiects they bee."

The accompanying text, which was supplied by Harriot, read in part…

> The marks which I obserued a monge them, are here put downe in order folowinge.
> The marke which is expressed by A. belongeth tho Wingino, the cheefe lorde of Roanoac.
> That which hath B. is the marke of Wingino his sisters husbande.
> Those which be noted with the letters, of C. and D. belonge vnto diverse chefe lords in Secotam.
> Those which have the letters E. F. G. are certaine cheefe men of Pomeiooc, and Aquascogoc.

It is noteworthy that of the seven markings representing the seven "cheefe" weroances, only Wingina was mentioned by name, and another of the seven was related to him through marriage. If Harriot listed these symbols "downe in order," meaning in order of importance, then the fact that Wingina's marking was listed first would be significant. Furthermore, Wingins's four vertical arrows were numerically greater than those of the other arrow markings and could represent either his ability to field a numerical superiority of warriors or his greater influence and authority than the other weroances. It is also worth noting that the arrow markings of the Secotan weroances, whose villages bordered Piemacum's territory, were numerically inferior to Wingina's.

The expansion of Wingina's authority and influence may have been a fairly recent or continuing transition which had begun about 1582, two years before the arrival of the English. In Barlowe's account, Piemacum's adversary in the war prior to 1582 was referred to as the "Lord of Secotan," apparently an unnamed Secotan weroance, not the "king of Wingandacoa," which was a consistent reference to Wingina in 1584. In 1582, however, a major event had occurred that upset the balance of intertribal leadership and may have ushered Wingina to the forefront of the conflict at that time. Barlowe recorded the following:

> about two yeeres past there was a peace made betweene the King Piemacum, and the Lord of Secotan, as these men which we haue brought with vs to England, haue giuen vs to vnderstand: but there remaineth a mortall malice in the Secotanes, for many iniuries and slaughters done vpon them by this Piemacum. They inuited diuers men, and thirtie women of the best of his countrey to their towne to

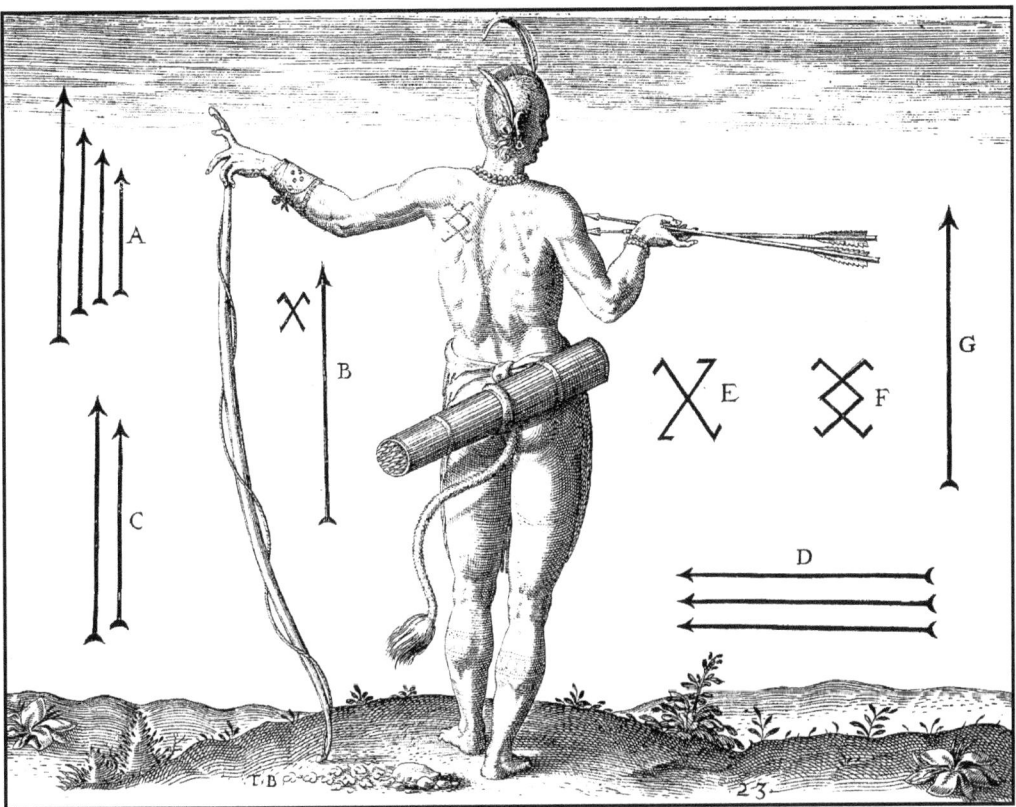

De Bry's engraving of "The Marckes of sundrye of the Chief mene of Virginia."

a feast: and when they were altogether merry, and praying before their Idol ... the captaine or Lord of the town came suddenly vpon them, and slewe them euery one, reseruing the women and children.[19]

If, as certainly seems plausible, the unnamed Lord of Secotan was one of the casualties in this slaughter conceived and carried out by Piemacum in 1582, the mantle of leadership would have fallen to another renowned and respected weroance, who could well have been Wingina. He was apparently held in high esteem, and it was reported to Barlowe that Wingina was "greately obeyed, and his brothers and children reuerenced." Wingina's succession would account for the fact that, by the time the Amadas-Barlowe reconnaissance ships arrived at the Outer Banks in early July of 1584, Wingina was many miles away on the mainland to the southwest, leading the "fight which hee had with the King of the next countrey," i.e., Piemacum. In fact Wingina had been "sore wounded" during the battle with Piemacum's warriors, having been "shot in two places through the body, and once cleane through the thigh but yet he recouered: by reason whereof and for that hee lay at the chiefe towne of the countrey, being six dayes iourney off, we saw him not at all."[20]

"The Tovvne of Secotan"

Neither the location nor the name of the "chiefe towne" where Wingina lay wounded was stated in Barlowe's account, and there has been little effort made to identify it. Quinn was of the opinion that Wingina had been wounded in a battle with one of the neighboring villages near Roanoac,[21] and presumably would have been recovering nearby, but that suggestion is implausible. For one thing it was based on Quinn's assumption that Wingina's authority was limited only to the immediate areas near the villages of Roanoac and Dasamonquepeuc. For another it is not at all consistent with the reports that Wingina was recovering at a "towne" quite a distance away, "six dayes iourney off," according to Barlowe. It also ignores the fact that he was fighting with "the King of the next countrey," not the next town or village. "Country" was a term used, much as it is today, for a large realm or territory governed by a recognized authority. Finally, there was only one known Indian conflict occurring at that time: the abovementioned "mortall warre" between Piemacum and Wingina.

Since the war was being waged by Wingina and the Secotans against Piemacum and his allies, it seems probable that Wingina had been wounded in a battle near the Pamlico River, which was the approximate territorial dividing line between the two forces. Therefore the "chiefe towne of the countrey" where Wingina was recuperating would in all likelihood have been a main village located in Secotan territory. Barlowe wrote that Wingina "lay at the chiefe towne, being six dayes iourney off." According to William Strachey, "from Hattorask [the inlet near Roanoke Island] to the so-ward four daies journey, [is] Secoto, the last towne southwardly of the bounds of Wingandacoa."[22] Ralph Lane, governor of the 1585–6 Roanoke colony, wrote, "The vttermost place to the Southward of any discouery was Secotan, being by estimation fourescore [80] miles distant from Roanoak," which is a fairly accurate estimate of the distance to the town of Secota(n) near the Pamlico River. It seems evident, then, that Wingina could not have been wounded in a battle near Roanoac, as Quinn suggested, because as mentioned above, when the English arrived in July of 1584, he lay recuperating "at the chiefe towne of the countrey, being six dayes iourney off, [and] we saw him not at all." Piemacum's main village was not mentioned in the text, but both Mook and ethnographer James Mooney believed it must have been Panauuaoic, on the White/de Bry map below, which was located in Pomouik territory somewhere south of the Pamlico River, although White's placement of the villages that far south was inconsistent.

On the White/de Bry map above (south is to the left), Secotan was the broad name for the Algonquian territory and the people living, generally speaking, between the present-day Pamlico River and Albemarle Sound. According to Mook, the villages in this tribal group would include Roanoac, Dasamonquepeuc, Pomeiock, Croatoan, Aquascogoc, Cotan, Secota, Mequopen, Tramaskecooc, and probably others not shown on White's map, all of which may be called Secotan villages. The town or village of Secota, the name of which echoes the larger Secotan territory, was—for that reason alone—very likely the principal Secotan village, or "the chiefe towne of the countrey."

There were a number of such examples like "Secotan" used to indicate the names of both the broad tribal groups and also the principal villages within those tribal territories. These villages or "townes" were the residences of the leading weroances and the centers of political activity.[23] Chawanoac, for example, was the name used for both the region near the Chowan River occupied by the Chawanoac tribe as well as its principal town where the Chawanoac weroance Menatonon dwelt. Weapemeoc was the name of both the main village and the larger territory north of present-day Albemarle Sound which the Weapemeoc tribe occupied. Moratuc was the primary village of the Moratuc tribe that dwelt along the Moratuc River to the west of Albemarle Sound. In the case of Secotan the spellings "Secota" and "Secotan" were used interchangeably. On de Bry's engraved map above "Secota" is

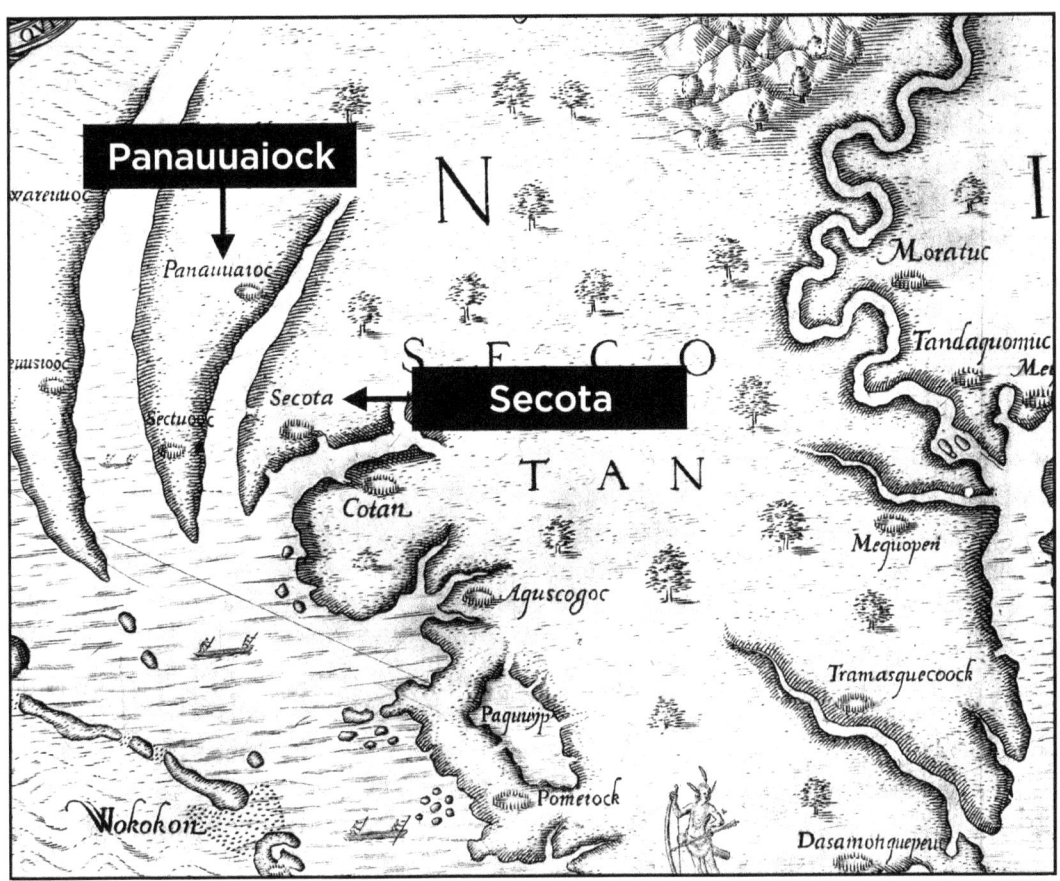

Part of the de Bry map showing the relative locations of Secota and Pananuaioc.

used to designate the name of the village, but when White visited and sketched that village during Grenville's tour of Pamlico Sound in 1585, he labeled it "Secoton." In the 1590 de Bry edition of Harriot's *Briefe and true report* the village is written as both "Secota" and "Secotan." Secotan was also the name used by both Ralph Lane in 1585 and the unnamed author of the 1585 Grenville account to designate the village.

The following is Thomas Harriot's text which accompanied this engraving:

Their townes that are not inclosed with poles aire commonlye fayrer. Then suche as are inclosed, as appereth in this figure which liuelye expresseth the towne of Secotam. For the howses are Scattered heer and ther, and they haue gardein expressed by the letter E. wherin groweth Tobacco which the inhabitants call Vppowoc. They haue also groaues wherin thei take deer, and fields vherin they sowe their corne. In their corne fields they builde as yt weare a scaffolde wher on they sett a cottage like to a rownde chaire, signiffied by F. wherin they place one to watch for there are suche number of fowles, and beasts, that vnless they keepe the better watche, they would soone deuoure all their corne. For which cause the watcheman maketh continual cryes and noyse. They sowe their corne with a certaine distance noted by H. otherwise one stalke would choke the grow the of another and the corne would not come vnto his rypeurs G. For the leaues therof are large, like vnto the leaues of great reedes. They haue also a seuerall broade plotte C. whear they meete with their neighbours, to celebrate their cheefe solemne feastes as the 18. picture doth declare: and a place D. whear after they haue ended their feaste they make merrie togither. Ouer against this place they haue a rownd plott B. wher they assemble themselues to make their solemne prayers. Not far from which place ther is a lardge buildinge A.

De Bry's engraving of "The Tovvne of Secotan."

wherin are the tombes of their kings and princes, as will appere by the 22. figure likewise they haue garden notted bey the letter I. wherin they vse to sowe pompions. Also a place marked with K. wherin the make a fyre att their solemne feasts, and hard without the towne a riuer L. from whence they fetche their water.[24]

Although de Bry's engraving of Secoton shows sixteen houses, Harriot noted above that villages like "the towne of Secotan" which were not encircled by a palisade of poles were "commonlye fayrer" and had "howses Scattered heer and ther." Such was the case with the main village of Chawanoac on the Chowan River where David Phelps's archaeological work in the 1980s uncovered evidence that the village was spread out along the western bank of the river for about a mile. Regarding the village of Secotan, Phelps wrote, "In the open plan of Secotan, it is probable that the houses of the nobility and the ruler cluster along the main street that connects the public and ceremonial areas and buildings. The commoners' residences or farmsteads were dispersed around the country-side."[25]

Unfortunately, archaeologists have not yet been able to locate the site of the village of Secotan, although a considerable amount of archaeological work has been undertaken over the years at prospective sites adjacent to the Pamlico River.[26] Complicating matters is the unreliable depiction of the rivers and waterways south of Aquascogoc on the White/de Bry map, as well as the fact that "Secotan" appears at varying locations on other contemporary maps shown below. The first, a rough "sketch map" drawn by an unknown member of the 1585 colonization venture, placed Secotan on the north side of the Pamlico River possibly near the present-day location of Bath. On White's *La Virginea Pars* map, however, Secotan is clearly situated on the south side of the Pamlico River, and on the later imprecise White/de Bry engraving Secotan also is situated on the south side of the Pamlico River.

Quinn suggested that White may have transposed "Secotan" with another similarly named village like Seco or Cotan or Sectuock, which also appear on the White/de Bry and *La Virginea Pars* maps. Note also that the village of Seco on *La Virginea Pars* map had become Cotan on the White/de Bry engraving and that both spellings are contained within the word "Secotan." According to Geary, the Algonquian words Seco and Cotan are "fragmentary designations" of the town of Secotan, and that they all mean "town at the bend of a river," and, in the case of Sectuock, they who dwell at the bend of a river."[27]

"There was neuer any people apparelled, or white of colour, either seene or heard of amongst these people"

On whichever side of the Pamlico River it was located, however, the village of Secotan was very likely the place where Wingina was recuperating from his wounds when the Amadas-Barlowe reconnaissance voyagers arrived in early July of 1584. Several days afterwards word would have reached him from the coast that oddly clothed white men with beards had arrived in two great vessels. He would soon learn much more from messengers undoubtedly sent by his brother Granganimeo about the Englishmen led by Philip Amadas and Arthur Barlowe. Initially, though, Wingina would only have heard puzzling and fragmentary second-hand information: The strangers had come to shore and had begun to examine the barrier island, where they took special note of the plants and trees. A few of the strangers climbed cedar trees and viewed the land from the top branches. They carried many remarkable instruments and weapons, one of which (a matchlock arquebus) made

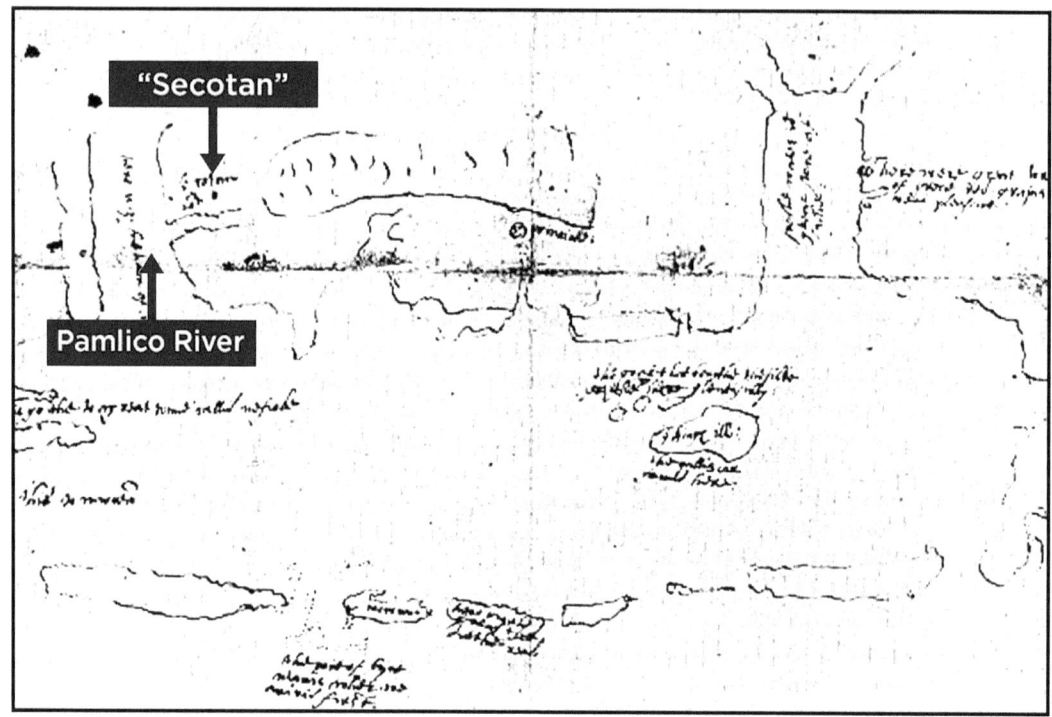

Barely legible 1585 rough, hand-drawn map with Secotan north of the Pamlico River (north is to the right).

such a loud and sudden noise that the ground seemed to shake and all the birds in the land arose at once and flew off screeching with fright.[28] Some of Wingina's people watched the strangers from concealment for two full days, saw them examine the island during the day, noted that they never ventured very far from their boats and never left that side of the barrier island. In the evening all the strangers returned to their ships where the breeze carried the scents from their onboard cooking inland. Throughout the night the dark outline of the ships rose and fell gently with the sea, and guards could be detected on both ships, their presence revealed by the occasional glimmer of moonlight on parts of their clothing and on the weapons they carried. What the native observers may not have seen, and certainly would not have understood if they had, was the ceremony the English had performed earlier by which they took possession of that island as well as all the "lands, countreis, or territories ... that shall abide within 200. Leagues [600 miles]" in the "right of the Queenes most excellent Maiestie."[29]

From a historical standpoint, it is important to note that, unlike tribal groups to the north and south of Secotan territory, Wingina and his people had no previous contact with Europeans—and virtually no knowledge about them—prior to the arrival of Amadas and Barlowe in 1584. More than two decades earlier, the Secotans had learned that a vessel had been wrecked in a storm along the coast south of Wokokon. The Indians there—perhaps elements of the Coree tribe—treated the few white survivors well, helping them prepare a makeshift craft with pieces of their clothing for sails and providing them with food for the voyage. Three weeks later the boat was found wrecked on the shore of another coastal island, the fate and identity of the whites unknown, although they were probably either Spaniards attempting to reach Santa Elena in present-day South Carolina, or possibly a French vessel attempting to locate Jean Ribault's earlier short-lived Charlesfort settlement which had been established in 1562. About six years later the remnants of another ship that had been wrecked in a storm were discovered on the beach along the Outer Banks in Secotan territory. The Indians managed to salvage nails and a few metal spikes, and with these "they made their best instruments."[30] These two-decades-old tools were the only partially metal "instruments" Wingina and his people possessed.

Wingina's people's scant knowledge about Europeans was limited to the single secondhand account about a few white shipwrecked survivors more than two decades earlier. "Other then these [the abovementioned white survivors]," Barlowe wrote, "there was neuer any people apparelled,

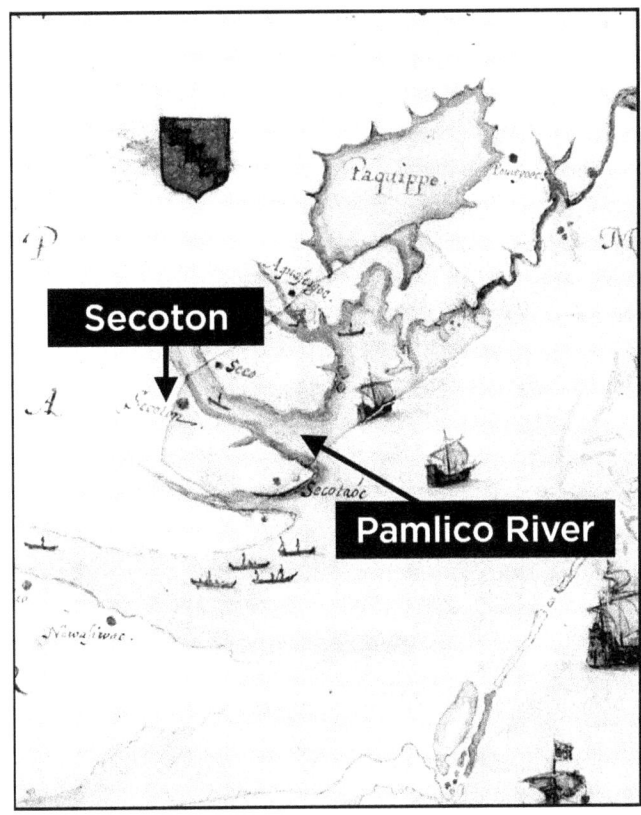

Portion of *La Virginea Pars* map showing Secotan south of the Pamlico River.

or white of colour, either seene or heard of amongst these people." The accuracy of this statement was manifested by the reactions of Wingina's people themselves to the English, "for they wondred maruelously when we were amongst them at the whitenes of our skins, euer coueting to touch our breasts, and to view the same."[31]

Given the considerable number of European explorations and contacts that had taken place in present-day Virginia and the Carolinas prior to 1584, it is both remarkable and initially difficult to understand how Wingina's people could have known or heard nothing at all about "people apparelled, or white of colour." For more than a half century before the arrival of Amadas and Barlowe, Europeans had been visiting the Atlantic coast to the north and south of Wingina's realm. In 1521 Francisco Gordillo sailed from Hispaniola in the West Indies perhaps as far north as Cape Fear and spent considerable time interacting with the native Indians at Winyah Bay in present-day South Carolina. In 1526 Vázquez de Ayllón established a Spanish colony in the same location at the mouth of the Pee Dee River. Sailing for King Francis I of France in 1524, the Italian explorer Giovanni da Verrazzano made contact with several coastal tribes just north of Cape Fear as he charted the Atlantic coast of North America. There is also evidence that Spaniards had made contact with the Woccon tribe far up the Neuse River by the 1520s.[32]

In 1540 Hernando de Soto led an expedition to the western part of present-day North Carolina during his exploration of North America. Two decades later the French briefly

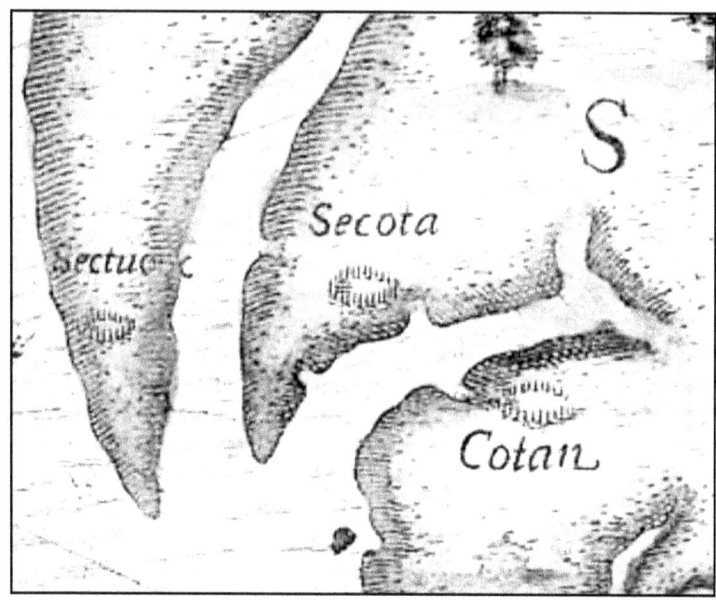

Portion of the White/de Bry map with Cotan, Secota and Sectuock.

settled Charlesfort at present-day Parris Island, South Carolina, and in 1566 the Spanish established Santa Elena, the first capital of La Florida, on the site of that abandoned French settlement. The Spanish town of Santa Elena, in fact, still existed at the time of the Amadas-Barlowe voyage in 1584. Between December of 1566 and March of 1568 the Spanish explorer Juan Pardo led two excursions from Santa Elena through the Piedmont of present-day North Carolina to the Appalachian Mountains. In January 1567 they reached Joara, the thriving Indian center of commerce near present-day Morganton, where they built Fort San Juan, the first European settlement in the interior of North Carolina, predating the Amadas-Barlowe voyage by seventeen years.

To the north of Wingina's territory, the Spanish had been active at what they called the Bahia de Santa Maria, or Chesapeake Bay, which is only about seventy miles from Wingina's village of Roanoac. It is believed by some historians that Vázquez de Ayllón discovered the Bahia de Santa Maria on one of his expeditions in the 1520s, but this is not definite. The Spanish were certainly at the Chesapeake in 1561, when a young native Indian whom the Spanish called Paquiquineo was abducted from the James River area, taken to Havana and then on to Spain. In 1570 Paquiquineo and a group of eight Jesuits returned to the Chesapeake to establish a settlement probably near the York River. Paquiquineo eventually killed the Jesuits but spared a young boy, as was the Algonquian custom, by the name of Alonso de Olmos. The Spanish returned in 1572 with a punitive expedition killing or capturing a number of Paquiquineo's tribesmen. Eight of the Indians were hanged from the ship's spars, one for each of the Jesuits.

Wingina and his people knew nothing whatsoever about any of this activity to the north and south of their territory, nor did they know that these previous contacts with Europeans had almost inevitably resulted in bloodshed. The Secotans' complete ignorance of Europeans, then, would partially explain the warm reception with which they greeted Amadas and Barlowe in 1584. Tribes to the north and south of Wingina had learned from past experience that the arrival of Europeans did not usually bode well for their people and should be met with extreme caution if not open hostility. This may possibly have been the case with Barlowe's co-captain, Philip Amadas, if he actually did make an excursion northward in 1584, as one questionable source later claimed. Little is known about the activities of Amadas in 1584, whose own account of the expedition, if he wrote one, has not been found. Years later, though, Richard Butler, who claimed to have been with the Amadas-Barlowe voyage in 1584, was captured and interrogated by the Spanish. In his deposition taken in 1596 he stated that Amadas explored the coast to the north and encountered hostile Indians. If Butler's account was accurate, Quinn suggested, Amadas could have entered Chesapeake Bay, and if so he may very well have encountered hostile tribes.[33] The native Indians there had already experienced bloody clashes with the Spanish, and so their instinctive reaction to the arrival of any European ships would likely have been hostile.

Previous experience with Europeans could also account for the seemingly unprovoked reaction of the Powhatan Algonquians when the Jamestown colonists arrived on April 26, 1607, at the entrance to the Chesapeake Bay. The English settlers landed at what they would soon call Cape Henry, and praised—in much the same glowing language as did Amadas and Barlowe—the "goodly tall Trees, with such Fresh-waters running through the woods." That same evening, however,

> there came the Savages creeping upon all foure, from the Hills, like Beares, with their Bowes in their mouthes, charged us very desperately in the faces, hurt Captaine Gabrill Archer in both hands, and a sayler in two places of the body very dangerous. After they had spent their Arrowes, and felt the sharpness of our shot, they retired into the Woods with great noise.[34]

All of this, then, begs the following question: how was it possible for the oral traditions of Wingina's people in 1584 to contain no memories or recollections whatsoever about any of the previous European activities to their north and south? The Powhatan Indians were able to relate memories to John Smith at Jamestown of Pardo's previously mentioned incursions nearly a half century earlier into the Piedmont of North and South Carolina.[35] How could it be that the oral traditions of the Powhatans to the *north* of Wingina's Roanoac village contained details of events that had never been "heard of amongst these [Wingina's] people," who dwelt much closer to the locations of those earlier Spanish incursions?

This phenomenon was likely a consequence of the coastal Carolina tribes' geographic isolation from what has been called the Great Trading Path. Also referred to as the Occaneechi Trail, which was actually just one segment of it, the Great Trading Path was an ancient interconnected network of Indian foot trails and waterways running from approximately the Chesapeake Bay area in present-day Virginia, southwest through the North Carolina Piedmont and continuing down into South Carolina. Long before the first arrival of Europeans to America the Great Trading Path had been the primary conduit connecting distant tribes not only for trade purposes but also for the exchange of information about significant events. Wingina's people were located about 100 miles east of the closest branch of the Great Trading Path. Most importantly, the Carolina Algonquians' access to the Great Trading Path was blocked by the tribal territorial boundaries of the hostile Iroquoian and Siouan tribes that dwelt to their west and south respectively. As shown on the map below, the tribes to the immediate north, south, and west of the Carolina Algonquians had direct access to the branches of the Great Trading Path indicated by the broken lines, but the shaded tidewater region where Wingina's people dwelt was far removed and effectively isolated.

As a result of their geographic confinement to the Coastal Plain, Wingina's people were never exposed to the stories about bearded men and their ships that were quite old and

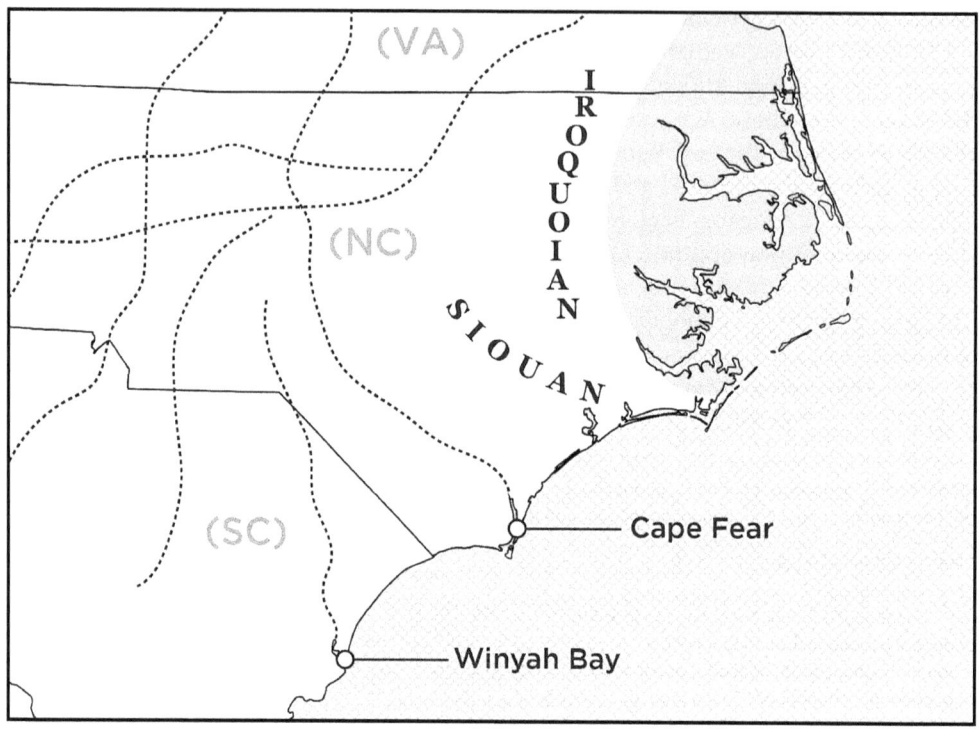

Branches of the Great Trading Path (courtesy Michael Gayle).

had been passed along the trading path for decades. Many of these memories were of the early Spanish explorations into the present-day Carolinas, particularly those of the above-mentioned expeditions by Juan Pardo. More than two decades after the Amadas-Barlowe reconnaissance voyage, the Powhatan Algonquians to the north could recall fragments of Pardo's 1566–68 expeditions in present-day North Carolina and relate them to John Smith and William Strachey at Jamestown. They were able to tell Smith about "certaine men cloathed like me [Smith]" who wore "short Coates, and Sleeves to the Elbowes" who had dwelt far to the south in the Carolina Piedmont. They told Strachey that the Indians there were taught by these clothed men how to build houses "one story above another," a fact confirmed by the journal of Pardo's expedition which relates how Pardo's men instructed the local Indians in the construction of wooden houses with second stories for the storage of corn.[36] As discussed elsewhere, however, both Smith and Strachey misinterpreted this information, erroneously concluding that they were clues to English survivors from the "lost" 1587 colony.[37]

Likewise in 1609, a native tribe far to the south of the Carolina Algonquians was able to relate current information about the two-year-old settlement at Jamestown. When in July of that year Francisco Fernández de Écija sailed from St. Augustine to the Rio Jordan, probably present-day Port Royal in South Carolina, the natives there provided him with remarkably detailed news about Jamestown which was acquired from their travels along the Great Trading Path. Although Rio Jordan was about 300 miles south of the Chesapeake Bay, the native Indians were able to give Écija a physical description of the Jamestown fort and its location, information about ships seen there, and the English habits of trading with the local Indians for food. Because Wingina's people were far removed and isolated from the Great Trading Path, it is understandable that "there was neuer any people apparelled, or white of colour, either seene or heard of amongst these people."

For Wingina's people the Amadas-Barlowe arrival was truly a "first contact" in the literal sense of the phrase and, as suggested, may provide some insight to the natural Secotan Algonquian mindset and explain to a great extent the very cordial reception offered to the English. These native people had had no previous contact with or even knowledge about Europeans, and consequently had not yet experienced or heard about any of the setbacks that plagued other contact locations and inevitably resulted in bloody conflicts and clashes. Although at first Wingina's Algonquians were understandably cautious about these odd strangers to their shores and were reluctant to show themselves, the actual contact was initiated by a bold but friendly, unnamed Indian who openly strode back and forth along the shore and addressed the English confidently as they approached. The Algonquian was then "brought ... with his owne good liking, aboord the ships" where he was given gifts, tasted English food and drink, and toured both ships. Upon returning to shore "he fell to fishing" and "diuided his fish into two parts, pointing one part to the ship, and the other to the pinnesse; which, after he had (as much as he might) requited the former benefites receiued, departed out of our sight."

The cultural traditions of native Indian hospitality have been described extensively by anthropologists, and nowhere was that practice more evident than in the Algonquians' welcome and subsequent treatment of the English during their month-long visit in 1584. Their friendly behavior no doubt also facilitated the trading arrangement with the English, who had many desirable items to offer, but that was only a beneficial byproduct of a longstanding cultural tradition of hospitality. Gift-giving and exchange was an integral part of hospitality, as author Seth Mallios has described[38]; nevertheless, hospitality was also freely offered to strangers who were unable to reciprocate. Note, for example, the hospitality and assistance given by the neighboring coastal tribe to the abovementioned shipwrecked survivors, who could do them no harm and who had nothing whatsoever to offer in exchange. Although Barlowe's account was certainly completed and edited after his return to England in order to present the most optimistic view to prospective investors and colonists, there is no hint whatsoever that this month long contact with Wingina's Algonquians was anything but friendly and productive.

Back at Secota or Secotan, the "chiefe towne" where Wingina most likely lay wounded, the startling news about the arrival of the English would have presented a dilemma of sorts. Wingina was currently preoccupied, either allied with or actually leading the Secotans in the "mortall warre" against Piemacum, and had become incapacitated, at least for the time being. He was physically unable to travel to the coast to evaluate and take personal charge of this unforeseen development involving strangers who had arrived in his domain, their purpose and intentions yet unclear. On the other hand, based on the preliminary news, these newcomers seemed to possess strange powers and instruments, and perhaps an association with them could prove to be beneficial, not only in terms of trade, but also as valuable allies in the ongoing war against his enemy Piemacum.

The subsequent reports that Wingina received from Grangamineo's messengers were encouraging. Good relations seemed to have been established with these strangers who called themselves "English," and many excellent trade goods had already been obtained from them. These English, he soon learned, planned to sail home perhaps with one or two Algonquian Indians and promised to return the following year. At this time it is possible that Wingina could have designated Wanchese, one of his own trusted Roanoac tribesmen, to go with the English, learn as much as he could about them, and report this intelligence to him upon his return. The last information relayed to Wingina in August was that the English had indeed departed, taking with them Wanchese and the Croatoan named Manteo.

"The two and twentieth of Iuly wee arriued safe at Hatorask"

By July 3, 1585, Wingina's wounds had long since healed, and he was back at his village of Roanoac, when he received word that the English had finally returned and were anchored near the inlet at Wokokon, about sixty miles to the south. Two weeks later, however, word had spread from the Indians fleeing from the village at Aquascogoc that these same English had burned their village and destroyed their corn crop. As already stated, this incident at Aquascogoc, in retaliation for the supposed theft of a silver cup, did far more damage than the English realized. To them it was simply a lesson taught to "the sauages" that positive relations with the English were possible—even desirable—as long as the Indians understood that offenses, however slight, would not be tolerated. What the Indians at Aquascogoc *did* clearly understand, was that the English had not only inexplicably destroyed their homes and their entire village, but their food supply as well. Although the English never fully understood its ramifications, the incident at Aquascogoc severely damaged the expectation, which had been established largely through the efforts of Granganimeo and his wife the previous summer, that the two peoples could be united in a bond of co-equal friendship and brotherhood. It was the first fracture in Anglo-Algonquian relations.

It is important to keep in mind that, unlike Granganimeo, Manteo, Wanchese and all the other Algonquians who had interacted with the English in 1584, this was Wingina's first contact with them. The return of the English must have been highly anticipated, but the reality was certainly a disappointment. First there was the abovementioned distressing report about the destruction of Aquascogoc on July 16, which had to have been relayed to Wingina at Roanoac days before the English arrived there. To make matters worse, Wanchese abandoned the English immediately upon his return from England, and he undoubtedly gave Wingina a negative assessment about his experiences in England and what they foretold about the future of the Roanoac tribe.

And then there was what could only have been seen as a blatant and offensive breach of traditional etiquette: the greeting ritual. There are two accounts of the first colony's 1585 voyage, Lane's and another by one of Grenville's men, and neither makes any reference at all to an initial greeting or meeting between Wingina and the English. On July 3, after the English ships anchored at Wokokon, Grenville "sent word of our arriuing at Wocokon, to Wingina at Roanoak." More than three weeks later, on July 27, the fleet finally anchored at the inlet off Roanoke Island, "and there we rested." On July 29 the first meeting was held aboard the 140 tun flagship *Tyger* with Granganimeo and Manteo. It is highly significant that Wingina was absent.

Algonquian tradition demanded that the initial arrival of any high-status persons to a leading weroance's territory be accompanied by a formal greeting ceremony complete with verbal and non-verbal rituals. An important part of the greeting required that mats of woven marsh reeds be placed in a particular arrangement to acknowledge the prominence of the visitor(s) and in order that "high-status individual[s] not be in direct contact with the ground."[39] The proper way to sit at the ceremony was cross-legged. A long speech was given by the hosting weroance which was accompanied by gestures such as the universal symbol of friendship and good will by placing a hand over the heart. An exchanging of gifts followed the ceremony. These were important and memorable occasions, organized as public events and attended by as many of the native community as was logistically possible. If the village of the hosting weroance was palisaded, as was Wingina's Roanoac village, the ceremony would be held outside the town in an open space large enough to accommodate the weroance, his guards, and a great retinue of attendants and onlookers.

Granganimeo had conducted such a ceremony the previous summer when the Amadas-Barlowe reconnaissance expedition arrived. At that time, however, Wingina was recuperating from his wounds at a village many days away, and so the greeting ritual was left to his brother. The ceremony was held on the beach, presumably at or near Wokokon, opposite the two anchored English ships and was attended by "fortie or fiftie men, very handsome and goodly people, and in their behauiour as mannerly and ciuill as any of Europe."[40] The arrival of the English at Hatorask on July 27, 1585, was a momentous event requiring a similar or perhaps even more elaborate greeting ceremony. The newly arrived English were not only more numerous than the previous group, but were led by Grenville and Lane, each of whom was of higher status and rank than Amadas and Barlowe. Furthermore, the English had anchored this time at the inlet near Roanoke Island and would soon come ashore on Wingina's island. Most importantly, this was to be Wingina's first contact with the leading Englishmen, requiring him to observe the tradition of a ceremonial greeting.

It can be presumed that Wingina expected Grenville to arrive at his Roanoac village soon after July 3, when he was informed that the English were anchored at Wokokon. Although he must have been perplexed by Grenville's three week delay, Wingina would have been prepared to conduct the formal greeting ceremony on July 27 when Grenville finally arrived at the inlet off Roanoke. However, Grenville rested aboard the *Tyger* on July 27, and he apparently spent July 28 organizing the governance of the colony and arranging his agenda for a meeting to be held on the flagship *Tyger* the following day. The failure of Grenville to follow the traditional etiquette of an arriving high status guest such as himself would have been a breach of etiquette and an insult, to say the least, to Wingina and the Roanoacs. In addition, by conducting the first formal meeting with the Algonquians on July 29 aboard the *Tyger*, Grenville usurped the role that was rightly Wingina's, that of hosting weroance. Although Grenville may or may not have been aware of the meaning of his actions, the message he sent was clear: The English did not see themselves as guests, but as colonizers.

It is not surprising, then, that Wingina did not personally attend what must have been announced as an important meeting aboard the flagship *Tyger* with Sir Richard Grenville, Governor Ralph Lane, and other prominent English colonists on July 29. He would have certainly been invited, but Grenville's flagrant breach of protocol would probably have precluded Wingina's attendance. Instead he sent his brother Granganimeo as his intermediary, accompanied by Manteo, whom the English fully trusted and who had acquired a facility with the English language during his stay at Raleigh's household. It is not known exactly what was discussed at the meeting aboard the *Tyger*, but, since Governor Ralph Lane began the construction of a fort on Roanoke Island shortly thereafter, one of the likely topics must have been the potential site for the new English settlement.

Prior to the meeting on July 29, it is probable that Lane, who was skilled in the construction of fortifications, had scouted the northern portion of Roanoke Island for a suitable location for a fort and settlement. As far as the English were concerned, Wingina's permission may neither have been required nor sought. Amadas and Barlowe had already "take[en] possession of the same, in the right of the Queenes most excellent Maiestie, as rightfull Queene, and Princesse of the same, and after deliuered the same ouer to your vse, according to her Maiesties grant, and letters patents, vnder her Highnesse great seale."[41] It was decided that the fort and settlement was to be located somewhere towards the northern end of the island, probably in part because Grenville had already explored much of Pamlico Sound to the south, and the northern part of Roanoke Island would give the English access to Albemarle Sound for exploration farther west. It was also close enough—perhaps a mile or so—to Wingina's corn fields, which the English would increasingly rely upon for a food source.

Considerable archaeological work has been undertaken at the north end of Roanoke Island since 1947, but neither the site of Lane's fort nor the colonists' settlement has been found. The location of Wingina's village also remains undiscovered. It had long been thought that Northwest Point may have been the location of Wingina's village, since archaeologist William Haag recorded the discovery of some early Indian potsherds there in 1958.[42] Many of the specimens, however, indicated a continuing Indian presence on the island for centuries before the arrival of the English, and nothing was found to suggest that a native village was located there. David Phelps later excavated the shoreline at Northwest Point and concluded that "the logical hypothesis is that this site was not inhabited in the 16th century, probably having been abandoned some centuries earlier because of low elevation and erosion."[43]

Similar problems have hindered the search for the 1585 English fort and settlement. Extensive archaeological excavations in and around the small earthwork seen along the Harriot Nature Trail at the Fort Raleigh National Historical Park have unearthed relatively few 16th century artifacts and nothing that could be associated with an occupied fort or settlement. The function and age of the earthwork has not been determined, and it has even been suggested that it was constructed in the 17th or 18th century.[44] A number of excavations have also been conducted over the years at what archaeologist J. C. Harrington termed the "outwork," located near the earthwork. Artifacts found at the outwork site are consistent with 16th century assaying materials, which indicate that metallurgy activity had probably been conducted there. Hakluyt had recommended that "Mynerall men" should accompany Raleigh's "Westerne discouerie," and a metallurgist named Doughan Gannes (also spelled Youghan or Joachim Ganz) was one of "the names of those as well Gentlemen as others, that remained one whole yeere in Virginia, vnder the Gouernement of Master Ralph Lane."[45] The outwork, then, could have been the site of a metallurgy lab or workshop where Gannes and possibly Harriot conducted scientific activities in 1585–6. The site, however, could not have been part of the fort or settlement since "there was nothing that could be attributed to the day-to-day living of 100 people."[46] As illustrated in the drawing below, based on a 1972 study and John White's depictions,[47] the northern end of Roanoke Island has been severely eroded since 1585, and it is likely that the sites of Lane's fort and the English settlement, as well as Wingina's village, are now submerged somewhere offshore.

There are several clues in the Roanoke accounts that, when pieced together, may provide at least a general idea of where Wingina's village and Lane's fort were located at the time of the Roanoke voyages. Barlowe wrote of his boat trip on Pamlico Sound to the village on Roanoke Island that it was "at the north end thereof," and as he and his men "came towardes it, [it was] standing neere vnto the waters side." Assuming Barlowe and his men rowed northward into present-day Roanoke Sound, which is most likely, they would have observed the palisaded village on their left not far from the shore line. That location would correspond with the de Bry engraving *"The Arrival of the Englishmen in Virginia"* as well

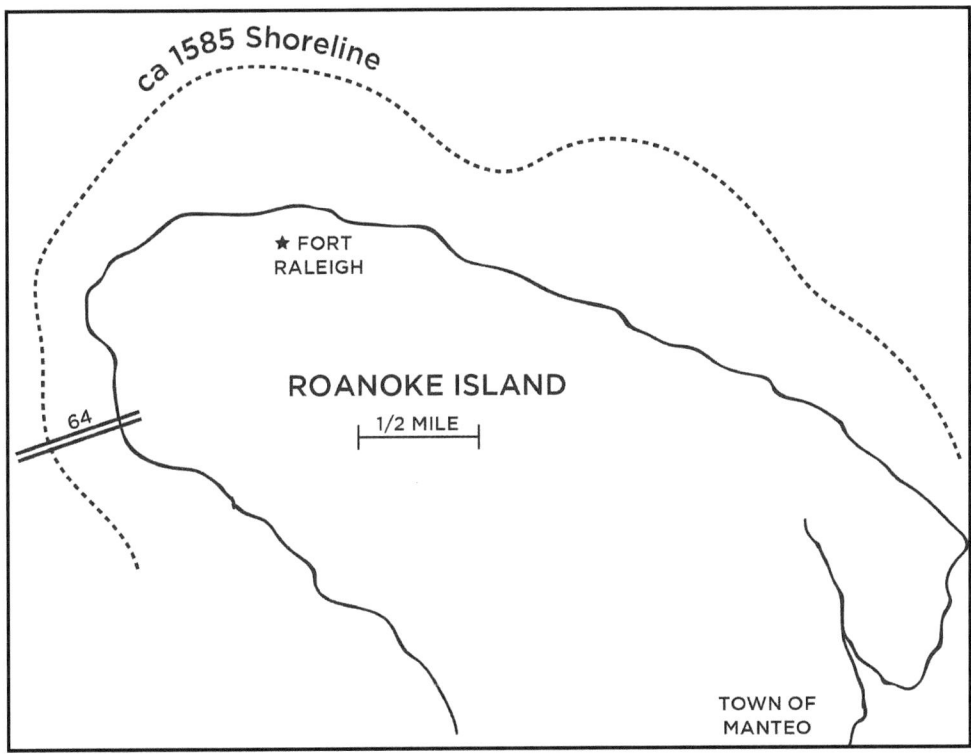

Approximate shoreline erosion since 1585 (courtesy Michael Gayle).

as White's *La Virginea Pars* map, both of which placed Wingina's village near the northeast end of the island, as illustrated below. If those maps are at all accurate, it seems clear that Wingina's village of Roanoac could not have been located at present-day Northwest Point.

When White finally returned to Roanoke Island in 1590 in search of his "lost" colonists, he provided a number of clues concerning the location of Lane's fort and nearby settlement. By using a representation of Roanoke Island and the location of Wingina's village as White drew it in 1585, and by tracing the route of White's search for his colonists in 1590, it may be possible to identify, at least in general terms, the location of Lane's fort. The following lines detailing White's search have been excerpted from his 1590 account and are listed numerically:

1. (Aug. 17) "We put off from Hatorask [inlet], being the number of 19 persons in both boates: but before we could get to the place where our planters were left, it was so exceeding darke, that we overshot the place a quarter of a mile."

2. (Aug. 17–18) "There we espied towards the North end of the Island the light of a great fire thorow the woods, to which we presently rowed: when wee came right ouer against it, we let fall our Grapnel neere the shore and sounded with a trumpet a Call, and afterwardes many familiar English tunes and Songs, and called to them friendly; but we had no answere, we therefore landed at day-breake, and comming to the fire, we found the grasse and sundry rotten trees burning about the place."

3. (Aug. 18) "From hence we went thorow the woods to that part of the Island directly ouer aguinst Dasamonqwepeuk."

Location of the village of Roanoac on the de Bry engraving "The Arrival of the Englishmen in Virginia."

    4. (Aug. 18) "From thence we returned by the water side, round about the North point of the Iland, vntill we came to the place, where I left our Colony."

    5. (Aug. 18) "And hauing well considered of this, we passed toward the place where they were left in sundry houses, but we found the houses taken downe, and the place very strongly enclosed with a high palisado of great trees, with cortynes and flankers very Fortlike."[48]

It was late afternoon on August 17, 1590, when White and the rest of the men set out from Hatorask for the fort and settlement where he had left his colonists three years earlier. By the time they neared the settlement location, it was too dark to see the shoreline clearly and they mistakenly went a quarter mile past their intended landing place (#1). This is an important piece of information because it means that the settlement was behind them at that point. They may have understandably overshot the settlement's location in the dark where the shoreline curved to

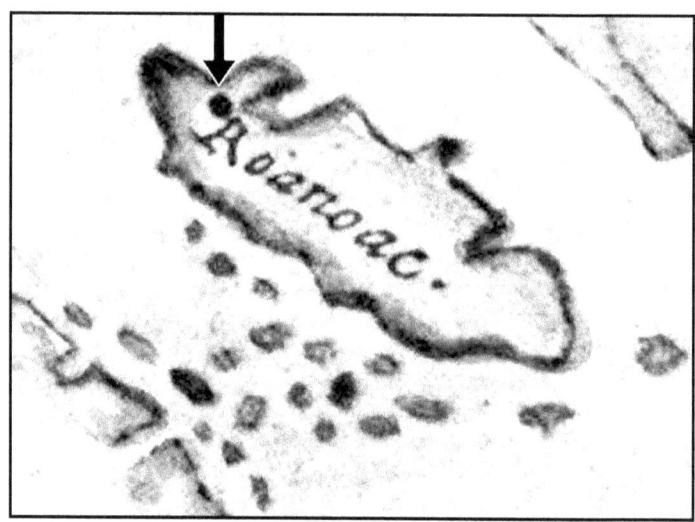

Location of the village of Roanoac, indicated by the dot on *La Virginea Pars* map.

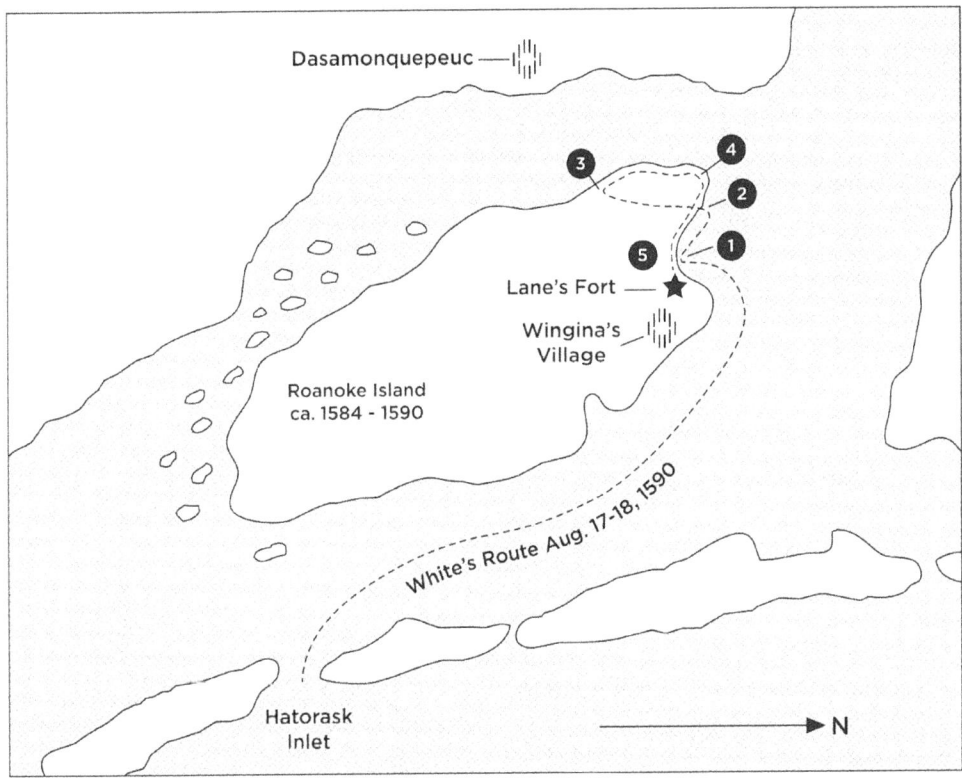

Proposed locations of the stops made by White en route to the English fort and settlement, August 17–18, 1590 (courtesy Michael Gayle).

the south and not realized their mistake until it started curving north again. Their investigation of the fire towards the north end of the island (#2) brought them, therefore, even farther away from the settlement location. At daybreak on August 18 they went ashore and, after determining that the fire was naturally caused, they walked through the woods until they reached the shoreline (#3) opposite the village of Dasamonquepeuc. From there they searched along the shoreline all the way around the north end of the island and had to have continued for a quarter mile beyond the point they first stopped on Aug 17 (#1) in order to reach the shoreline location (#5) which was just a short walk inland to the settlement and fort site. The suggested location would also concur with Lane's estimate that Dasamonquepeuc was "within two leagues [six miles]" of the fort. Wingina's village of Roanoac, long since abandoned by the time White returned, may have been located about a mile east of the fort's suggested location.

"From the New Fort in Virginia"

The English spent the first few weeks of August 1585, ferrying supplies and materials to the settlement site where their dwellings and the fort were under construction. The construction of the fort, as well as the settlement houses and other outbuildings, was most likely completed before Grenville's departure on August 27, and certainly by "this third of September, 1585," the date on which Lane wrote a letter to Hakluyt "from the new fort in

Virginia." Wingina must have watched this entire process with both amazement and apprehension as he, for the first time, witnessed some of the remarkable capabilities of the English. He surely marveled at the quality and effectiveness of their metal tools and weapons, particularly their firearms, but he undoubtedly also worried about their intentions, which were not yet clear, and their capacity to harness forces he could not understand. Equally troubling was the uncertainty surrounding the origins of these newcomers, especially in light of Wanchese's disturbing report about the vast English towns across the sea, towns filled with houses and people too numerous to count.

Harriot commented on the technological inferiority of the Indians. Although Wingina's people "haue no such tooles, nor any such craftes, sciences and artes as wee," Harriot wrote, "in those thinges they doe, they shewe excellencie of wit." Furthermore, he went on to say:

> And by howe much they vpon due consideration shall finde our manner of knowledges and craftes to exceede theirs in perfection, and speed for doing or execution, by so much the more is it probable that they shoulde desire our friendships & loue, and haue the greater meanes of good gouernment bee vsed, that they may in short time be respect for pleasing and obeying vs. Whereby may bee hoped if brought to ciuilitie, and the imbracing of true religion.[49]

Based on the encouraging reports he had received from his brother Granganimeo, Wingina had reason to expect that the English would be a source of useful and valuable trade goods as well as a potentially powerful ally in the "mortall warre" against his enemy Piemacum far to the south. Trade and gift exchanges had played a prominent part during the previous visit of the English in 1584, when initial Anglo-Algonquian relations were established. In addition, there was the promise of a "great store of commodities" to be had if the English could be persuaded to attack Piemacum.[50] It is interesting to note that trade goods and gift exchanges were barely mentioned again in the Roanoke accounts, and there was no further reference made to a potential alliance with Wingina against Piemacum.

The English had returned in 1585 with a specific agenda, and "colonization" is too broad a term to accurately describe it. Richard Hakluyt had already published his *Discourse of Western Planting* in which he expounded on twenty objectives and benefits to be gained by colonizing America. They can generally be summarized by the following: explore the land in search of valuable natural resources, attempt to find the fabled all-water passage westward to "Cathaio and China," and establish a foothold in America from which privateering expeditions could be launched against Spanish shipping. Regarding their habitation and relations with the native Indians, the English claimed that they "are not to be feared, but that they shall haue cause both to feare and loue vs, that shall inhabite with them."[51] In time, however, that claim would be put to the test.

From his observation of the activities taking place perhaps a mile or so from his village, Wingina soon realized that the English settlement and fort were intended to be permanent installations. Wingina was also acutely aware that a divergence of opinions about the English was already developing within the tribe. His father Ensenore and brother Granganimeo, both of whose words carried considerable weight, urged him to cooperate with Grenville and Lane and the rest of the English, and he did so, if warily, through the remainder of the summer and into the fall. No doubt Wanchese's warnings about the nature of the English and their potential dangers also ran through his mind at this early stage, but Wanchese's opinions were clearly in the minority. Of concern, too, was the fact that by the time Grenville sailed for England on Aug 25, the English had already made requests of Wingina to supplement the colony's food stores. In addition, the English had started sending expeditions to other tribal provinces, particularly to the north and the west, where Wingina had already established an alliance with the Chawanoacs and probably with the Moratucs and the Weapemeocs. Wingina would have been concerned, with good reason, that his alliances could be threatened or weakened by potential English interference.

Both puzzling and remarkable to Wingina was the message that the English claimed was contained in a book about "the true and onely God, and his mightie works." Among Hakluyt's objectives for English colonization, he had listed "thinlargement of the Gospell of Christe, whereunto the princes of the refourmed religion are chefely bounde, amongst whome her Majestie ys principall." Harriot took a particular interest in this pursuit, noting that "Some religion they haue already, which although it be farre from the trueth, yet being as it is, there is hope it may be the easier and sooner reformed."[52] To that end he began preaching to the Indians from a bible which "therein … conteined the true doctrine of saluation through Christ, with many particularities of Miracles and chiefe points of Religion, as I was able then to vtter [Harriot having acquired some fluency in Algonquian].… Many times and in euery towne where I came, according as I was able, I made declaration of the contents of the Bible." According to Harriot his proselytizing was rather effective. Many Indians, he wrote, attempted "to touch it [the bible], to embrace it, to kisse it, to holde it to their breastes and heads."[53]

Harriot specifically mentioned Wingina, "the Wiroans with whom we dwelt," whose "people would bee glad many times to be with vs at our Prayers," and Wingina himself often joined them. In the late summer and fall, as the English explored the area, Wingina "sometimes accompanied vs" to other villages "to pray and sing Psalmes, hoping thereby to be partaker of the same effects which we by that meanes also expected." On one occasion a number of Indians, fearing that they might have offended the English in some unintended way, asked them to pray to their God for relief "when their corne began to wither by reason of a draught." If the "God of England … would preserue their Corne," the Indians promised, "when it was ripe we also should be partakers of the fruit."[54]

"The people began to die very fast…"

The events that occurred during the winter of 1585–6 were unrecorded in the Roanoke accounts, or perhaps purposefully deleted, but it is evident that relations between Wingina and the English deteriorated significantly during that time. That portion of Lane's account was doubtless revised and edited later so that future investment and participation in Raleigh's colonization enterprises would not be discouraged. Nothing specific is mentioned in Harriot's *A Briefe and true report* either, except for a vague reference noting that "some of our company towards the ende of the yeere, shewed themselues too fierce in slaying some of the people in some Townes."

It is very possible that the worsening relations and eventual conflicts resulted from an inexplicable "power" the English seemed to possess, one that even they themselves did not fully understand: the transmission of infectious diseases among an Indian population that had no natural immunities. The seemingly supernatural ability to "kill and slay whom we would without weapons" struck fear in the hearts of the Indians. Wingina himself had fallen ill on two occasions and called upon the English to pray to their God for his recovery:

> Twise this Wiroans was so grieuously sicke that he was like to die, and as he lay languishing, doubting of any helpe by his owne priestes, and thinking hee was in such danger for offending vs and thereby

our God, sent for some of vs to pray and bee a meanes to our God that it would please him either that he might liue, or after death dwell with him in blisse, so likewise were the requests of many others in the like case.[55]

Wingina survived these illnesses, but most who contracted English diseases were not so fortunate. Wherever the English traveled, it seemed, "within a few dayes after our departure from euery such Towne, the people began to die very fast." Word soon circulated among the native people that some incident had to have occurred at these towns that provoked the wrath of the English. As referenced above, it was already believed, at least among "the common and simple sort of people," as Harriot wrote, that even unintentional offenses against the English could result in droughts and crop failure. "The oldest men in the Countrey" reported that such a strange occurrence had never happened before. This "marueilous accident in all the Countrey," as Harriot called the mysterious deaths, led many of the native people to believe that the English were not men but gods.

Old Ensenore's continued pleas to Wingina for cooperation with the English were based mainly on his belief in their supernatural powers and that these strange occurrences had been preordained. He had concluded that the English were "dead men returned into the world againe," and "were not subiect to bee destroyed by them."

There was universal wonder among the native Indians about the strange ability of the English to strike their enemies down from afar. According to Harriot the Indians were also amazed that "there was no man of ours knowen to die, or that was specially sicke." This was not completely accurate, since he also commented in his report that "there were but foure of our whole company (being one hundred and eight) that died all the yeere and that but at the latter ende thereof." Harriot was careful to minimized the significance of these few deaths, however, by explaining that of "all foure especially three were feeble, weake, and sickly persons before euer they came thither, and those that knewe them much marueyled that they liued so long beeing in that case, or had aduentured to trauaile." This comment, like so much of his *Briefe and true report*, was written with a particular audience in mind—prospective colonists for Raleigh's next colonization attempt. In any case English deaths appear to have been few during 1585–86, and they probably hid them from the Indians to maintain the façade that they were indeed supernatural beings. The assumption among some of Wingina's people that the English were gods of some sort was aided by the fact that there were no women among them and that they did not "care for any of theirs." Several of the native Indians concluded from this that the Englishmen must not have been "borne of women, and therefore [were] not mortal." It was thought by some that the Englishmen could be from an ancient generation who had "risen againe to immortalitie."

Wingina himself had observed the aftereffects of the Englishmen's "inuisible bullets" in several villages, and for a while he seemed convinced that they had the power to strike down those who may have given some cause for offense. Like many others, he was "perswaded that it was the worke of our God through our meanes," and that the English were capable of killing their enemies "and not come neere them." These occurrences, however, seemed random and unrelated to any transgressions, intended or not, and doubts about the supernatural qualities of the English eventually began to surface. For Wingina, those suspicions were enhanced considerably by a response given by the English to a logical request he made. In view of the love and friendship the English professed for him and his people, Wingina asked, would the English use their power to kill his own distant enemies, perhaps Piemacum and the Pomouiks? The English balked at Wingina's request. It took a great deal of rationalizing on Harriot's part to explain that "our God would not subiect himselfe to any such prayers and requests of men: that indeede all things haue bene and were to be done according to his good pleasure as he had ordeined." In fact, Harriot continued, God's "true seruants ought rather to make petition for the contrary, that they with them might liue together with vs, be made partakers of his trueth, and serue him in righteousnesse."[56] Wingina must have found this response unsatisfactory and contradictory, particularly since it had been concluded that the deaths were caused directly and intentionally by the English. It is not known when Wingina made this request, but the inadequate response certainly would have made him question the belief that cooperation and obedience to the English would protect him and his people.

By now Wingina harbored suspicions about the English colonists, who seemed far less invincible than Ensenore and others believed. Many of the English, in fact, appeared to be idle and lazy, and even Harriot noted that some "had litle or no care of any other thing but to pamper their bellies." Yet they were unable to provide their own food, which they increasingly expected to be supplied by Wingina. Despite their advanced tools and efficiencies, they were incapable of constructing the most basic weirs for catching fish, which could have provided a continuous supply for the colony. As Lane noted, "at that time wee had no weares for fish, neither coulde our men skill of the making of them." Instead they made ever-increasing demands upon Wingina's tribe to supply corn and other foodstuffs, which even under normal circumstances would barely sustain the Indians themselves through the winter. Memories of the summer assault at Aquascogoc and the destruction of that village's corn supply by these same Englishmen must have been particularly galling to Wingina as he anticipated the inevitable food shortages that would occur in the months to come.

In addition to "their [the Englishmen's] misdemeanour and ill dealing in the countrey," the mounting death toll from English diseases must have been a contributing factor in the clashes that eventually erupted. Harriot hinted at "their [the Indians'] wicked practices" committed against the English, but, as mentioned, he provided no details whatsoever and Lane's account was almost certainly revised in order to exclude those bloody conflicts that had occurred "towards the ende of the yeere." Harriot acknowledged that some of the unspecified retaliatory measures taken by the English "might easily ynough haue bene borne withal," but added "yet notwithstanding ... it was on their [the Indians'] part iustly deserued." By this time Wingina's attitude toward the English was on the decline, and he was gradually coming to the realization that the once promising English presence was proving to be destructive to the Indians and their way of life.

"Wingina changeth his name"

At some time after the outbreak of the terrible sickness, Wingina's brother Granganimeo died. Although nothing was said about the circumstances of his death, it is most likely that he succumbed to the one of these infectious diseases spread through contact with the English. Based on Wingina's reaction, it is clear that he placed the blame for his brother's death squarely on the mysterious, but malevolent, influence of the English. Granganimeo's death brought about a transformation in Wingina that would have critical consequences in the months ahead: Upon his brother's death Wingina changed his name to Pemisapan, an important event which thereafter redefined himself as a committed enemy of the English, dedicated to their destruction. Geary interpreted the Algonquian name "Pemisapan" to mean "a wolf who watches from a distance,"[57] an appropriate term for one who would thereafter be prepared to strike at the English when the time was right. Lane was unaware of the significance of this name-change, citing it simply as a chronological occurrence rather than the pivotal event it was. Names held far more relevance to the Indians than they did for Europeans and name *changes*, in fact, were transformational experiences in the Algonquian world. As already noted, the name "Manteo" had spiritual connotations and was very possibly a new name acquired by the Croatoan weroance before he embarked on his transformational journey to acquire the powerful "manitou" of the English. A later name change with historical parallels to Wingina's was that of the Powhatan weroance Opechancanough, whose new war name "Mangopeesoman" preceded his coordinated massacre of the English colonists in 1622.

Although the English never fully understood the transitional nature of Algonquian name changes, it is interesting to compare the different contexts in which "Wingina" and/or "Pemisapan" were mentioned by Harriot and Lane in their accounts of the 1585 colonization venture. In Harriot's *Briefe and true report* Wingina was mentioned by name twice, both in very complimentary terms. The first was to tell how glad Wingina was to join the English in their prayers both at the Roanoke settlement and elsewhere. The second was to mention "especially the Wiroans Wingina" as one "of the inhabitants which were our friends." Harriot referred to "this Wiroans" on one other occasion, as mentioned above, when he was sick and, "doubting of any helpe by his owne priestes," sent for some of the English to pray for him. "Pemisapan" was not mentioned at all. Anyone reading Harriot's report would come away knowing nothing about Wingina's transition and its deadly aftermath ... which is precisely what Harriot intended. Lane on the other hand referred to Wingina just once, to note his name change, but mentioned Pemisapan twenty-one times, virtually all of which dealt with "the conspiracie of Pemisapan" against the English.

When Lane's account continues in early March of 1586, Pemisapan was already in the process of organizing a confederacy of various tribes from near and far to destroy the English. It was at this time that Ralph Lane and about fifty armed men arrived unexpectedly at the town of Chawanoac on Chowan River, where a meeting of various Chawanoacs, Mangoaks, and Moratuks had all gathered, according to Lane, as part of Pemisapan's plot against the English. Lane and his men forcibly dispersed the group of Indians and captured the Chawanoac weroance, Menatonon. The weroance then told Lane about a place called Chaunis Temoatan, which was far up the Moratuc River in the land of the Mangoaks. There, Menatonon told Lane, he might find "a marueilous mineral," called wassador, which was probably copper but which Lane may have thought was the elusive gold or silver that the English were anxious to find. Spanish treasure ships had already been transporting gold and silver from their La Florida colonies farther south, and the lure of similar riches was a primary motivation for many participants in Raleigh's 1585 venture. As mentioned above, Hakluyt had recommended that "mynerall men" should accompany Raleigh's ventures and a metallurgist named Doughan Gannes or Joachim Ganz was part of the 1585 enterprise.

It is just possible that the story about precious metals at Chaunis Temoatan was embellished as part of a deception orchestrated by Pemisapan and Menatonon, who were allies, to lure Lane and his men into a trap. It is clear that, while preparations were being made for Lane's voyage up the Moratuc River, Pemisapan was planning the expedition's annihilation. He sent messengers ahead to the villages along the river warning them about Lane's approach and instructing them on what actions to take in order to defeat them. One of these tribes was the Moratucs, who were also by this time allied with Pemisapan, and whose territory Lane would have to pass through as he ventured up the Moratuc River towards Chaunis Temoatan. Pemisapan was well aware that Lane's trip against the current up the Moratuc River would be an arduous one from the start. It was said of "this Riuer of Moratoc" that it "hath so violent a current from the West and Southwest," that "with oares it would scarse be nauigable: it passeth with many creekes and turnings and … the current runneth … strong."[58] Appropriately, "Moratuc" is translated from the Algonquian to mean "dangerous river."[59]

According to Pemisapan's plan the Lane expedition, which consisted of about thirty-five men plus a few Indian guides and two mastiffs in two double wherries [oared boats used for river transport], would first face exhaustion, then starvation, and finally annihilation as they extended their journey far up the river. Pemisapan's plan was to be carried out in two stages. First, as Lane advanced up the river, the Moratucs would abandon their riverside villages, taking their food stores with them. The English would thus be denied a chance to resupply their provisions, which would quickly run out, and they would soon be faced with starvation. Then, as the Englishmen weakened, the Indians would attack from a high river bank and massacre them.

Back at Roanoac in the meantime, Pemisapan would work to dispel the stubbornly persistent belief among Ensenore's followers that the English were supernatural beings and could not be destroyed. Pemisapan spread the word that the Moratucs and the Mangoaks had slain Lane and his men, proving not only that the English were not supernatural, but also that "our Lorde God was not God, since hee suffered vs to sustaine much hunger, and also to be killed." He then commanded that no corn was to be planted for the remaining seventy or so Englishmen at Roanoke that spring nor any weirs built for them. The weirs were especially crucial at this time, for as Harriot had written, "For foure moneths of the yeere, February, March, Aprill and May, there are plenty of Sturgeons. And also in the same moneths of Herrings … both these kinds of fish in those moneths are most plentifull, and in best season, which we found to be most delicate and pleasant meat."[60] In short time the English at Roanoke would weaken and starve and become easy prey for Pemisapan's forces.

The plan nearly succeeded. After rowing against the current for three or four days on the river, Lane's provisions had run out and they could not find even "a graine of Corne" in any of the abandoned villages near the riverside. Finally one evening the English heard Indian voices calling from beyond the steep river bank and, thinking they were being welcomed and would be provided with food, the two boats headed towards the shore. It was only then that Manteo, who was aboard Lane's boat, recognized that this was an ambush and warned the English off. The Indians then attempted to shower them with arrows, but the English managed to escape the ambush. Facing starvation, Lane decided to return to Roanoke, but not before resorting to killing the two mastiffs and making a "Dogges porridge" mixed with sassafras leaves.

Lane made good time rowing downriver and "came the next day by night to the Riuers mouth within foure or fiue miles of the same, hauing rowed in one day downe the current, much as in foure dayes wee had done against the same." On April 4 they "lodged vpon an Iland," probably one of the two near the mouth of the Moratuc on the White/de Bry map, "where wee had nothing in the world to eate but pottage of Sassafras leaues." A storm blew in the next day, preventing Lane from continuing into Albemarle Sound, where "there was no possibilitie of passage without sinking of our boates." On April 6, Easter morning, they entered the sound and by four o'clock they made it to the Weapemeoc village of Chipanum. Like the Moratucs, the Weapemeocs had also abandoned their villages, but the Englishmen found a few fish in the weirs near Chipanum, "as God was pleased not vtterly to suffer vs to be lost: for some of our company … were farre spent." On the following morning, April 7, Lane and his men arrived back at Roanoke Island.

Lane's safe arrival at Roanoke Island completely thwarted Pemisapan's plans. However weakened and nearly starved Lane and his men appeared, their return contradicted what Pemisapan had said about their fate and actually reinforced the belief that the English indeed had supernatural powers. Pemisapan now was forced to accede to Ensenore's urging to build weirs for the English and to sow the fields with enough corn to feed them. Grenville was scheduled to return to Roanoke Island soon—he had promised to return by Easter—with fresh supplies and additional colonists, and it now appeared that a widening English occupation of Pemisapan's territory was inevitable.

On April 20, however, less than two weeks after Lane's return from the trip up the Moratuc, old Ensenore died. As was the case with Granganimeo, the circumstances surrounding his death were not stated, but the effect was significant. The English lost their last friendly, influential voice among the Roanoacs and the only weroance who had stood against the

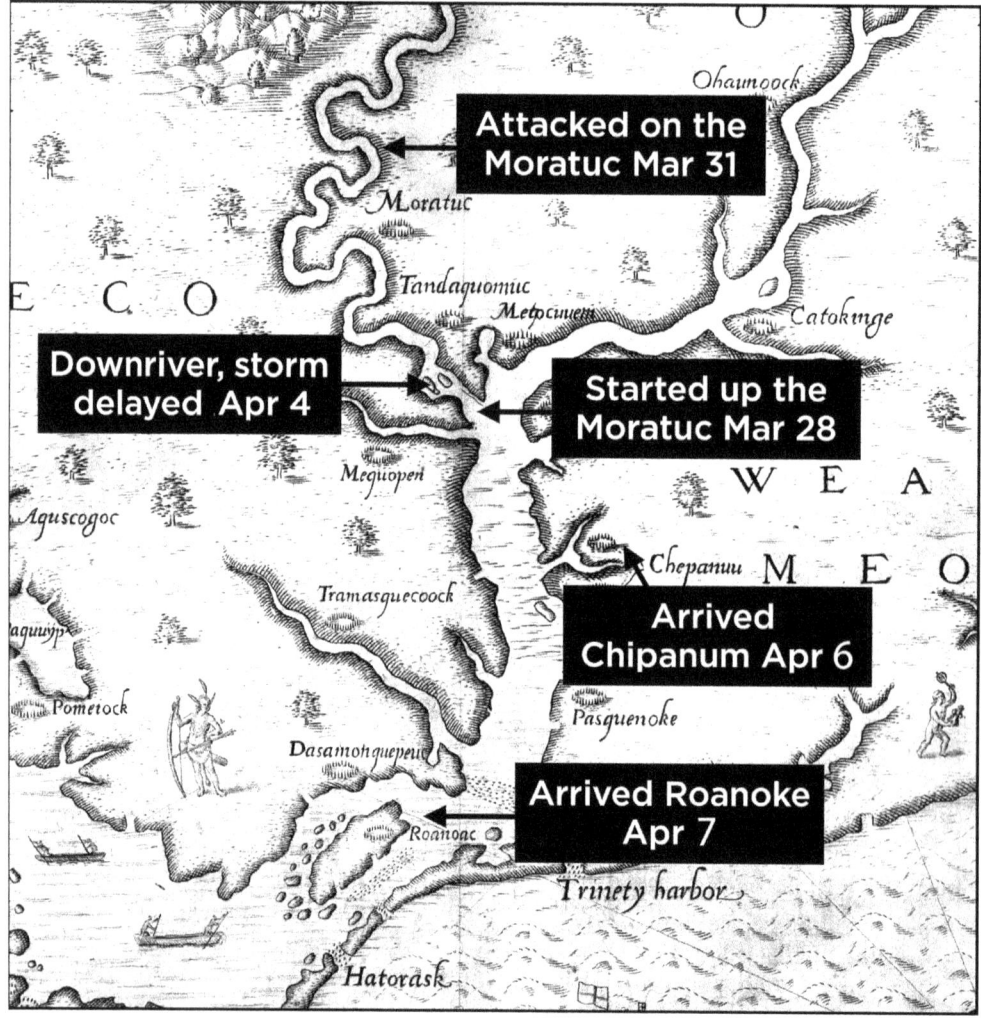

Lane's Moratuc expedition, March 28–April 7, 1586.

growing resentment of the English. Furthermore, assuming that Ensenore's death resulted from one of the English contagions that had so afflicted the tribes, his death would have been inexplicable and extremely troubling to his followers. As mentioned, it was widely held that the strange "inuisible bullets" responsible for so many deaths among the Indians were intentionally targeted by the English against wrongdoers who had committed some offense, real or imaginary, against them. If the English had deliberately directed this deadly force against Ensenore, their greatest ally among the Roanoacs, then no one was safe from the lethal powers of the English. Perhaps even more frightening was the possibility that this deadly power was indiscriminate, a deduction that must have occurred to many by this time. In either case, for the Indians the inescapable conclusion was that sickness and death were byproducts of simply associating with the English.

Ensenore's death erased most of the lingering support for the English, and Pemisapan quickly renewed his plan to assemble a coalition of tribes to annihilate them. He sent word to the weroances of the neighboring tribes to gather their warriors several weeks later at Dasamonquepeuc, ostensibly to participate in a great celebration in remembrance of Ensenore. The great assembly would not arouse English suspicions because such gatherings were common following the death of an important weroance. In the meantime he ordered that the weirs recently built for the English be broken up. At the same time he prohibited the Indians from providing any sustenance whatsoever to the English. As a result Lane wrote, "the famine grew so extreeme among vs" that he was forced to divide his numbers by sending some of his men to Hatorask and Croatoan and elsewhere in search of food. With the English force at Roanoke thus diminished, as Pemisapan anticipated, his assault on them would be far more effective.

The details of Pemisapan's strategy were as follows: After all the warriors had assembled at Dasamonquepeuc and some were strategically placed at Roanoac, which was expected to be accomplished by early June, Pemisapan's assault would commence. Signal fires were to be lit during the night on the west shore of the island opposite Dasamonquepeuc, alerting the forces there to launch their canoes and reassemble at the Roanoke Island shoreline. The first stage of the attack would be led by two of Pemisapan's subordinates, Tarraquine and Andacon, along with twenty other Indians, who would target Lane's house first. His dwelling was to be set afire, and then—according to Lane—when he came "running out of a sudden amazed in my shirt without armes, ... they would haue knocked out my braines." The same tactic was to be employed on the other principal Englishmen. Once the English leaders were killed, the main force of Pemisapan's coalition would fall upon the rest of the Englishmen, who would be quickly overwhelmed in the darkness and confusion. Any survivors who fled into the woods would be easily dispatched afterwards.

Pemisapan's plan was well thought out and strategically sound, and it may very well have been successful had not Skiko, who had been imprisoned at Roanoke Island since March, been divulging information to his captors about Indian activities and plots against the English. Ironically, the failure of Pemisapan's plan, and his own demise for that matter, resulted from the betrayal by an Indian whom he never suspected. Skiko was the "best beloued sonne" of Menatonon, the weroance of the Chawanoac tribe, who had been Pemisapan's ally since before the arrival of the Amadas-Barlowe reconnaissance voyage in 1584. Pemisapan had recruited these Chawanoacs, probably in early 1586, as part of his coalition against the English. The imprisonment of Skiko, however, effectively prevented Menatonon from taking part in any action against the English. It was likely for that reason that Pemisapan visited with Skiko on occasion and may have played a role in his attempted escape.

At one point Pemisapan had actually interceded with Lane on Skiko's behalf after the boy "attempted to run away." Lane subsequently chained him to the floor, "threatening to cut off his head," and only "remitted at Pemisapans request." Unbeknownst to Pemisapan, however, Skiko was gradually befriended by his English captors during his three month captivity, and he kept them informed about the Roanoac weroance's plans and intentions.

Lane decided to act before the coalition of Indians had sufficient time to gather at Dasamonquepeuc. He sent word to Pemisapan that Grenville's resupply fleet had arrived at Croatoan, a ruse intended to confuse and delay Pemisapan's plans. Lane informed Pemisapan that he was headed to Croatoan presently, but before leaving he wished to visit him at Dasamonquepeuc "to borrow of his men to fish for my company, and to hunt for me at Croatoan, as also to buy some foure dayes prouision to serue for my voyage." Pemisapan sent word back to Lane that he would deliver the provisions himself, but he delayed from day to day in order to allow time for his allied tribes to reach Dasamonquepeuc. It is also likely that Pemisapan dispatched scouts to Croatoan at this time to verify Lane's report about the English fleet's arrival.

Lane was aware that Pemisapan had Indians constantly watching his movements and that they "held as good espial vpon vs, both day and night, as we did vpon them." One of the spies for the English was an unidentified Roanoac Indian, "one of Pemisapans owne men" according to Lane, who kept the English informed about Pemisapan's progress and apparently divulged further details of the plot to Lane on May 31. The identity of this informant was not mentioned in the account, but he may have been a former follower of Pemisapan's father, old Ensenore, who had always advised against resisting the English. Quinn seems to have misinterpreted the passage in Lane's account regarding this unnamed Roanoac Indian. Lane stated that Pemisapan's plan "was reueiled vnto me by one of Pemisanans owne men, that night before he was slaine."[61] Quinn wrote, "We are not told the name of this Indian who was, it would seem, executed for treachery by Wingina [Pemisapan]."[62] Lane's "that night before he was slaine," however, was almost certainly a reference to Pemisapan himself, who was killed during Lane's surprise attack on June 1, the day after the unnamed Indian updated Lane on the progress of the plot, which would have been on the night of May 31. Lane went to great lengths to prevent any Indians from leaving Roanoke Island for Dasamonquepeuc the night before his attack, and therefore Pemisapan could not have learned anything about what had transpired that night. Furthermore, there is no evidence whatsoever that Pemisapan executed anyone for treachery or for anything else. As noted, on the night of May 31 Lane sent men to seize the canoes at Roanoke's western shore to prevent any Indians from bringing word about the English plans to Pemisapan at Dasamonquepeuc, located about two miles across present-day Croatan Sound. As the English guarded the shoreline they came upon two Indians who tried to leave in a canoe and "ouerthrew the canoa, and cut off two Sauages heads." This encounter alerted other Indians near the shore and a skirmish quickly ensued during which "some three or foure of them at the first were slaine with our shot; the rest fled into the woods."

On the following morning, June 1, Pemisapan was sitting in his village of Dasamonquepeuc conferring with a number of his weroances and others, when one of his scouts reported that Lane had arrived at the shore with about thirty men and wished to speak with him. The pressing topic Lane supposedly wanted to discuss was one of Pemisapan's weroances, Osacon, who had apparently attempted to free Lane's prisoner, Skiko, the previous night. Pemisapan sent word back to Lane that he would meet with him. As soon as the Englishmen approach Pemisapan, however, Lane shouted out the watchword "Christ our victory," and the English opened fire on the Indians. Pemisapan was "shot thorow" immediately and lay on the ground, assumed to be dead. As the attack continued, though, he jumped up and ran for the protection of the woods. He was shot again "thwart the buttocks" as he ran, but managed to reach the woods. Two of Lane's men chased after him and sometime later one of them, Edward Nugent, emerged from the woods carrying Pemisapan's severed head in his hand.

Although Pemisapan's plan to annihilate the English ultimately failed, its effect was, ironically, a contributing factor in the collapse of Lane's colony. With the exception of the Croatoans on the Outer Banks, all the tribes in the surrounding area had by now turned against the English, which was the tipping point that led Lane to conclude that the prospects for continuing the colonization effort at Roanoke were severely jeopardized. Exactly one week after Pemisapan's death, "a great fleet of three and twentie sailes" was seen approaching Roanoke Island. The fleet was led by Sir Francis Drake, who had just completed a series of successful raids on Spanish towns to the south, and now stopped at Roanoke to offer "not only of victuals, munition, and clothing, but also of barks, pinnesses, and boats; they also by him to be victualled, manned and furnished to my contentation." [63] After considering his options and deliberating with the "Captaines and gentlemen of my company" for days, Lane decided to abandon Roanoke Island and return to England with Drake.

There are a few details in Lane's account regarding the conspiracy against the English which further support the earlier proposition that Wingina's/Pemisapan's influence extended much farther than the villages of Roanoac and Dasamonquepeuc, as Quinn supposed. For one thing, among the conspiring tribes Lane mentioned were "the Mandoaks [Mangoaks] … with the Chesepians and their friends to the number of 700." These two tribes resided a considerable distance from Roanoke Island. The Iroquoian Mangoaks dwelt far to the west and the Algonquian Chesepians to the north, both of whom were considerably distant from Roanoke Island and well beyond what has been thought to be Pemisapan's sphere of influence. Also part of Pemisapan's confederacy were the Moratucs and the Weapemeocs, who had already demonstrated their fidelity to Pemisapan by participating in his plot to starve Lane and his men during their quest to find Chaunis Temoatan. The Chawanoacs, too, were part of Pemisapan's conspiracy, as Lane noted, when he interrupted the "generall assembly … made by Menatonon at Chawanook of all his Weroances, and allies … preparing to come vpon vs at Roanoak." Menatonon's active participation was prevented only because Lane had imprisoned "his sonne that he best loued" and threatened "to cut off his head." Even if Lane occasionally exaggerated the number of warriors aligned against him—"three thousand bowes" he wrote on one occasion—it seems clear that Pemisapan was an Algonquian leader whose influence has been generally underestimated.

Wingina/Pemisapan: Postscript

Ethnographers James Mooney and Cyrus Thomas wrote the following about the nature and characteristics of the eastern Algonquian tribes:

> The eastern Algonquian tribes probably equaled the Iroquois in bravery, intelligence, and physical powers, but lacked their … capability of organization, and do not appear to have appreciated the power and influence they might have wielded by combination. The alliances between the tribes were generally temporary and without real cohesion. There seems, indeed, to have been some element in their character which rendered them incapable of combining in large bodies, even against a common enemy. Some

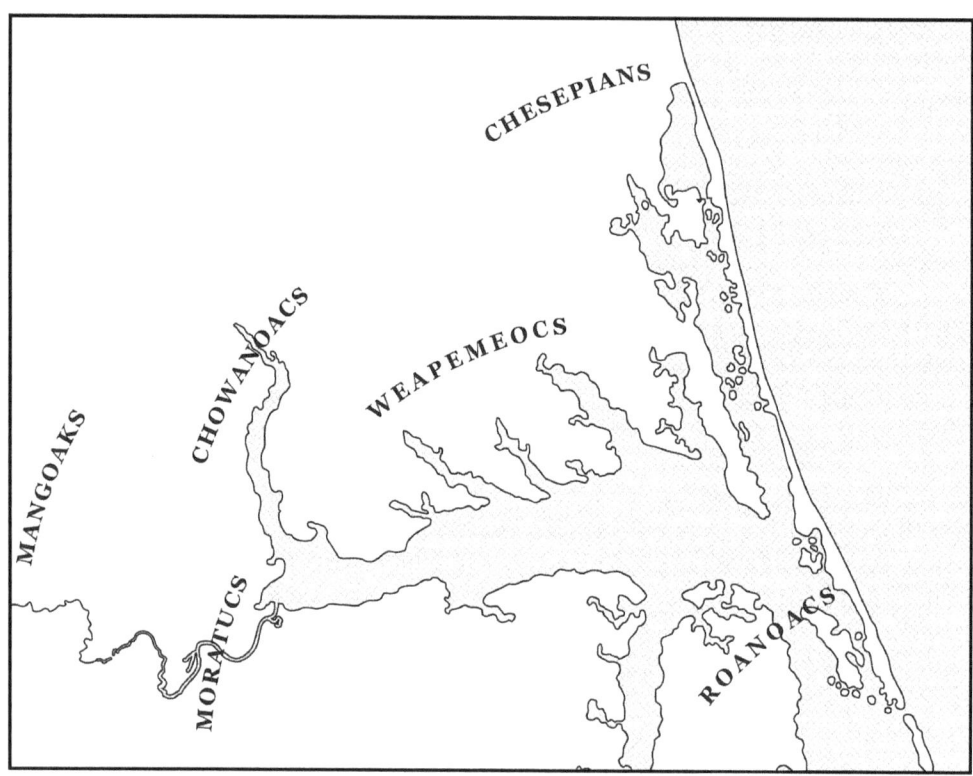

Tribes involved in Pemisapan's conspiracy against the English (courtesy Michael Gayle).

of their great chieftains, as Philip, Pontiac, and Tecumseh, attempted at different periods to unite the kindred tribes in an effort to resist the advance of the white race; but each in turn found that a single great defeat disheartened his followers and rendered all his efforts fruitless, and the former two fell by the hands of deserters from their own ranks. The Virginia tribes, under the able guidance of Powhatan and Opechancanough, formed an exception to the general rule. They presented a united front to the whites, and resisted for years every step of their advance until the Indians were practically exterminated.[64]

If the Mooney/Thomas comments about the Algonquians' inherent inability to form tribal confederacies against a common enemy are in any way accurate, then Wingina/Pemisapan stands as a remarkable exception. Whether or not the Roanoacs, Croatoans, and Secotans were all one tribe, as Mook believed, Wingina was the principal weroance who united and led them in the "mortall warre" against Piemacum and his allies before the arrival of the English in 1584. In 1586 Pemisapan united six tribes—the Roanoacs, Chesepians, Moratucs, Weapemeocs, Chawanoacs, and the Iroquoian Mangoaks—in a confederation to destroy the English.

There are a number of parallels between Pemisapan and the "great chieftains" mentioned by Mooney and Thomas. Each of these chieftans established historically rare coalitions of tribes to resist the English, and all but Powhatan were killed in the process. The story of one of the chieftains in particular, Philip, invites a closer comparison with Pemisapan. In 1675 Metacom or Metacomet, a Wampanoag Algonquian chief known to the English as Philip, formed a coalition of five tribes—the Wampamoags, Narragansetts, Abenakis, Nipmucs, and Mohawks to drive the English from New England in what was called

King Philip's War. Metacomet's father Massasoit had supported the Mayflower Pilgrims and was a trusted friend to the Plymouth colonists, echoing Ensenore's cooperative relationship with the 1585 English colonists at Roanoke Island. Like Pemisapan's confederation, Metacomet's was made up of Algonquian tribes except for one, the Mohawks, who—like the Mangoaks—were Iroquoian. The details of Pemisapan's plot were divulged to Lane by Skiko and an unnamed Roanoac Indian, resulting in Lane's preemptive attack at Dasamonquepeuc during which Pemisapan was shot twice and beheaded. Metacomet was killed in 1676 by an Indian who had sided with the English, after which Metacomet was beheaded, and his severed head was staked on a pole for public display at Plymouth.[65] Coincidentally, about a month after Metacomet was killed, three Indians were hanged in Boston for their part in an assault and slaughter at the Eames Farm during King Philip's War. These three Indians were the Jackstraws, who were claimed by William T. Forbes to be Manteo's direct descendants (see *Manteo*).

In the final analysis Wingina's/Pemisapan's place in the historical record remains largely unrecognized today. Part of the reason, of course, is the fact that his conspiracy was betrayed to Lane by Skiko and one of his own Roanoac tribesmen, and consequently his carefully crafted plan to destroy the English failed even before it could be initiated. A broader reason Wingina's/Pemisapan's importance is overlooked today is that a permanent English settlement was never established at Roanoke Island, and the focus of colonial historians soon shifted to Jamestown and then to Plymouth Plantation and the Massachusetts Bay Colony. At Jamestown Powhatan and then Opechancanough resisted English expansion starting in about 1610, and at Plymouth Plantation and the Massachusetts Bay Colony Philip/Metacomet and his allied tribes rebelled against the English in 1675. From a chronological perspective at least, the coalition assembled by Pemisapan in 1586 was the first attempt by an Algonquian chief to unify separate and independent tribes into a cohesive force against the English. For that reason alone Wingina/Pemisapan deserves to be ranked among the "great chieftains" cited by Mooney and Thomas.

Wingina's name is infrequently recalled today: There is a small unincorporated community in Nelson County, Virginia, which was named "Wingina" in 1880 when the Richmond and Allegheny Railroad purchased property there. More geographically relevant is "Wingina Avenue" which runs north-south through the town of Manteo on Roanoke Island and intersects Ananias Dare, Barlowe, and Harriot Streets. And Wingina is appropriately mentioned on North Carolina marker B-69 titled "Dasemunkepeuc" near the intersection of U.S. 264 and U.S. 64, just southwest of Manns Harbor, where he resided in 1586 and was killed on June 1.

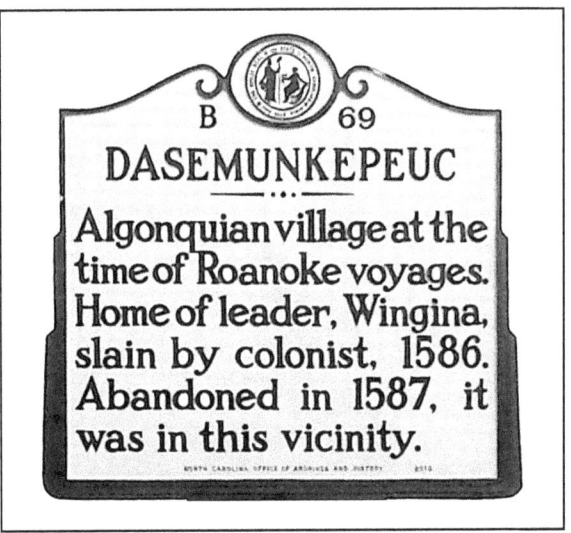

North Carolina Historical Marker no. B-69.

Appendix A:
"Manteo and Jack Straw"

"MANTEO AND JACK STRAW," by William T. Forbes; Full text as it appeared in the *Proceedings of the American Antiquarian Society*, New Series, Vol XIV, October 1900–October 1901. Pages 240–250. Worcester, published by the Society, 1902:

The shire town of Dare County, North Carolina, is situated on Roanoke Island, between Albemarle and Pamlico Sounds, and bears the name of an Indian, Manteo, who was for several years in the service of Sir Walter Raleigh.

This island is, and doubtless always will be, associated with Raleigh's five unsuccessful attempts to make a permanent settlement in Virginia.

In the southeasterly part of Westborough, in this Commonwealth, a hill has borne the name of Jack Straw for more than two hundred years.

As a boy, the writer played in Jack Straw Brook, climbed Jack Straw Hill, and watched the cattle feeding in Jack Straw Pasture. A deed, dated 1723, granting eighty acres of land to Jonathan Forbes, an ancestor of the writer, described the premises as situated "at Jack Straw's Hill." Other ancient deeds of land in the vicinity refer to the south line of Marlborough as "Jack Straw's old line."

Efforts to ascertain the origin of this name have led me back through registries of deeds in Worcester, Middlesex and Suffolk counties, in each of-which, successively, this hill was located. I find among the Massachusetts archives at the State House, proof that many years prior to the first white settlement in that vicinity, Jack Straw's Hill was a well-known landmark.

In all early deeds, maps and grants of the General Court the name is written "Jack Straw's Hill." During the last half-century, in all printed documents and among the people of its vicinity, it has been known and is now called," Jackstraw Hill."

It is the purpose of this paper to show that Manteo, the faithful friend of Sir Walter Raleigh and his colonists, from 1584 to 1587, the first Christian Indian in the English Colonies, and Jack Straw, who in his old age enjoyed the hospitality of Gov. Winthrop, in Boston, and of Gov. Bradford, in Plymouth, were probably the same person,—that the county seat of Dare County, North Carolina, and this Worcester County hill, bear the names of the same Indian.

In 1584, Queen Elizabeth granted to Sir Walter Raleigh the land in America from latitude 33° to 40° north, which he named Virginia. That very year he sent two vessels, under Capt. Amadas and Capt. Barlow, to explore the country.

They were cordially received, and returned with the products of the soil and also "two of the savages, being lusty men, whose names were Wanchesc and Manteo."

They were taken to Sir Walter Raleigh, who presented them and a great pearl and other products of Virginia to Queen Elizabeth.

The following year, 1585, Sir Richard Grenville sailed to Virginia with seven vessels, the four largest from 50 to 140 tons. He left 108 men, under Ralph Lane, to found—a colony in Roanoke. Lane says, "The natives which were taken to England returned with this expedition. One of them. Manteo, did good service in opening the way for the landing and friendly reception of the fleet."

Referring to one of his exploring expeditions. Lane Writes:—

> "In the evening, about three of the clock, we heard certain savages call, as we thought, Manteo, who was also at that time with me in the boat, whereof we all being very glad hoping of some friendly conference with them & making him to answer them they presently began a song, as we thought, in token of our welcome to them.
>
> But Manteo presently betook him to his piece & told me that they meant to fight with us.
>
> Which word was not so soon spoken by him, & the light horseman ready to put to shore, but their alighted a volley of their arrows among them in the boat."

In the second part, touching the conspiracy of King Wangina, otherwise called Pemisapan, Lane refers to an expedition in which he was accompanied by Manteo.

In the troubles with the Indians which followed, Wanchese, Manteo's companion in England, is referred to as "one of our great enemies." He aided in the killing of George Howe, who was ambushed on Roanoke Island.

In one of the numerous fights with the savages, their king, Pemisapan, formerly named Wangina, who had been shot through by the colonel and left for dead, suddenly started up and outran his captors, while Lane was looking out for the safety of Manteo's friends among the Indians. He was overtaken and beheaded by an Irishman named Nugent.

In 1586, Sir Francis Drake, with a large fleet, appeared and, at their request, took the discouraged colonists back to England.

A few days after they sailed, Sir Walter Raleigh's relief expedition, of three vessels, under Sir Richard Grenville, arrived, immediately preceded by a ship of 100 tons. The fifteen men left on the island by this third expedition were killed by the Indians. "Their houses were found standing, and deer feeding on the melons of divers sorts growing in the deserted fort."

The fourth" and best equipped expedition sent out by Raleigh sailed in 1587, under Capt. John White. Manteo, who had gone to England with Lane the previous year, returned with White. There were 150 persons with White, including his daughter and 16 other women.

The following narrative is taken from White's report:—

> "July 30th. Mr. Stafford & twenty of our men passed by water to the island of Croatoan" (Cape Lookout, about 75 m. S. of Roanoke) "with Manteo, who had his mother and many of his kindred dwelling in that Island, of whom we hoped to understand some news of our fifteen men, but especially to learn the disposition of the people of the country towards us & to renew our old friendship with them." The natives at first appeared hostile and then fled, but returned at the call of Manteo, who spoke to them in their own language.
>
> In revenge for the death of George Howe, who was slain by Wangina's men in Roanoke Island, Manteo conducted a night expedition, under Capt. Stafford, who surprised and killed some friendly Indians who were encamped in the enemies' country for the purpose of gathering their abandoned "corn, peas, pompions and tobacco."

Lane says that Manteo behaved himself towards us as a most faithful Indian, and adds:—

"August 13th, our savage. Manteo, by the commandment of Sir Walter Raleigh, was christened in Roanoke, and called lord thereof and of Dasamonguepeuk, in reward of his faithful services."

Another eye witness writes that they arrived at Hatarask July 22, and "the Governor, accompanied with forty of his best men in a small pynnace, stood in for Roanoke where, having christened a grandchild of his own born there (his daughter being married to one of the company), and calling it Virginia" (this was Virginia Dare, born August 18, 1587), "he caused, likewise, Manteo, the savage, to be christened, by Sir W. Raleigh his appointment, and, in reward of his faithfulness, entitled him Lord of Roanok and of Dasamonguepeuk."

So far as I can learn, Manteo was the first Indian baptized in the English colonies or under English auspices.

So Manteo succeeded Wangina, the beheaded king of Roanoke and Dasamonguepeuk. The latter place was the large peninsula west of Roanoke.

The fifth and last expedition for the relief of the Roanoke Colony, under John White, in 1590, after various vicissitudes, sailed north from the West Indies, past Cape Lookout on the island of Croatoan, and reached Roanoke in August.

They encountered rough weather, lost seven men, and returned to England without seeing a colonist. They found on a tree three fair Roman letters, "C. R. O.," which letters, White writes, "we knew to signify the place where I should find the planters seated, according to a secret token agreed upon between them and me. If in distress, they should carve a cross over the letters or name; but no sign of distress was found. At the entrance to the fort, in fair capital letters, graven on one of the chief posts, they found the word "CROATOAN." Capt. White was but a passenger on Watts's fleet with supplies, and was broken-hearted when his associates decided to leave the colonists, including his daughter and granddaughter Virginia Dare, to their fate. He writes, however, "I greatly joyed that I had safely found a certain token of their safe being at Croatoan, which is the place where Manteo was born, and the savages of the islands our friends."

This is the last certain information that we have of the fate of the colonists. A tradition among the Hatteras Indians a hundred years after suggests that they intermarried with the natives and, finally, were absorbed by the savages, having lost every vestige of Christianity and civilization.

This seems probable to Dr. Francis K. Hawkes, author of a History of North Carolina, printed in 1856.

His principal reasons for believing this tradition are the grey eyes and other signs of white blood found among the savages.

The story told by Strachey, first Secretary of the Jamestown Colony, is much more credible. He says that they were killed a few years before the landing at Jamestown by Powhatan, who was influenced by his priests.

In the year 1674, Maj.-Gen. Daniel Gookin makes this report:—

"Magunkaquog (Magunco) is the seventh town where the praying Indians do inhabit.
The number of its inhabitants are about eleven families and about fifty-five souls, of whom eight are church members and fifteen baptized."

This Indian town was included later within the limits of Hopkinton, adjoining Westborough.

Among them were William Jackstraw and his two sons, Joseph Jackstraw and John Jackstraw.

They were all hanged on Boston Common, September 21, 1676.

The story of the Indian attack on the family of Thomas Eames of Framingham, February 1, 1675–6; is well known. In his absence, a party of eleven Indians burned his house, barn and cattle, killed his wife and five children, and carried off five others.

William Jackstraw and his two sons were present, under the lead of the famous Netus, who, with a few other praying Indians escaped to the woods when their associates were deported to Deer Island, at the beginning of King Philip's War.

After the proclamation of June 19, promising life to such of the enemy as would come in and submit, the three Jackstraws gave themselves up, with their wives and children.

They relied on these words of the Council: "Those that have been drawn into the war and acting only as soldiers shall have their lives spared."

William Jackstraw and his two sons were examined before Mr. Thomas Danforth, August 14. His minutes of the examination are as follows :—

> "Joseph, Indian, son of William, of Mogoncocke, being examined, do say & confess that himself with these others named in the margent (see list above) were the persons that destroyed Thomas Eames' family in the beginning of Feb. last : that the same was occasioned by their missing of corn which they expected to have found at Moguncocke, & by that means were provoked to come & do that spoil, killing of some & carrying captive of the rest, and burning house, barn and cattle ; and do confess that he carried away on his back one of Eames's sons.
>
> "Apumatquin, alias John, being examined, do confess the same thing.
>
> "William Jackstraw, being examined, do confess the same thing as above: owns that his sons Joseph and John were present at the desolation of Goodman Eames's family, and that himself was of the company, but kept at a distance a little way off in the cornfields.
>
> "Isaac Beech being present at this examination, do say Joseph, above-named, confessed the same thing to him and Jno. Prentice.
>
> "For encouragement to Joseph, who was first examined, to tell the truth (they at first denying all), I told him I would speak to the Governor to spare his life in case he would tell me plainly how all this said matter was acted.
>
> "Taken the day and year above said. Before Thomas Danforth, John Speen, Interpreter.
>
> "Confessions were owned by the prisoners at the barr, 18, 6, 76.
>
> E. R. Sec."

Copy of Indictment. "We the grand jury for our Sovereign Lord the King do present and indict Joseph Indian of Maguncog by the name of Joseph Indian, for that he not having the fear of God before his eyes and being instigated by the devil did with other his accomplices on the beginning of Feb. 6 last burn the house and cattle of Thomas Eames and killed his wife and children contrary to the peace of our Sovereign Lord the King his crown and dignity, the laws of God and of this jurisdiction.

"The Jury finds this bill, and have him to forthwith tryal. Richard Colicott fforeman for the name of the rest of the Jury."

They were all convicted August 18, 1676. They sent in to the Court of Assistants on the fifth day of September following, a petition reciting the terms of their surrender, and claiming that, although present, they did not assist in the massacre, and asking for their lives. Sixteen days later, the diary of Samuel Sewall contains this item:—

> "Stephen Goble of Concord was executed for murder of Indians. Three Indians for firing Eames his house and murder. The weather was cloudy and rawly cold, though little or no rain. Mr. Mighil prayed; four others sat on the gallows, two men and two impudent women, one of which at least laughed on the gallows as several testified."

The remaining eight Indians were killed, pardoned, or escaped. The Indians frequently used the first name of the father as the surname of the son or daughter.

In the diary of the Rev. Ebenezer Parkman of Westborough, Mass., great-grandfather of the historian Francis Parkman, under the date of March 23, 1737, is this entry:—

"Cold northerly wind. P. M. visited old David Monanaow, he tells me he was 104 last Indian Harvest. Says the name of Boston was not Shawmut but Shaw-waw-muck."

His son was named Abimeleck David, and the latter's daughter Sue Abimeleck. Her fate is noted in the same diary, under date of Jan. 31, 1779. "Hear that Sue Bimeleck was lately frozen to Death. This whole month has been cold to admiration."

Sarah Boston, the Indian giantess of Grafton, Mass., still remembered by persons living in the land of the Hassanamiscoes, was the daughter of Boston Phillips.

It seems, therefore, probable that the children of Jack Straw the elder used his name as one word for a surname, and the children of his son William, who would naturally be adults in 1675, still retained the family name derived from their famous ancestor. Phinehas Pratt was one of sixty sent to Massachusetts to found a Colony, by Thomas Weston, in the year 1622. In his Narrative, published in the Massachusetts Historical Society Collections, Vol. IV., Fourth Series, are these words:

"Neare unto y place is a Town of Lator Time caled Brantry. Not long after this oferthrow of the first plantation in this bay Capt. Louit cam to y[our] Cuntry.

"At the Time of his being at Piscataway a Saeham or Sagamor Gave two of his men, on to Capt Louit & an other to Mr. Tomson, but on [it] was ther said 'How can you trust these Salvagis & call the nam of on Watt Tylor & [the] other Jack Straw after [the] names of the two greatest Rebills [that] ever weare in Eingland.'"

"Wott Tylor said when he was a boy Capt. Doomer found him upon an Island in great distress."

Watt Tyler and Jack Straw led insurgent peasants of the counties of Essex and Kent, and Tyler was killed by the Lord Mayor Walworth while treating with Richard II.

Gov. Winthrop's Journal, p. 25.

April 4, 1631:

"Wahginacut a Sagamore upon the river Quonehtacut which lies W. of Naraganset came to the Governor at Boston, with John Sagamore and Jack Strawe (an Indian which had lived in England and had served Sir Walter Raleigh and was now turned Indian again) and divers of their sannops and brought a letter to the Governor from Mr. Endieot to this effect; that the said Wahginacut was very desirous to have some Englishmen to come plant in his country and offered to find them corn and give them yearly eighty skins of beaver, and that the country was very fruitful, &c. and wished that there might be two men sent with him to see this country.

"The Governor entertained them at dinner but would send none with him. He discovered afterwards that the said sagamore is a very treacherous man and at war with the Pekoath (a far greater Sagamore): His country is not above five days journey from us by land."

To sum up : The literature of the Roanoke Colony and of Sir Walter Raleigh's connection with Virginia is very minute and voluminous, and based on detailed narratives of those who participated in the events narrated, which cover the years 1584 to 1590, inclusive. Raleigh had nothing to do with Virginia after the latter date. All contemporary and other writers agree that two natives, Manteo and Wanchese, were taken to England in 1584, presented by Raleigh to Queen Elizabeth, and returned to Roanoke in 1585.

Wanchese immediately joined the hostile natives, assisted in killing George Howe, remained an implacable enemy of the English, and was never in the service of Raleigh.

Manteo twice visited England; "was a firm friend to the English"; was of the greatest service to the Colony; was baptized and made king of Roanoke and Dasamonguepeuk by command of Sir Walter Raleigh himself, who never visited the infant settlement. No writer mentions the visit of any other North American Indian to England and of his serving Raleigh.

According to Capt. Lovit, an Indian on the coast of Maine, in the early part of the seventeenth century, was given the name of Jack Straw and went to Braintree. His companion when a boy (and very possibly Jack Straw himself), was rescued from peril on an island by Capt. Doomer. A large proportion of the ships of that time sailed direct from England to the West Indies, and then followed the coast north and passed in sight of the island of Croatan, Manteo's home.

A few years later he is employed to negotiate a treaty with the colonies of Massachusetts Bay and Plymouth, is dined by Gov. Winthrop and by Gov. Bradford, and the following year is given a coat worth twelve shillings (paid for out of the Colony Treasury), by order of Governor Winthrop.

According to Winthrop, this Indian, Jack Straw, had once served Raleigh, and had doubtless once lived as a civilized Christian, or Winthrop would not have observed that he "had turned Indian again."

He was so well known in the Massachusetts Bay Colony that his humble wigwam made a landmark in the wilderness and his name still marks the place of his abode. Contrary to the usual Indian custom in the vicinity, his descendants, for at least two generations, retained his Christian and surname as a family name.

Does it not seem probable that Manteo and Jack Straw were two names of the same man, and he one of the most famous Indians of the English Colonies in America?

Appendix B:
"The Legend of the Coharie"

"The Legend of the Coharie," by Ernest M. Bullard; full text as it appeared in *Huckleberry Historian*, a quarterly publication of the Sampson County Historical Society, Volume XXXVI, Number 1, Jan 2014:

Only this much of truth I know to be; I tell the tale as 'twas told to me...

About the end of the year 1588 or early in the year 1589 the remnant of the Lost Colony which had taken up their abode with Manteo on Croatoan Island, the place of Manteo's birth, accompanied by Manteo and all that survived a tremendous tidal wave left the island for the mainland beyond the sound to the west.

One of the colonists making this sojourn was young George Howe, whose father George Howe, Sr., was slain by the Indians on Roanoak Island on July 28, 1587.

These migrants of whites and Indians, it is believed, landed in what is now Carteret or Pamlico County, because, so goes the legend, they tried early the next. year, probably 1589, to ascend the "Neus" River farther inland in order to reach higher land on which they could grow Indian corn, for the tidal wave had salted the earth where they first settled so that it would not grow corn. Many of the colonists grew sick for lack of bread to eat with sea foods and game which were abundant.

Before they could get settled on a desirable location they were attacked by an unfriendly tribe and a few of the migrants were wounded.

A consultation was held before leaving Croatoan Island and it was decided that some of the colonists would bypass Wanchese's hostile tribe by going to the north and some would go to the south. Our legend concerns only those choosing the southern route.

According to the legend as it was told to me, about 1892, Manteo and most of his tribe, which was small, chose the southern route. This seems reasonable since the hostile tribe of Wanchese was to the north and west of Croatoan Island, and since he in all probability knew much of the coastline and fishing waters to the south of the island of his nativity.

On meeting resistance in their attempt to establish themselves inland, they turned south and for many moons dwelt along the coast, finally establishing themselves on the east side of the Cape Fear River where they lived in peace for many seasons.

Finally a colony of white people settled across the river, possibly the Clarendon Colony (1664). Manteo's tribe very much desiring peace and tranquility, once again began to migrate farther inland. How many years, or moons, as they counted time, passed before they reached the confluence of the Deep and Haw Rivers, which forms the Cape Fear River, may never be known.

They established themselves on the eastern prong, which they named Howe River in honor of George Howe III who, according to legend, was the grandson of Manteo. (George Howe II married one of the daughters of Manteo.)

The legend continues: They lived in the "Howe" River section about 170 moons when a severe drought came and dried the river and all the springs. When they felt they could no longer survive there, they began the journey down stream and migrated in keeping with the receding water supply until they reached what is now Cumberland County. Here, they encountered scattered Scotch settlements along the Cape Fear River.

With peace and tranquility still uppermost in their minds, they dispatched two runners, one of which was George Howe IV. The two men started eastward and crossed South River and Big Swamp, both of which they found dry. They continued on and soon came into a dense forest with black and mucky soil. Within a few hundred paces one of the two stepped out of the thick brush to the bank of a sparkling clear stream of water several feet wide. With delight he cried out to his companion, "co-her-ah." (Come here ah).

The colonists, or rather the descendants of the colonists and Manteo's tribe of Croatoan Indians, settled along the two Coheras, (now Coharies), and South River where many of their descendants still reside.

This ends the legend of Cohera, but not the people whose origin this legend is intended to explain, nor that segment of these people which is responsible for handing it down by word of mouth for more than three hundred years before one word of it was ever put into writing, so far as this writer has ever been able to learn.

It has been reported that some of the Manors who have to a considerable degree preserved their Indian blood and characteristics, and who now reside in the central western section of Sampson County, North Carolina, and on both sides and between the two "Coheras," claim to be the direct descendants of Manteo. The definition of Manor furnishes a clue as to why the surname Manteo was changed to Manor after he was christened Lord of Roanoke by order of Sir Walter Raleigh and given dominion over all the Indians in those entire areas.

A fact that lends support to the theory that the descendants of the "Lost Colony" have resided and still reside in Sampson and adjoining counties is that of the more than eighty surnames of the colonists, considerably more than half are today found in the census roll of Sampson County and more than two-thirds can be found among the peoples of southeastern North Carolina.

Of the remaining twenty-five or thirty, names of eight are known to have been changed on the records to names as spelled today. Several others are so similar that it is quite reasonable to conclude that they too may have been changed.

One of these names is Howe, which according to the legend, was the name given to the eastern prong of the Cape Fear River. The name Howe has since been changed to Haw River, possibly because of the more harsh sound given in usage and because of the influence of the Indian dialect.

Near the center of a small clearing on which these early people produced Indian corn and perhaps potatoes and collards, on top of a knoll overlooking the lowland of Big Swamp in the western part of what was known at that time (1779) as "The Territory" of Duplin County, there stood a small log cabin belonging to Enoch Hall. Hall was said to have been a lineal descendant from George Howe of the "Lost Colony," the name having been changed from Howe to Haw, then to Hall. Little better could have been expected from a people who had survived the hardships of more than a century and a half without a school.

I believe that the descendants of a substantial number of those 96 men, 16 women and 9 boys of the "Lost Colony" have lived and are now living in Sampson County and adjoining counties and many have moved to every state in the Union and some to foreign countries.

They survived the hardships of their time and in so doing exemplified courage, perseverance and stamina seldom equaled and never surpassed in the annals of the history of man. Nor were these attributes confined to the colonists alone. The friendly Indians who met them and through every danger, every hardship, and every misfortune accompanied them all the way manifested a loyalty and devotion seldom equaled among the children of men.

E. M. Bullard

Chapter Notes

Manteo

1. Strachey, William, *The Historie of Travaile Into Virginia Britannia* (London: Printed for the Hakluyt Society, 1849), p. 111.
2. *Ibid.*, p. 48.
3. Quinn, David B., *The Roanoke Voyages 1584–1590*, Vol. II (London: The Hakluyt Society, 1955), p. 893.
4. For a commentary on the practice and significance of Algonquian naming, see Rountree, Helen C., "Uses of Personal Names by Early Virginia Indians," Encyclopedia Virginia, available online.
5. Kupperman, Karen Ordahl, *Indians & English, Facing Off in Early America* (Ithaca, NY: Cornell University Press, 2000), p. 185.
6. Harriot, Thomas, *A Briefe and True Report of the New Found Land of Virginia* (Francoforti: Theodor De Bry, 1590), p. 25.
7. Kupperman, pp. 185–89.
8. Quinn, *The Roanoke Voyages*, Vol. II, p. 866.
9. Haag, William G., *The Archaeology of Coastal North Carolina*, Coastal Studies Series 2, Part 4 (Baton Rouge: Louisiana State University Press, 1958).
10. Quinn, pp. 865–66.
11. Haag, Coastal Studies Series 2, Part 11.
12. Hakluyt, Richard, "The first voyage made to the coasts of America, with two barks, wherein were Captaines M. Philip Amadas, and M. Arthur Barlowe, who discouered part of the Countrey now called Virginia Anno 1584. Written by one of the said Captaines, and sent to sir Walter Ralegh knight, at whose charge and direction, the said voyage was set forth." *The Principal Navigations, Voyages, Traffiques, and Discoveries of the English Nation*, edited by Edmund Goldsmid, Vol. XIII America Part II (Edinburgh: E. and G. Goldsmid, 1889), pp. 282–293.
13. Von Klarwill, Victor, editor, *Queen Elizabeth and Some Foreigners* (London: John Lane, 1928), p. 323.
14. Blackmore, Josiah, *Moorings: Portuguese Expansion and the Writing of Africa* (Minneapolis: University of Minnesota Press, 2009), pp. 3–4; also Harvey, L.P. *Islamic Spain 1250–1500* (Chicago: University of Chicago Press, 1990), p. 1.
15. Quinn, David B., "The [June, 1585] Relation of Hernando de Altamirano" from *The Roanoke Voyages 1584–1590*, Vol. II (London: The Hakluyt Society,1955), pp. 740–43.
16. Smith, John, *The Generall Historie of Virginia, New England & The Summer Isles* Library of Congress (New York: Macmillan Company, 1907), pp. 62 & 77.
17. *Ibid.*, p. 30.
18. Strachey, p. 63.
19. Harriot, *A Briefe and True Report...*, text accompanying de Bry's engraving no. III, "A weroan or great Lorde of Virginia," 1590.
20. Rountree, Helen C., *Pocahantas, Powhatan, Opechancanough: Three Indian Lives Changed by Jamestown* (Charlottesville: University of Virginia Press, 2005), p. 32; also Rountree, *Pocahantas's People*, pp. 8–9.
21. Harriot, *A Briefe and True Report...*, text from de Bry's engraving No. XII, "The manner of making their boates." 1590.
22. An English "tun" referred to an old wine cask measurement of volume equivalent to 954 litres of wine, which weighed roughly a ton.
23. Paul Hulton, Introduction to the 1972 Dover Edition of Harriot's *Briefe and True Report...*, p. ix.
24. Quinn, David B., *The Roanoke Voyages 1584–1590*, Vol. I (London: The Hakluyt Society, 1955), p. 348. See also Vaughn, Alden T, *Transatlantic Encounters: American Indians in Britain 1500–1776* (Cambridge and New York: Cambridge University Press, 2006), p. 23.
25. Hakluyt, "A letter from John White to M. Richard Hakluyt. 1593," *The Principal Navigations...*, p. 373.
26. Harriot, *A Briefe and True Report...*, Cover page for de Bry's engravings "The Trve Pictvres" following p. 33 of the text.
27. Harriot, *A Briefe and True Report...*, p. 24.
28. Hakluyt, "The first voyage made to the coasts of America...," *The Principal Navigations...*, p. 290.
29. Scholefield, Joshua and Hill, G.R., editors, "London Building Legislation and its Administration," *The Justice of the Peace and Local Government Review* Vol. LXXI (London: Charles Bond, 1907), pp. 421–22.
30. "The Holinshed Notice of the 1584 Voyage," from Quinn's *The Roanoke Voyages 1584–1590*, Vol. I, pp. 90–1; for the early English newsletters by Arthur Collins see "The Newspapers of the United Kingdom," *Encyclopaedia Britannica Ninth Edition*, Vol. XVII (Philadelphia: J.M. Stoddart Co., 1884), p. 424.
31. "December 1584 Bill to Confirm Raleigh's

Patent, as Passed by the House of Commons," from Quinn, Vol. I, pp. 126–29.

32. Hakluyt, "The Letters Patents, granted by the Queenes Maiestie to M. Walter Ralegh now Knight, for the discovering and planting of new lands and Countries, to continue the space of 6. yeeres and no more. 1584," *The Principal Navigations*…, p. 276.

33. Trevelyan, Raleigh, *Sir Walter Raleigh: Being a True and Vivid Account of the Life and Times of the Soldier, Scholar, Poet, and Courtier* (New York: Henry Holt, 2002), p. 59.

34. Dyson, Humphrey, collector, *A Booke containing all svch Proclamations, as were pvblished during the Raigne of the late Queene Elizabeth* (London: Bonham, Norton, and Iohn Bill, 1618), p. 35. See also: Secara, Maggie. "Elizabethan Sumptuary Statutes of May 1562 and June 1574," http://elizabethan.org/sumptuary/index.html#statutes.

35. Lewandowski, Elizabeth J. *The Complete Costume Dictionary* (Toronto: Scarecrow, 2011), p. 295.

36. Harriot, *A Briefe and True Report*…, p. 25.

37. Hakluyt, Richard, "A Discourse of Western Planting, written by M. Richard Hakluyt, 1584" *The Principal Navigations*…, Chapter 18, p. 169.

38. *Ibid.*

39. Harriot, *A Briefe and True Report*…, p. 25.

40. Hakluyt, "A Discourse of Western Planting…" *The Principal Navigations*…, p. 169.

41. Hakluyt, Richard, "The voiage made by Sir Richard Greenuile, for Sir Walter Ralegh, to Virginia, in the yeere 1585." The Principal Navigations…, p. 293.

42. Harriot, *A Briefe and True Report*…, p. 59.

43. Milton, Giles. *Big Chief Elizabeth* (New York: Farrar, Straus and Giroux, 2000), p. 53.

44. Hakluyt, Richard, "The imployments of the English men left in Virginia by Richard Greenuill vnder the charge of Master Ralph Lane," *The Principal Navigations*…, p. 302.

45. "The Legal Consequences of an Incident on the Thames early in 1585," from Quinn, *The Roanoke Voyages* Vol. I, pp. 139–144.

46. Hakluyt, "The first voyage made to the coasts of America…," *The Principal Navigations*…, p. 282.

47. Rountree, Helen, *The Powhatan Indians of Virginia* (Norman: University of Oklahoma Press, 1989), p. 47.

48. Harriot, A Briefe and True Report…, pp. 10–11.

49. Hakluyt, Richard, "An extract of Master Ralph Lanes letter to M. Richard Hakluyt Esquire, and another Gentleman of the middle Temple From the New Fort in Virginia, this third of September, 1585," *The Principal Navigations*…, p. 301.

50. Hakluyt, Richard, "The first voyage made to the coasts of America…," *The Principal Navigations*…, p. 282.

51. *Ibid.*

52. Harriot, A Briefe and True Report…, p. 28.

53. *Ibid.*, p. 30.

54. Hakluyt, Richard. "The third voyage made by a ship, sent in the yeere 1586 to the reliefe of the Colonie planted in Virginia, at the sole charges of Sir Walter Ralegh," *The Principal Navigations*…, p. 325.

55. Hakluyt, Richard, "The imployments of the English men left in Virginia by Richard Greenuill vnder the charge of Master Ralph Lane," *The Principal Navigations*…, p. 302.

56. *Ibid.*

57. *Ibid.*

58. *Ibid.*

59. Trevelyan, R., *Sir Walter Raleigh*…, pp. 96–9.

60. Quinn, David B., The Roanoke Voyages 1584–1590, Vol. II, pp. 828–9.

61. Stow, John, *A Summarie of the Chronicles of England, Diligently collected, abridged, & continued vnto this present yere of Christ, 1598* (London: Richard Bradocke, 1598), p. 1217.

62. *Ibid.* pp. 1217–18.

63. *Ibid.*, p. 1239.

64. Trevelyan, R., *Sir Walter Raleigh*…, p. 104.

65. *Ibid.*, pp. 103–5.

66. *Ibid.*, pp. 118–19.

67. *Ibid.*, pp. 100–1.

68. Harriot, *A Briefe and True Report*…, p. 32.

69. Quinn, Vol. II. pp. 502–3.

70. Hakluyt, Richard, "The Fourth Voyage Made to Virginia with Three Ships, in Yere 1587. Wherein was transported the second Colonie, "*The Principal Navigations*…, p. 358.

71. Fullam, Brandon, The Lost Colony of Roanoke: New Perspectives (Jefferson, NC: McFarland, 2017), pp. 25–37.

72. Hakluyt, Richard, "The Fourth Voyage Made to Virginia…," *The Principal Navigations*…, p. 358.

73. *Ibid.*

74. *Ibid.*

75. Fullam, pp. 25–32.

76. Hakluyt, Richard, *The Principal Navigations*…, p. 358, "The Fourth Voyage Made to Virginia…"

77. Fullam, pp. 25–37.

78. Hakluyt, Richard, "The Fourth Voyage Made to Virginia…," The Principal Navigations…, p. 358.

79. The precise number of colonists left at Roanoke in 1587 is disputed. Most authors have settled on 115 "lost" colonists, but author Andrew Powell has done an examination of this topic and arrived at 119, the number used here. See Powell, Andrew T. *Grenville & The Lost Colony of Roanoke* (UK: Matador/Troubador Publishing, 2011), pp. 209–218.

80. Quinn, David Beers, Set Fair for Roanoke, Voyages and Colonies 1584–1606 (Chapel Hill: University of N.C. Press, 1985), pp. 53 & 85.

81. Haag, William G., *The Archaeology of Coastal North Carolina*, Coastal Studies Series (Louisiana State University, Baton Rouge: 1958).

82. Rudes, Blair A., "The First Description of an Iroquoian People: Spaniards among the Tuscaroras before 1522" University of North Carolina at Charlotte, n.d., p. 14.

83. Haag, "Physiography of the Coastal Region, Pamlico Sound," *The Archaeology of Coastal North Carolina*, Coastal Studies Series 2, p. 47.

84. Fullam, "A Critical Gamble at Sea," *The Lost Colony of Roanoke*…, Chapt. 3.

85. Fullam, "The Great Hurricane and the Col-

lapse of the Colony," *The Lost Colony of Roanoke...*, Chapt. 8.

86. Hosmer, James Kendall ed., "Winthrop's Journal 1630–1649" Entry for April 4, 1631, Original Narratives of Early American History (New York: Charles Scribner's Sons, 1908), p. 61.

87. Drake, Samuel G., *Book of the Indians, Biography and History of the Indians of North America from its First Discovery to the Year 1841* (Boston: Antiquarian Bookstore 56 Cornhill, 1841), pp. 49–50.

88. De Forest, Heman Packard, *The History of Westborough, Massachusetts* Part I (Cambridge: John Wilson and Son, 1891), p. 7.

89. Hurd, D. Hamilton, *The History of Worcester County, Massachusetts* (Philadelphia: J.W. Lewis & Co., 1889), pp. 1335–6.

90. Forbes, William T., "Manteo and Jack Straw," *Proceedings of the American Antiquarian Society*, New Series, Vol. XIV, October 1900–October 1901 (Worcester: published by the Society, 1902), p. 241.

91. "Phinehas Pratt's Petition," *Collections of the Massachusetts Historical Society*, Vol. IV of the Fourth Series (Boston: Little, Brown, and Company, 1858), p. 487.

92. De Forest, *The History of Westborough...*, pp. 6–7, p. 461.

93. Hurd, *The History of Worcester County...*, p. 1335.

94. *Ibid.*

95. Hosmer, "Winthrop's Journal 1630–1649." Entry for Dec 5, 1633, *Original Narratives...*, pp. 114–15.

96. Barry, William, *A History of Framingham, Massachusetts: Including the Plantation, from 1640 to the Present Time* (Boston: James Munroe and Company, 1847), pp. 28 & 32.

97. Temple, Josiah Howard, *History of Framingham, Massachusetts* (Framingham: Published by the Town of Framingham, 1887), p. 78. The records concerning the executions are confusing. According to Temple three Indians were executed on Sept. 21, presumably the Jackstraws, but there were four who were "on the gallows, two men and two impudent women, one of which, at least laughed on the gallows, as several testified." There are three Jackstraw entries in the Family Search Genealogies database which record the deaths of William Jackstraw and his wife Mrs. William Jackstraw on September 18, 1676. Their son Joseph Jackstraw's death is recorded three days later on September 21, 1676. There is no record for John Jackstraw. See https://www.familysearch.org/search/tree/results?count=20&query=%2Bsurname%3AJackstraw~&https://www.familysearch.org/search/family-trees=undefined.

98. Haulley, Fletcher, *A Primary Source History of the colony of New Hampshire* (New York: The Rosen Publishing Group, 2006), p. 10.

99. Forbes, *Proceedings of the American Antiquarian Society*, p. 249.

100. Vaughn, Alden T., *Transatlantic Encounters: American Indians in Britain 1500–1776* (New York: Cambridge University Press, 2006), pp. 42–3.

101. *Ibid.*, p. 65.

102. Forbes, *Proceedings of the American Antiquarian Society*, p. 250.

103. *Ibid.*

104. Hosmer, "Winthrop's Journal...," entry for March 21, 1637, *Original Narratives...*, p. 212.

105. Lossing, Benson J., *Lives of Celebrated Americans* (Hartford, CT: Thomas Belknap, 1869), p. 15.

106. McMillan, Hamilton, Sir Walter Raleigh's Lost Colony. An Historical Sketch of the Attempts of Sir Walter Raleigh to Establish a Colony in Virginia, With the Traditions of an Indian Tribe in North Carolina (Wilson, N.C.: Advance Press, 1888), p. 20.

107. Email from W. Stephen Lee to the author, Dec. 21, 2014.

108. Bullard, Ernest M., "The Legend of the Coharie," reprinted in *Huckleberry Historian*, a quarterly publication of the Sampson County Historical Society, Volume XXXVI, Number 1, January, 2014.

109. Email from W. Stephen Lee to the author, 2014.

110. Johnson, Gordon, and Phillip Sylvester, "Salt Water Inundation from Hurricane Sandy," University of Delaware College of Agricultural and Natural Resources, 2012. http://extension.udel.edu/kentagextension/2012/11/07/salt-water-inundation-from-hurricane-sandy/

111. *Ibid.*

112. McMillan, pp. 18, 20.

113. Mooney, James, *The Siouan Tribes of the East* (Washington, DC: Government Printing Office, 1894), p. 66.

114. Bullard, Ernest M., "The Legend of the Coharie."

115. McMillan, p. 34.

116. "Brief Sketch of a Few Prominent Indian Families of Sampson County" by Enoch Emanuel and C. D. Brewington, from Butler, George Edwin, *The Croatan Indians of Sampson County, North Carolina. Their Origin and Racial Status. A Plea for Separate Schools...*, (Durham, NC: The Seeman Printery, 1916), p. 47.

117. Brewington, C. D., *The Five Civilized Indian Tribes of Eastern North Carolina.* Edited by Oscar M. Bizzell (Newton Grove, NC: Sampson County Historical Society, 1994), p. 15.

118. Dial, Adolph L., and Elaides, David K., *The Only Land I Know* (New York: Syracuse University Press, 1996), pp. 23–4.

119. Grady, Don A., "The Coharie Indians of Sampson County, NC: A Collectrion of Oral Folk History." Thesis Submitted to the Faculty of the University of North Carolina at Chapel Hill. 1981, p. 41.

120. Lawson, John, *A New Voyage to Carolina* (London: N.p., 1709), p. 62.

121. Johnson, Gordon and Sylvester, Phillip, "Salt Water Inundation from Hurricane Sandy," University of Delaware College of Agricultural and Natural Resources, 2012. Also: Weaver, J. Curtis and Zembrzuski Jr., Thomas J. "August 31, 1993, Storm Surge and Flood of Hurricane Emily on Hatteras Island, North Carolina." Water Supply Paper 2499, U.S. Department of the Interior, U.S. Geological Survey.

122. Bullard, Ernest M, "The Legend of the Coharie."

123. Hakluyt, Richard, "The fift voyage of M. Iohn White into the West Indies and parts of America called Virginia, in the yeere 1590, entry for August 17, *Principal Navigations*..., p. 375.
124. *Ibid.*, August 18.
125. *Ibid.*
126. *Ibid.*
127. *Ibid.* August 19.
128. *Ibid.*, August 12–13.
129. Quinn. *The Roanoke Voyages*..., Vol. II. p. 866.
130. Hakluyt, "The Letters Patents, granted by the Queenes Maiestie to M. Walter Ralegh now Knight, for the discovering and planting of new lands and Countries, to continue the space of 6. yeeres and no more. 1584," *The Principal Navigations*..., p. 276.
131. Hakluyt, "The fift voyage of M. Iohn White ... in the yeere 1590," entry for August 18, *Principal Navigations*..., p. 375.
132. France, Kevin, "Top Five U.S. Cities Most Vulnerable to Hurricanes," from AccuWeatherc.com, June 25, 2015.
133. Landsea, Chris, of the National Hurricane Center, "Chronological List of All Hurricanes which Affected the Continental United States 1851–2014." NOAA Hurricane Research Division, 2014.
134. Hann, John H., "Translation of the Écija Voyages of 1605 and 1609 and the Gonzalez Derrotero of 1609," *Florida Archaeology No. 2* (Florida Bureau of Archaeological Research, Nov. 2, 1986), pp. 33–34.
135. Hakluyt, "The fift voyage of M. Iohn White into the West Indies and parts of America called Virginia, in the yeere 1590," *Principal Navigations*..., p. 375.
136. "Francis Yeardley's Narrative of Excursions into Carolina, 1654" from Salley, Alexander S., Jr., editor, *Narratives of Early Carolina, 1650–1708* (New York: Charles Scribner's Sons, 1911), pp. 25–6.
137. *Ibid.*, p. 27.
138. Lawson, John, *A New Voyage to Carolina* (London: 1709), p. 54.
139. Brooks, Baylus C., "John Lawson's Indian Town on Hatteras Island, North Carolina," The North Carolina Historical Review. Vol. 91, No. 2 (April, 2014), pp. 171–207; See also Quinn, David B. The Roanoke Voyages 1584–1590, Vol. II, p. 864.
140. Lawson, p. 192.
141. *Ibid.*, p. 62.
142. Brooks, pp. 182–3.
143. Lee, E. Lawrence, *Indian Wars in North Carolina 1663–1763* (Raleigh: Office of Archives and History/North Carolina Department of Cultural Resources, 2011), p. 3.
144. *Ibid.*, p. 224.
145. La Vere, David, *The Tuscarora War* (Chapel Hill: University of North Carolina Press, 2013), p. 185.
146. *The Colonial Records of North Carolina*. Edited by William S. Saunders, Secretary of State. Vol. II 1713–178 (Raleigh, NC: P.M. Hale, Printer to the State, 1886), p. 129.
147. La Vere, p. 176.
148. *Colonial Records...* Vol. II, p. 172.
149. *Colonial Records...* Vol. III, p. 153.
150. Torres, Louis, *Historic Resource Study of Cape Hatteras National Seashore* (U.S. Department of the Interior: National Park Service, Denver Service Center, 1985), pp. 17–18.
151. *Colonial Records...* Vol. VI (Raleigh, NC: Joseph Daniels, Printer to the State, 1888), p. 563.
152. *Ibid.*, p. 995.
153. *Ibid.*, pp. 197–200.
154. Torres, pp. 27–8.
155. Private Laws of the State of North Carolina, Passed by the General Assembly, Session of 1899 (Raleigh: Edwards & Broughton, and E. M. Uzzell, State Printers and Binders, 1899), pp. 112–14.

Ensenore

1. Harriot, Thomas, text from illustration no. IX, "An ageed manne in his winter garment," A Briefe and True Report of the New Found Land of Virginia (Francoforti: Theodor De Bry, 1590).
2. Hakluyt, "The first voyage made to the coasts of America...," *The Principal Navigations*..., p. 282.
3. Harriot, *A Briefe and True Report*..., p. 43.
4. Hakluyt, "The imployments of the English men left in Virginia by Richard Greenuill vnder the charge of Master Ralph Lane," *The Principal Navigations*..., p. 302.
5. Harriot, *A Briefe and True Report*..., p. 41.
6. Harriot, *A Briefe and True Report*..., text from illustration no. III, "A weroan or greate Lorde of Virginia."
7. *Ibid.*, p. 43.
8. *Ibid.* pp. 41–3.
9. Hakluyt, "The imployments of the English men left in Virginia...," *The Principal Navigations*..., p. 302.
10. Kocher, Paul H., *Science and Religion in Elizabethan England* (New York: Octagon Books, 1969), p. 166.
11. Hackett, David, editor, *Religion and American Culture* (Routledge: New York, 2003), p. 38.
12. Harriot, p. 43.
13. "Hussey's Catalog of Comets," *Philosophical Magazine and Journal of Science* Vol. IV, January—June, 1834, p. 352.
14. Miguel Granada, Adam Mosley and Nicholas Jardine, eds., *Christoph Rothmann's Discourse on the Comet of 1585: an edition and translation with accompanying essays* (Leiden, Netherlands: Brill Academic Publishing, 2014), pp. 24–7.
15. Harriot, p. 41.
16. Hakluyt, "The imployments of the English men left in Virginia...," *The Principal Navigations*..., p. 302.

Eracano

1. Harriot, Thomas, A Briefe and True Report of the New Found Land of Virginia (Francoforti: Theodor De Bry, 1590), illustration no. VII.
2. Hakluyt, Richard, "The imployments of the

English men left in Virginia by Richard Greenuill vnder the charge of Master Ralph Lane," *The Principal Navigations...*, p. 302.

Granganimeo

1. Hakluyt, Richard, "The Letters Patents, granted by the Queenes Maiestie to M. Walter Ralegh now Knight, for the discovering and planting of new lands and Countries, to continue the space of 6. yeeres and no more. 1584," The Principal Navigations..., p. 276.
2. Hakluyt, "The first voyage made to the coasts of America...," *The Principal Navigations...*, p. 282.
3. *Ibid.*
4. Harriot, Thomas, *A Briefe and True Report of the New Found Land of Virginia* (Francoforti: Theodor De Bry, 1590,) p. 23.
5. *Ibid.*, p. 51, notes accompanying the White/de Bry engraving of "manner of fishynge in Virginia."
6. *Ibid.*, p. 20.
7. *Ibid.*, p. 51.
8. Hakluyt, "The first voyage made to the coasts of America...," *The Principal Navigations...*, p. 282.
9. Quinn, David Beers, *Set Fair for Roanoke, Voyages and Colonies 1584–1606* (Chapel Hill: University of North Carolina Press, 1985), p. 28.
10. Hakluyt, "The first voyage made to the coasts of America...," p. 282.
11. *Ibid.*
12. Quinn, *Set Fair...*, p. 102. See also Fullam, Brandon, *The Lost Colony of Roanoke: New Perspectives* (Jefferson, NC: McFarland, 2017), pp. 54, 58.
13. Quinn, David B., *The Roanoke Voyages 1584–1590*, Vol. I (London: The Hakluyt Society, 1955), p. 79.
14. Hakluyt, "The first voyage made to the coasts of America...," p. 282.
15. *Ibid.*
16. Bartlet, Guillermo, "On the Ethnohistory of Powhatan Ritual Gestures," *Anthropos Journal* Vol. 105, No. 1 (2010), pp. 47–56.
17. *Ibid.*
18. Ralegh, Sir Walter, Knight, *The History of the World in Five Bookes*, "The First Booke of the First Part," Chapter 8 (London: Printed for Walter Burre, 1614), pp. 175–176.
19. See Mallios, Seth, *The Deadly Politics of Giving* (Tuscaloosa: University of Alabama Press, 2006).
20. Hakluyt, "The first voyage made to the coasts of America...," p. 282.
21. Kupperman, Karen Ordahl, *Roanoke, The Abandoned Colony* (Totowa, NJ: Rowman & Allanheld, 1984), p. 69.
22. Hakluyt, "The first voyage made to the coasts of America...," p. 282.
23. Harriot, "A cheiff Ladye of Pomeioc," illustration no. VII, *A Briefe and True Report...*
24. Hakluyt, "The first voyage made to the coasts of America...," p. 282.
25. *Ibid.*
26. Hakluyt, "The imployments of the English men left in Virginia by Richard Greenuill vnder the charge of Master Ralph Lane," *The Principal Navigations...*, p. 302.
27. Harriot, *A Briefe and True Report...*, p. 28.
28. Hakluyt, "The imployments of the English men left in Virginia...," *The Principal Navigations...*, p. 302.

Menatoan

1. Hakluyt, Richard, "The Fourth Voyage Made to Virginia with Three Ships, in Yere 1587. Wherein was transported the second Colonie," *The Principal Navigations...*, p. 358.
2. *Ibid.*

Menatonon

1. Quinn, David B., *The Roanoke Voyages 1584–1590*, Vol. II (London: The Hakluyt Society, 1955), p. 891.
2. Hakluyt, Richard, "The imployments of the English men left in Virginia by Richard Greenuill vnder the charge of Master Ralph Lane," *The Principal Navigations...*, p. 302.
3. *Ibid.*
4. Harriot, Thomas, *A Briefe and True Report of the New Found Land of Virginia* (Francoforti: Theodor De Bry, 1590), p. 35.
5. *Ibid.*, p. 7.
6. Swanton, John Reed, *The Indian Tribes of North America* (Washington, DC: U.S. Government Printing Office, 1952), pp. 77–78.
7. Dillard, Richard, M.D., "The Indian Tribes of Eastern Carolina," *The North Carolina Booklet*, Vol. VI No. 1, compiled and edited by Mrs. E.E. Moffitt (Raleigh: The North Carolina Society, 1906), pp. 3–26.
8. Ashe, Samuel A'Court, *The History of North Carolina From 1584 To 1783*, Vol. I (Greensboro: Charles L. Van Noppen, 1908), pp. 86–87.
9. Mintz, John J., Beaman, Thomas E., and Mohler, Paul J., "'They in respect of troubling our inhabiting and planting, are not to be feared': Archaeology and Ethnohistory of Native Coastal Populations before and after European Contact," *The Archaeology of North Carolina: Three Archaeological Symposia*, North Carolina Archaeological Council Publication Number 30, 2011, pp. 8–2, 8–3.
10. Phelps, David S., "Archaeology of the Native Americans: The Carolina Algonkians: Final Report," Department of Sociology, Anthropology and Economics (Greenville: East Carolina University, 1984).
11. Hakluyt, "The imployments of the English men left in Virginia...," *The Principal Navigations...*, p. 302.
12. Phelps, David S., "Archaeology of the Native Americans..."
13. Hakluyt, "The Letters Patents, granted by the Queenes Maiestie to M. Walter Ralegh now Knight, for the discovering and planting of new lands and

Countries, to continue the space of 6. yeeres and no more. 1584," *The Principal Navigations…*, p. 276.
  14. Hakluyt, "The imployments of the English men left in Virginia by Richard Greenuill vnder the charge of Master Ralph Lane," *The Principal Navigations…*, p. 302.
  15. *Ibid.*
  16. *Ibid.*
  17. Hodge, Frederick W., editor, *Handbook of American Indians North of Mexico* Part 1 (Washington, DC: Government Printing Office, 1907), p. 840.
  18. Smith, John, *The Generall Historie of Virginia, New England & The Summer Isles* Library of Congress (New York: Macmillan Company, 1907), p. 74.
  19. *Ibid.*, p. 87.
  20. Saunders, William S., Secretary of State, editor, *The Colonial Records of North Carolina*, Vol. I 1662–1712 (Raleigh: P.M. Hale, Printer to the State, 1886), p. 5.
  21. LaVere, David, *The Tuscarora War* (Chapel Hill: University of North Carolina Press, 2013), p. 15.
  22. *Ibid.*, p. 204.

Okisko

  1. Quinn, David B., *The Roanoke Voyages 1584–1590*, Vol. II (London: The Hakluyt Society, 1955), p. 892.
  2. Quinn, David B., *Set Fair for Roanoke, Voyages and Colonies 1584–1606* (Chapel Hill: University of North Carolina Press, 1985), p. 73.
  3. *Ibid.*
  4. Mook, Maurice A., "Algonquian Ethnohistory of the Carolina Sound," *Journal of the Washington Academy of Sciences*, Vol. 34, No. 6 (June 15, 1944), p. 187.
  5. Hakluyt, "The imployments of the English men left in Virginia by Richard Greenuill vnder the charge of Master Ralph Lane," *The Principal Navigations…*, p. 302.
  6. Quinn, "The Map of Raleigh's Virginia," *The Roanoke Voyages…*, Vol. II, p. 860.
  7. Mook, p. 188.
  8. Quinn, p. 847.
  9. *Ibid.*, p. 849.
  10. Hakluyt, p. 302.
  11. *Ibid.*
  12. *Ibid.*
  13. Mook, p. 221.
  14. *Ibid.*

Piemacum

  1. Quinn, David B., *The Roanoke Voyages 1584–1590*, Vol. II (London: The Hakluyt Society, 1955), p. 894.
  2. Fullam, Brandon, *The Lost Colony of Roanoke: New Perspectives* (Jefferson NC: McFarland, 2017), pp. 148–9.
  3. McMillan, Hamilton, *Sir Walter Raleigh's Lost Colony. An Historical Sketch of the Attempts of Sir Walter Raleigh to Establish a Colony in Virginia, With the Traditions of an Indian Tribe in North Carolina* (Wilson, NC: Advance Press, 1888), p. 14.
  4. Smith, "A True Relation," edited by Lyon G. Tyler, *Narratives of Early Virginia, 1606–1625* (New York: Charles Scribner's Sons, 1907), p. 53.
  5. Wolf, Brendan, "The Roanoke Colonies," *Encyclopedia Virginia*. June 13, 2014. https://www.encyclopediavirginia.org/Roanoke_Colonies_The#start_entry.
  6. Oberg, Michael Leroy, *The Head in Edward Nugent's Hand* (Philadelphia: University of Pennsylvania Press, 2008), p. 12.
  7. See notation accompanying "A cheife Herowans wyfe of Pomeoc," *The Virginia Indian Archive*, a project of the Virginia Indian Heritage Program at the Virginia Humanities headquarters at the University of Virginia in Charlottesville, VA. http://virginiaindianarchive.org/items/show/165.
  8. Oberg, p. 63.
  9. Hakluyt, "The first voyage made to the coasts of America…," *The Principal Navigations…*, p. 282.
  10. Mook, Maurice A., "Algonquian Ethnohistory of the Carolina Sound," *Journal of the Washington Academy of Sciences* 34 (1944), pp. 6–7. See also Feest, Christian F., "North Carolina Algonquians," *Handbook of North American Indians* Vol. 15, Bruce Trigger, editor (Washington, DC: Smithsonian Institute, 1978), pp. 271–281.
  11. Speck, Frank, G., "The Ethnic Position of the Southeastern Algonquian," *American Anthropologist* 26 (1924), pp. 184–200.
  12. Hakluyt, "The first voyage made to the coasts of America…," *The Principal Navigations…*, p. 282.
  13. *Ibid.*
  14. Fullam, "Simon Fernandez and the Aborted Chesapeake Plan," *The Lost Colony of Roanoke: New Perspectives* (Jefferson NC: McFarland, 2017), pp. 25–37.
  15. Smith, John, "A True Relation," *Narratives of Early Virginia, 1606–1625*, edited by Lyon G. Tyler (New York: Charles Scribner's Sons, 1907), p. 53.
  16. "Archdale's Description of Carolina, 1707," *Narratives of Early Carolina, 1650–1708*, Salley, Alexander S., Jr., editor (New York: Charles Scribner's Sons, 1911), p. 286.

Pooneno

  1. Hakluyt, "The imployments of the English men left in Virginia by Richard Greenuill vnder the charge of Master Ralph Lane," *The Principal Navigations…*, p. 302.
  2. Mook, Maurice A., "A Newly Discovered Algonkian Tribe of Carolina," *American Anthropologist*, October-December 1943, pp. 635–37.
  3. Hodge, Frederick W., editor, *Handbook of American Indians North of Mexico*, Part 2 (Washington, DC: Government Printing Office, 1912), p. 942.

"Raleigh"

  1. "The Relation of Pedro Diaz" as translated in Quinn, *The Roanoke Voyages 1584–1590*, Vol.II, p. 793.

2. "1588–9 Entries in the Bideford Parish Register," *The Roanoke Voyages,* Vol. I, p. 495.

Skiko

1. Quinn, David B., *The Roanoke Voyages 1584–1590,* Vol. II (London: The Hakluyt Society, 1955), p. 857.
2. Hakluyt, "The imployments of the English men left in Virginia by Richard Greenuill vnder the charge of Master Ralph Lane," *The Principal Navigations…,* p. 302.
3. Quinn, Vol. I, p. 285.
4. *Ibid.,* p. 293.

Tarraquine

1. Quinn, David B., *The Roanoke Voyages 1584–1590,* Vol. II (London: The Hakluyt Society, 1955), p. 890.

Tetepano

1. Quinn, David B., *The Roanoke Voyages 1584–1590,* Vol. II (London: The Hakluyt Society, 1955), p. 897.
2. *Ibid.,* p. 857.

Towaye

1. Hakluyt, "The names of all the men, women and children, which safely arriued in Virginia, and remained to inhabite there. 1587 Anno regni Reginæ Elizabethæ. 29," *The Principal Navigations…,* p. 371.
2. Quinn, David B., *The Roanoke Voyages 1584–1590,* Vol. II (London: The Hakluyt Society, 1955), p. 897.

Wanchese

1. Quinn, David B., *The Roanoke Voyages 1584–1590,* Vol. II (London: The Hakluyt Society, 1955), p. 898.
2. Hakluyt, "The first voyage made to the coasts of America…," *The Principal Navigations…,* p. 282.
3. Quinn, "The [June, 1585] Relation of Hernando de Altamirano," *The Roanoke Voyages 1584–1590,* Vol. II (London: The Hakluyt Society,1955), p. 741.
4. Hakluyt, "A Discourse of Western Planting, written by M. Richard Hakluyt, 1584," *The Principal Navigations…,* p. 169.
5. Quinn. *The Roanoke Voyages…,* Vol. I, p. 280.
6. Milton, Giles, *Big Chief Elizabeth* (New York: Farrar, Straus and Giroux, 2000), pp. 61, 68.
7. Hakluyt, "The imployments of the English men left in Virginia by Richard Greenuill vnder the charge of Master Ralph Lane," *The Principal Navigations…,* p. 302.
8. See Fullam, "Simon Fernandez and the Aborted Chesapeake Plan," *The Lost Colony of Roanoke: New Perspectives* (Jefferson, NC: McFarland, 2017), pp. 25–37.
9. Phelps, David S., "Archaeology of the Tillett Site: The First Fishing Community at Wanchese, Roanoke Island," 1984, *Archaeological Research Report* No. 6, Archaeology Laboratory, East Carolina University, Greenville, North Carolina, pp. 1–2. See also "The Will of Wanchese" by Susan West. *Working Waterfront Archives,* May 17, 2012. http://www.workingwaterfrontarchives.org/2012/05/17/the-will-of-wanchese/

Wingina

1. Harriot, Thomas, text accompanying illustration no. VII, "A cheiff Lorde of Roanoac," *A Briefe and True Report of the New Found Land of Virginia* (Francoforti: Theodor De Bry, 1590).
2. Quinn, *The Roanoke Voyages 1584–1590,* Vol. II (London: The Hakluyt Society, 1955), p. 862.
3. Hakluyt, "The first voyage made to the coasts of America…," *The Principal Navigations…,* p. 282.
4. Quinn, Vol. II, p. 869.
5. Mook, Maurice A., "A Newly Discovered Algonkian Tribe of Carolina," *American Anthropologist,* October-December 1943, pp. 635–37.
6. Hodge, Frederick W., editor, *Handbook of American Indians North of Mexico,* Part 2 (Washington, DC: Government Printing Office, 1912), p. 958.
7. Strachey, William, *The Historie of Travaile Into Virginia Britannia* (London: Printed for the Hakluyt Society, 1849), p. 195.
8. Ralegh, Sir Walter, Knight, "The First Booke of the First Part," Chapter 8, *The History of the World in Five Bookes* (London: Printed for Walter Burre, 1614), pp. 175–176.
9. Quinn, Vol. I, p. 147; Vol. II, pp. 508, 570.
10. "The Bill for Confirmation of Letters Patents made unto Walter Rawleigh…," Quinn, Vol. I, p. 122.
11. Hakluyt, "The first voyage made to the coasts of America…," *The Principal Navigations…,* p. 282.
12. Strachey, pp. 142–3.
13. "Act for the confermacion of lettres patentes graunted to Walter Raleghe esquire," Quinn, Vol. I, pp. 126–29.
14. Quinn, Vol. I, p. 100, fn 1.
15. Mook, Maurice A., "Algonquian Ethnohistory of the Carolina Sound," *Journal of the Washington Academy of Sciences* Vol. 34, No. 6 (June 15, 1944), p. 213.
16. Quinn, Vol. I, p. 100.
17. Mallios, Seth, *The Deadly Politics of Giving* (Tuscaloosa: University of Alabama Press, 2006), p. 65.
18. *Ibid.* See also Mooney, James, *The Siouan Tribes of the East* (Washington, DC: Government Printing Office, 1894), pp. 64–5.
19. Hakluyt, "The first voyage made to the coasts of America…," *The Principal Navigations…,* p. 282.
20. *Ibid.*
21. Quinn, David Beers, *Set Fair for Roanoke: Voyages and Colonies, 1584–1606* (University of North Carolina Press, 1985), p. 32.

22. Strachey, *The Historie of Travaile Into Virginia Britannia*, p. 43.
23. Mook. "Algonquian Ethnohistory of the Carolina Sound," p. 215.
24. Harriot, *A Briefe and True Report…*, p. 61.
25. Phelps, David S., "Archaeology of the Native Americans: The Carolina Algonkians: Final Report," Department of Sociology, Anthropology and Economics (Greenville, NC: East Carolina University, 1984).
26. Abbott, Lawrence E., "An Archaeological Inspection of Site 31BF25: Beaufort County, North Carolina," *A Report of Field Inspections: PCS Phosphate Company, Inc.* (Raleigh: Office of State Archaeology, June 2016).
27. Quinn, *The Roanoke Voyages…*, Vol. II, pp. 870–1.
28. Hakluyt, "The first voyage made to the coasts of America…," The Principal Navigations…, p. 282.
29. *Ibid.*
30. *Ibid.*
31. *Ibid.*
32. Rudes, Blair A., "The First Description of an Iroquoian People: Spaniards among the Tuscaroras before 1522," University of North Carolina at Charlotte, n.d. http://www.coastalcarolinaindians.com/research/BlairARudes/The%20First%20Description%20of%20An%20Iroquoian%20People.pdf
33. Quinn, *Set Fair for Roanoke…*, pp. 42–3.
34. Percy, George, "Observations by Master George Percy 1607," *Narratives of Early Virginia, 1606–1625*, edited by Lyon G. Tyler (New York: Charles Scribner's Sons, 1907), pp. 9–10.
35. Fullam, *The Lost Colony of Roanoke: New Perspectives* (Jefferson, NC: McFarland, 2017), pp. 139–141.
36. Hudson, Charles, *The Juan Pardo Expeditions* (Tuscaloosa: University of Alabama Press, 2005), p. 146.
37. Fullam, "The 'Men Cloathed' at Ocanahonan and Pakrakanick," *The Lost Colony of Roanoke: New Perspectives*, pp. 134–144.
38. Mallios, *The Deadly Politics of Giving*, p. 60.
39. Bartlet, Guillermo, "On the Ethnohistory of Powhatan Ritual Gestures," Anthropos, vol. 105, no. 1, 2010, pp. 47–56.
40. Hakluyt, "The first voyage made to the coasts of America…," *The Principal Navigations…*, p. 282.
41. *Ibid.*
42. Haag, William G., "Physiography of the Coastal Region, Roanoke Island," *The Archaeology of Coastal North Carolina*, Coastal Studies Series 2 (Baton Rouge: Louisiana State University Press, 1958), p. 62.
43. Phelps, David S., "Roanoke Island," *Archaeology of the Native Americans: The Carolina Algonkians* (Greenville: East Carolina University Press, 1984), p. 19.
44. Luccketti, Nicholas M., Klingelhofer, Eric C., and Evans, Phillip W., "Archaeological Research at Fort Raleigh—Past and Present," *The Archaeology of North Carolina: Three Archaeological Symposia*, North Carolina Archaeological Council Publication Number 30, 2011, ch. 9, p. 6.
45. Hakluyt, "The voiage made by Sir Richard Greenuile, for Sir Walter Ralegh, to Virginia, in the yeere 1585," *The Principal Navigations…*, p. 293.
46. Luccketti, Klingelhofer, and Evans, p. 6.
47. Drawing based on: Dolan, Robert, and Kenton Bosserman, "Shoreline Erosion and the Lost Colony," *Annals of the Association of American Geographers*, vol. 62, no. 3, 1972, pp. 424–426; also based on depictions of Roanoke Island on de Bry's engravings of White's *The Arrival of the Englishmen in Virginia* and on *Americæ pars, nunc Virginia dicta*.
48. Hakluyt, "The fourth voyage made to Virginia with three ships, in yere 1587. Wherein was transported the second Colonie," *The Principal Navigations…*, p. 358.
49. Harriot, A Briefe and True Report, p. 25.
50. Hakluyt, "The first voyage made to the coasts of America…," *The Principal Navigations…*, p. 282.
51. Hakluyt, "A Discourse of Western Planting, written by M. Richard Hakluyt, 1584," *The Principal Navigations…*, p. 169.
52. Harriot, p. 25.
53. *Ibid.*
54. *Ibid.* pp. 27–8.
55. Harriot, *A Briefe and True Report*, p. 27.
56. *Ibid.*, p. 42.
57. Quinn, The Roanoke Voyages 1584–1590, Vol. II (London: The Hakluyt Society, 1955), p. 893.
58. Hakluyt, "The imployments of the English men left in Virginia by Richard Greenuill vnder the charge of Master Ralph Lane," *The Principal Navigations…*, p. 302.
59. *Ibid.*, p. 859.
60. Harriot, *A Briefe and True Report*, p. 29.
61. Hakluyt, "The imployments of the English men left in Virginia…," p. 302.
62. Quinn, *The Roanoke Voyages*, Vol. I, p. 285.
63. Hakluyt, p. 302.
64. Hodge, Frederick W., editor, Handbook of American Indians North of Mexico, Part 2 (Washington, DC: U.S. Government Printing Office, 1912), p. 43.
65. Lepore, Jill, *King Philip's War and the Origin of American Identity* (New York: Alfred A. Knopf, 1998), p. 174.

Bibliography

Primary Sources

Brewer, J. S., and William Bullen. *Calendar of the Carew Manuscripts Preserved in the Archiepiscopal Library at Lambeth 1575–1588.* London: Longmans, Green, Reader, & Dyer, 1868.

Dyson, Humphrey, collector. *A Booke containing all svch Proclamations, as were pvblished during the Raigne of the late Queene Elizabeth.* London: Bonham, Norton, and Iohn Bill, 1618.

Granada, Miguel, Adam Mosley, and Nicholas Jardine. *Christoph Rothmann's Discourse on the Comet of 1585: An Edition and Translation with Accompanying Essays.* Leiden, Netherlands: Brill Academic Publishing, 2014.

Hakluyt, Richard. *The Principal Navigations, Voyages, Traffiques, and Discoveries of the English Nation.* Edited by Edmund Goldsmid, Vol. XIII America Part II. Edinburgh: E. and G. Goldsmid, 1889.

_____. "An account of the particularities of the imployments of the English men left in Virginia by Richard Greenuill vnder the charge of Master Ralph Lane Generall of the same, from the 17. Of August 1585. Vntil the 18. Of Iune 1586 at which time they departed the Countrey; sent and directed to Sir Walter Ralegh." *The Principal Navigations, Voyages, Traffiques, and Discoveries of the English Nation.* Edited by Edmund Goldsmid, Vol. XIII America Part II. Edinburgh: E. and G. Goldsmid, 1889.

_____. "A Discourse of Western Planting, written by M. Richard Hakluyt, 1584." *The Principal Navigations, Voyages, Traffiques, and Discoveries of the English Nation.* Edited by Edmund Goldsmid, Vol. XIII America Part II. Edinburgh: E. and G. Goldsmid, 1889.

_____. "An extract of Master Ralph Lanes letter to M. Richard Hakluyt Esquire, and another Gentleman of the middle Temple" "...From the New Fort in Virginia, this third of September, 1585."

_____. "The fift voyage of M. Iohn White into the West Indies and parts of America called Virginia, in the yeere 1590." *The Principal Navigations, Voyages, Traffiques, and Discoveries of the English Nation.* Edited by Edmund Goldsmid, Vol. XIII America Part II. Edinburgh: E. and G. Goldsmid, 1889.

_____. "The first voyage made to the coasts of America, with two barks, wherein were Captaines M. Philip Amadas, and M. Arthur Barlowe, who discouered part of the Countrey now called Virginia Anno 1584. Written by one of the said Captaines, and sent to sir Walter Ralegh knight, at whose charge and direction, the said voyage was set forth." *The Principal Navigations, Voyages, Traffiques, and Discoveries of the English Nation.* Edited by Edmund Goldsmid, Vol. XIII America Part II. Edinburgh: E. and G. Goldsmid, 1889.

_____. "The Fourth Voyage Made to Virginia with Three Ships, in the Yere 1587. Wherein was transported the second Colonie." *The Principal Navigations, Voyages, Traffiques, and Discoveries of the English Nation.* Edited by Edmund Goldsmid, Vol. XIII America Part II. Edinburgh: E. and G. Goldsmid, 1889.

_____. "A letter from John White to M. Richard Hakluyt. 1593." *The Principal Navigations, Voyages, Traffiques, and Discoveries of the English Nation.* Edited by Edmund Goldsmid, Vol. XIII America Part II. Edinburgh: E. and G. Goldsmid, 1889.

_____. "The Letters Patents, granted by the Queenes Maiestie to M. Walter Ralegh now Knight, for the discovering and planting of new lands and Countries, to continue the space of 6. yeeres and no more." *The Principal Navigations, Voyages, Traffiques, and Discoveries of the English Nation.* Edited by Edmund Goldsmid, Vol. XIII America Part II. Edinburgh: E. and G. Goldsmid, 1889.

_____. "The third voyage made by a ship, sent in the yeere 1586 to the reliefe of the Colonie planted in Virginia, at the sole charges of Sir Walter Raleigh." *The Principal Navigations, Voyages, Traffiques, and Discoveries of the English Nation.* Edited by Edmund Goldsmid, Vol. XIII America Part II. Edinburgh: E. and G. Goldsmid, 1889.

_____. "The voiage made by Sir Richard Greenuile, for Sir Walter Ralegh, to Virginia, in the yeere 1585." *The Principal Navigations, Voyages, Traffiques, and Discoveries of the English Nation.* Edited by Edmund Goldsmid, Vol. XIII America Part II. Edinburgh: E. and G. Goldsmid, 1889.

Hann, John H. "Translation of the Écija Voyages of 1605 and 1609 and the Gonzalez Derrotero of 1609." *Florida Archaeology No. 2.* Florida Bureau of Archaeological Research, Nov. 2, 1986.

Harriot, Thomas. *A Briefe and True Report of the New*

Found Land of Virginia. Francoforti: Theodor De Bry, 1590.
Hosmer, James Kendall, ed. "Winthrop's Journal 1630-1649." *Original Narratives of Early American History,* Vol. 2. New York: Charles Scribner's Sons, 1908.
Hudson, Charles M., and Herbert E. Ketcham. "Translation of the 1569 Spanish account with Documents Relating to the Pardo Expeditions." *The Juan Pardo Expeditions: Spanish Explorers and the Indians of the Carolinas and Tennessee, 1566-1568.* Washington: Smithsonian Institution Press, 1990.
Kingsbury, Susan Myra, editor. *The Records of the Virginia Company of London.* Washington, DC: Government Printing Office, 1906.
Lawson, John. *A New Voyage to Carolina.* London: [s.n.], 1709.
Percy, George. "Observations by Master George Percy 1607." *Narratives of Early Virginia, 1606-1625.* Edited by Lyon G. Tyler. New York: Charles Scribner's Sons, 1907.
"Phinehas Pratt's Petition." *Collections of the Massachusetts Historical Society,* Vol. IV, Fourth Series. Boston: Little, Brown, and Company, 1858.
Private Laws of the State of North Carolina, Passed by the General Assembly, Session of 1899. Raleigh: Edwards & Broughton, and E.M. Uzzell, State Printers and Binders, 1899.
Public Laws of the State of North Carolina, Passed by the General Assembly. Session 1869-70. Raleigh: Jo. W. Holden, State Printer and Binder, 1870.
Quinn, David B. *The Roanoke Voyages 1584-1590.* 2 vols. London: The Hakluyt Society, 1955.
_____. "Act for the confermacion of lettres patentes grauntedto Walter Raleghe esquire." *The Roanoke Voyages 1584-1590.* London: The Hakluyt Society, 1955.
_____. "The Bill for Confirmation of Letters Patents made unto Walter Rawleigh…" *The Roanoke Voyages 1584-1590.* London: The Hakluyt Society, 1955.
_____. "December 1584 Bill to Confirm Raleigh's Patent, as Passed by the House of Commons." *The Roanoke Voyages 1584-1590.* London: The Hakluyt Society, 1955.
_____. "The Holinshed Notice of the 1584 Voyage." *The Roanoke Voyages 1584-1590.* London: The Hakluyt Society, 1955.
_____. "The [June, 1585] Relation of Hernando de Altamirano." *The Roanoke Voyages 1584-1590,* London: The Hakluyt Society, 1955.
_____. "The [March, 1589] Relation of Pedro Diaz." *The Roanoke Voyages 1584-1590,* Vol. II. London: The Hakluyt Society, 1955.
Ralegh, Sir Walter, Knight. *The History of the World in Five Bookes.* London: Printed for Walter Burre, 1614.
Salley, Alexander S., Jr., editor. "Archdale's Description of Carolina, 1707." *Narratives of Early Carolina, 1650-1708.* New York: Charles Scribner's Sons, 1911.
_____. "Francis Yeardley's Narrative of Excursions into Carolina, 1654." *Narratives of Early Carolina, 1650-1708.* New York: Charles Scribner's Sons, 1911.
Saunders, William S., editor. *The Colonial Records of North Carolina.* Vol. I, 1662-1712. Raleigh: P. M. Hale, Printer to the State, 1886.
_____. *The Colonial Records of North Carolina,* Vol. II 1713-1728. Raleigh: P. M. Hale, Printer to the State, 1886.
_____. *The Colonial Records of North Carolina,* Vol. VI. Raleigh: Joseph Daniels, Printer to the State, 1888.
Smith, John. *The Generall Historie of Virginia, New England & The Summer Isles.* Library of Congress. New York: Macmillan Company, 1907.
Stow, Iohn. *A Summarie of the Chronicles of England, Diligently collected, abridged, & continued vnto this present yere of Christ, 1598.* London: Richard Bradocke, 1598.
Strachey, William. *The Historie of Travaile lInto Virginia Britannia.* London: Printed for the Hakluyt Society, 1849.
Von Klarwill, Victor, editor. "A Knight Errant," the Journal of Leopold von Wedel. *Queen Elizabeth and Some Foreigners.* London: John Lane, 1928.

Secondary Published Sources

Abbott, Lawrence E. "An Archaeological Inspection of Site 31BF25: Beaufort County, North Carolina." *A Report of Field Inspections: PCS Phosphate Company, Inc.* Raleigh: Office of State Archaeology, June 2016.
Allen, Thomas. *The History and Antiquities of London, Westminster, Southwark, and Parts Adjacent,* Vol. IV. London: Cowie and Strange, 1829.
Annual Report of the Chief of Engineers to the Secretary of War. Washington, DC: Government Printing Office, 1876.
Ashe, Samuel A'Court. *The History of North Carolina from 1584 to 1783,* Vol. I. Greensboro, NC: Charles L. Van Noppen, 1908.
Baldwin, Frances Elizabeth. "Sumptuary Legislation and Personal Regulation in England." PhD dissertation. Baltimore: Johns Hopkins University, 1923.
Barry, William. *A History of Framingham, Massachusetts: Including the Plantation, from 1640 to the Present Time.* Boston: James Munroe and Company, 1847.
Bartlet, Guillermo. "On the Ethnohistory of Powhatan Ritual Gestures." *Anthropos Journal* Vol. 105, No. 1, 2010.
Blackmore, Josiah. *Moorings: Portuguese Expansion and the Writing of Africa.* Minneapolis: University of Minnesota Press, 2009.
Bragdon, Kathleen J. *The Columbia Guide to the Indians of the Northeast.* New York: Columbia University Press, 2001.
Brevoort, James Carson. "Notes on Giovanni da Verrazano and on a Planisphere of 1529, Illustrating His American Voyage in 1524, with a Reduced Copy of the Map." *Journal of the American Geographical Society of New York,* Volume 4, 1871.

Brewington, C.D. *The Five Civilized Indian Tribes of Eastern North Carolina*, Edited by Oscar M. Bizzell. Newton Grove, NC: Sampson County Historical Society, 1994.

Brooks, Baylus C. "John Lawson's Indian Town on Hatteras Island, North Carolina." *The North Carolina Historical Review*, Vol. 91, No. 2, April, 2014.

Bullard, Ernest M. "The Legend of the Coharie," as reprinted in *Huckleberry Historian*, a quarterly publication of the Sampson County Historical Society. Volume XXXVI, Number 1, January, 2014.

Burrage, Henry S. *The Beginnings of Colonial Maine*. Portland: Marks Printing House, 1914.

Butler, George Edwin. *The Croatan Indians of Sampson County, North Carolina. Their Origin and Racial Status. A Plea for Separate Schools...* Durham, NC: The Seeman Printery, 1916.

Carrier, Lyman. "The Veracity of John Lederer." *The William and Mary Quarterly*, Vol.19, No. 4, Oct. 1939.

Carter, Codell. *The Decline of Therapeutic Bloodletting and the Collapse of Traditional Medicine*. New Brunswick, NJ: Transaction Publishers, 2012.

Cobb, Samuel, and Burrage, Henry. *Register of the Officers and Members of the Society of Colonial Wars in the State of Maine*. Portland: Marks Printing House, 1905.

Cogswell, Rev. William, editor. *The New England Historical & Genealogical Register*. Volume 1 & 2. Boston: Samuel P. Drake, 1847–8.

Collins, Arthur Collins, news-letters of. "The Newspapers of the United Kingdom." *Encyclopaedia Britannica*, Ninth Edition, Vol. XVII. Philadelphia: J.M. Stoddart Co., 1884.

Cox, Noel. "Tudor Sumptuary Laws and Academical Dress: An Act against Wearing of Costly Apparel 1509 and An Act for Reformation of Excess in Apparel 1533." *Transactions of the Burgon Society*, Vol. 6, 2006.

Crosby, Alfred W. "Virgin Soil Epidemics as a Factor in the Aboriginal Depopulation in America." *The William and Mary Quarterly* 33, no. 2, 1976.

De Forest, Heman Packard. *The History of Westborough, Massachusetts*, Part I. Cambridge: John Wilson and Son, 1891.

Dial, Adolph L. and Elaides, David K. *The Only Land I Know*. New York: Syracuse University Press, 1996.

Dillard, Richard, M.D. "The Indian Tribes of Eastern Carolina." *The North Carolina Booklet*, Vol. VI No. 1, compiled and edited by Mrs. E.E. Moffitt. Raleigh: The North Carolina Society, 1906.

Dolan, Robert, and Kenton Bosserman. "Shoreline Erosion and the Lost Colony." *Annals of the Association of American Geographers*, vol. 62, no. 3, 1972.

Donegan, Kathleen. "What Happened in Roanoke: Ralph Lane's Narrative Incursion." *Early American Literature*, vol. 48, no. 2, 2013.

Drake, Samuel G. *Book of the Indians, Biography and History of the Indians of North America from its First Discovery to the Year 1841*. Boston: Antiquarian Bookstore 56 Cornhill, 1841.

"Ethnohistorical Description of the Eight Villages adjoining Cape Hatteras National Seashore and Interpretive Themes of History and Heritage." Prepared for the Cape Hatteras National Seashore by Impact Assessment, Inc. National Park Service. U.S. Department of the Interior, November, 2005.

Feest, Christian F. "North Carolina Algonquians." *Handbook of North American Indians*, Vol. 15. Bruce Trigger, editor. Washington, D.C.: Smithsonian Institute, 1978.

Forbes, William T. "Manteo and Jack Straw." *Proceedings of the American Antiquarian Society*. New Series, Vol. XIV, October 1900–October 1901. Worcester: Published by the Society, 1902.

France, Kevin. "Top Five US Cities Most Vulnerable to Hurricanes." AccuWeatherc.com, June 25, 2015.

Fullam, Brandon. *The Lost Colony of Roanoke: New Perspectives*. Jefferson NC: McFarland, 2017.

Geary, Rev. James A. "The Language of the Carolina Algonkian Tribes." In David B. Quinn, ed., *The Roanoke Voyages 1584–1590*, Vol II. London: The Hakluyt Society, 1955.

Grady, Don A. "The Coharie Indians of Sampson County, North Carolina: A Collectrion of Oral Folk History." Thesis Submitted to the Faculty of the University of North Carolina at Chapel Hill, 1981.

Green, Paul R. *The Archaeology of 31HY43, "Pomeiooc."* Department of Sociology and Anthropology. Greenville, NC: East Carolina University, 1987.

_____. *The Archaeology of "Chowanoke."* Department of Sociology and Anthropology and Economics. Greenville, NC: East Carolina University, 1986

Grofe, Francis. *Military Antiquities Respecting A History of the English Army*. London: S. Hooper, 1786.

Haag, William G. "Physiography of the Coastal Region, Roanoke Island," *The Archaeology of Coastal North Carolina*, Coastal Studies Series 2. Louisiana State University: Baton Rouge, 1958.

Hackett, David, editor. *Religion and American Culture*. Routledge: New York and London, 2003.

Hall, David D. *A World of Wonders: The Mentality of the Supernatural in Seventeenth-Century New England*. Boston: The Colonial Society of Massachusetts, 1984.

Harvey, L.P. *Islamic Spain 1250–1500*. Chicago and London: University of Chicago Press, 1990.

Haulley, Fletcher. *A Primary Source History of the colony of New Hampshire*. New York: The Rosen Publishing Group, 2006.

Hawks, Francis L. *The History of North Carolina*. Fayetteville NC: E. J. Hale & Son, 1859.

Hodge, Frederick W., editor. *Handbook of American Indians North of Mexico*. Parts 1 and 2. Washington, DC: Government Printing Office, 1907 and 1912.

Hooper, Wilfrid. "The Tudor Sumptuary Laws." *The English Historical Review*, Vol. 30, No. 119. London: Oxford University Press, July 1915.

Hosmer, James Kendall, editor. "Winthrop's Journal 1630–1649." *Original Narratives of Early American History*, Vol. 2. New York: Charles Scribner's Sons, 1908.

Hough, Franklin B. *Papers Relating to Pemaquid*. Albany: Weed, Parsons & Companie, 1856.

Hudson, Charles. *The Juan Pardo Expeditions.* Tuscaloosa: University of Alabama Press, 2005.

Hulton, P.H. "White, John (fl. 1577–93)." *Dictionary of Canadian Biography,* vol. 1. Toronto: University of Toronto/Université Laval, 1979.

Hurd, D. Hamilton. *The History of Worcester County, Massachusetts.* Philadelphia: J.W. Lewis & Co., 1889.

"Hussey's Catalog of Comets." *Philosophical Magazine and Journal of Science,* Vol. IV, January-June, 1834.

Johnson, Gordon and Sylvester, Phillip. *Salt Water Inundation from Hurricane Sandy.* Wilmington: University of Delaware, College of Agricultural and Natural Resources, 2012.

Kidder, Frederic. "Historical Sketch of the Indians Who Inhabited the Eastern Part of North Carolina from 1524 to the Present." *The Historical Magazine,* Vol I, No. 6. June 1857.

Kocher, Paul H. *Science and Religion in Elizabethan England.* New York: Octagon Books, 1969.

Kupperman, Karen Ordahl. *Indians & English, Facing Off in Early America.* Ithaca, NY: Cornell University Press, 2000.

_____. *Roanoke, The Abandoned Colony.* Totowa, NJ: Rowman & Allanheld, 1984.

La Vere, David. *The Tuscarora War.* Chapel Hill: University of North Carolina Press, 2013.

Landsea, Chris, contributor. "Chronological List of All Hurricanes which Affected the Continental United States 1851–2014." NOAA Hurricane Research Division, National Hurricane Center, n.d.

Lee, E. Lawrence. *Indian Wars in North Carolina 1663–1763.* Raleigh: Office of Archives and History/North Carolina Department of Cultural Resources, 2011.

Lepore, Jill. *King Philip's War and the Origin of American Identity.* New York: Alfred A. Knopf, 1998.

Lewandowski, Elizabeth J. *The Complete Costume Dictionary.* Lanham, MD: Scarecrow, 2011.

Lossing, Benson J. *Lives of Celebrated Americans.* Hartford, CT: Thomas Belknap, 1869.

Luccketti, Nicholas M, Klingelhofer, Eric C., and Evans, Phillip W. "Archaeological Research at Fort Raleigh—Past and Present." *The Archaeology of North Carolina: Three Archaeological Symposia.* North Carolina Archaeological Council Publication Number 30, 2011.

MacCord, Sr., Howard A. "Wingina Site, Nelson County, Virginia." *Archeological Society of Virginia Quarterly Bulletin.* 28 (4), 1974.

Mallios, Seth. *The Deadly Politics of Giving.* Tuscaloosa: University of Alabama Press, 2006.

McMillan, Hamilton. *Sir Walter Raleigh's Lost Colony. An Historical Sketch of the Attempts of Sir Walter Raleigh to Establish a Colony in Virginia, With the Traditions of an Indian Tribe in North Carolina.* Wilson, NC: Advance Press, 1888.

Milton, Giles. *Big Chief Elizabeth.* New York: Farrar, Straus and Giroux, 2000.

Mintz, John J., Beaman, Thomas E., and Mohler, Paul J. "'They in respect of troubling our inhabiting and planting, are not to be feared': Archaeology and Ethnohistory of Native Coastal Populations before and after European Contact." *The Archaeology of North Carolina: Three Archaeological Symposia.* North Carolina Archaeological Council Publication Number 30, 2011.

Mook, Maurice A. "Algonquian Ethnohistory of the Carolina Sound." *Journal of the Washington Academy of Sciences,* Vol. 34, No. 6. June 15, 1944.

_____. "A Newly Discovered Algonkian Tribe of Carolina." *American Anthropologist,* October–December, 1943.

Mooney, James. *The Siouan Tribes of the East.* Washington, DC: Government Printing Office, 1894.

Mosley, Adam. *Bearing the Heavens: Tycho Brahe and the Astronomical Community of the Late Sixteenth Century.* Cambridge: Cambridge University Press, 2007.

Oberg, Michael Leroy. *Dominion and Civility: English Imperialism and Native America, 1585–1685.* Ithaca, NY: Cornell University Press, 1999.

_____. *The Head in Edward Nugent's Hand.* Philadelphia: University of Pennsylvania Press, 2008.

Otis, James. *The Story of Pemaquid.* New York: Thomas Y. Crowell & Co., 1908

Petrey, Whitney R. "Weapemeoc Shores: The Loss of Traditional Maritime Culture among the Weapemeoc Indians." A Thesis Presented To the Faculty of the Department of History East Carolina University in Partial Fulfillment of the Requirements for the Master of Arts in Maritime Studies, April 2014.

Phelps, David S. *Archaeology of the Native Americans: The Carolina Algonkians: Final Report.* Department of Sociology, Anthropology and Economics, East Carolina University: Greenville, NC, 1984.

_____. "Archaeology of the Tillett Site: The First Fishing Community at Wanchese, Roanoke Island," *Archaeological Research Report* No. 6, Archaeology Laboratory, East Carolina University: Greenville, North Carolina, 1984.

_____. "The Carolina Algonkians: Archaeology and History." America's Four Hundredth Anniversary Slide and Narrative Presentation. East Carolina University: Greenville, NC, 1984

_____. "Roanoke Island." *Archaeology of the Native Americans: The Carolina Algonkians.* Greenville: East Carolina University, 1984.

Powell, Andrew T. *Grenville & The Lost Colony of Roanoke.* London: Matador/Troubador Publishing, 2011.

Price, David A. *Love and Hate in Jamestown.* New York: Alfred A. Knopf, 2003.

Quinn, David B. *The Roanoke Voyages 1584–1590,* Vols. I & II. London: The Hakluyt Society, 1955.

_____. *Set Fair for Roanoke, Voyages and Colonies 1584–1606.* Chapel Hill: University of North Carolina Press, 1985.

Ribeiro, Aileen. *Dress and Morality.* Oxford: Berg Publishers, 2003.

Rountree, Helen C. *Pocahantas, Powhatan, Opechancanough: Three Indian Lives Changed by Jamestown.* Charlottesville: University of Virginia Press, 2005.

_____. *Pocahantas's People, The Powhatan Indians of Virginia Through Four Centuries*. Norman: University of Oklahoma Press, 1990.

_____. *The Powhatan Indians of Virginia*. Norman: University of Oklahoma Press, 1989.

_____. "Uses of Personal Names by Early Virginia Indians." *Encyclopedia Virginia*, May 30, 2014.

Rudes, Blair A. *The First Description of an Iroquoian People: Spaniards among the Tuscaroras before 1522*. Charlotte: University of North Carolina at Charlotte, n. d.

Scales, John, editor. *Piscataqua Pioneers 1622–1775*. Dover, NH: C.F. Whitehouse, 1919.

Scholefield, Joshua, and Hill, G.R., editors. "London Building Legislation and its Administration." *The Justice of the Peace and Local Government Review,* Vol. LXXI. London: Charles Bond, 1907.

Secara, Maggie. *Compendium of Common Knowledge, 1558–1603*. Los Angeles: Popinjay Press, 2008.

Smith, John. "A True Relation." Edited by Lyon G. Tyler. *Narratives of Early Virginia, 1606–1625*. New York: Charles Scribner's Sons, 1907.

Speck, Frank G. "The Ethnic Position of the Southeastern Algonquian." *American Anthropologist* 26, 1924.

Stith, William. *The History of the First Discovery and Settlement of Virginia*. Williamsburg, VA: William Parks, 1747.

Swanton, John Reed. *The Indian Tribes of North America*. Washington, DC: U.S. Government Printing Office, 1952.

Temple, Josiah Howard. *History of Framingham, Massachusetts*. Framingham: Published by the Town of Framingham, 1887.

Torres, Louis. *Historic Resource Study of Cape Hatteras National Seashore*. U.S. Department of the Interior: National Park Service, Denver Service Center, 1985.

Trevelyan, Raleigh. *Sir Walter Raleigh: Being a True and Vivid Account of the Life and Times of the Soldier, Scholar, Poet, and Courtier*. New York: Henry Holt, 2002.

Tucker, Spencer, Arnold, James R., and Wiener, Roberta, editors. *The Encyclopedia of North American Indian Wars, 1607–1890: A Political, Social, and Military History*. Santa Barbara, CA: ABC-CLIO, 2011.

Vaughn, Alden T. *Transatlantic Encounters: American Indians in Britain 1500–1776*. New York: Cambridge University Press, 2006.

Waldman, Carl. *Encyclopedia of Native American Tribes*. New York: Checkmark Books, 2006.

Weaver, J. Curtis, and Zembrzuski, Thomas J., Jr. "August 31, 1993, Storm Surge and Flood of Hurricane Emily on Hatteras Island, North Carolina." Water Supply Paper 2499, U.S. Department of the Interior, U.S. Geological Survey, 1993.

West, Susan. "The Will of Wanchese." *Working Waterfront Archives*. Rockland, ME: Island Institute, May 17, 2012.

Winthrop, Robert C. *Life and Letters of John Winthrop, Governor of the Massachusetts-Bay Company at their Emigration to New England*. Boston: Little, Brown, and Company, 1869.

Index

Abenaki tribe 10, 60, 62, 64–66, 190
Aid (ship) 19
Allen, Thomas 43
Altamirano, Hernando 12, 14, 26
Amadas, Philip: and 1584 reconnaissance 5–6, 9, 11, 16–19, 21–22, 25, 26, 93, 102–3, 108–10, 135, 139, 149, 151, 163, 168–73, 175, 187; the 1585 colony 26, 32, 37, 122, 125, 193; incident at Aquascogoc 29–32, 47
Amoret 65
Andacon 2, 89, 90, 145, 187
Apumatquin 63, 196; *see also* Jackstraw, John
Aquascogoc (village) 27, 29–31, 47, 110, 112, 122, 136, 152, 162, 164, 167, 174, 183
Archdale, Gov. John 138
Arquebus 34, 40, 46, 149, 167; *see also* Caliver
Arundel, John 27
Ashe, Samuel A'Court 114
Aubry, Captain 27
Ayllón, Vázquez de 169–170

Babington Plot 41–2
Bailey, Roger 52
Bark Raleigh (ship) 17
Barlowe, Arthur: and 1584 reconnaissance 6, 12, 18–21, 29–30, 34, 93, 103–4, 106–9, 115, 132–33, 135, 139, 149, 151–2, 158–164, 167, 169, 171, 173, 176
Barlowe Street 88, 191
Batts, Nathaniel 128
Bearcroft, Philip 82
Beaufort County (NC) 55, 58, 132, 135, 138
Bell, Albert 87
Boniten, Captain 27
Boyd, Col. Thomas 82
Bradford, Gov. William 59, 67, 193, 198
Brave (ship) 19
Brewington, C.D. 73
Brooks, Baylus 81
Bullard, Ernest M. 68–72, 74, 199–201
Burrington, Gov. George 82
Butler, Richard 103, 122, 171
Buxton, NC 11, 76

Caliver 34–5, 46; *see also* Arquebus
Camden County (NC) 122
Canonicus 67
Cape Creek (archaeological site) 11, 76, 81
Cape Hatteras 11, 79
Carey, George 26, 44
Carteret County (NC) 55, 58, 69–70, 134, 199
Catoking, Cautaking (village) 113–14, 124–25
Cavendish, Thomas 26, 43
Cayoworaco 66
Chacandepeco (inlet) 11, 76–78, 81
Chaunis Temoatan 37, 90, 117–118, 126, 140, 142, 184–185, 189
Chawanoac, Chawanooc, Chawanook (village) 37, 114–117, 119–120, 122, 125, 142–143, 164, 167, 184
Chawanoac tribe 5, 113–114, 117, 119–121, 123–127, 129, 139, 142, 144, 164, 181, 184, 187, 190
Chepanoc, Chepanuu (village) 122, 124, 126
Chesepian tribe 5, 19, 33, 36–37, 98, 115–116, 124–125, 189–190
Chipanum (village) 118, 185–186
Chowan County (NC) 122
Coharie tribe 67–70, 72–74, 80
Collins, Arthur 20
Comet of 1585 95–96
Cooke, Abraham 74–76
Cooper, Christopher 51
Coree tribe 54–55, 136, 168; *see also* Cwareuuock
Cossine 2, 90–91, 100, 146
Cotan (village) 167
Craven County (NC) 55, 58, 134, 138
Croatoan tribe 1, 5, 9–13, 19, 27, 30, 38, 40, 44–50, 55–56, 67–70, 73–74, 76, 79–83, 112, 136, 141, 148, 154, 189–190; village/island 9–13, 17, 26–27, 39–40, 46, 50, 53–55, 57–58, 67, 69, 74–78, 80–81, 120, 123, 136, 150, 187–188, 194–195, 199
Cumberland County (NC) 72, 200
Currituck County (NC) 83, 122
Cwareuuock 54–55; *see also* Coree tribe

Danforth, Thomas 63–64, 196
Dare, Ananias 51–52, 83; Ananias Street 88, 191
Dare, Elyoner 51–52
Dare, Virginia 51, 75, 83–87, 195
Dare County (NC) 83, 156, 193
Dasamonquepeuc (village) 11–12, 19, 32, 39–40, 44–52, 54–56, 58, 66, 89, 98, 101–102, 112, 119, 126, 129–130, 136, 143, 145, 147, 149, 153–162, 164, 179, 187–189
De Bry, Theodor: engraved drawings 14–17, 19, 27–28, 92–93, 95, 103, 108, 157–158, 162–164, 166–167, 176, 178; engraved map *America Pars* 2–3, 11–13, 53, 104–105, 113–115, 123–125, 132–134, 162, 164–165, 167, 170, 185–186
de Forest, Heman Packard 59
Desmond Rebellion 21, 43
Dial, Adolph 73
Dillard, Dr. Richard 114
disease 7, 33, 35–36, 81, 94, 96–97, 110–111, 181–183, 187
Dorothy (ship) 17
Drake, Sir Francis 40–41, 47, 57, 80, 83, 98–99, 119, 141, 143, 148, 153, 189, 194; Sir Francis Drake Street 88
Drake, Samuel Gardner 59
Durham House 19, 21–22, 25–26, 34, 41–43, 66, 148, 150, 160

Eames Massacre 63–64, 191, 196
Écija, Francisco Fernández de 79–80, 172
Eliades, David 73
Eliot, John 63; *see also* "praying towns/Indians"
Elizabeth I, Queen 3, 6, 20–23, 25–26, 41–43, 77, 109, 118, 126–127, 143, 151, 160, 193–194, 197; Queen Elizabeth Avenue 88
Elks, Mary 83
Emanuel, Enoch 73
Ensenore 2, 35, 38–39, 90, 92–99, 102, 111, 119, 126–127, 129, 143, 145, 153, 180, 182–183, 185–188, 191
Eracano 2, 90, 100–101, 146

Fernandez, Simon 45, 49
Forbes, William T. 59–67, 74, 80,

191; "Manteo and Jack Straw" 193–198
Frobisher, Martin 19

Ganz, Joachim 176, 184
Geary, the Rev. James 102, 113, 122–123, 147–148, 158, 167, 183
George Howe Street 88
Gilbert, Sir Humphrey 6, 21, 57
Gordillo, Francisco 169
Grady, Don A. 73
Granganimeo 2, 102–111; death 35–36, 38, 96–98, 125, 129, 131,153, 183, 186; 1584 first contact 11–12, 92–93, 97, 149, 167, 175, 180; 1585 colony 32, 152–153, 174–175
Great Trading Path 93, 171–173
Green, Paul 86–87
Grenville, Sir Richard: and 1585 voyage 12–13, 26–27, 29–34, 47, 53, 57, 80, 95–96, 104, 109–110, 114, 122, 133, 150, 152, 165, 174–176, 179–180, 194; 1586 relief voyage 36, 38–41, 44–45, 45, 48, 57, 64, 136, 141, 153, 186, 188
Grenville Street 88

Haag, William G. 11, 55–56, 176
Hakluyt, Richard (the younger) 2, 11, 15, 18, 20–21, 25–26, 33, 43, 47, 50–5, 66, 103–104, 109, 111, 132, 145, 150, 152, 176, 179–181, 184; *Discourse of Western Planting* 25, 109, 180; *Principal Navigations* 11, 21, 33, 44
Hall, Enoch 70–71, 200
Hall, Everett 69
Hall, Lucy Bullard 69
Harrington, J.C. 176
Harriot, Thomas 1, 7, 10; *A Briefe and true Report...* 15, 19, 36, 43, 113, 181; descriptive text for de Bry's engravings 92–93, 100, 102–103, 107, 157–158, 162–163, 165–167; 1585-6 colony 27, 32–33, 36, 39–40, 113–114, 148, 176, 180–185; in London 1584–5 20–23, 25–26, 66, 106, 149–150, 160; post-1586 43–44, 50; on sickness among the Indians 94–96, 110, 181–182
Harriot Street 88, 191
Haruie, Dyonis 51
Haruie, Margery 51
Hatorask (inlet) 32–33, 39–41, 44, 57, 74, 81, 104, 109–110, 119, 152–153, 174–175, 177–178, 187
Hatteras tribe 68, 73, 81–84, 195
Hilton, William 70–71
Hobbomock 10
Hopewell (ship) 74–76
Hosmer, James Kendall 59
Howe, George, Jr. 71, 74, 200
Howe, George, Sr. 46–49, 68, 112, 130, 138, 154
Howe, George III 71–72, 200
Howe, George IV 72, 200
Hues, Robert 43
Hurd, Hamilton D. 59, 62

Hussey, the Rev. T.J. 96
Hyde County (NC) 82–83, 132–133

Ibarra, Pedro de 79
Irish, William 44

"Jack Straw" Indian 58–67, 74, 78, 193–198; English rebel 61–62
Jackstraw, John 195
Jackstraw, Joseph 195
Jackstraw, William 63–64, 195–196, 205
Jackstraw Brook 62
Jackstraw family 59, 63–64, 191, 196
Jackstraw Hill 62, 193
Jerome, John 79

King Philip's War 63, 191, 196
Kiscutanewh, King 128
Kupperman, Karen 10, 106

Lane, Ralph: attack at Dasamonquepeuc 39–41, 46, 48–49, 89, 98, 112, 127, 129, 143, 145, 153, 188; at Chawanoac 113, 115–120, 123–126, 142, 189; departure with Drake 40, 46, 98–99, 141, 148, 189; and 1585-6 colony 5, 7, 32–41, 66, 94, 110, 115, 175, 179–184, 188, 191; the Moratuc expedition 29–38, 90–91, 97, 100–101, 118, 126, 140, 142, 147, 159, 184–185, 194
Lawson, John 71, 73–74, 81–82, 138
Lee, W. Stephen 68
"Legend of the Coharie" 67–74, 78, 80, 199–201
Levett, Christopher 60–62, 65
Lowrie, George 68
Lumbee tribe 67–68, 70, 72–73

Mace, Samuel 64, 79
Machumps 65
Magunkook (village) 63
Mallios, Seth 173
Mamanatowick 10, 157
Manedo 10, 65
Mangoak tribe 5, 37, 54–55, 90–, 97, 101, 115, 117–118, 123, 126, 134, 142, 147, 159, 162, 184–185, 189–191
Mangopeesoman 10, 184; *see also* Opechancanough
Manitou, Mantóac 10, 18, 21, 25, 27, 51, 150, 184
Manteo 1–3; 9–88; at Croatoan in 1584 9–16, 160–161, 174, 184; 1587 colony 43–50; 1st voyage to England 20–26, 149–152; Grenville's tour of Pamlico Sound 27–31; installment as Lord of Roanoke and Dasamonquepeuc 50–52; Jack Straw 58–67, 193–198; Legend of the Coharie 67–74, 199–201; Manteo, NC 83–88, 156; Moratuc expedition 37–38, 90, 118, 147, 185; post-1587 52–58, 74–79, 135–136, 148, 191; return to "Virginia" in 1585 26–27, 110, 174–175; role in the 1586 attack at Dasamonquepeuc 39–40, 112; 2nd voyage to England 40–43, 141, 148; status among the English 34–36
Maraton (village) 113–114
Mary, Queen of Scots 41–42
Massasoit 63, 191
Mattamuskeet tribe 82
McMillan, Hamilton 67–68, 70, 72, 132
Menatoan 112, 119
Menatonon 2, 113–121; Chaunis Temoatan 37, 90, 118, 126, 184; and Okisko 38, 118, 127; realm of Chawanoac 113–117, 139–140, 158–159, 164; seized by Lane 36–39, 90, 115, 120, 126, 184; Skiko's imprisonment 37, 118, 127, 129, 142–143, 187, 189
Metackwem, Metocaum (village) 113, 122–123
Metacom, Metacomet ("Philip") 190–191; *see also* King Philip's War
Miantuunomoh 67
Midgett, Nathan 83
Mohawk tribe 16, 190–191
Molyneux, Emery 43
Monanaow, David (Indian) 62, 197
Mook, Maurice A. 122–123, 139, 158, 160–162, 164, 190
Mooney, James 71, 139, 164, 189–191
Moonlight (ship) 76
Moratuc tribe 5, 37, 90, 100, 126, 139–140, 142, 146, 158–159, 164, 181, 184–185, 189–190; river 29, 37–40, 90, 97, 100–101, 117–118, 123, 126, 129, 139–140, 142, 146, 159, 164, 184–185; village 37, 118, 164
Munetute 10
Muscamunge, Mascomenge, Mascoming (village) 122–124

Namontack 65
Narragansett tribe 76, 190
Nelson County (VA) 191
Netus 63, 196
Neusiok tribe 5, 54–55, 134, 136, 162
Newfoundland 57–58, 64, 67, 74–78, 81
Nipmuc tribe 63, 190
Nugent, Edward 189, 194

Ocracoke 11, 53, 104, 135
Ohanoak (village) 113
Okisko 122–128; pledges loyalty to Queen Elizabeth 126–127, 143; realm of Weapemeoc 122–125, 139; subordinate to Menatonon 38, 118, 126
Olmos, Alonso de 170
Opechancanough 10, 14, 184, 190–191
Osacan, Osocon 129–130, 143, 145

Index

Pamlico County (NC) 55, 58, 69, 132, 135, 138, 199
Pamlico tribe 82, 132, 138; *see also* Pomouik tribe
Panauuaioc, Pananuaioc, Pananaioc, Pananiock, Panawicke (village) 132-133, 137-138, 161, 165
Paquiquineo 172
Pardo, Juan 170-172
Parkman, the Rev. Ebenezer 62, 197
Parry, William 25, 41
Paspahegh tribe 137-138; king of 137; *see also* Wowinchopunk
Pasquenoke (village) 123-124
Pasquotank County (NC) 122
Pasquotank river 124, 128
Pasquotank tribe 122
Pemaquid (village) 65
Pemisapan 131; conspiracy 5, 10, 35-40, 89, 97-98, 115, 119, 122, 125-127, 129, 132-134, 136, 140, 142-143, 145, 147, 152-153, 189-193; death 39, 89, 91, 98, 143, 153, 188-189; Moratuc plot 37-38, 90, 97, 100-101, 123, 129, 142, 145, 146, 184-186; *see also* Wingina
Percy, Henry (Earl) 43
Perquimans County (NC) 122
Perquimans tribe 122; river 123-124, 128
Phelps, David 81, 115, 117, 167, 176
Piemacum 132-138; realm/location 30, 54, 132-137; war with Wingina/Secotan 25, 30, 54, 136, 149-150, 161-165, 173, 180, 182, 190
Piscataqua settlement 60-62, 65
Plymouth Plantation 59-60, 67, 191, 193, 198
Pocahontas 65
Pokanoket tribe 10
Pomeiock (village) 27-31, 47, 104-105, 112, 132-134, 139, 161, 164
Pomouik tribe 5-6, 54-55, 132-134, 136, 138, 162, 182; territory 54, 132-133, 135-137, 161, 164; *see also* Piemacum
Pooneno, Pooneho 139-140; Moratuc weroance 139
Popham, George 65
Pory, John 120, 144
Poteskeet tribe 122, 128
Powhatan (Wahunsunacock) 5, 10, 13, 64-65, 116, 127, 157, 190-191; tribe/chiefdom 5, 16, 65, 137, 171-172
Pratt, Phinehas 59-62, 197
"Praying Town/Indians" 63, 195-196

Quinn, David Beers 2; 1584 voyage 18-19, 104, 160-161, 163-164; 1585-6 colony 122-123, 143, 167, 188-189

Ragopo, Leonard (chief) 66
"Raleigh," "Rawly" (Indian) 141
Raleigh, Sir Walter: charter expiration and the 1590 voyage 77; 1584 voyage 5-6, 12, 17-25, 102, 150-152, 159-160; 1585-6 colony 26, 40-41, 83, 89, 99, 109, 111, 113, 115, 125, 148; 1587 colony 42-45, 49-50, 58, 87, 148, 154; Gov. Bradford's reference to 58-59, 64-67, 193-198; Sir Walter Raleigh Street 88
Ramushonok (village) 113
Raymond, George 27
Red Lyon (ship) 27
Ricahokene (village) 124
Richard (ship) 65
Roanoac 3; tribe 5, 11, 30, 32, 35, 38-39, 48, 54, 90, 92-94, 98, 1-1, 110-111, 122, 127, 143, 153, 157-158, 173-174, 186-187, 190-191; village 11, 19, 27, 32, 44, 49-50, 52, 55-56, 58, 66, 81, 105, 109-110, 115, 150, 153, 157, 159-160, 164, 170-171, 175, 185-186, 189; site of 177-170; weroance(s) of 10, 32, 35, 44-46, 48, 54, 81, 92, 100, 102, 119, 129, 131, 142, 149, 152-153, 161-162
Robeson County (NC) 67-68, 70, 72
Rocque, Bertrand 79
Rothman, Christopher 96
Rowse, Anthony 26
Rudes, Blair 55

Sagamore, John (Indian) 58, 62-63, 197
Sampson County (NC) 67-68, 72-73, 199-201
Sanderson, William 26
Sassacomoit 65
Sassamon, John (Indian) 63
Saunders, W.O. 85
Savage, James 59
Sea Venture(ship) 65
Seco (village) 167
Secotan tribe 5-6, 25, 55, 58, 135-136, 161-162, 168, 170, 173, 190; territory 54, 133, 160-165, 168-169; village (also Secotan, Secota, Secoton) 27, 29-31, 47, 109, 132-134, 161-169, 173
Sectuock (village) 167, 170
Sicklemore, Michael 120
Sissipahau, Saxapahaw tribe 71
Skicoak (village) 19, 33, 125, 139
Skicowaros tribe 65
Skiko, Skyco, Skico 142-144; abduction 37, 118, 120, 126, 142; in captivity 129, 143, 187-188; Chaunis Temoatan 142; Pemisapan's plot divulged 143, 188, 191; post-1586 144
Smith, John 13-14, 64-65, 116, 120, 132-133, 137-139, 160, 171-172; *Generall Historie of Virginia* 14, 120, 137-139
Solar Eclipse of 1585 95
Soto, Hernando de 169
Spicer, Edward 74
Squanto 10

Stafford, Edward 39, 46-48, 52, 57, 194
Stewart, Alexander 82-83
Stick, Frank 85
Strachey, William 6, 9-10, 159-160, 164, 172, 195; *Historie of Travaile Into Virginia Britannia* 14
Sumptuary Laws 3, 23-24
Swanton, John 113-114

Tahanedo 65
Tandaquomuc (village) 113-114
Tarraquine, Tanaquiny 89, 145
Tetepano 90, 100, 146-147
Thomas, Dr. Cyrus 119, 189
Thompson, David 60-62, 65
Torporley, Nathaniel 43
Torres, Louis 83
Towaye 40-41, 49, 64, 148
Tuscarora War 82, 138,
Tyger(ship) 26, 32, 109-110, 149, 152, 174-175
Tyler, Watt 197

Uttamatomakkin 65

Verrazzano, Giovanni da 169
Von Wedel, Leopold 12-13, 22-23

Wahginnacut 58, 62
Wahunsonacock, Wahunsenacawh 157; *see also* Powhatan
Walsingham, Francis 26, 41-42, 109
Wampanoag tribe 63, 190
Wanchese 149-157, 1-2, 10, 173-174; in England 20-26, 30, 34, 160-161; 1584 voyage 11, 16, 18-19, 54-55, 59, 108; return to Roanoac 13, 26-27, 32; turned against the English 32, 47, 66, 110, 129, 145, 175, 180, 194, 199; *see also* Pemisapan
Wanchese, NC 156
Warner, William 43
Wanuckhow 63; *see also* Jackstraw, William
Warowtani, Waratan (village) 113-114, 124-125
Warraskoyack (village) 120, 137
Warren, Lindsay 87
Waymouth, George 65
Weapemeoc tribe 5, 118, 122-127, 143, 159, 181, 185; village(s) 32-33, 38, 118, 122-127, 139, 164, 185
Webster, Noah 59
Wessagusset 60
White, John: drawings 2, 14-16, 27, 30, 40, 92-93, 100, 157-158, 162-163, 166, 176, 178; the 1577 voyage 18-19; 1585 voyage 19, 32-33, 40, 44, 134; 1587 voyage 19, 43-53, 112, 119, 136, 148, 153-154, 194; 1588 resupply attempt 19; 1590 voyage 19, 57, 69, 74-79, 82, 120, 138, 155, 177-179, 195; maps 3, 11, 13, 53-54, 104-105, 114-116, 123-

125, 132–134, 146–147, 159, 162, 164–165, 167, 169–170, 185–186
Wingandacoa, Wingandacoia 22, 106, 108, 139, 157, 159–162, 164
Wingina 157–191; 1, 18, 27, 35; conspiracy 157–191; death 157–191; and the English (1585) 32, 109–110, 152; interpretation of disease 94, 97; legacy 157–191; name change 10, 36, 98, 111, 115, 125, 140, 152 (*see also* Pemisapan); realm of 11, 22, 54, 106, 132, 139–140; war with Piemacum 6, 54, 135–136, 149–150
Wingina, VA, Wingina Avenue 191
Winthrop, Gov. John 2, 58–59, 61–64, 66–67, 193, 197–198
Woccon tribe 54, 169
Wokokon (inlet) 11, 13, 27, 53, 55–57, 76–78, 103–105, 109,115, 135–136, 152, 168, 174–175

Wowinchopunck 137–138; *see* Paspahegh

Yeardley, Francis 80
Yeopim river 123
Yeopim tribe 122, 128; *see also* Weapemeoc

Zúñiga map 137–138

www.ingramcontent.com/pod-product-compliance
Ingram Content Group UK Ltd.
Pitfield, Milton Keynes, MK11 3LW, UK
UKHW050529150426
5217IPUK00026B/1866